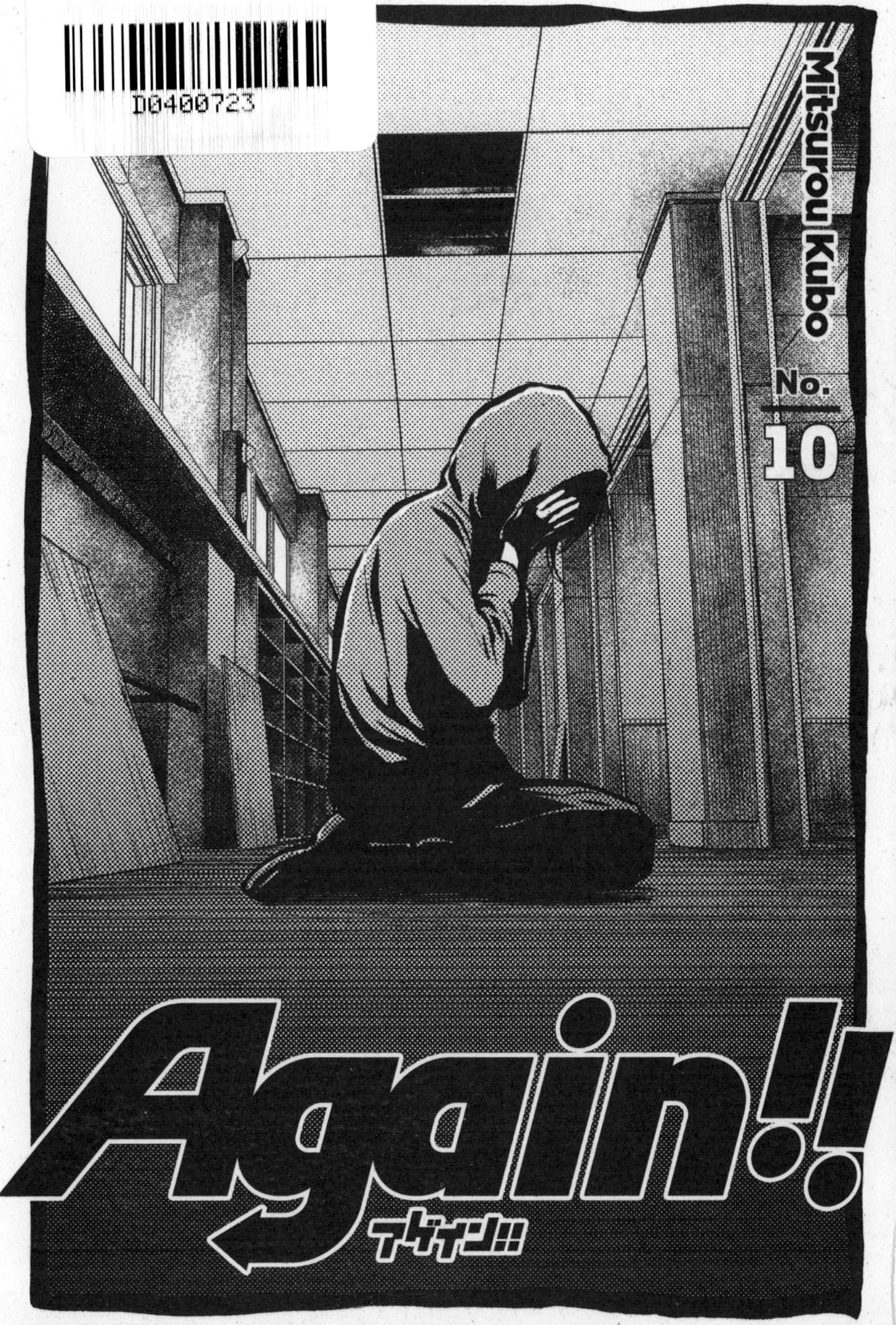
Mitsurou Kubo
No.
10
Again!!
アゲイン!!

c o n t e n t s

99. THIS LAST ONE'S FOR YOU

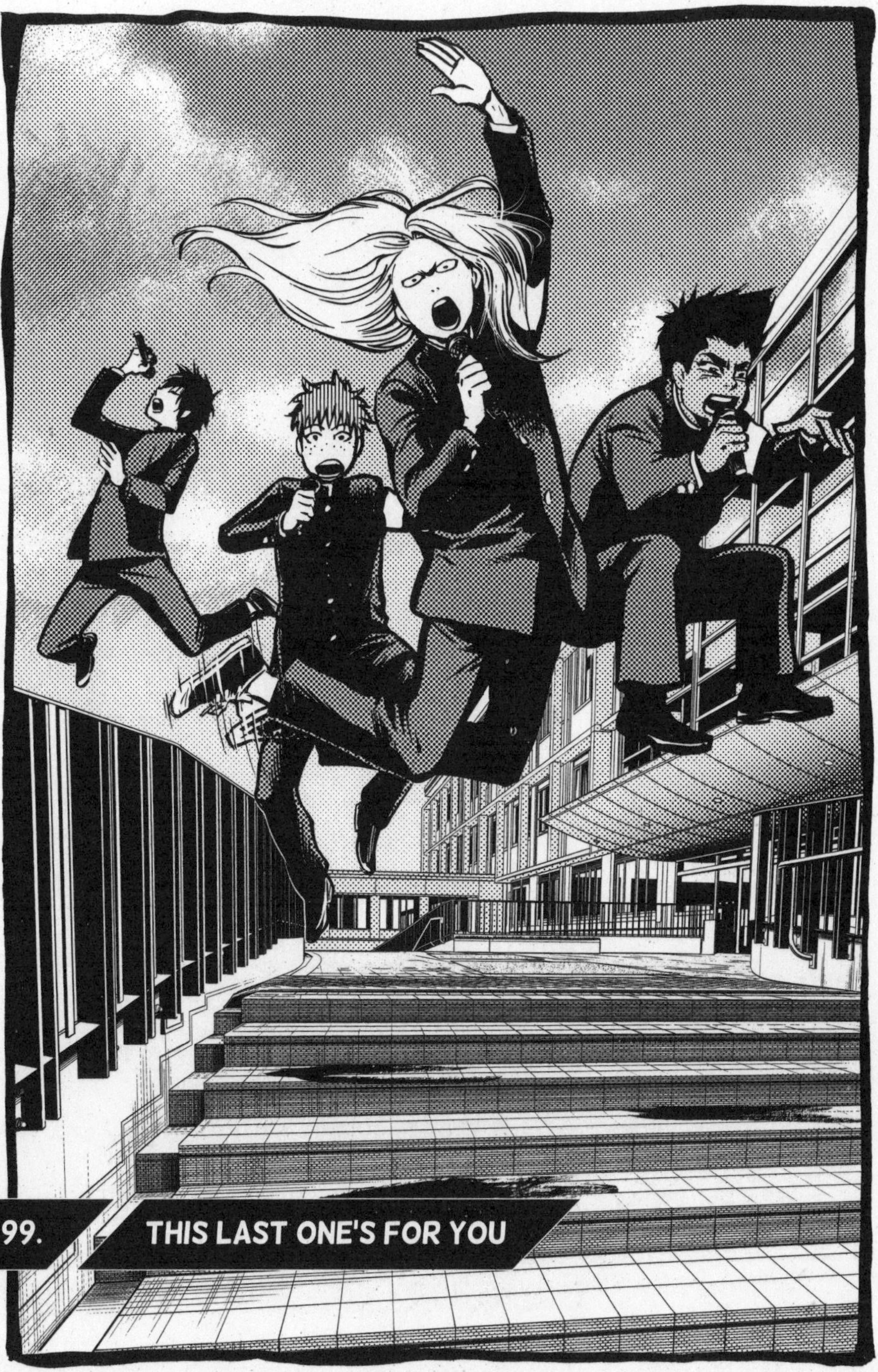

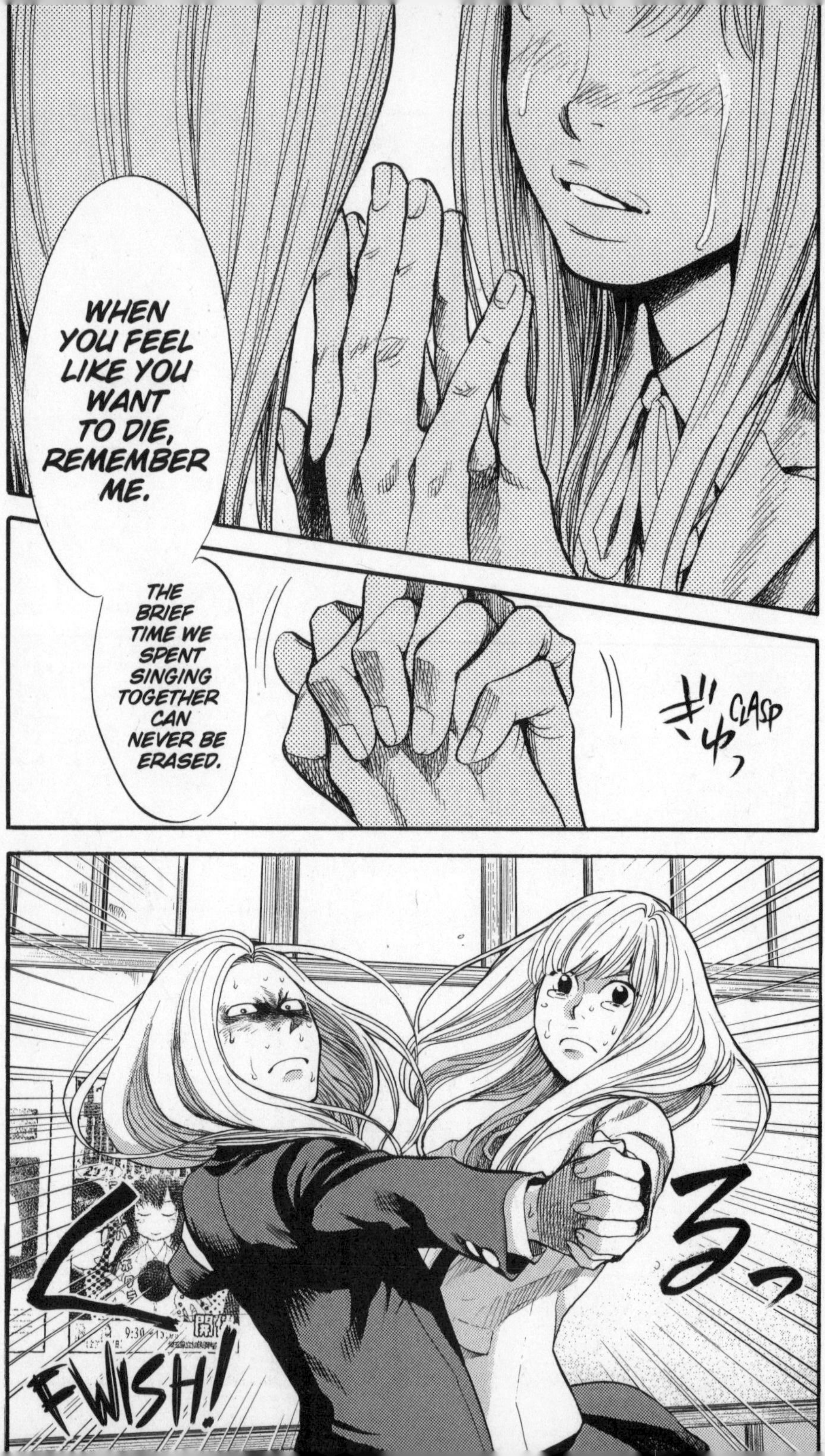
WHEN YOU FEEL LIKE YOU WANT TO DIE, REMEMBER ME.
THE BRIEF TIME WE SPENT SINGING TOGETHER CAN NEVER BE ERASED.
ぎゅっ
CLASP
FWISH!

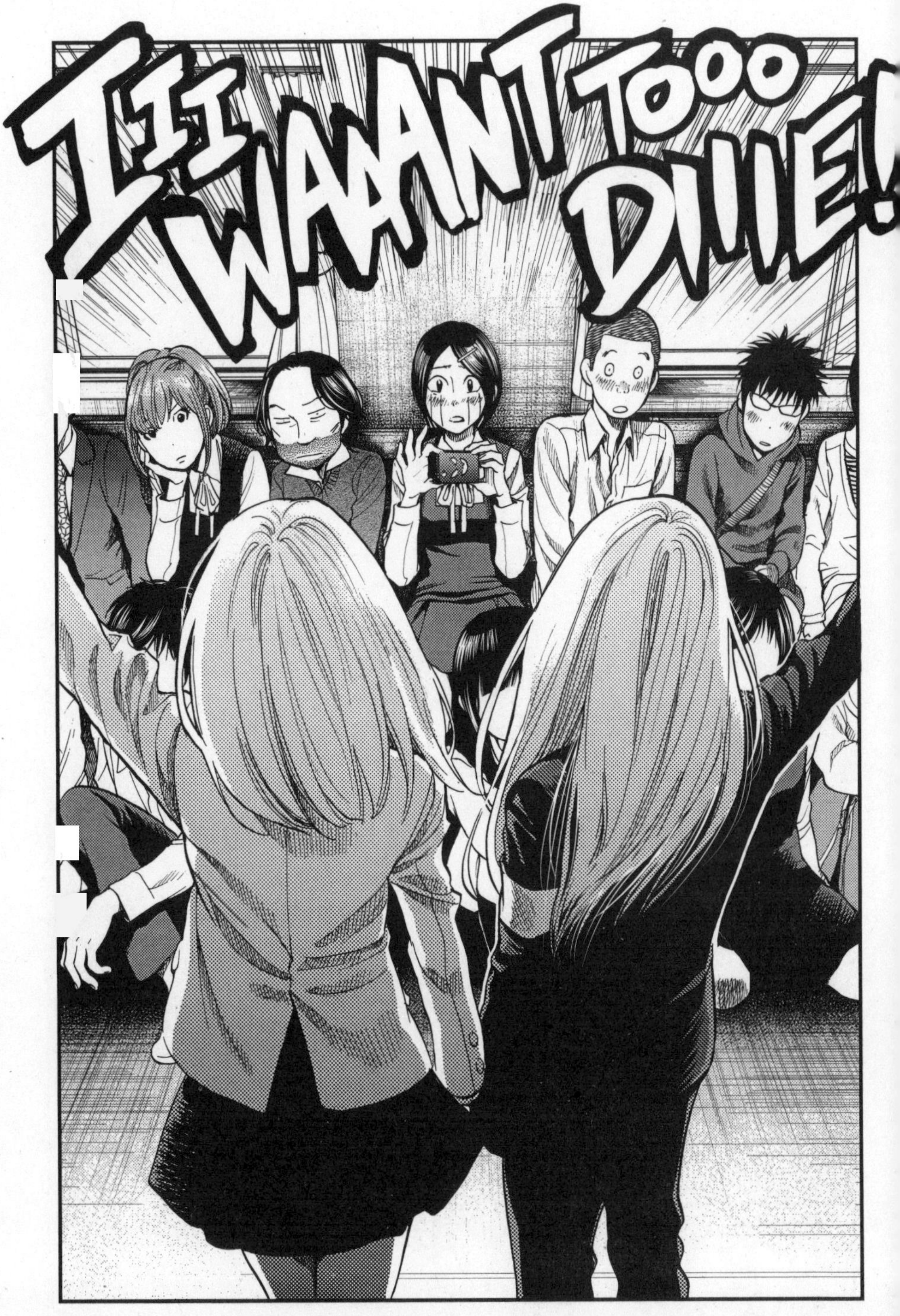
IIII WAAANT TOOO DIIIE!

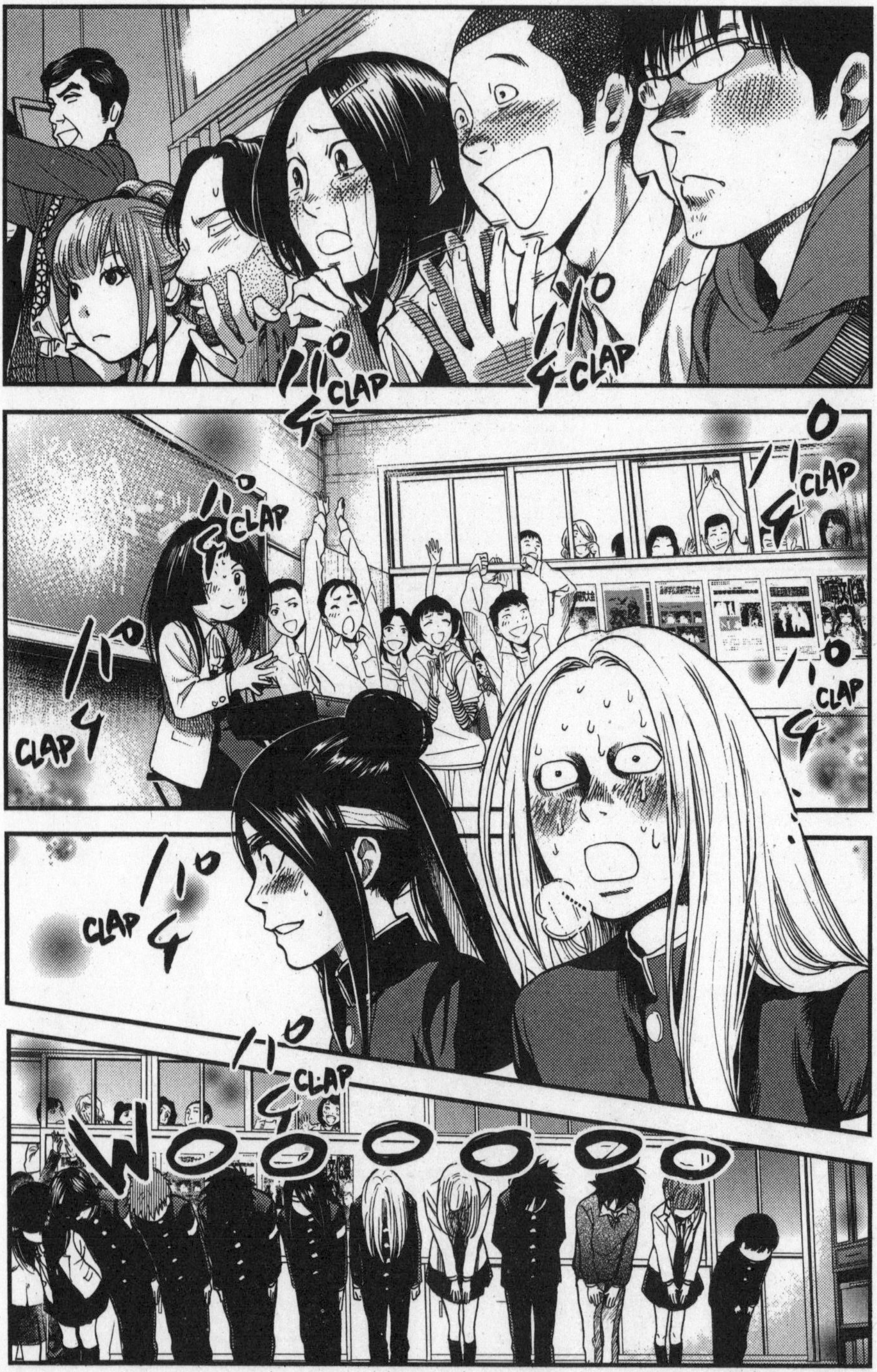
CLAP
CLAP
CLAP
CLAP
CLAP
CLAP
CLAP
CLAP
WOOOOOOO

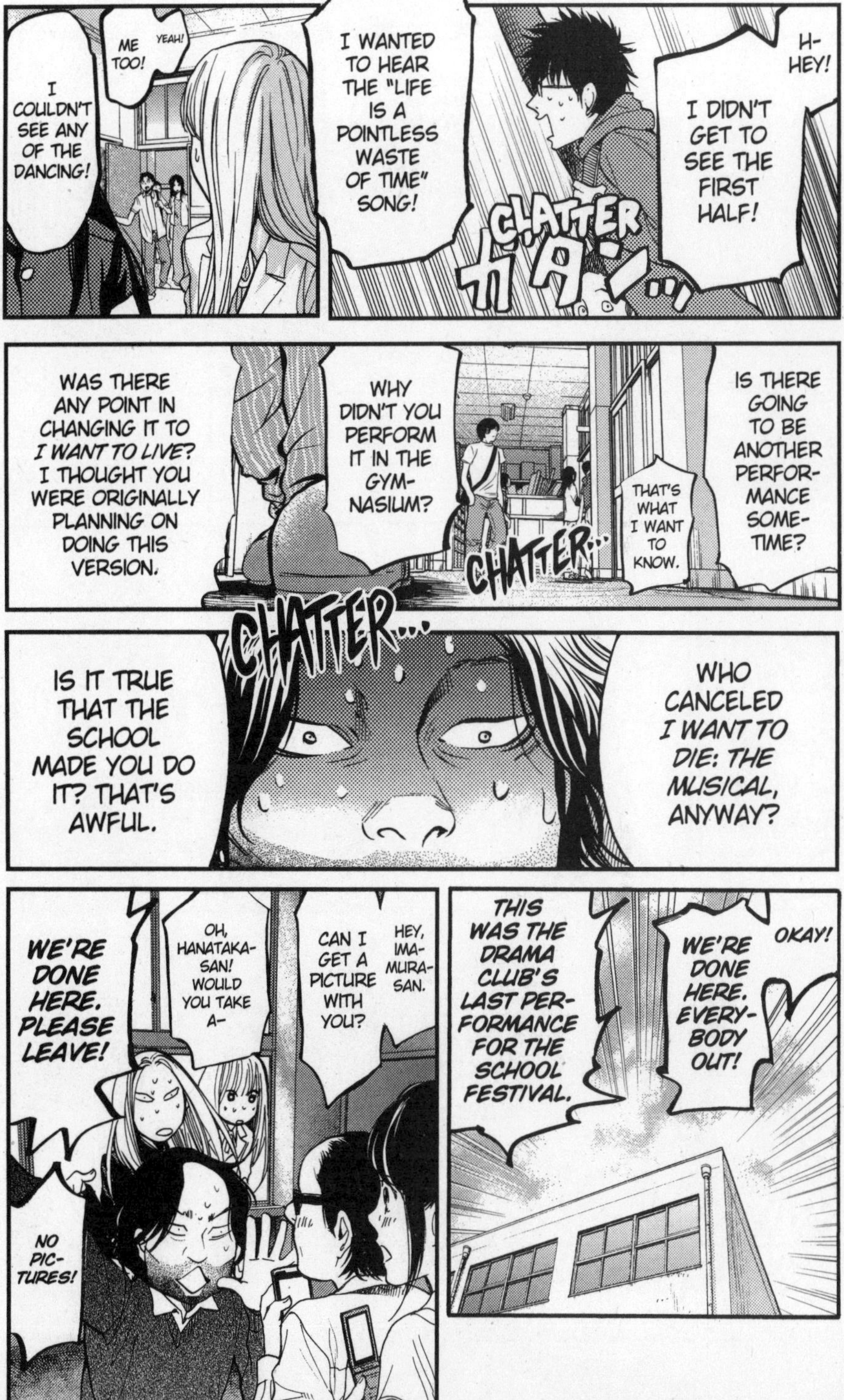
H-HEY!
I DIDN'T GET TO SEE THE FIRST HALF!
CLATTER
カタン…
I WANTED TO HEAR THE "LIFE IS A POINTLESS WASTE OF TIME" SONG!
YEAH!
ME TOO!
I COULDN'T SEE ANY OF THE DANCING!
IS THERE GOING TO BE ANOTHER PERFORMANCE SOMETIME?
THAT'S WHAT I WANT TO KNOW.
CHATTER...
WHY DIDN'T YOU PERFORM IT IN THE GYMNASIUM?
WAS THERE ANY POINT IN CHANGING IT TO *I WANT TO LIVE*? I THOUGHT YOU WERE ORIGINALLY PLANNING ON DOING THIS VERSION.
CHATTER...
WHO CANCELED *I WANT TO DIE: THE MUSICAL*, ANYWAY?
IS IT TRUE THAT THE SCHOOL MADE YOU DO IT? THAT'S AWFUL.
OKAY!
WE'RE DONE HERE. EVERYBODY OUT!
THIS WAS THE DRAMA CLUB'S LAST PERFORMANCE FOR THE SCHOOL FESTIVAL.
HEY, IMAMURA-SAN.
CAN I GET A PICTURE WITH YOU?
OH, HANATAKA-SAN! WOULD YOU TAKE A-
WE'RE DONE HERE. PLEASE LEAVE!
NO PICTURES!

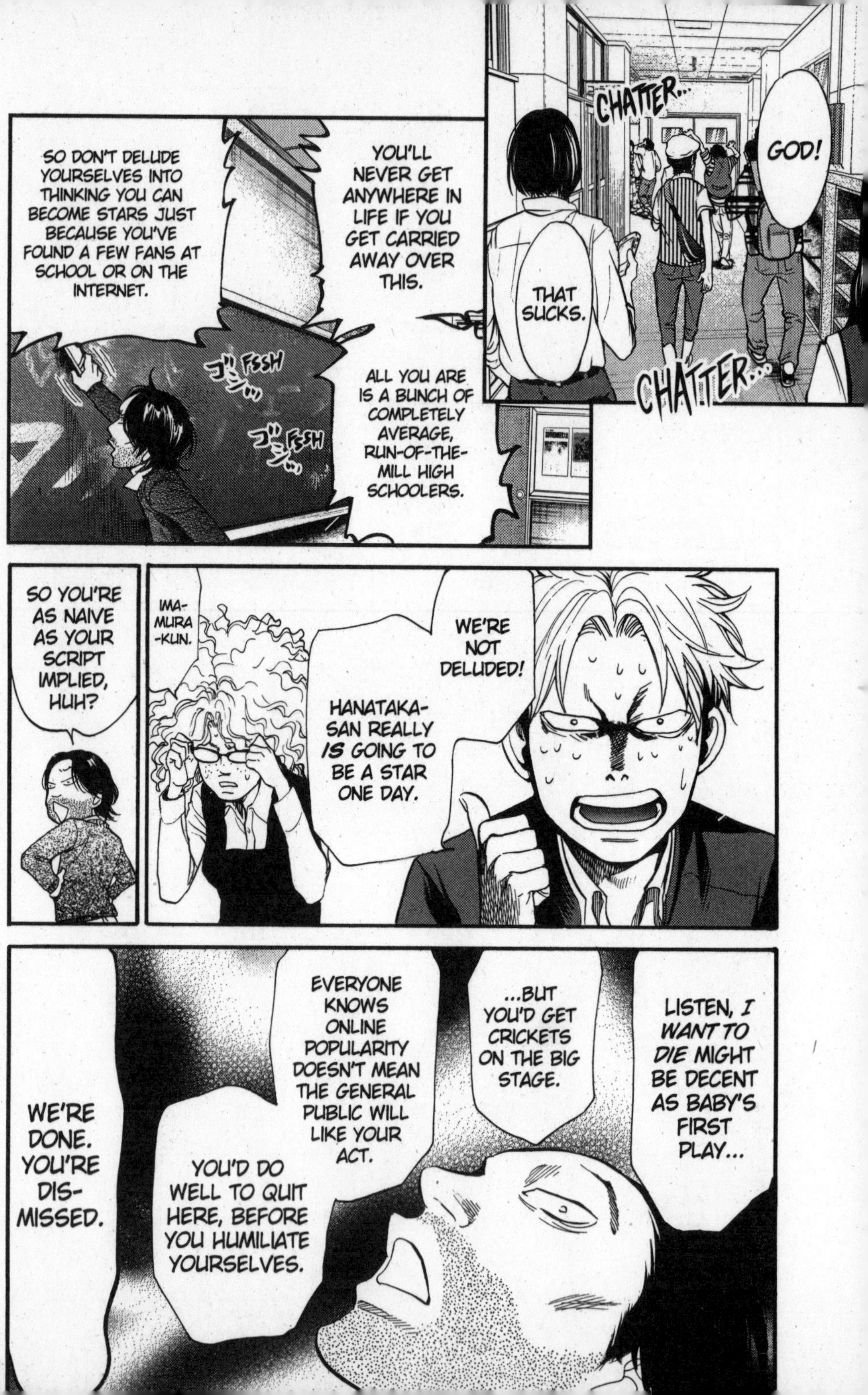
GOD!
CHATTER...
THAT SUCKS.
CHATTER...
YOU'LL NEVER GET ANYWHERE IN LIFE IF YOU GET CARRIED AWAY OVER THIS.
SO DON'T DELUDE YOURSELVES INTO THINKING YOU CAN BECOME STARS JUST BECAUSE YOU'VE FOUND A FEW FANS AT SCHOOL OR ON THE INTERNET.
FSSH
FSSH
ALL YOU ARE IS A BUNCH OF COMPLETELY AVERAGE, RUN-OF-THE-MILL HIGH SCHOOLERS.
WE'RE NOT DELUDED!
HANATAKA-SAN REALLY *IS* GOING TO BE A STAR ONE DAY.
IMA-MURA-KUN.
SO YOU'RE AS NAIVE AS YOUR SCRIPT IMPLIED, HUH?
LISTEN, *I WANT TO DIE* MIGHT BE DECENT AS BABY'S FIRST PLAY...
...BUT YOU'D GET CRICKETS ON THE BIG STAGE.
EVERYONE KNOWS ONLINE POPULARITY DOESN'T MEAN THE GENERAL PUBLIC WILL LIKE YOUR ACT.
YOU'D DO WELL TO QUIT HERE, BEFORE YOU HUMILIATE YOURSELVES.
WE'RE DONE. YOU'RE DIS-MISSED.

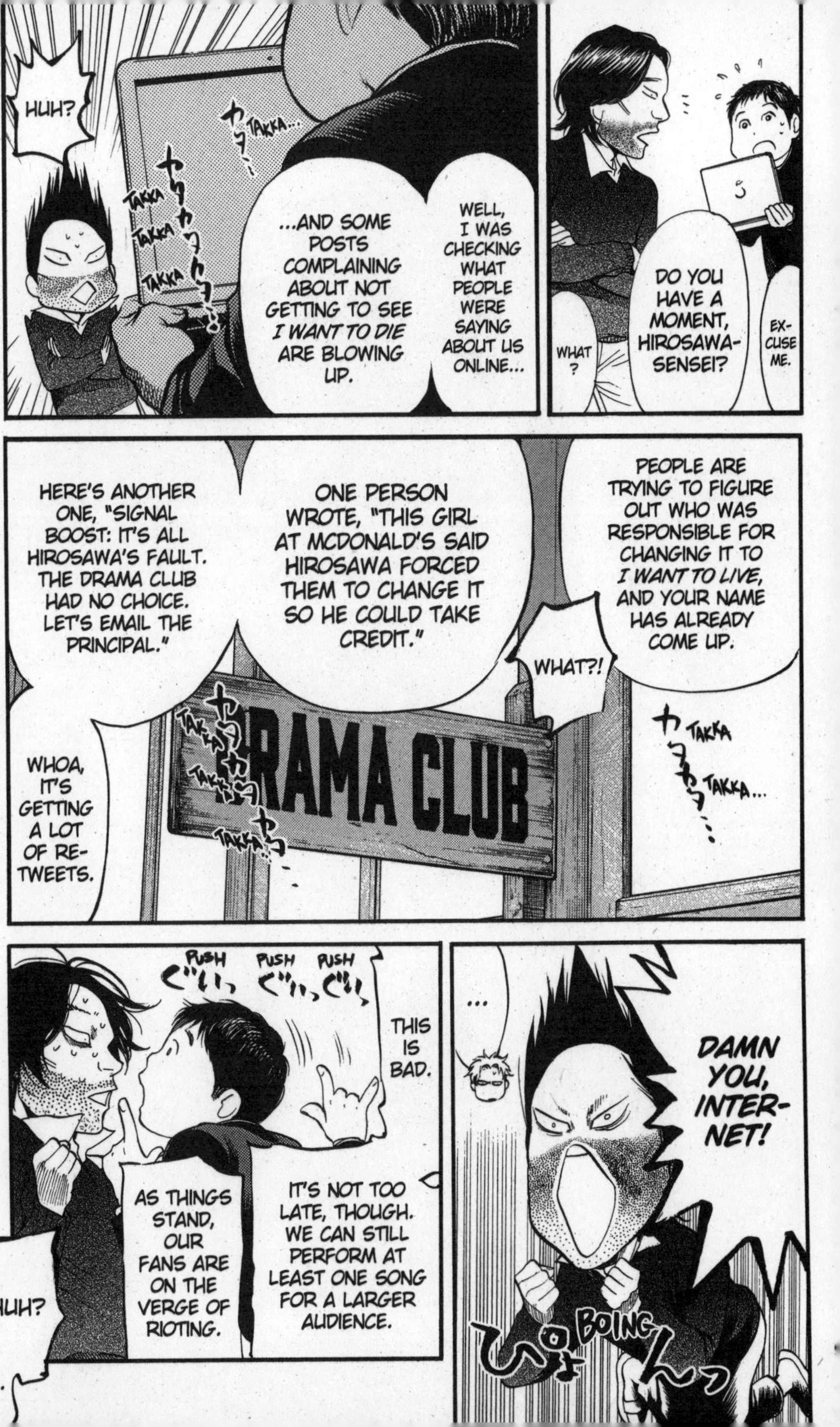
EX-CUSE ME.
DO YOU HAVE A MOMENT, HIROSAWA-SENSEI?
WHAT?
WELL, I WAS CHECKING WHAT PEOPLE WERE SAYING ABOUT US ONLINE...
...AND SOME POSTS COMPLAINING ABOUT NOT GETTING TO SEE *I WANT TO DIE* ARE BLOWING UP.
TAKKA...
TAKKA
TAKKA
TAKKA
HUH?
PEOPLE ARE TRYING TO FIGURE OUT WHO WAS RESPONSIBLE FOR CHANGING IT TO *I WANT TO LIVE,* AND YOUR NAME HAS ALREADY COME UP.
WHAT?!
TAKKA
TAKKA...
ONE PERSON WROTE, "THIS GIRL AT MCDONALD'S SAID HIROSAWA FORCED THEM TO CHANGE IT SO HE COULD TAKE CREDIT."
HERE'S ANOTHER ONE, "SIGNAL BOOST: IT'S ALL HIROSAWA'S FAULT. THE DRAMA CLUB HAD NO CHOICE. LET'S EMAIL THE PRINCIPAL."
DRAMA CLUB
TAKKA
TAKKA
TAKKA
WHOA, IT'S GETTING A LOT OF RE-TWEETS.
...
DAMN YOU, INTERNET!
BOING
PUSH
PUSH
PUSH
THIS IS BAD.
IT'S NOT TOO LATE, THOUGH. WE CAN STILL PERFORM AT LEAST ONE SONG FOR A LARGER AUDIENCE.
AS THINGS STAND, OUR FANS ARE ON THE VERGE OF RIOTING.
HUH?
UH...

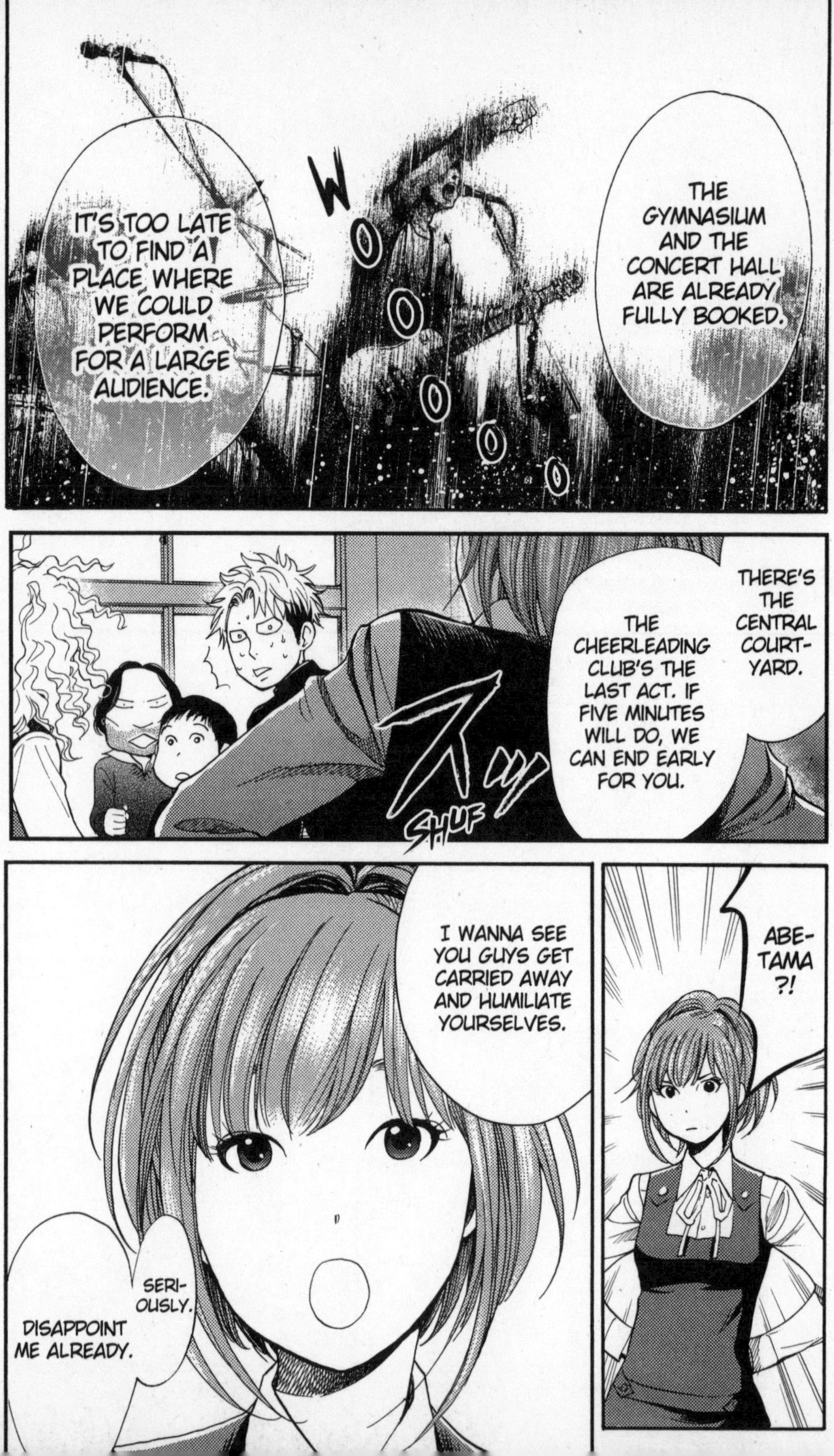
THE GYMNASIUM AND THE CONCERT HALL ARE ALREADY FULLY BOOKED.
IT'S TOO LATE TO FIND A PLACE WHERE WE COULD PERFORM FOR A LARGE AUDIENCE.
WOOOOO
THERE'S THE CENTRAL COURT-YARD.
THE CHEERLEADING CLUB'S THE LAST ACT. IF FIVE MINUTES WILL DO, WE CAN END EARLY FOR YOU.
SHUF
ABE-TAMA?!
I WANNA SEE YOU GUYS GET CARRIED AWAY AND HUMILIATE YOURSELVES.
SERI-OUSLY.
DISAPPOINT ME ALREADY.

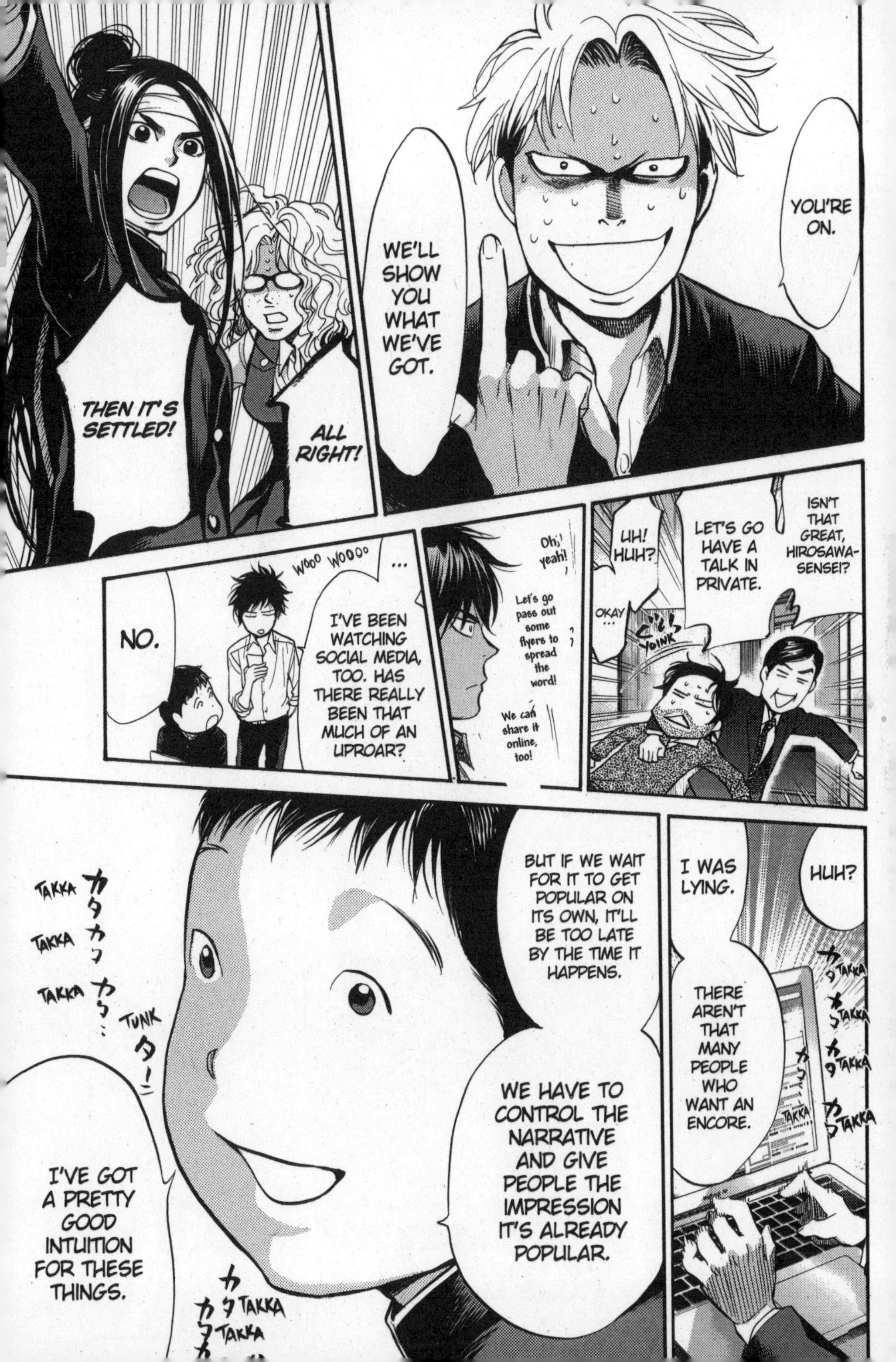

YOU'RE ON.
WE'LL SHOW YOU WHAT WE'VE GOT.
THEN IT'S SETTLED!
ALL RIGHT!
ISN'T THAT GREAT, HIROSAWA-SENSEI?
LET'S GO HAVE A TALK IN PRIVATE.
UH! HUH?
OKAY...
YOINK
Oh, yeah!
Let's go pass out some flyers to spread the word!
We can share it online, too!
WOOO WOOOO
...
I'VE BEEN WATCHING SOCIAL MEDIA, TOO. HAS THERE REALLY BEEN THAT MUCH OF AN UPROAR?
NO.
HUH?
I WAS LYING.
THERE AREN'T THAT MANY PEOPLE WHO WANT AN ENCORE.
TAKKA TAKKA TAKKA TAKKA TAKKA
BUT IF WE WAIT FOR IT TO GET POPULAR ON ITS OWN, IT'LL BE TOO LATE BY THE TIME IT HAPPENS.
WE HAVE TO CONTROL THE NARRATIVE AND GIVE PEOPLE THE IMPRESSION IT'S ALREADY POPULAR.
TAKKA TAKKA TAKKA
TUNK
I'VE GOT A PRETTY GOOD INTUITION FOR THESE THINGS.
TAKKA TAKKA

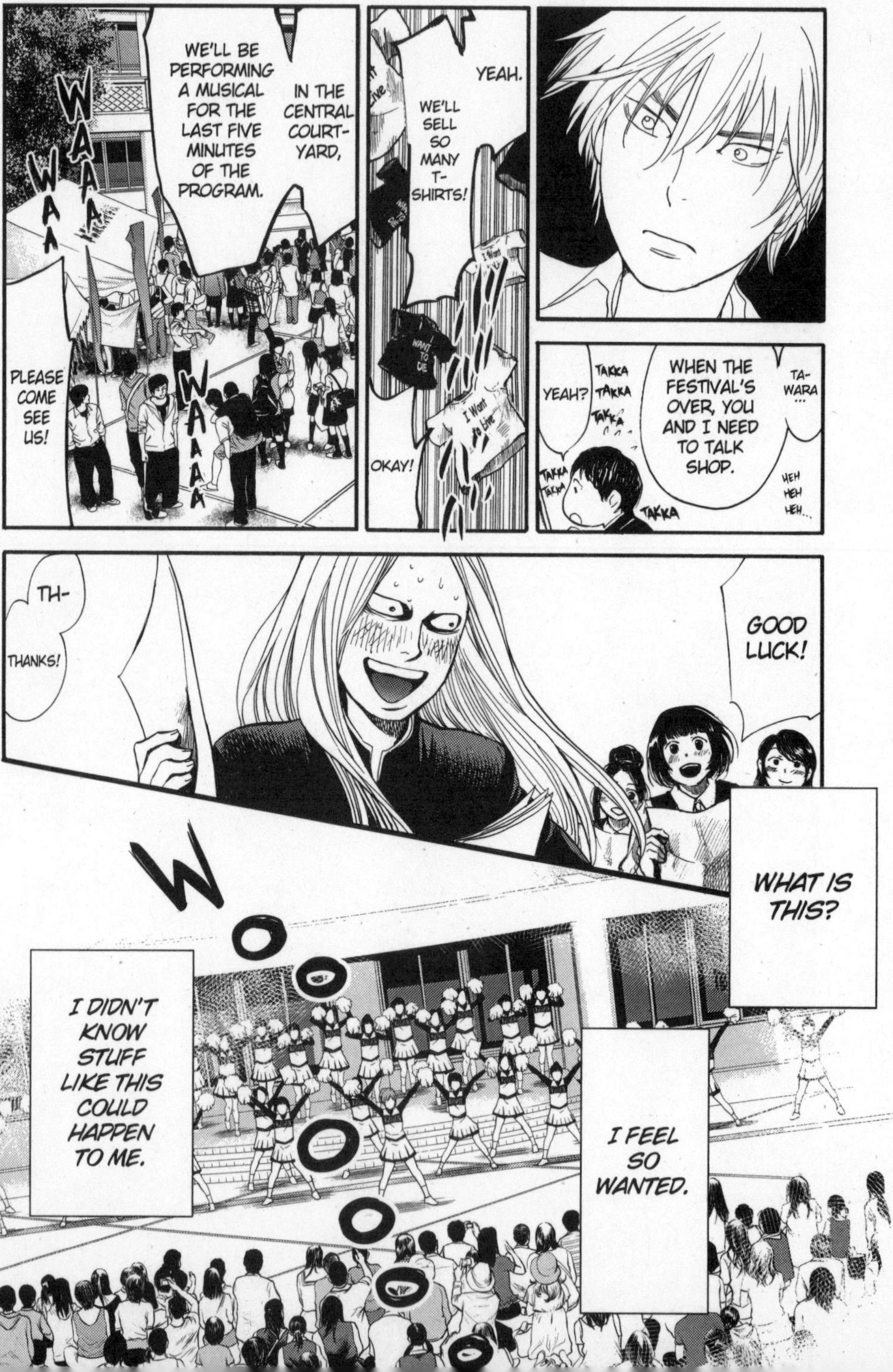
TA-WARA ...
WHEN THE FESTIVAL'S OVER, YOU AND I NEED TO TALK SHOP.
YEAH?
TAKKA TAKKA TAKKA
HEH HEH HEH...
TAKKA TAKKA
TAKKA
YEAH.
WE'LL SELL SO MANY T-SHIRTS!
I WANT TO DIE
I Want to Live
OKAY!
WE'LL BE PERFORMING A MUSICAL FOR THE LAST FIVE MINUTES OF THE PROGRAM.
IN THE CENTRAL COURT-YARD,
WAAAA
WAAA
PLEASE COME SEE US!
WAAAA
GOOD LUCK!
TH- THANKS!
WHAT IS THIS?
I FEEL SO WANTED.
I DIDN'T KNOW STUFF LIKE THIS COULD HAPPEN TO ME.
WOOOOO

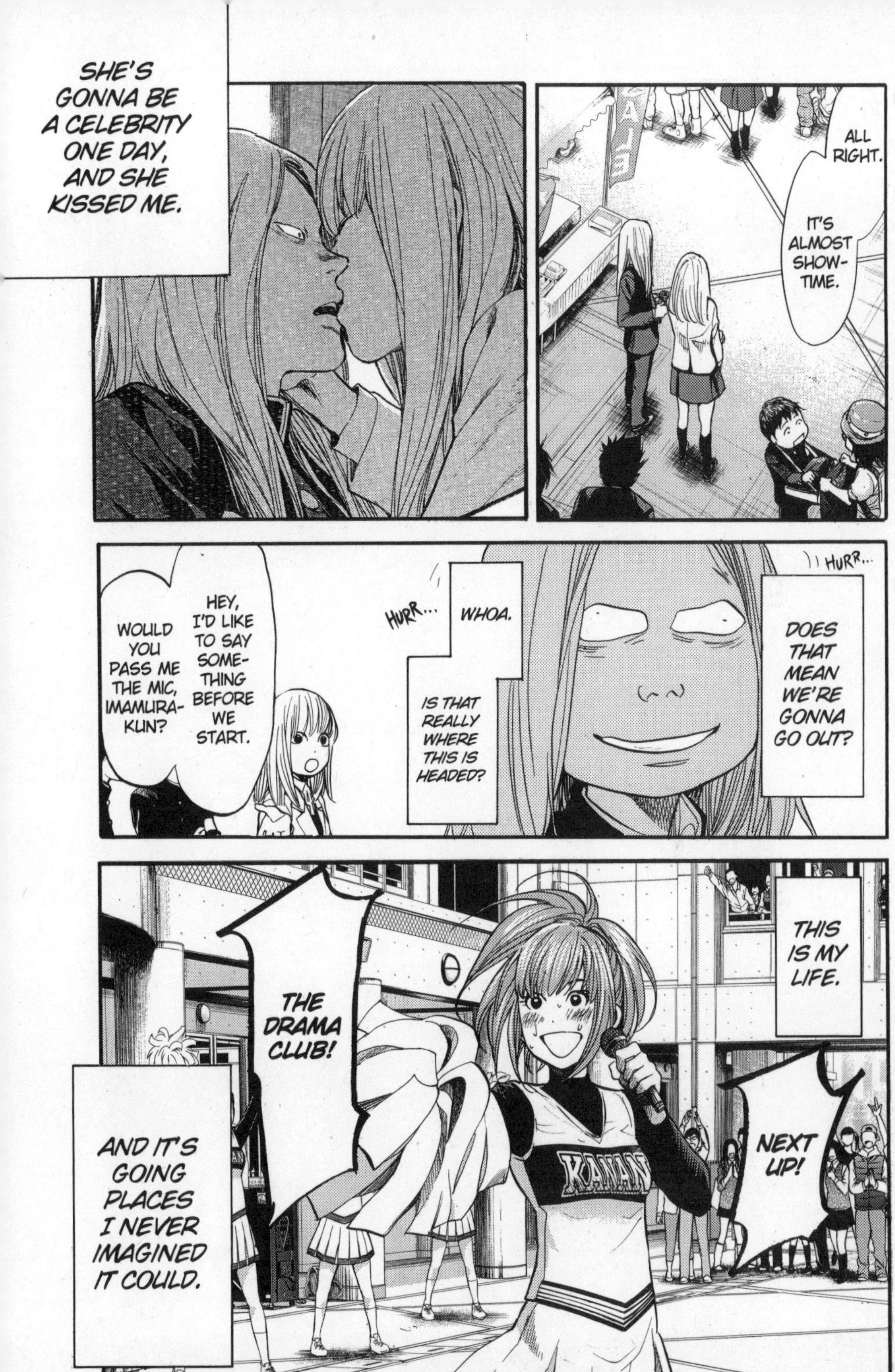
ALL RIGHT.
IT'S ALMOST SHOW-TIME.
SHE'S GONNA BE A CELEBRITY ONE DAY, AND SHE KISSED ME.
HURR...
DOES THAT MEAN WE'RE GONNA GO OUT?
WHOA.
IS THAT REALLY WHERE THIS IS HEADED?
HURR...
HEY, I'D LIKE TO SAY SOME-THING BEFORE WE START.
WOULD YOU PASS ME THE MIC, IMAMURA-KUN?
THIS IS MY LIFE.
NEXT UP!
THE DRAMA CLUB!
AND IT'S GOING PLACES I NEVER IMAGINED IT COULD.

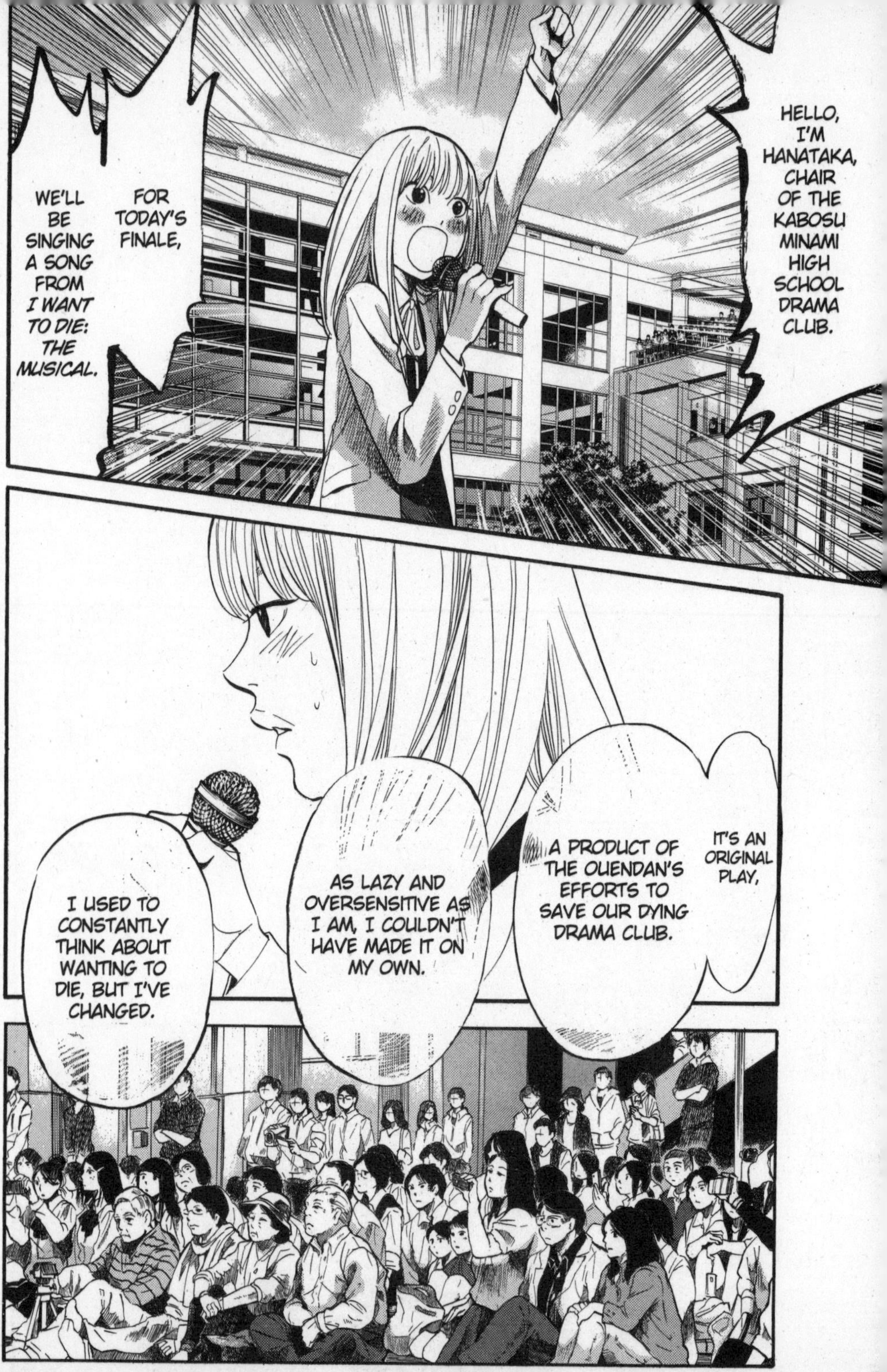
HELLO, I'M HANATAKA, CHAIR OF THE KABOSU MINAMI HIGH SCHOOL DRAMA CLUB.
FOR TODAY'S FINALE,
WE'LL BE SINGING A SONG FROM *I WANT TO DIE: THE MUSICAL.*
IT'S AN ORIGINAL PLAY,
A PRODUCT OF THE OUENDAN'S EFFORTS TO SAVE OUR DYING DRAMA CLUB.
AS LAZY AND OVERSENSITIVE AS I AM, I COULDN'T HAVE MADE IT ON MY OWN.
I USED TO CONSTANTLY THINK ABOUT WANTING TO DIE, BUT I'VE CHANGED.

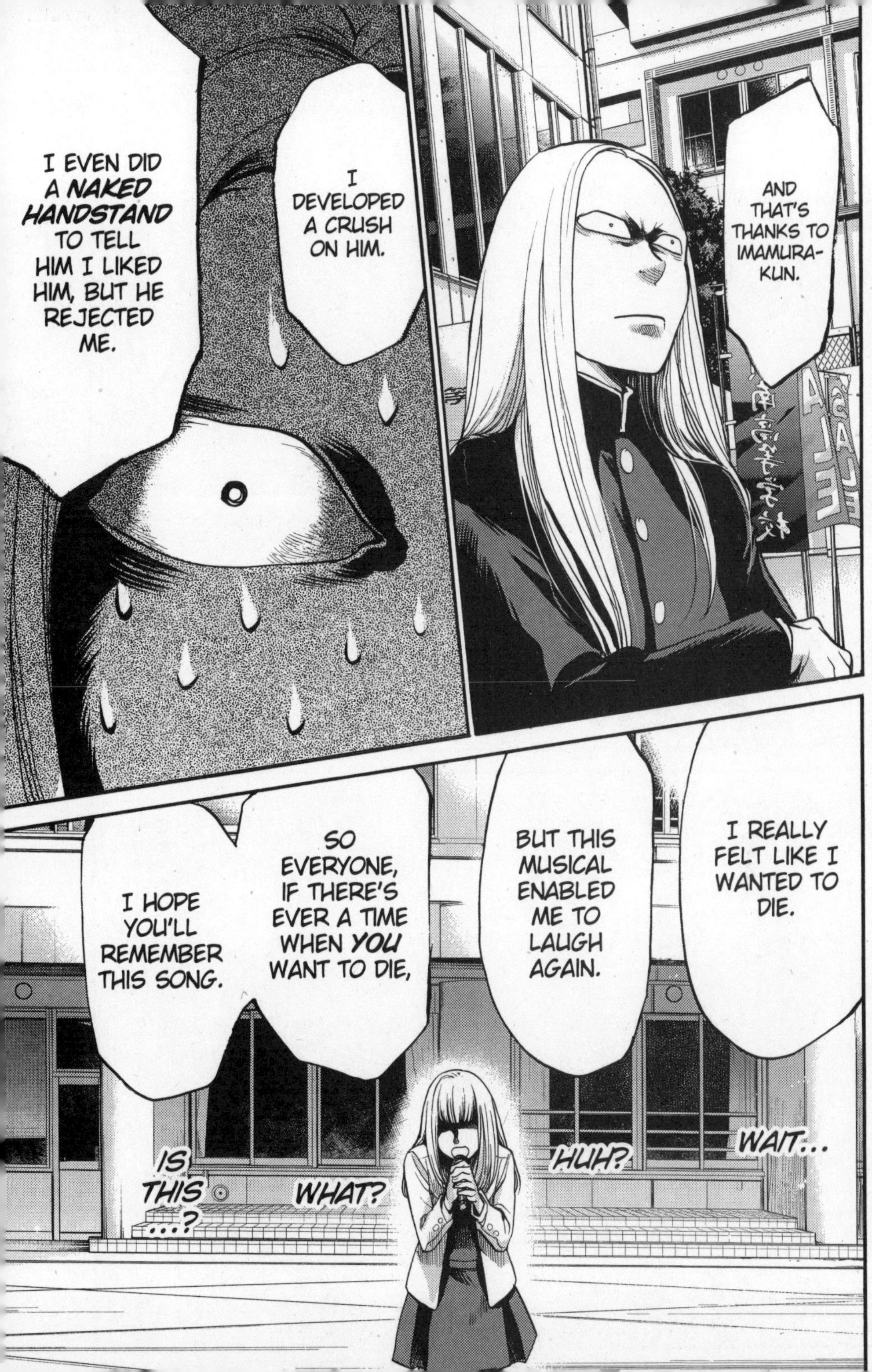
AND THAT'S THANKS TO IMAMURA-KUN.
I DEVELOPED A CRUSH ON HIM.
I EVEN DID A **NAKED HANDSTAND** TO TELL HIM I LIKED HIM, BUT HE REJECTED ME.
I REALLY FELT LIKE I WANTED TO DIE.
BUT THIS MUSICAL ENABLED ME TO LAUGH AGAIN.
SO EVERYONE, IF THERE'S EVER A TIME WHEN *YOU* WANT TO DIE,
I HOPE YOU'LL REMEMBER THIS SONG.
WAIT...
HUH?
WHAT?
IS THIS ...?

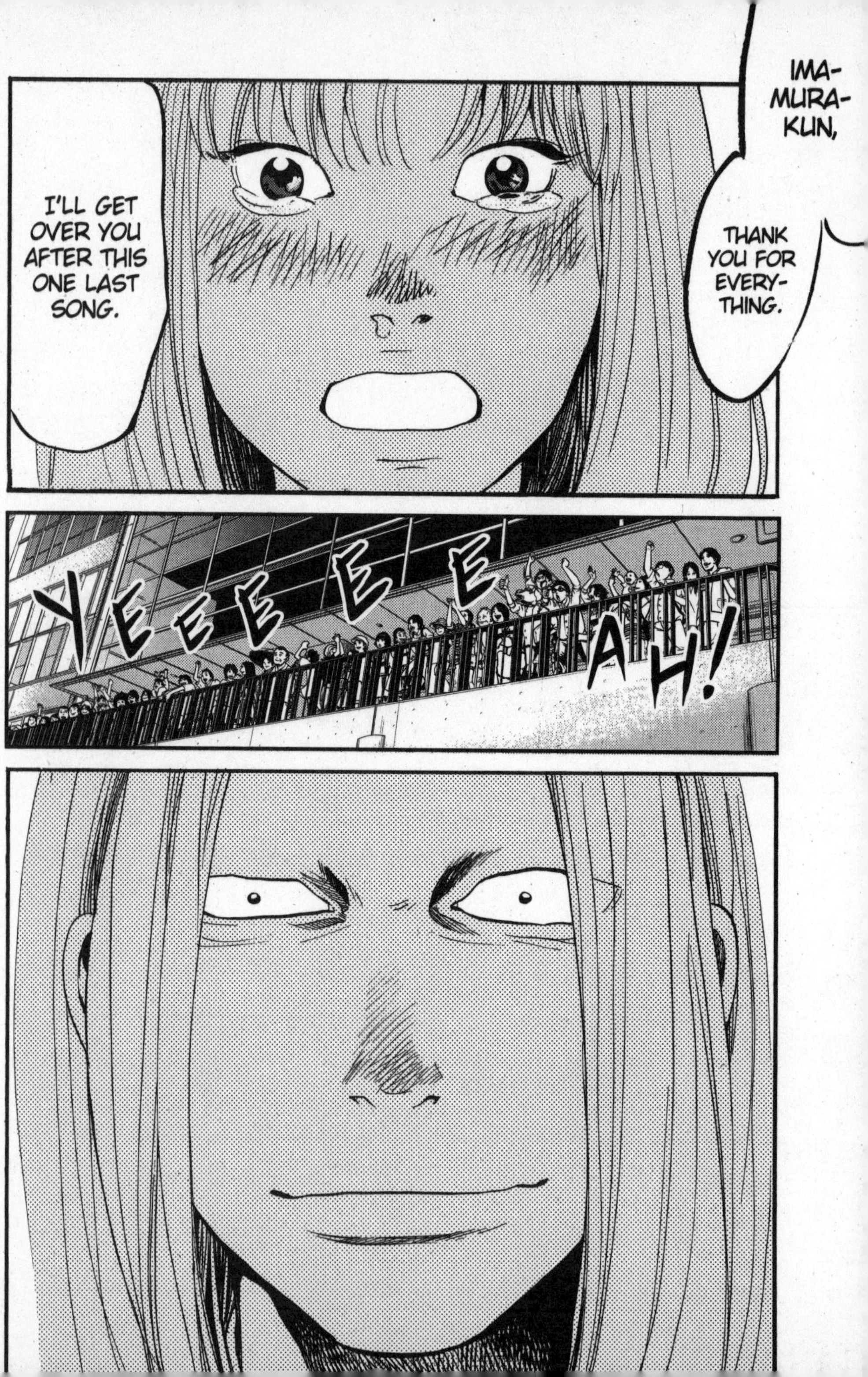
IMA-MURA-KUN,
THANK YOU FOR EVERY-THING.
I'LL GET OVER YOU AFTER THIS ONE LAST SONG.
YEEEEEAH!

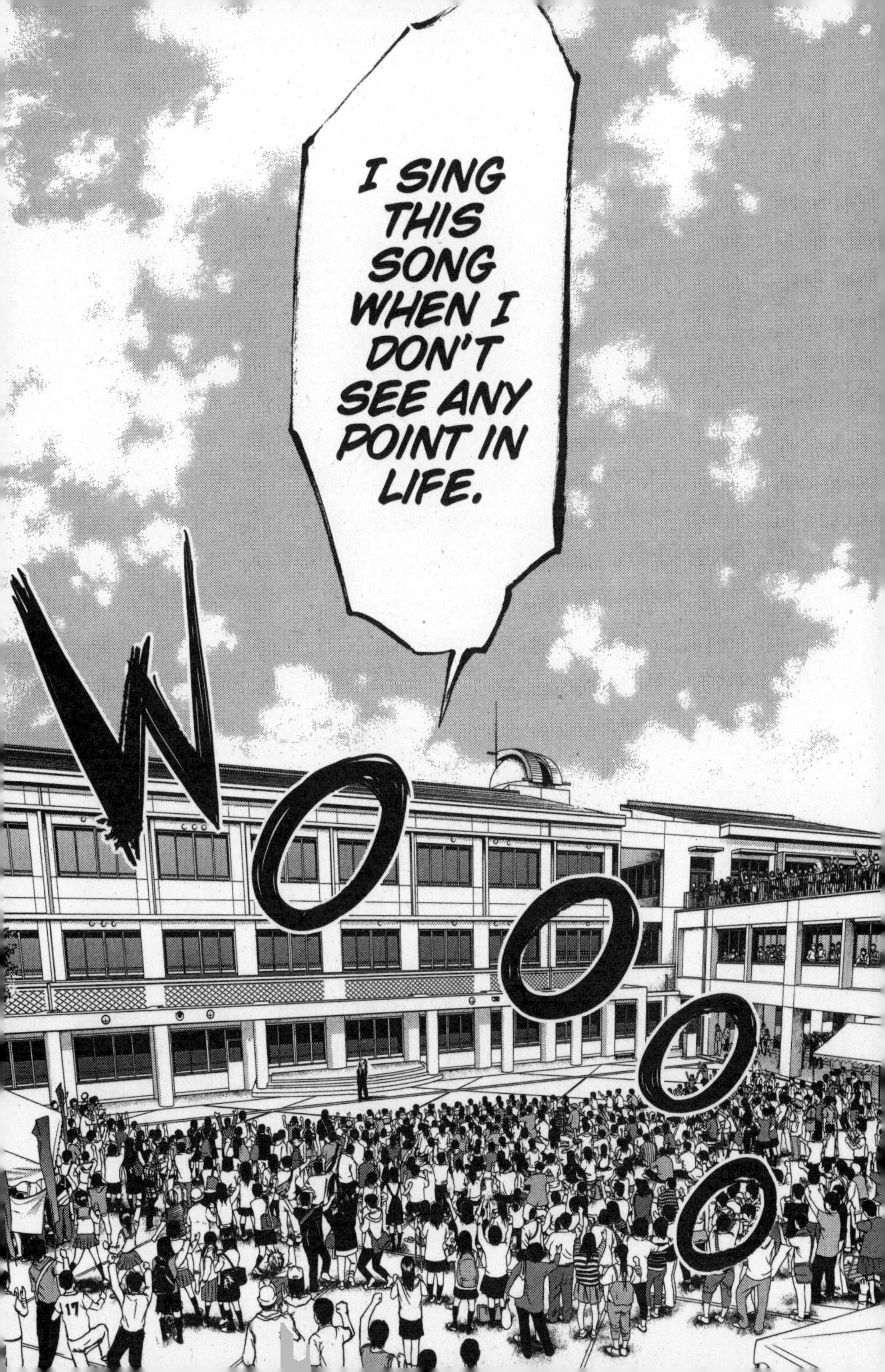
I SING THIS SONG WHEN I DON'T SEE ANY POINT IN LIFE.
WOOOO

Again!!
アゲイン!!

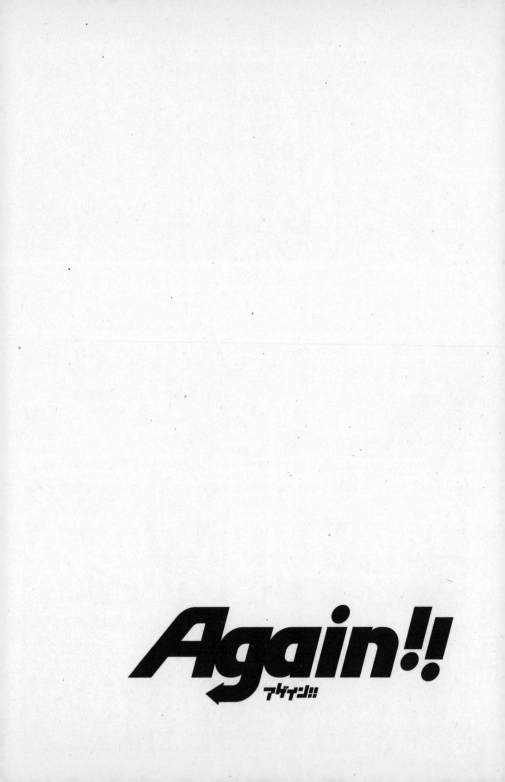

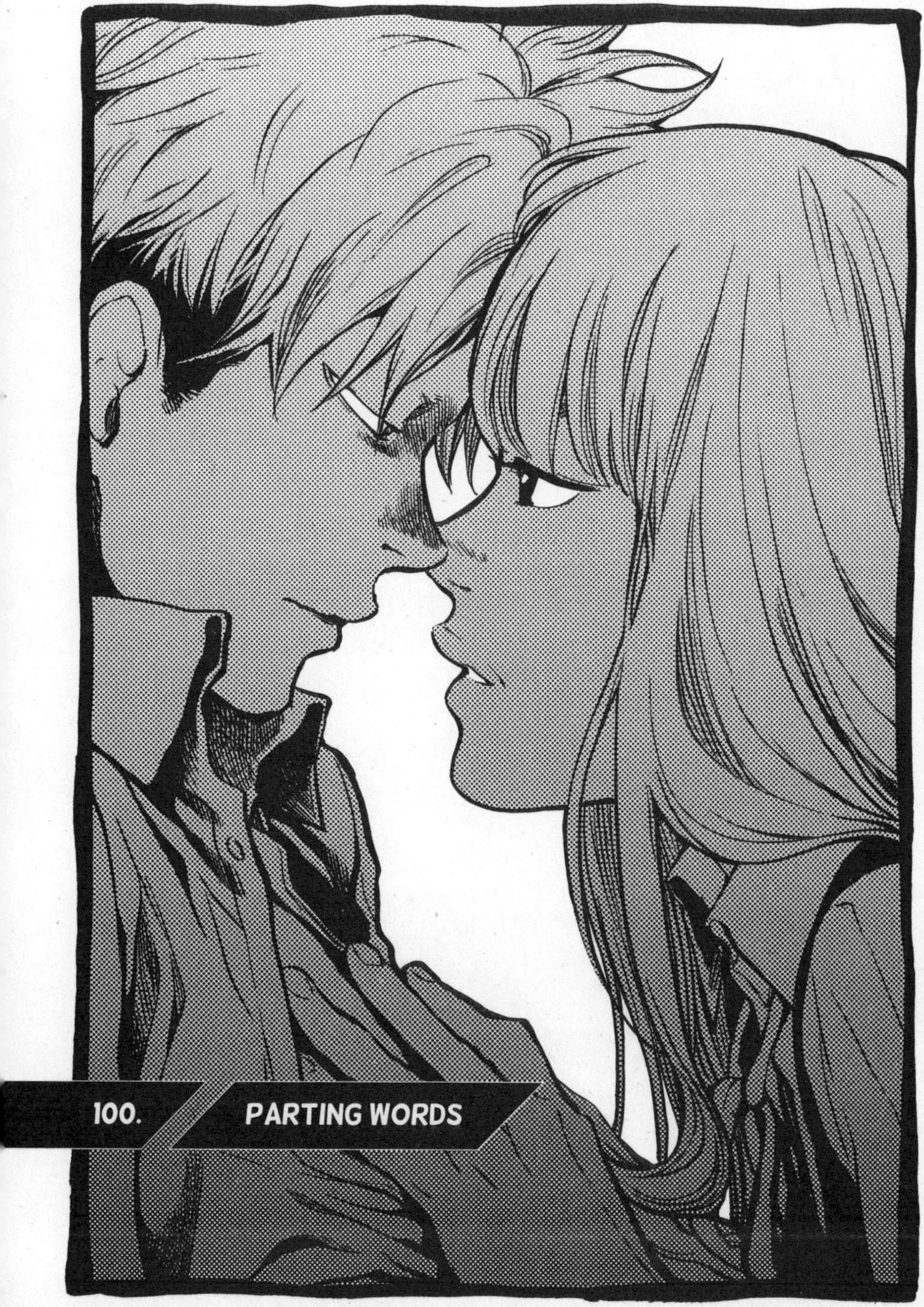
100.
PARTING WORDS

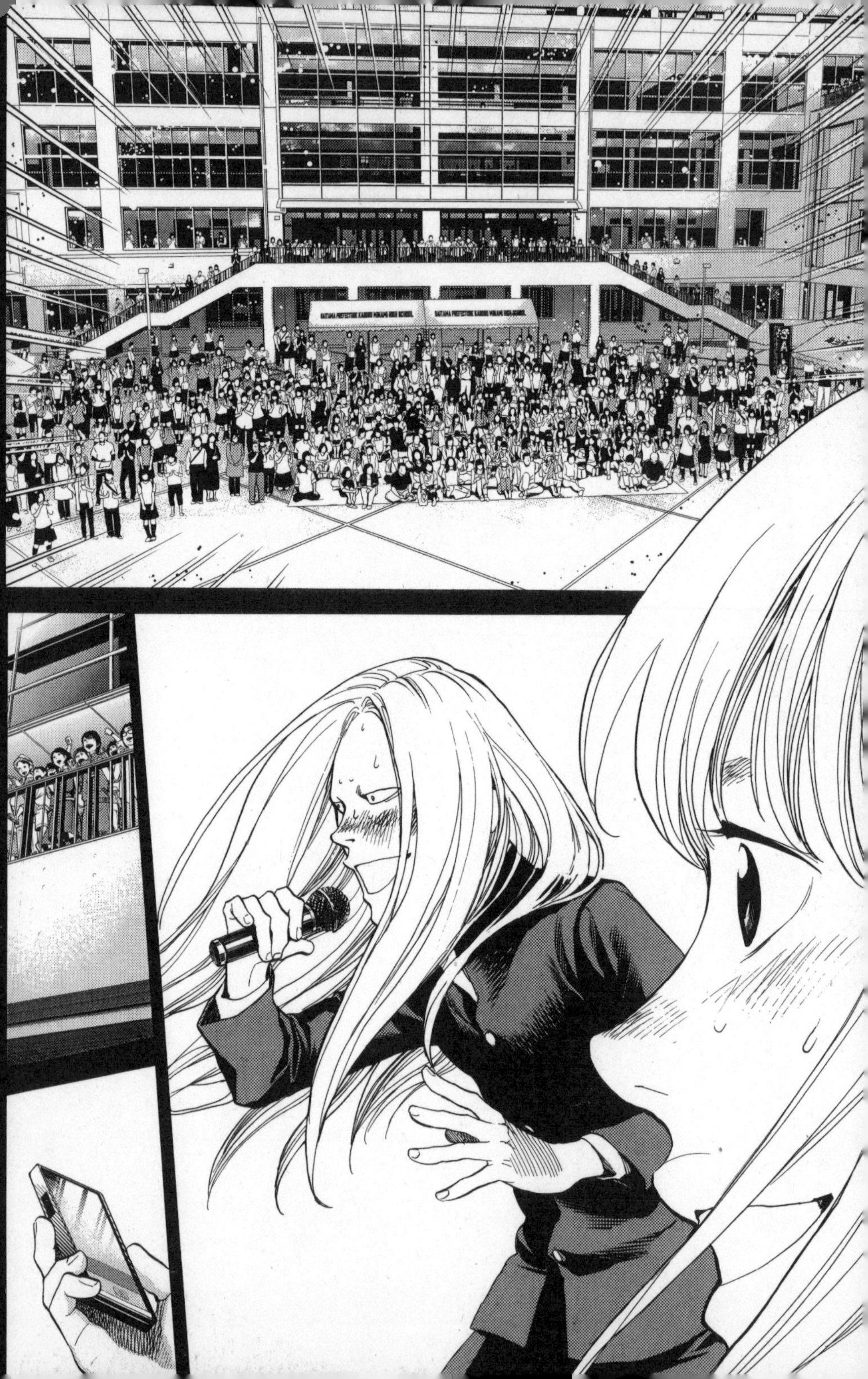

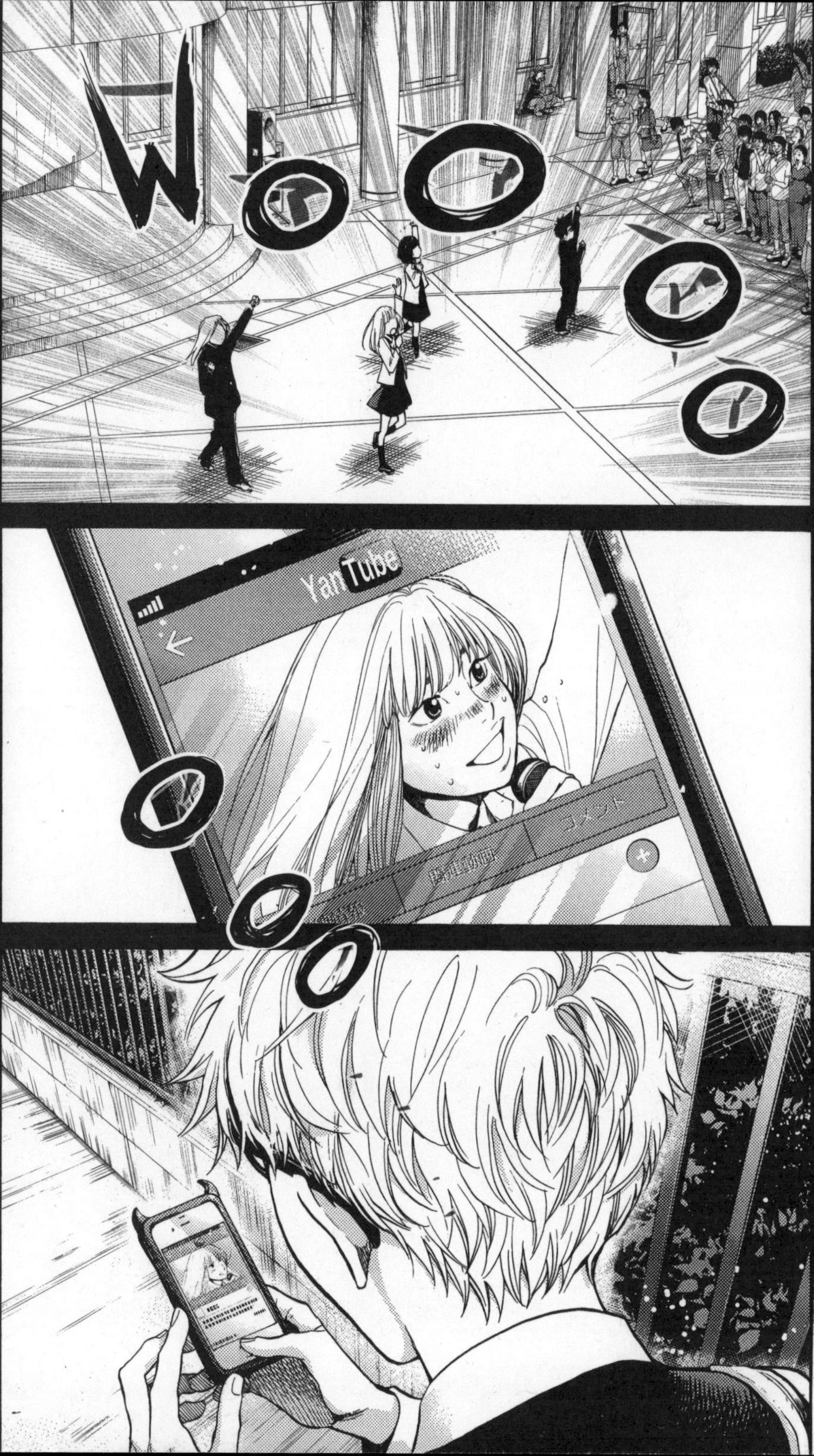
WOOOOOOO
YanTube
コメント
関連動画

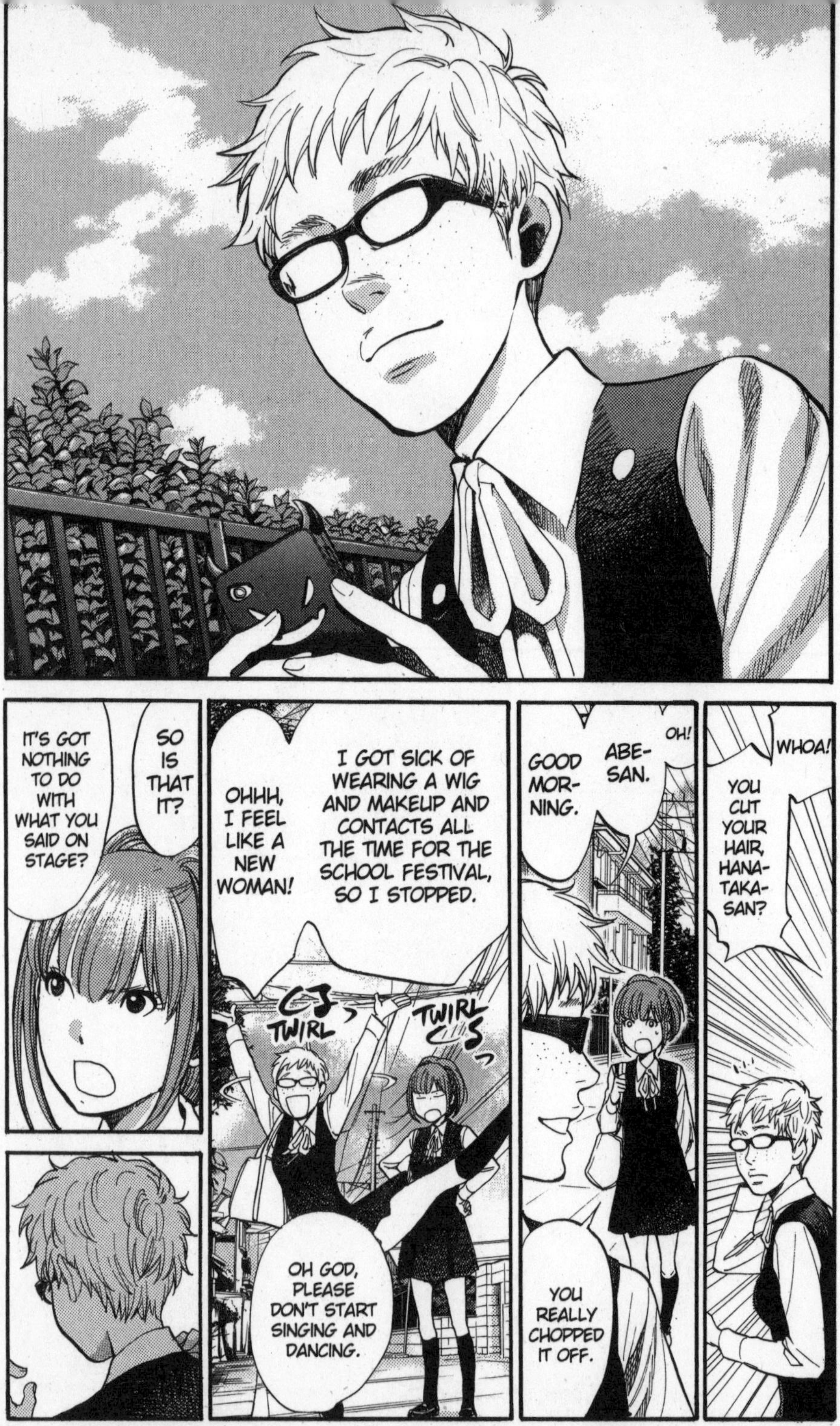
WHOA!
YOU CUT YOUR HAIR, HANA-TAKA-SAN?
OH!
ABE-SAN.
GOOD MOR-NING.
YOU REALLY CHOPPED IT OFF.
I GOT SICK OF WEARING A WIG AND MAKEUP AND CONTACTS ALL THE TIME FOR THE SCHOOL FESTIVAL, SO I STOPPED.
OHHH, I FEEL LIKE A NEW WOMAN!
TWIRL
TWIRL
OH GOD, PLEASE DON'T START SINGING AND DANCING.
SO IS THAT IT?
IT'S GOT NOTHING TO DO WITH WHAT YOU SAID ON STAGE?

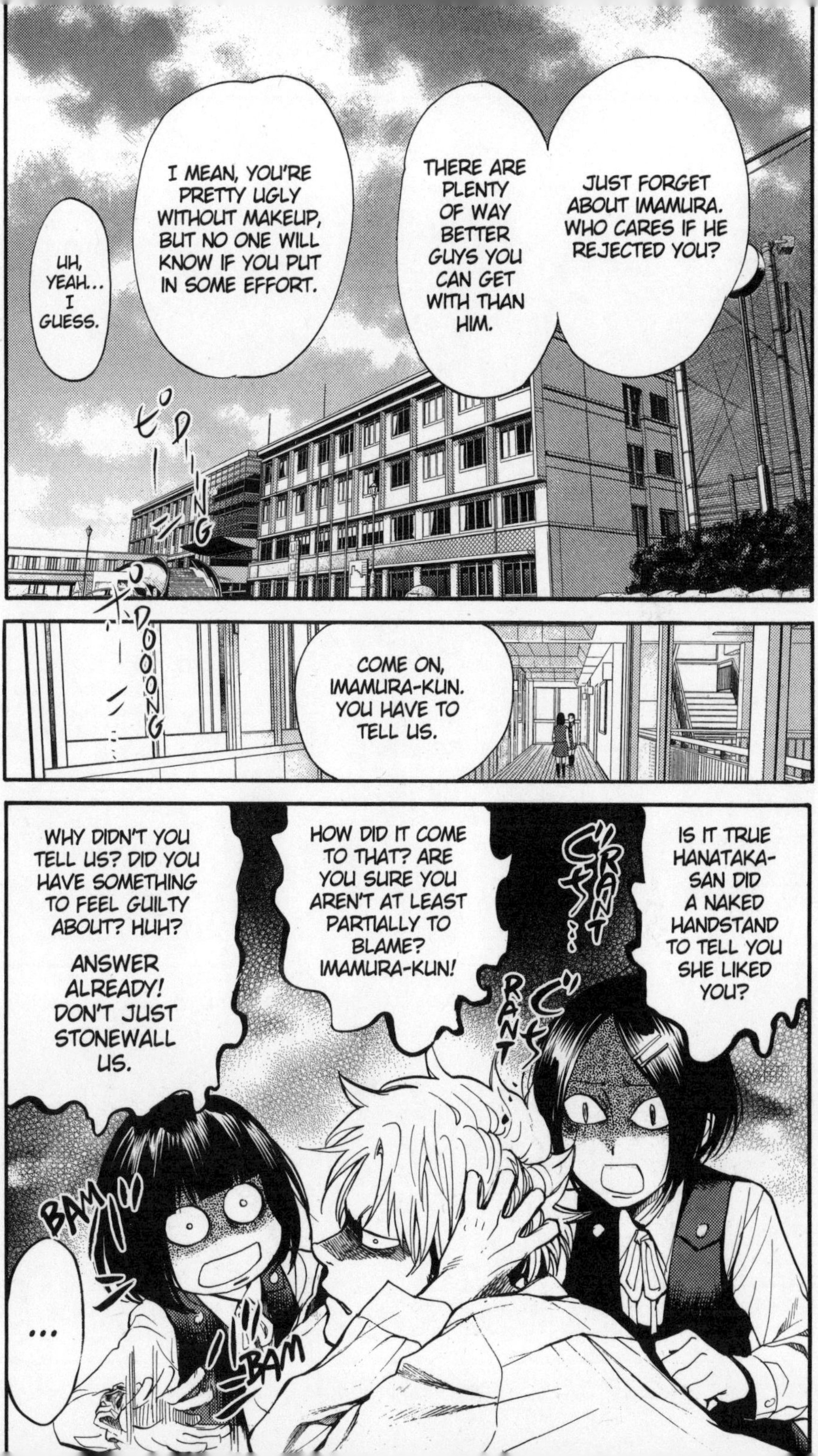
JUST FORGET ABOUT IMAMURA. WHO CARES IF HE REJECTED YOU?
THERE ARE PLENTY OF WAY BETTER GUYS YOU CAN GET WITH THAN HIM.
I MEAN, YOU'RE PRETTY UGLY WITHOUT MAKEUP, BUT NO ONE WILL KNOW IF YOU PUT IN SOME EFFORT.
UH, YEAH... I GUESS.
DI-I-ING
DOOOONG
COME ON, IMAMURA-KUN. YOU HAVE TO TELL US.
IS IT TRUE HANATAKA-SAN DID A NAKED HANDSTAND TO TELL YOU SHE LIKED YOU?
RANT
RANT
HOW DID IT COME TO THAT? ARE YOU SURE YOU AREN'T AT LEAST PARTIALLY TO BLAME? IMAMURA-KUN!
WHY DIDN'T YOU TELL US? DID YOU HAVE SOMETHING TO FEEL GUILTY ABOUT? HUH?
ANSWER ALREADY! DON'T JUST STONEWALL US.
BAM
BAM
...

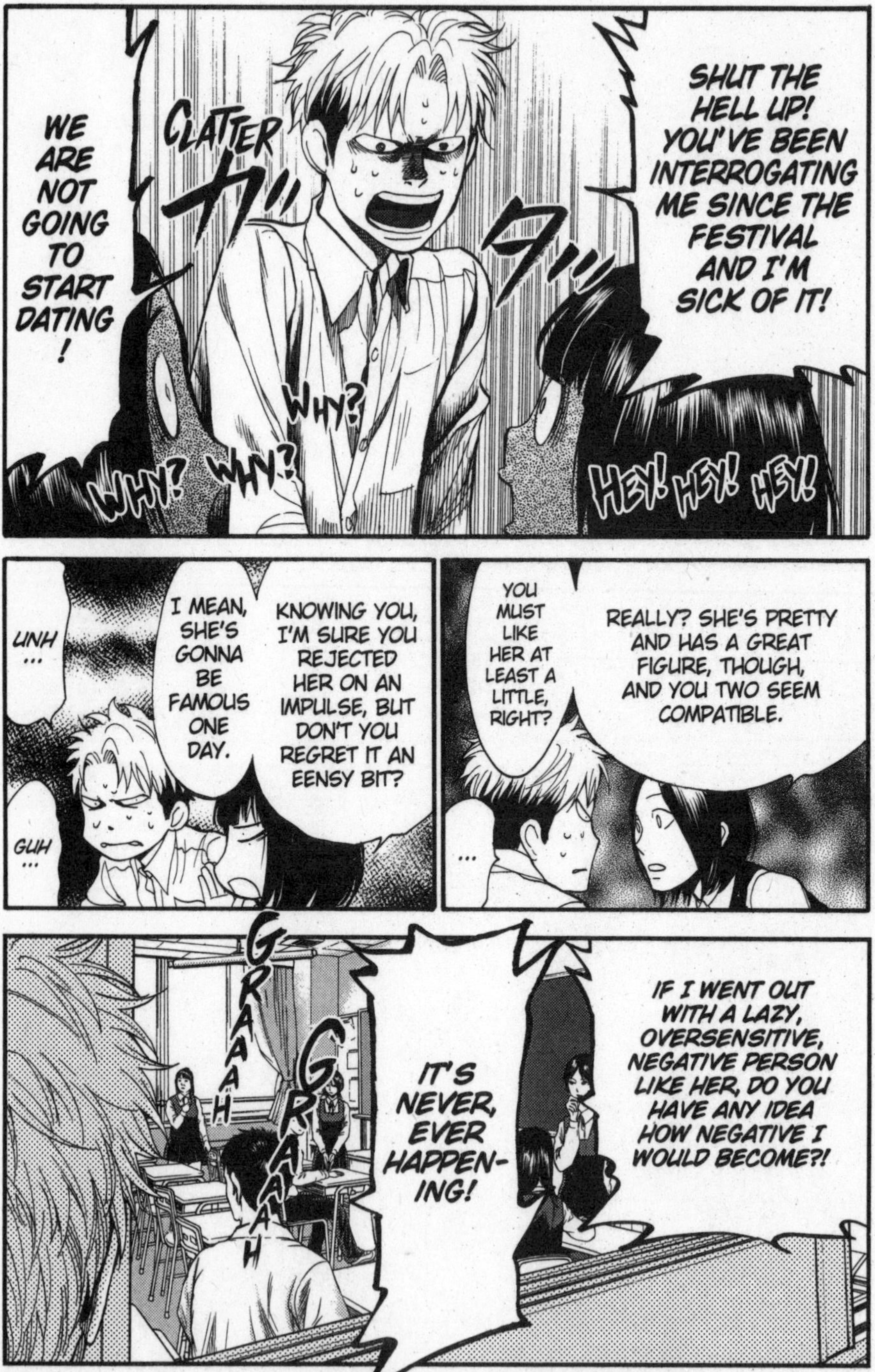
SHUT THE HELL UP! YOU'VE BEEN INTERROGATING ME SINCE THE FESTIVAL AND I'M SICK OF IT!
CLATTER
WE ARE NOT GOING TO START DATING!
WHY?
HEY! HEY! HEY!
WHY? WHY?
REALLY? SHE'S PRETTY AND HAS A GREAT FIGURE, THOUGH, AND YOU TWO SEEM COMPATIBLE.
YOU MUST LIKE HER AT LEAST A LITTLE, RIGHT?
...
KNOWING YOU, I'M SURE YOU REJECTED HER ON AN IMPULSE, BUT DON'T YOU REGRET IT AN EENSY BIT?
I MEAN, SHE'S GONNA BE FAMOUS ONE DAY.
UNH ...
GUH ...
IF I WENT OUT WITH A LAZY, OVERSENSITIVE, NEGATIVE PERSON LIKE HER, DO YOU HAVE ANY IDEA HOW NEGATIVE I WOULD BECOME?!
IT'S NEVER, EVER HAPPEN-ING!
GRAAAAH
GRAAAAH

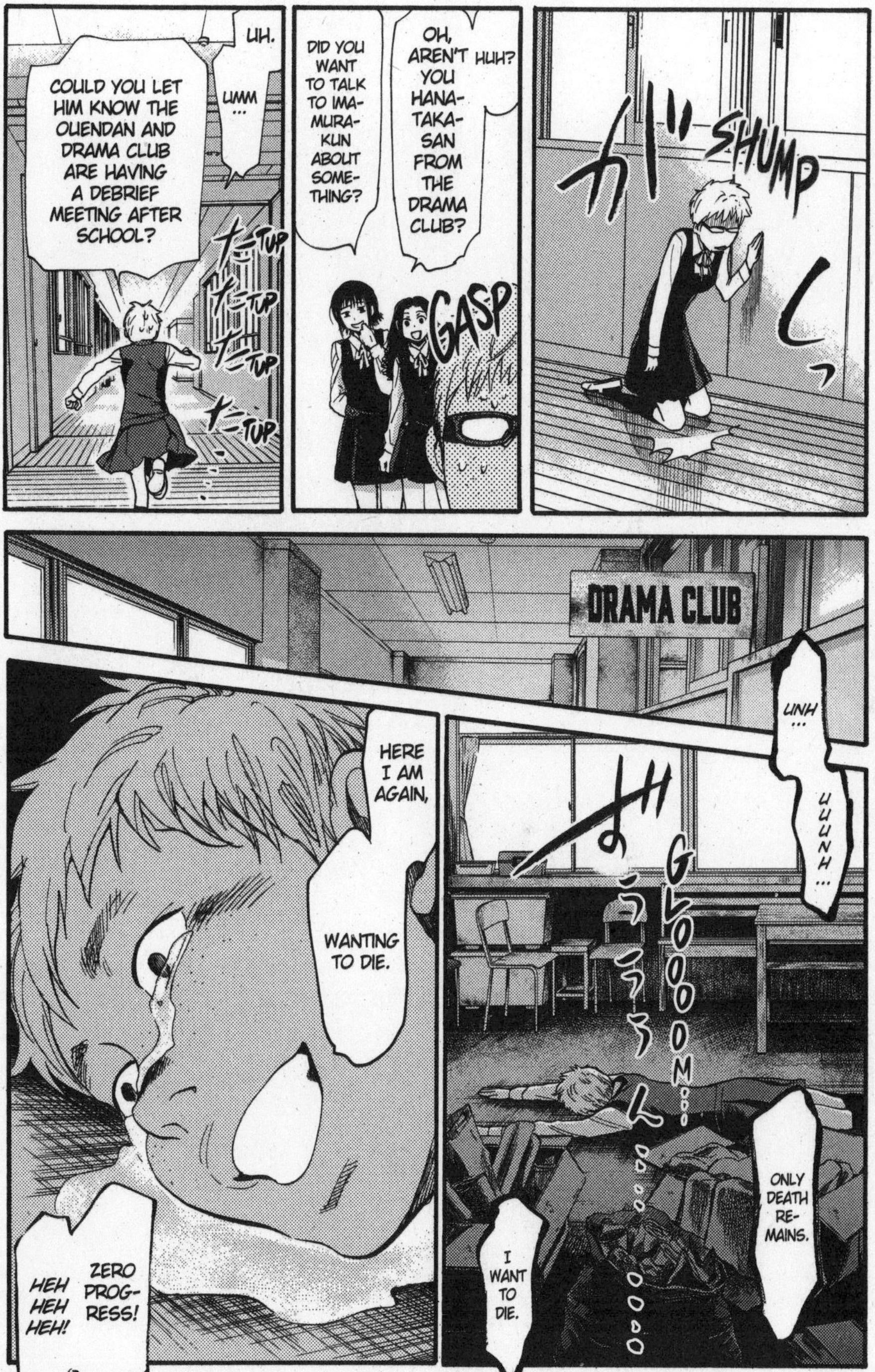
SHUMP
HUH?
OH, AREN'T YOU HANA-TAKA-SAN FROM THE DRAMA CLUB?
DID YOU WANT TO TALK TO IMA-MURA-KUN ABOUT SOME-THING?
GASP
UH.
UMM ...
COULD YOU LET HIM KNOW THE OUENDAN AND DRAMA CLUB ARE HAVING A DEBRIEF MEETING AFTER SCHOOL?
TUP
TUP
TUP
TUP
DRAMA CLUB
UNH ...
UUUNH ...
GLOOOOOM...
ONLY DEATH RE-MAINS.
I WANT TO DIE.
HERE I AM AGAIN,
WANTING TO DIE.
ZERO PROG-RESS!
HEH HEH HEH!

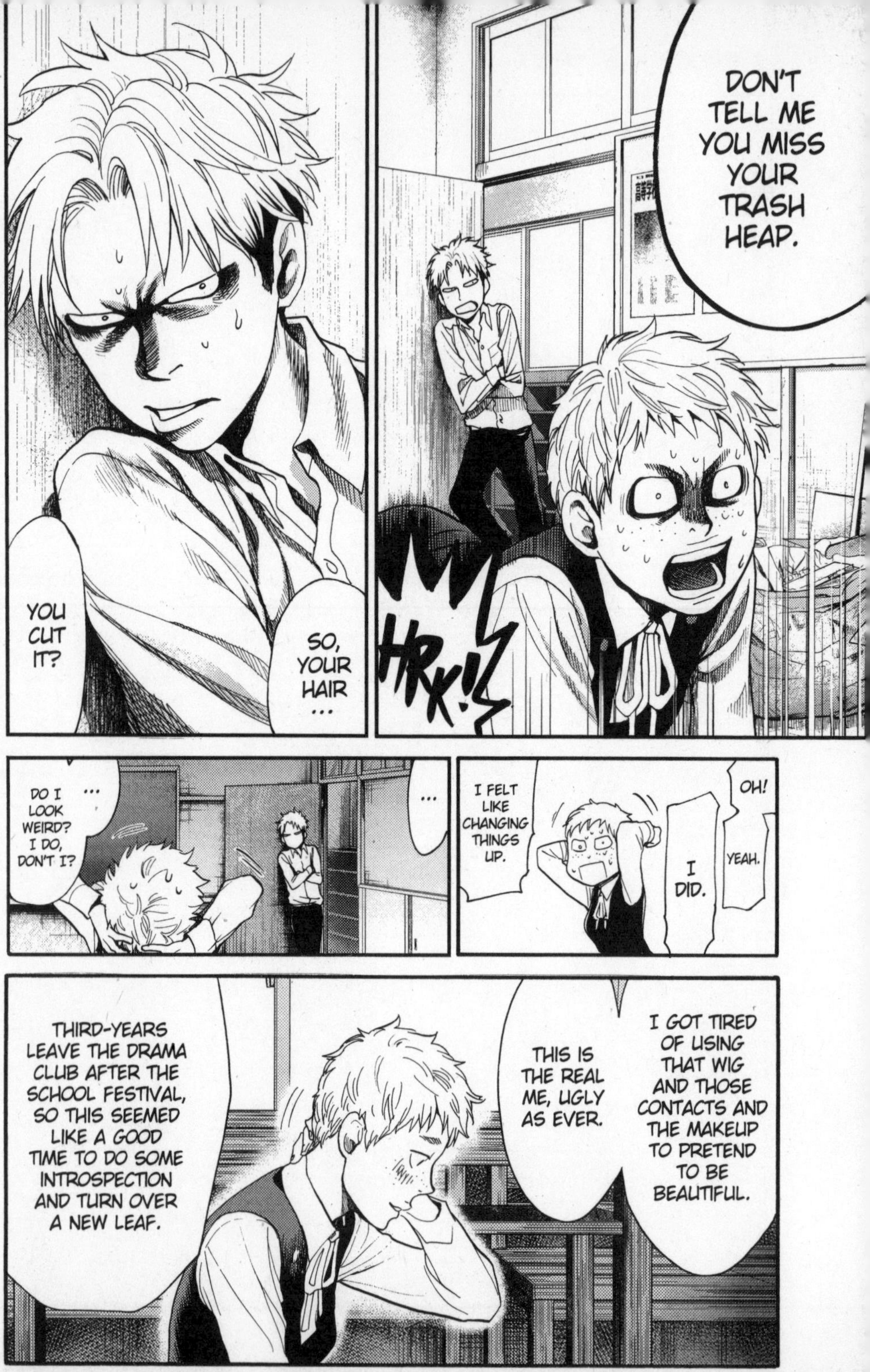
DON'T TELL ME YOU MISS YOUR TRASH HEAP.
HRK!!
SO, YOUR HAIR...
YOU CUT IT?
OH!
YEAH.
I DID.
I FELT LIKE CHANGING THINGS UP.
...
...
DO I LOOK WEIRD? I DO, DON'T I?
I GOT TIRED OF USING THAT WIG AND THOSE CONTACTS AND THE MAKEUP TO PRETEND TO BE BEAUTIFUL.
THIS IS THE REAL ME, UGLY AS EVER.
THIRD-YEARS LEAVE THE DRAMA CLUB AFTER THE SCHOOL FESTIVAL, SO THIS SEEMED LIKE A GOOD TIME TO DO SOME INTROSPECTION AND TURN OVER A NEW LEAF.

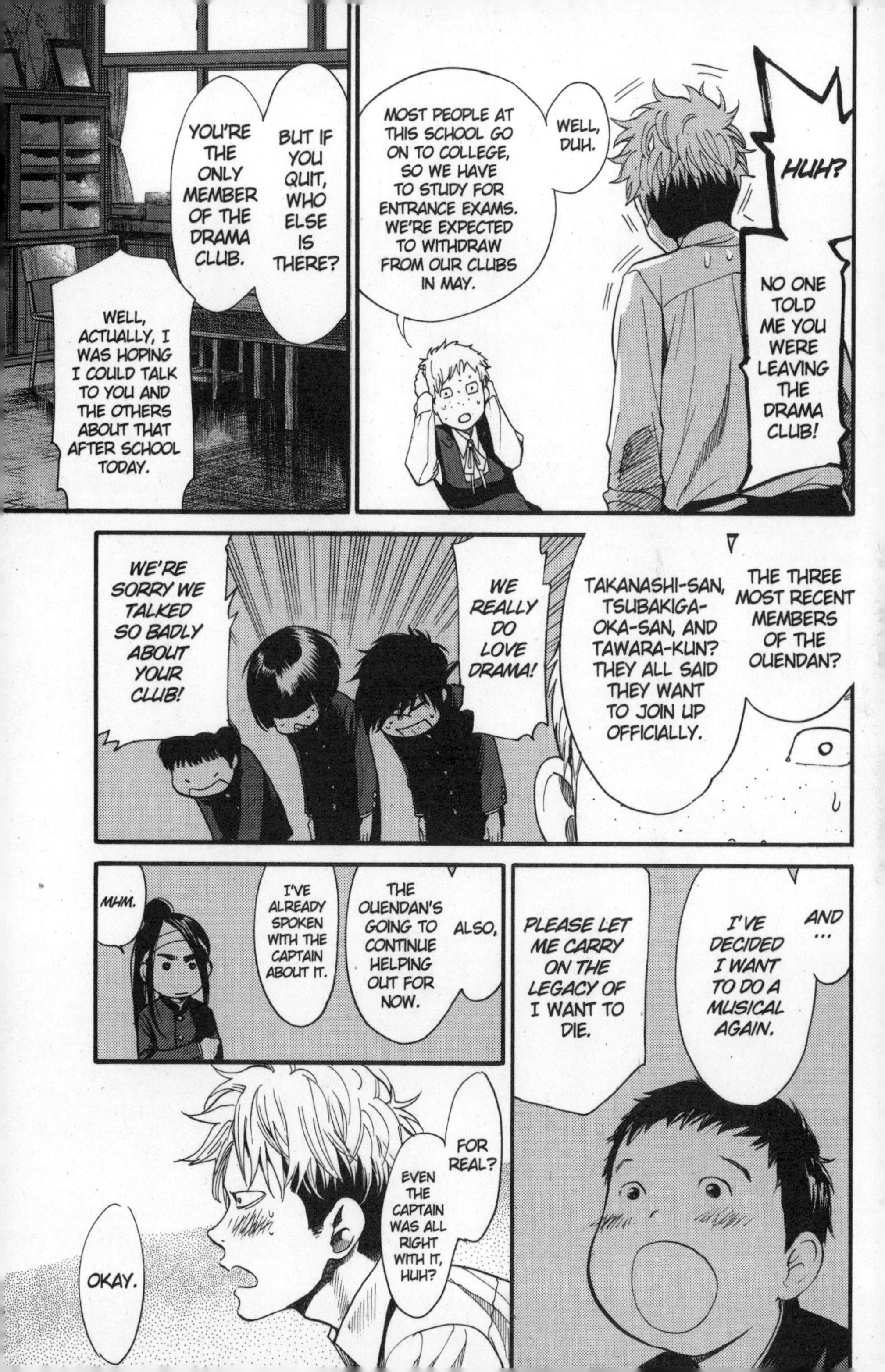
HUH?
NO ONE TOLD ME YOU WERE LEAVING THE DRAMA CLUB!
WELL, DUH.
MOST PEOPLE AT THIS SCHOOL GO ON TO COLLEGE, SO WE HAVE TO STUDY FOR ENTRANCE EXAMS. WE'RE EXPECTED TO WITHDRAW FROM OUR CLUBS IN MAY.
BUT IF YOU QUIT, WHO ELSE IS THERE?
YOU'RE THE ONLY MEMBER OF THE DRAMA CLUB.
WELL, ACTUALLY, I WAS HOPING I COULD TALK TO YOU AND THE OTHERS ABOUT THAT AFTER SCHOOL TODAY.
THE THREE MOST RECENT MEMBERS OF THE OUENDAN?
TAKANASHI-SAN, TSUBAKIGA-OKA-SAN, AND TAWARA-KUN? THEY ALL SAID THEY WANT TO JOIN UP OFFICIALLY.
WE REALLY DO LOVE DRAMA!
WE'RE SORRY WE TALKED SO BADLY ABOUT YOUR CLUB!
AND ...
I'VE DECIDED I WANT TO DO A MUSICAL AGAIN.
PLEASE LET ME CARRY ON THE LEGACY OF I WANT TO DIE.
ALSO,
THE OUENDAN'S GOING TO CONTINUE HELPING OUT FOR NOW.
I'VE ALREADY SPOKEN WITH THE CAPTAIN ABOUT IT.
MHM.
FOR REAL?
EVEN THE CAPTAIN WAS ALL RIGHT WITH IT, HUH?
OKAY.

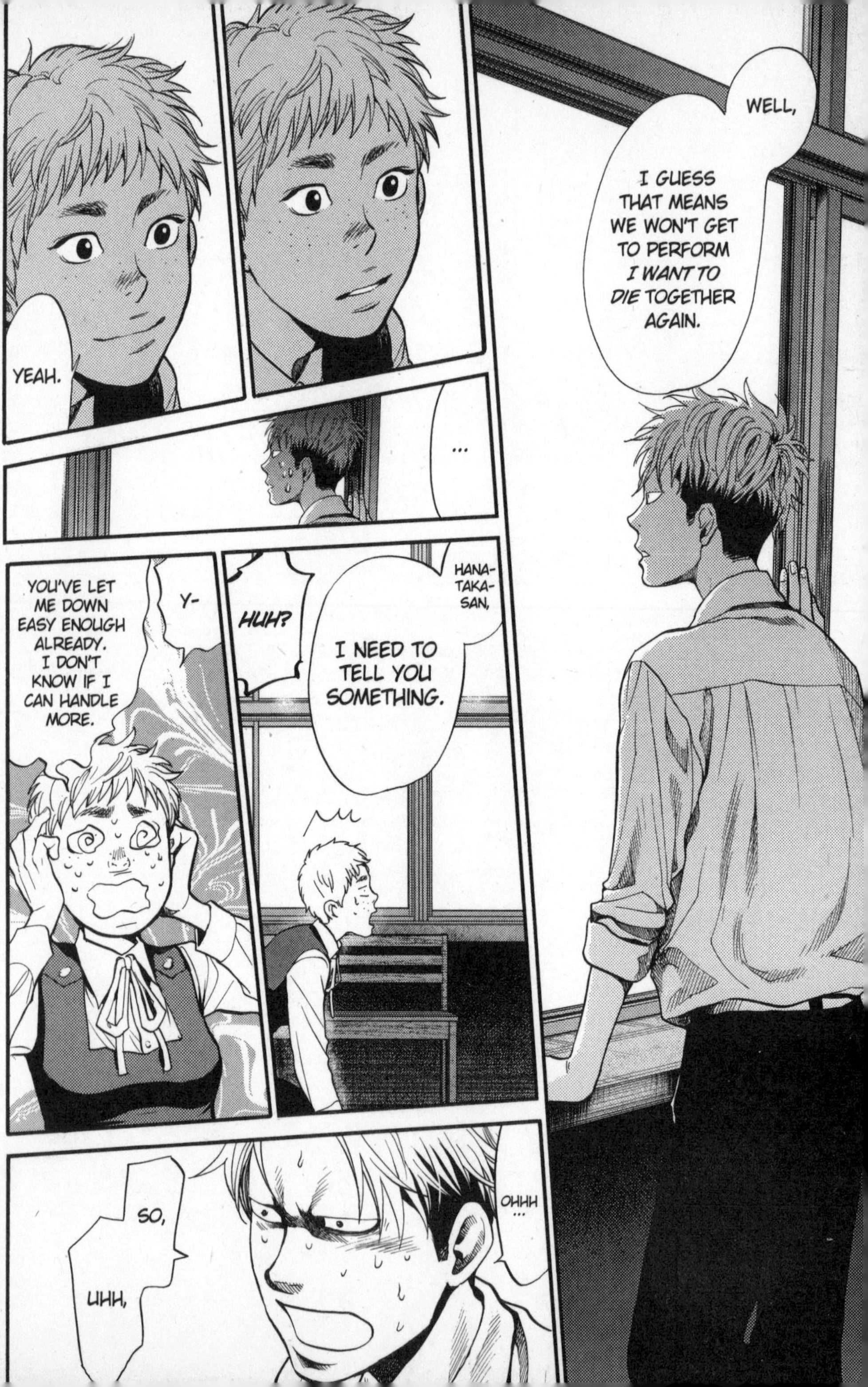
WELL,
I GUESS THAT MEANS WE WON'T GET TO PERFORM *I WANT TO DIE* TOGETHER AGAIN.
YEAH.
...
HANA-TAKA-SAN,
I NEED TO TELL YOU SOMETHING.
HUH?
Y-
YOU'VE LET ME DOWN EASY ENOUGH ALREADY. I DON'T KNOW IF I CAN HANDLE MORE.
OHHH ...
SO,
UHH,

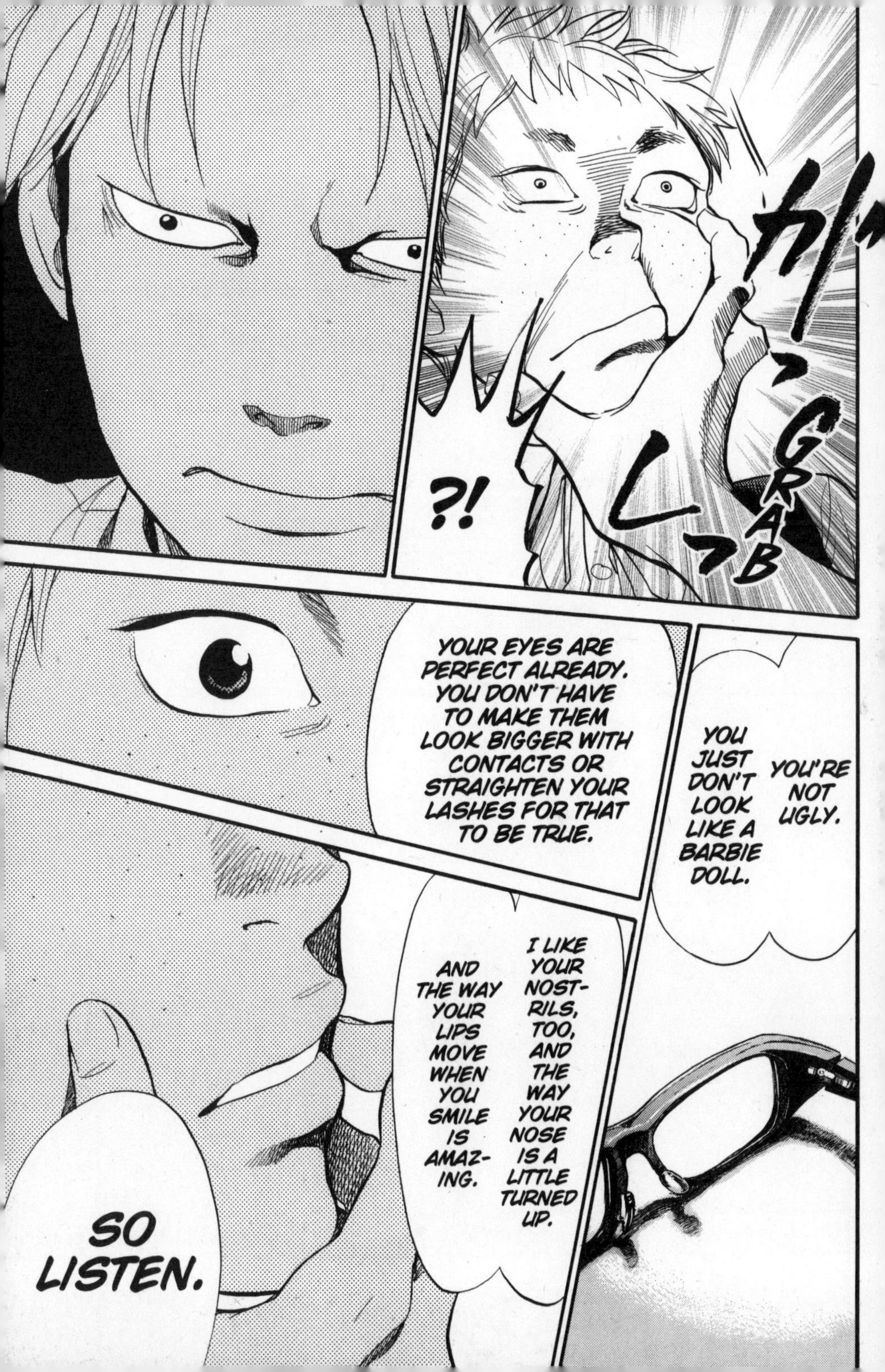
GRAB
?!
YOU'RE NOT UGLY.
YOU JUST DON'T LOOK LIKE A BARBIE DOLL.
YOUR EYES ARE PERFECT ALREADY. YOU DON'T HAVE TO MAKE THEM LOOK BIGGER WITH CONTACTS OR STRAIGHTEN YOUR LASHES FOR THAT TO BE TRUE.
I LIKE YOUR NOST-RILS, TOO, AND THE WAY YOUR NOSE IS A LITTLE TURNED UP.
AND THE WAY YOUR LIPS MOVE WHEN YOU SMILE IS AMAZ-ING.
SO LISTEN.

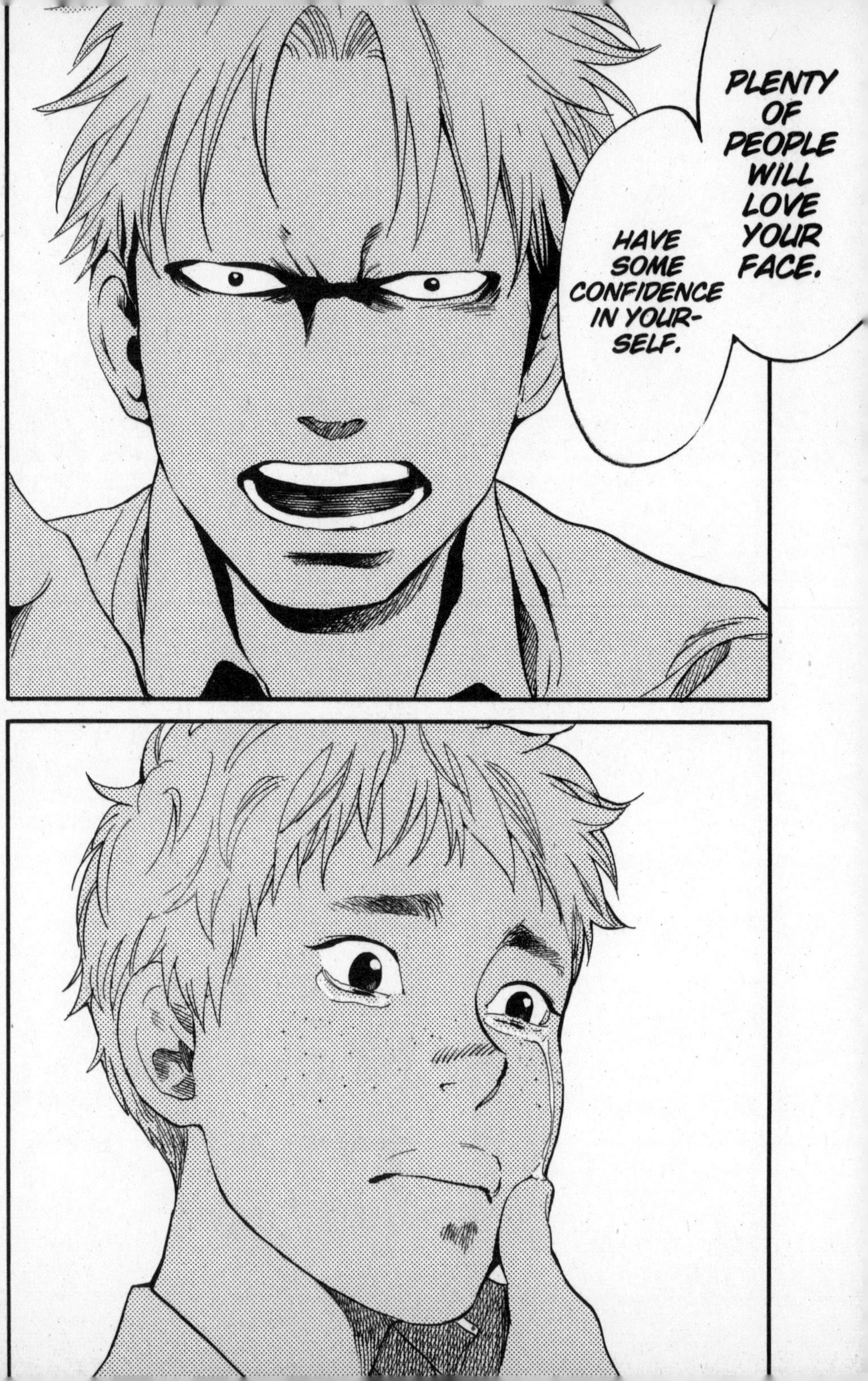
PLENTY OF PEOPLE WILL LOVE YOUR FACE.
HAVE SOME CONFIDENCE IN YOUR-SELF.

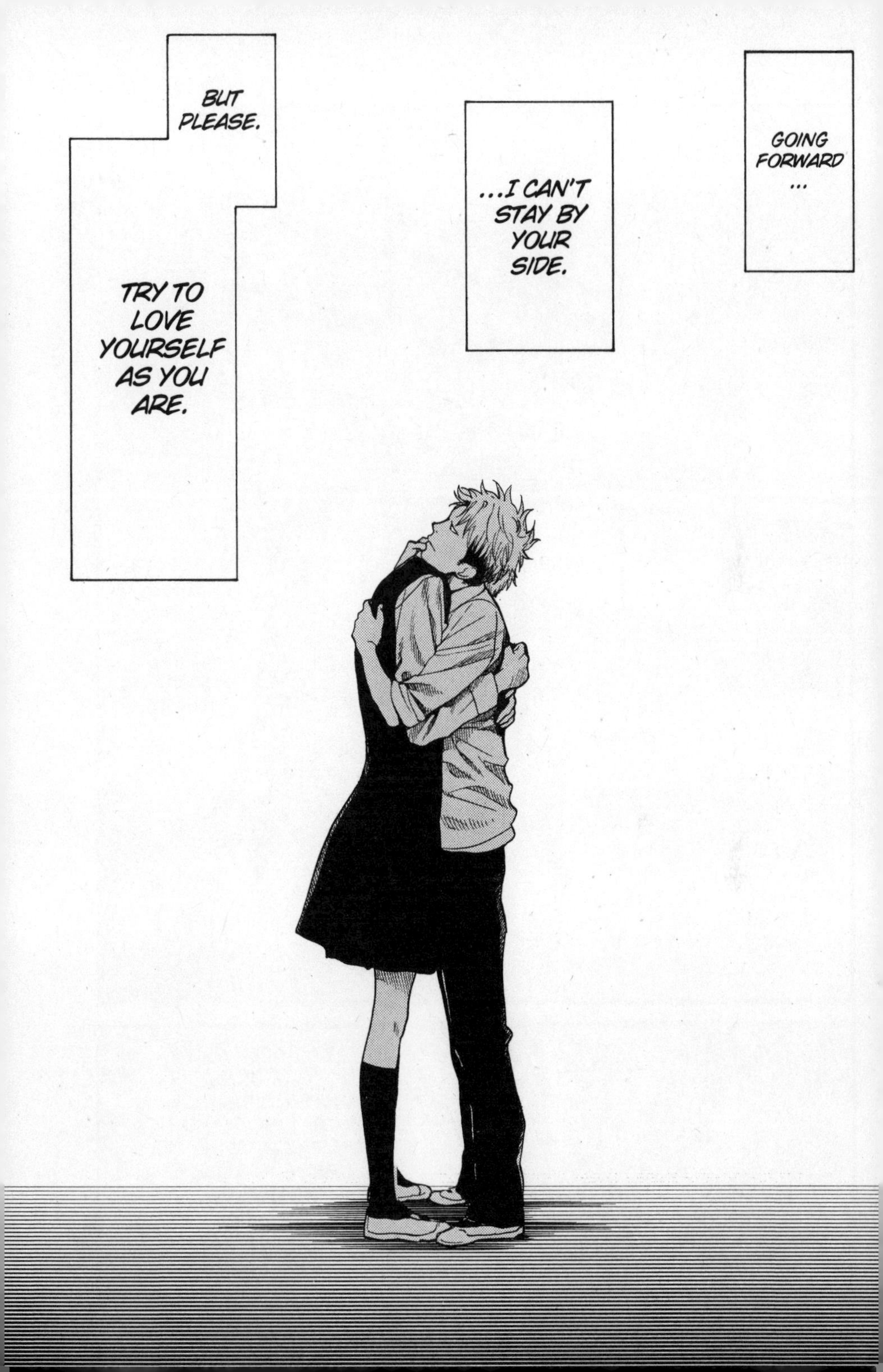
GOING FORWARD ...
...I CAN'T STAY BY YOUR SIDE.
BUT PLEASE.
TRY TO LOVE YOURSELF AS YOU ARE.

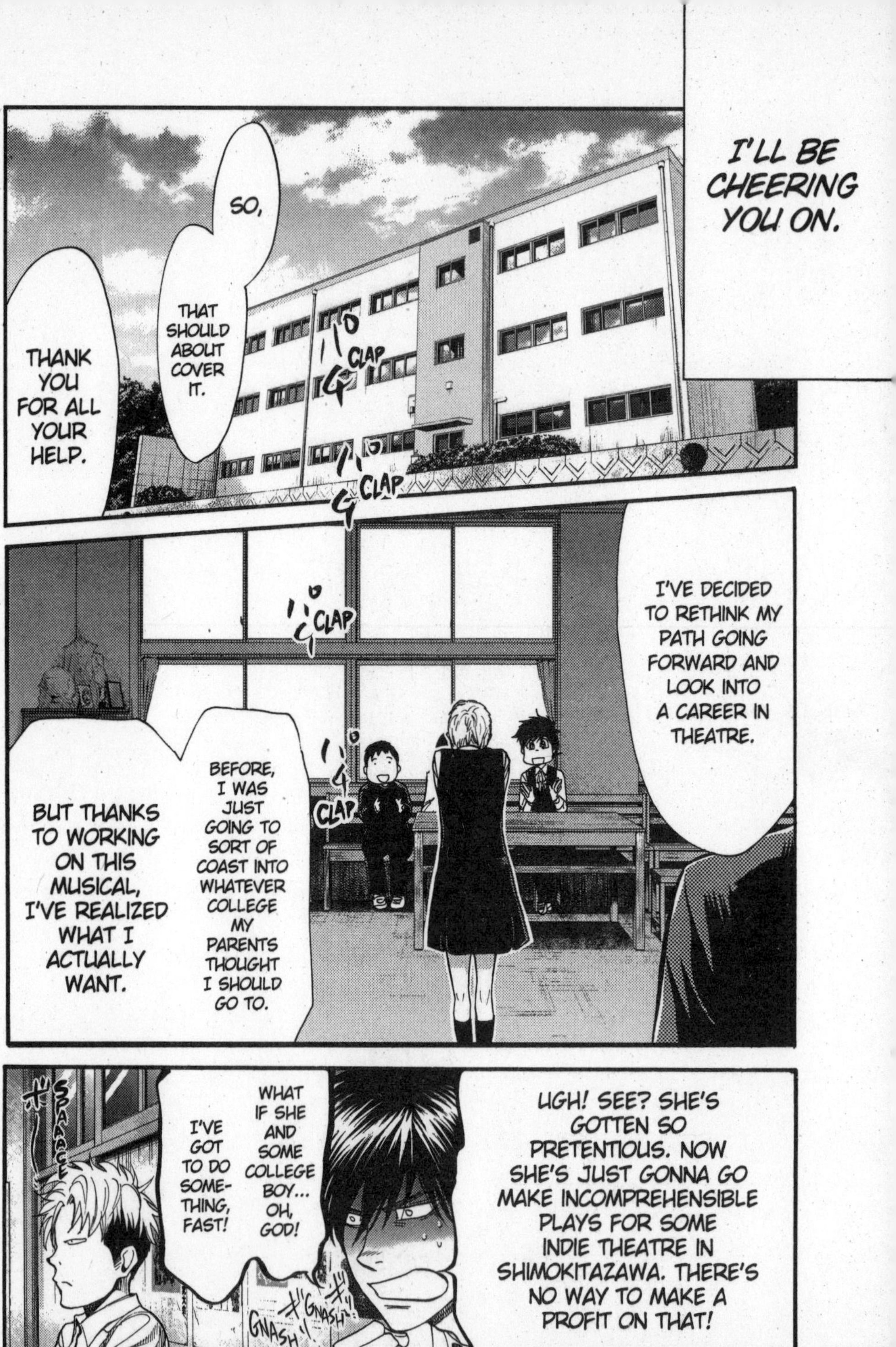
I'LL BE CHEERING YOU ON.
SO,
THAT SHOULD ABOUT COVER IT.
CLAP
CLAP
THANK YOU FOR ALL YOUR HELP.
I'VE DECIDED TO RETHINK MY PATH GOING FORWARD AND LOOK INTO A CAREER IN THEATRE.
CLAP
CLAP
BEFORE, I WAS JUST GOING TO SORT OF COAST INTO WHATEVER COLLEGE MY PARENTS THOUGHT I SHOULD GO TO.
BUT THANKS TO WORKING ON THIS MUSICAL, I'VE REALIZED WHAT I ACTUALLY WANT.
UGH! SEE? SHE'S GOTTEN SO PRETENTIOUS. NOW SHE'S JUST GONNA GO MAKE INCOMPREHENSIBLE PLAYS FOR SOME INDIE THEATRE IN SHIMOKITAZAWA. THERE'S NO WAY TO MAKE A PROFIT ON THAT!
GNASH
GNASH
WHAT IF SHE AND SOME COLLEGE BOY... OH, GOD!
I'VE GOT TO DO SOME-THING, FAST!
SPAAACE

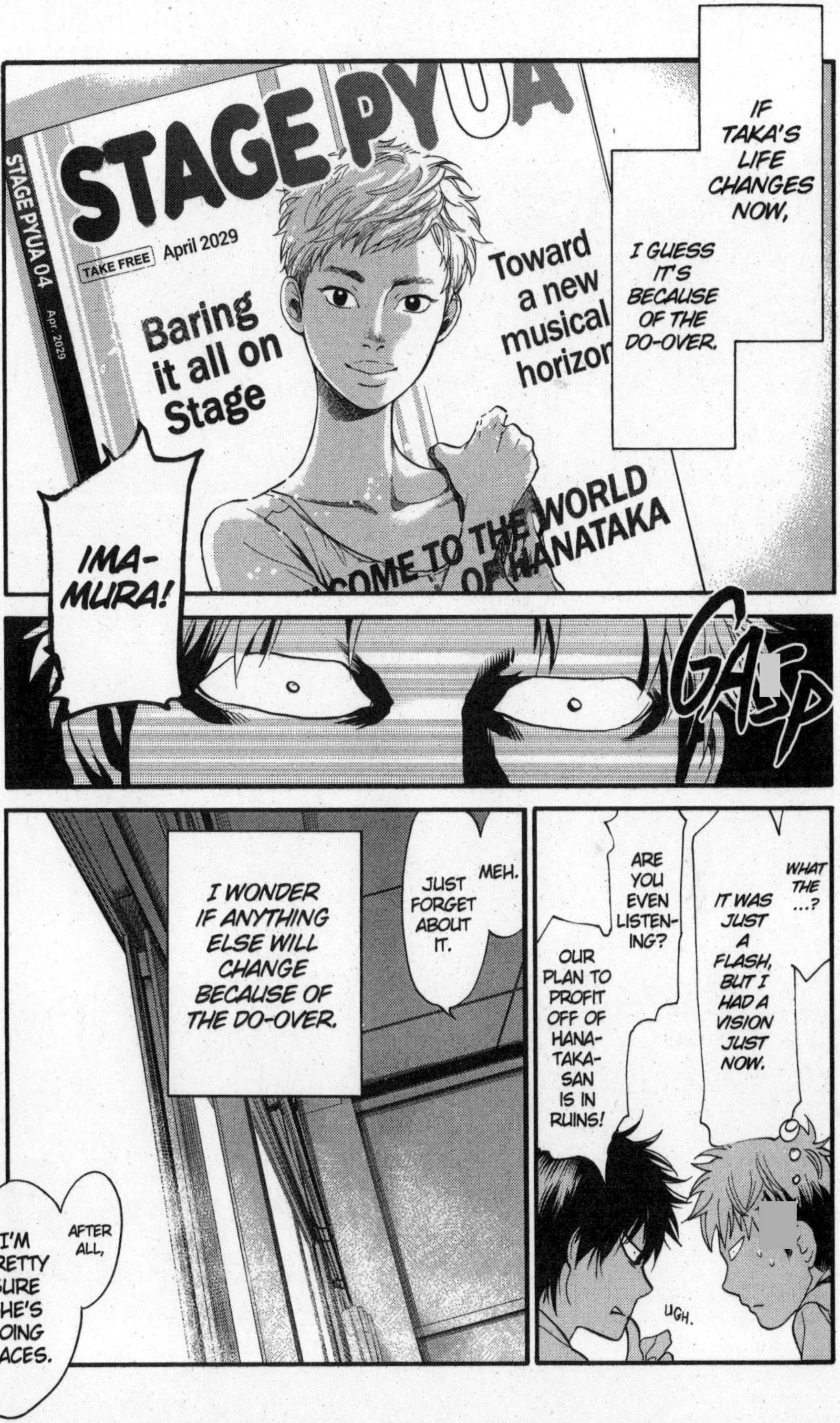
IF TAKA'S LIFE CHANGES NOW,
I GUESS IT'S BECAUSE OF THE DO-OVER.
STAGE PYUA
STAGE PYUA 04
Apr. 2029
TAKE FREE April 2029
Toward a new musical horizon
Baring it all on Stage
COME TO THE WORLD OF HANATAKA
IMA-MURA!
GASP
WHAT THE ...?
IT WAS JUST A FLASH, BUT I HAD A VISION JUST NOW.
ARE YOU EVEN LISTENING?
OUR PLAN TO PROFIT OFF OF HANA-TAKA-SAN IS IN RUINS!
UGH.
MEH.
JUST FORGET ABOUT IT.
I WONDER IF ANYTHING ELSE WILL CHANGE BECAUSE OF THE DO-OVER.
AFTER ALL,
I'M PRETTY SURE SHE'S GOING PLACES.

Again!!

アゲイン!!

101. BLISSFUL TEEN IDENTITY CRISIS

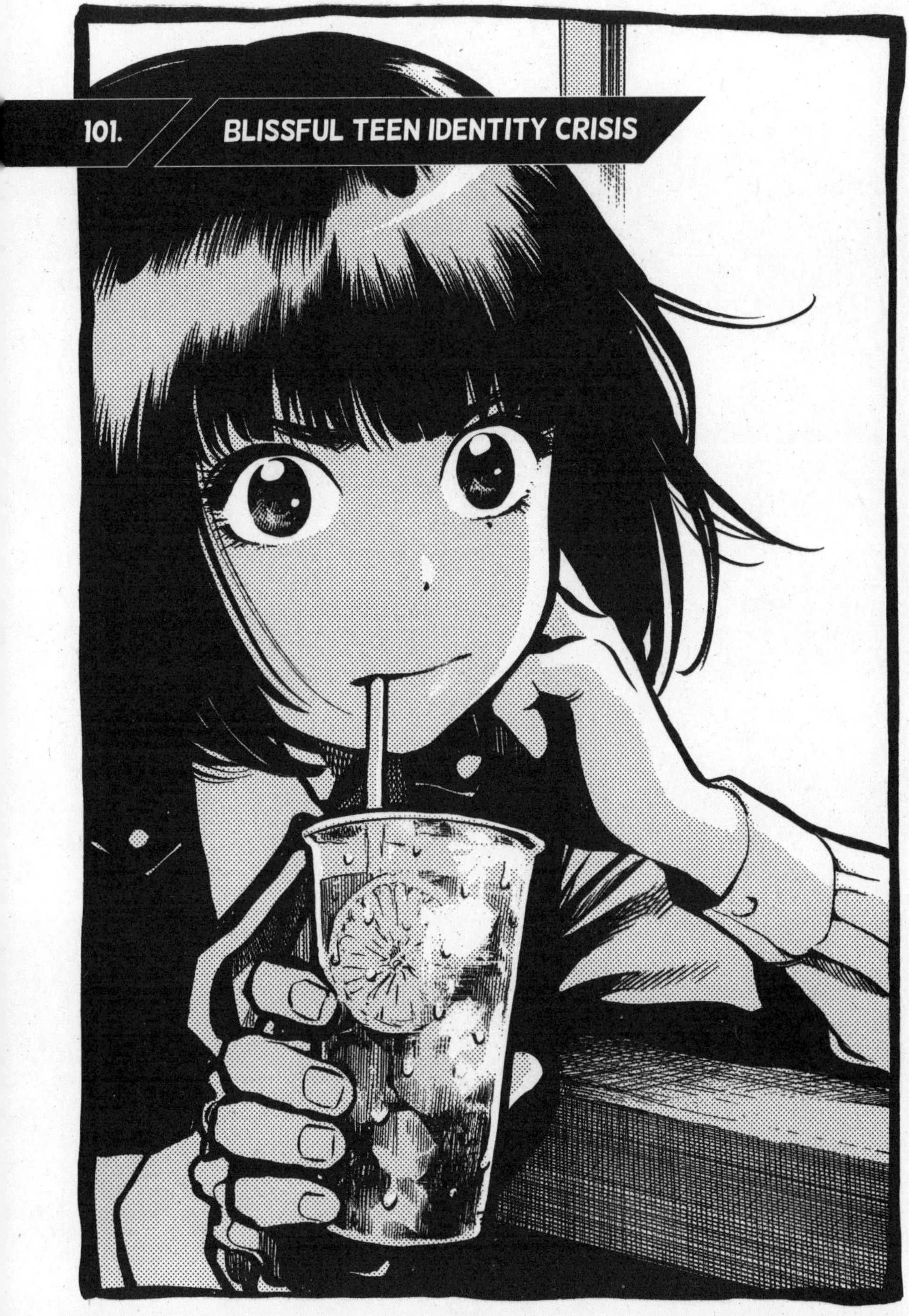

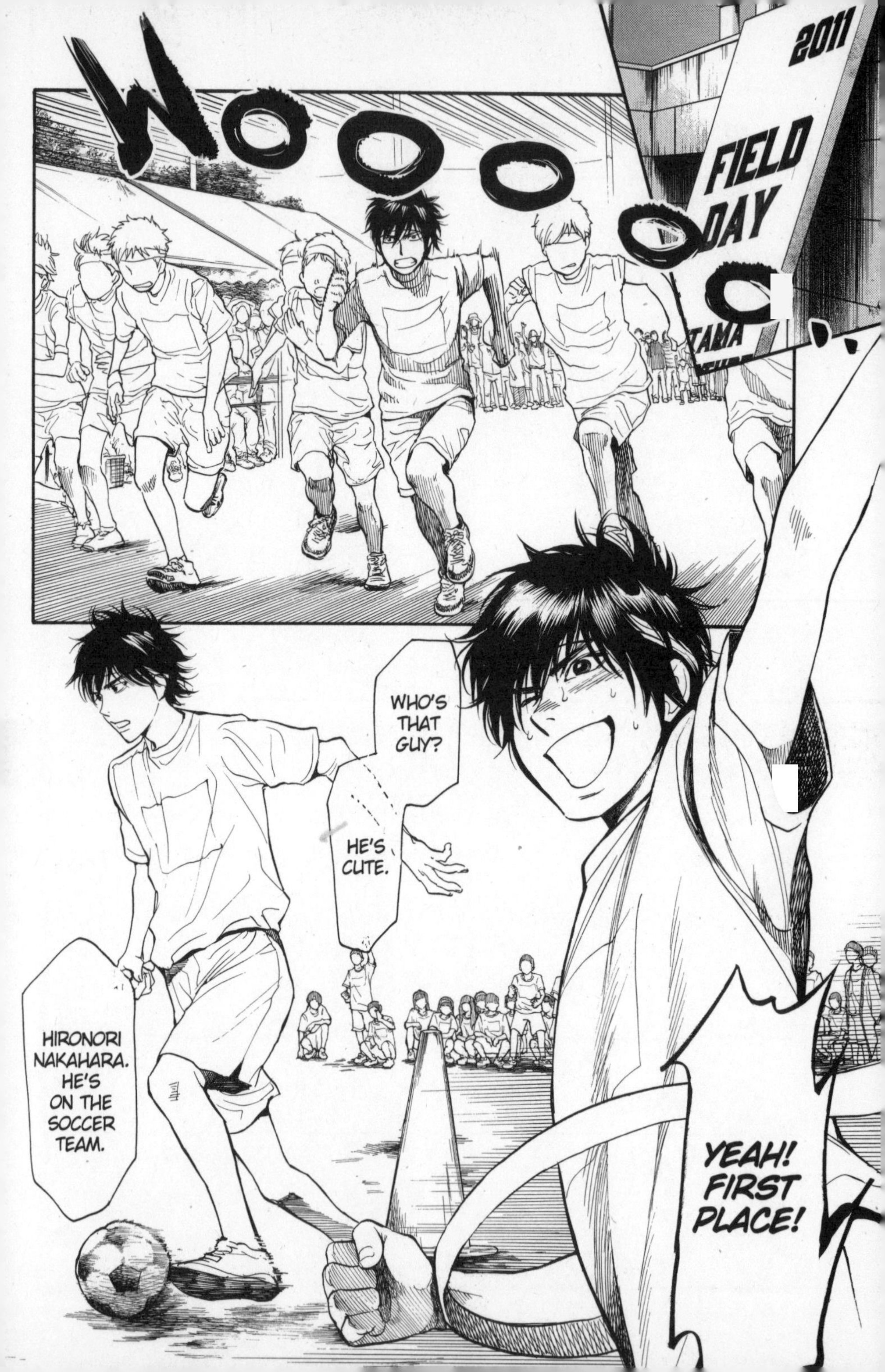
2011
FIELD DAY
TAMA
WOOOOOO..
YEAH! FIRST PLACE!
WHO'S THAT GUY?
HE'S CUTE.
HIRONORI NAKAHARA. HE'S ON THE SOCCER TEAM.

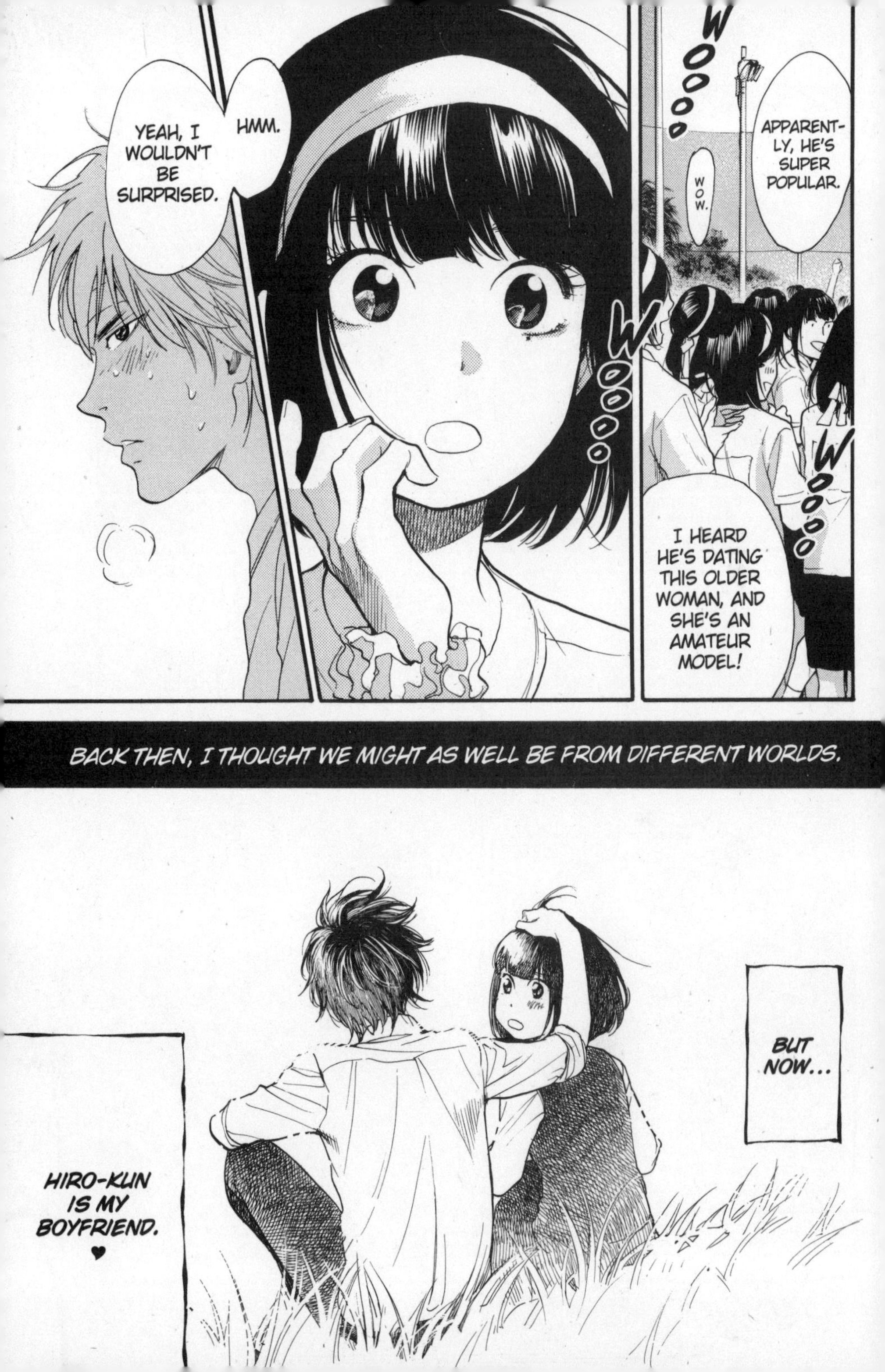
WOOOOO
APPARENTLY, HE'S SUPER POPULAR.
WOW.
I HEARD HE'S DATING THIS OLDER WOMAN, AND SHE'S AN AMATEUR MODEL!
WOOOOO
WOOOOO
HMM.
YEAH, I WOULDN'T BE SURPRISED.
BACK THEN, I THOUGHT WE MIGHT AS WELL BE FROM DIFFERENT WORLDS.
BUT NOW...
HIRO-KUN IS MY BOYFRIEND. ♥

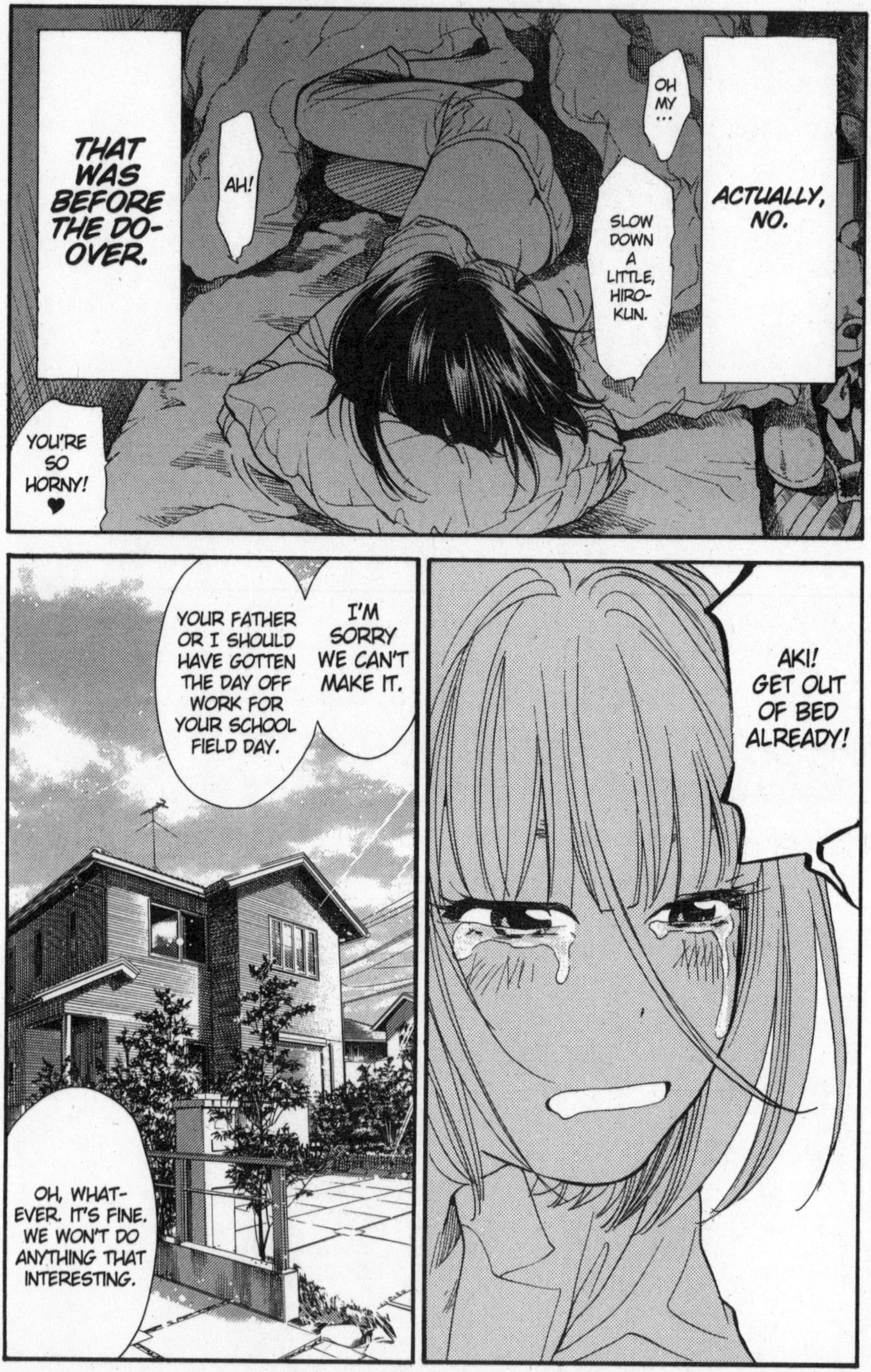
ACTUALLY, NO.
OH MY...
SLOW DOWN A LITTLE, HIRO-KUN.
AH!
THAT WAS BEFORE THE DO-OVER.
YOU'RE SO HORNY! ♥
AKI! GET OUT OF BED ALREADY!
I'M SORRY WE CAN'T MAKE IT.
YOUR FATHER OR I SHOULD HAVE GOTTEN THE DAY OFF WORK FOR YOUR SCHOOL FIELD DAY.
OH, WHAT-EVER. IT'S FINE. WE WON'T DO ANYTHING THAT INTERESTING.

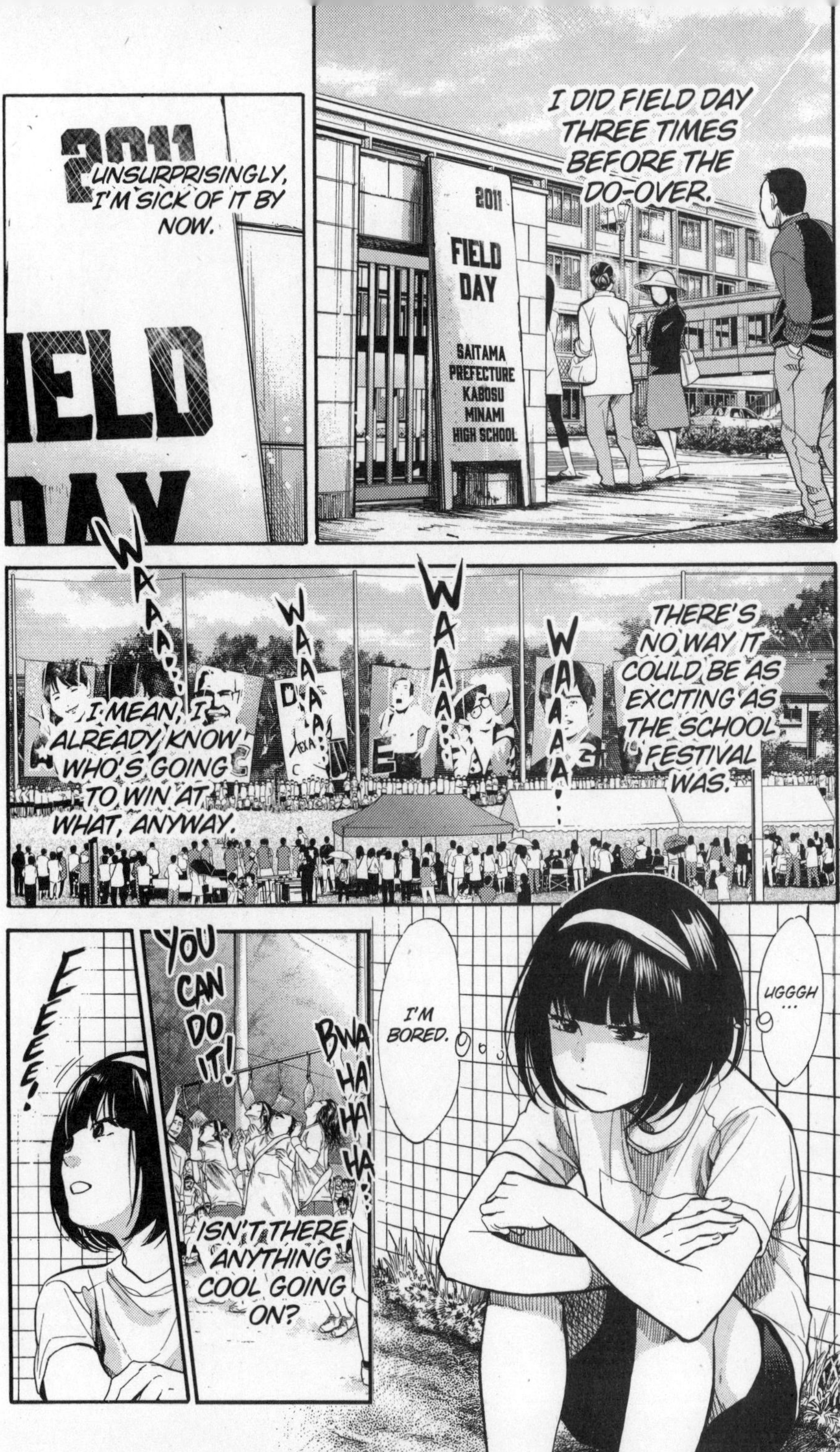
I DID FIELD DAY THREE TIMES BEFORE THE DO-OVER.
2011
FIELD DAY
SAITAMA PREFECTURE KABOSU MINAMI HIGH SCHOOL
2011
UNSURPRISINGLY, I'M SICK OF IT BY NOW.
THERE'S NO WAY IT COULD BE AS EXCITING AS THE SCHOOL FESTIVAL WAS.
WAAAA...
WAAAA...
WAAAAAA...
WAAAAA...
WAAA...
I MEAN, I ALREADY KNOW WHO'S GOING TO WIN AT WHAT, ANYWAY.
UGGGH...
I'M BORED.
YOU CAN DO IT!
BWAHAHAHA!
EEEEE!
ISN'T THERE ANYTHING COOL GOING ON?

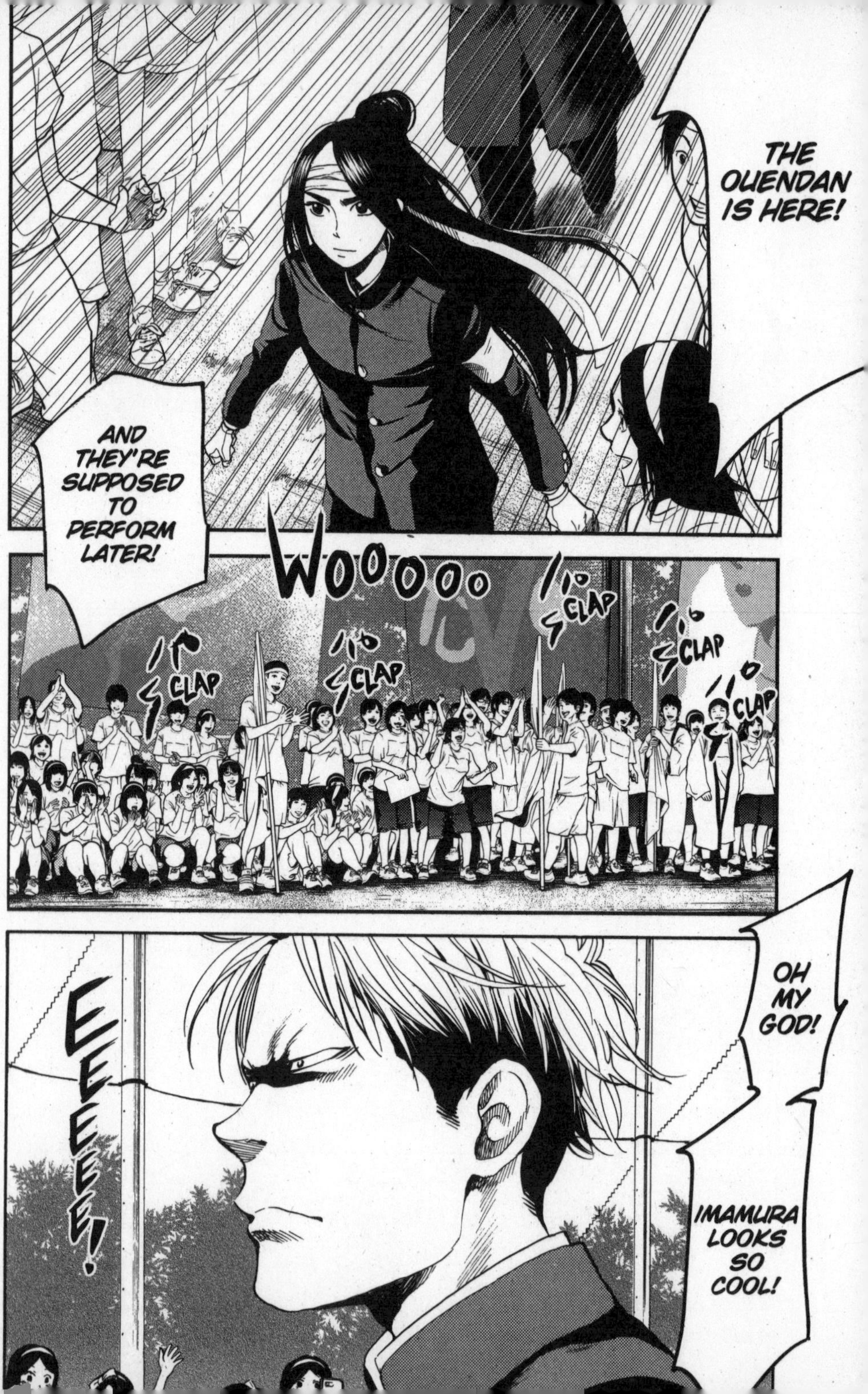
THE OUENDAN IS HERE!
AND THEY'RE SUPPOSED TO PERFORM LATER!
WOOOOO
CLAP
CLAP
CLAP
CLAP
CLAP
OH MY GOD!
IMAMURA LOOKS SO COOL!
EEEEEE!

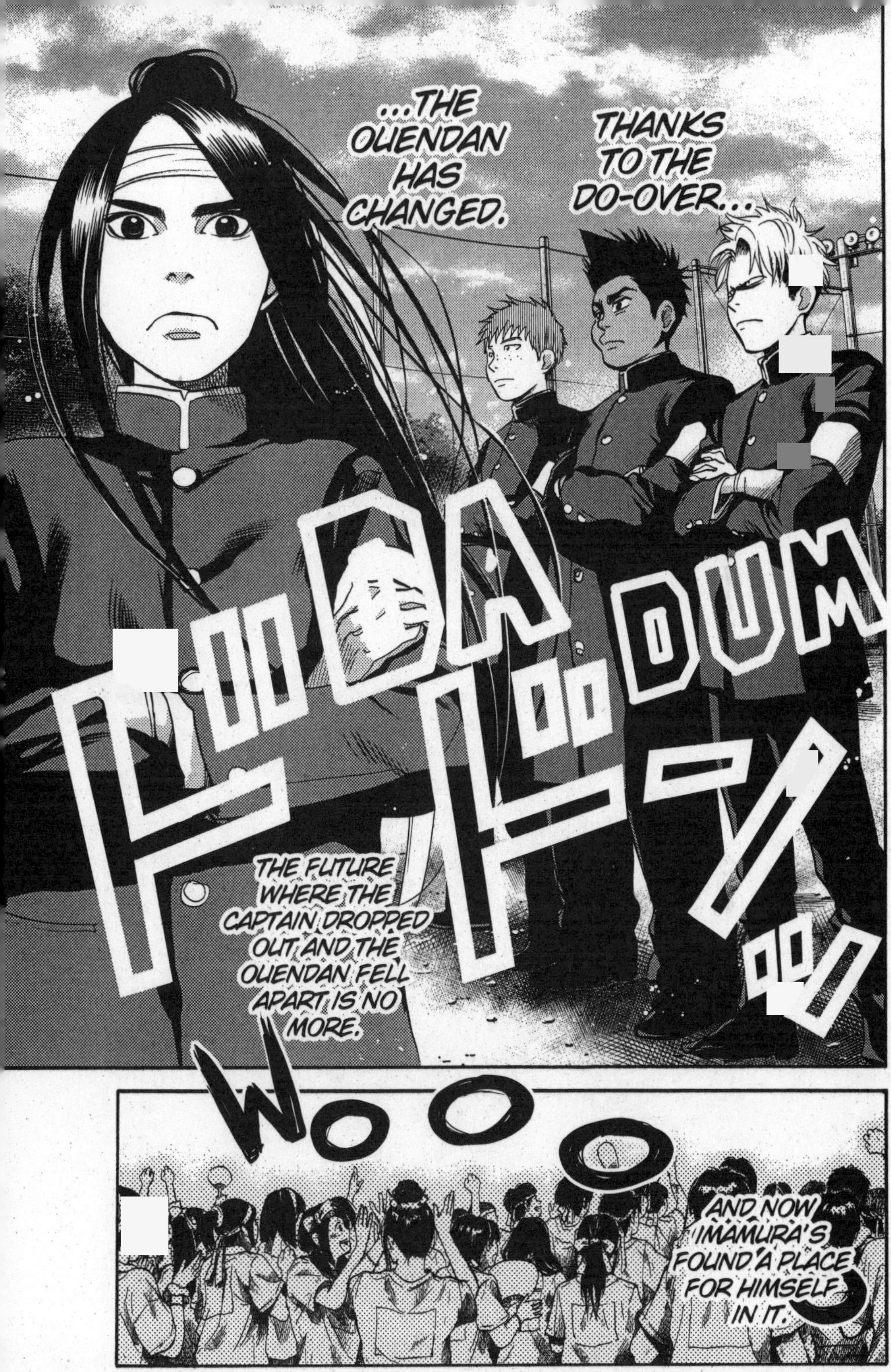
THANKS TO THE DO-OVER...
...THE OUENDAN HAS CHANGED.
THE FUTURE WHERE THE CAPTAIN DROPPED OUT AND THE OUENDAN FELL APART IS NO MORE.
WOOO
AND NOW IMAMURA'S FOUND A PLACE FOR HIMSELF IN IT.

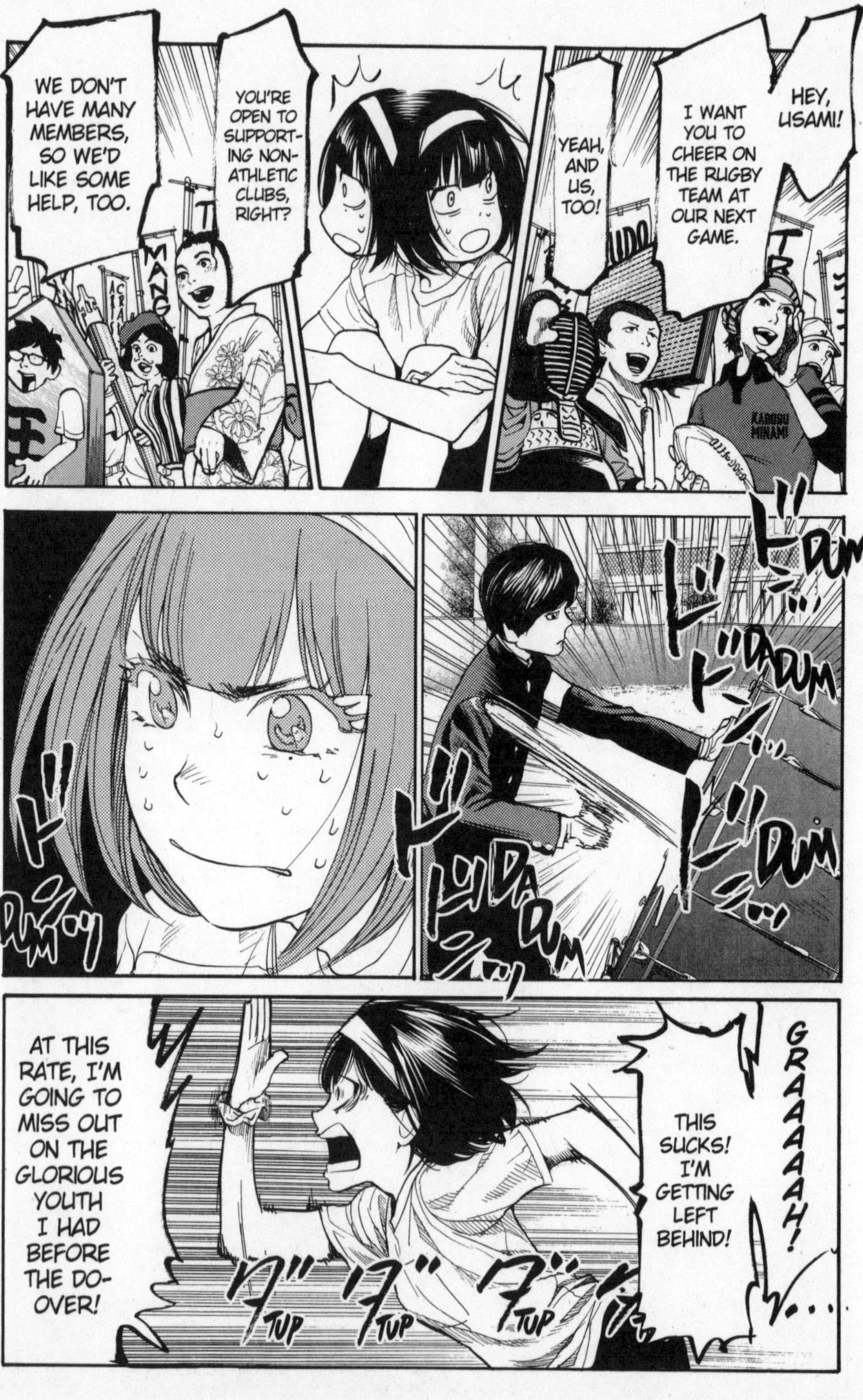
HEY, USAMI!
I WANT YOU TO CHEER ON THE RUGBY TEAM AT OUR NEXT GAME.
YEAH, AND US, TOO!
YOU'RE OPEN TO SUPPORTING NON-ATHLETIC CLUBS, RIGHT?
WE DON'T HAVE MANY MEMBERS, SO WE'D LIKE SOME HELP, TOO.
DUM
DADUM
DUM
DADUM
DUM
GRAAAAAAH!
THIS SUCKS! I'M GETTING LEFT BEHIND!
AT THIS RATE, I'M GOING TO MISS OUT ON THE GLORIOUS YOUTH I HAD BEFORE THE DO-OVER!
TUP
TUP
TUP

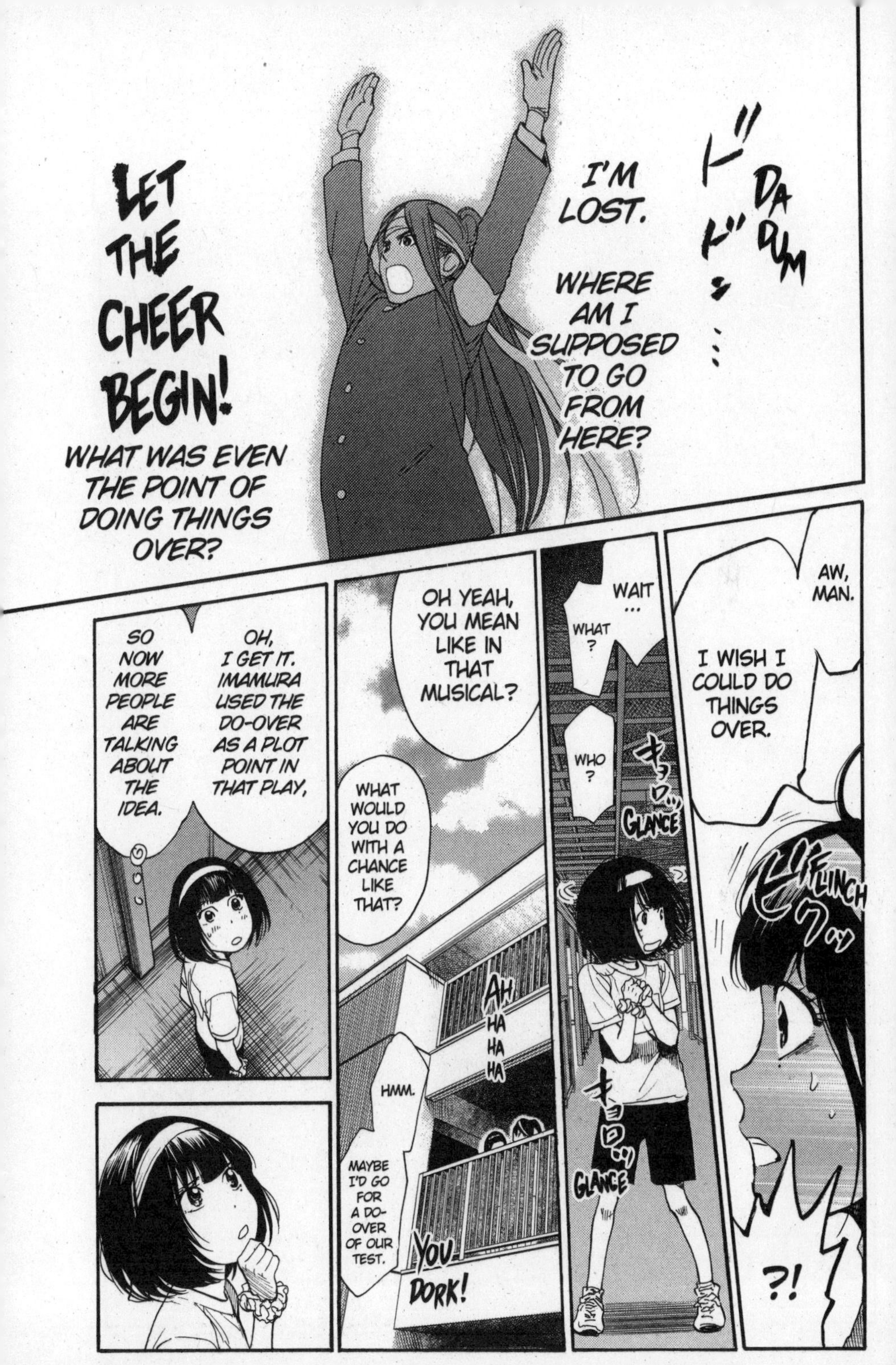
DA DUM
I'M LOST.
WHERE AM I SUPPOSED TO GO FROM HERE?
LET THE CHEER BEGIN!
WHAT WAS EVEN THE POINT OF DOING THINGS OVER?
AW, MAN.
I WISH I COULD DO THINGS OVER.
FLINCH
?!
WAIT ...
WHAT ?
WHO ?
GLANCE
GLANCE
OH YEAH, YOU MEAN LIKE IN THAT MUSICAL?
WHAT WOULD YOU DO WITH A CHANCE LIKE THAT?
AH HA HA HA
HMM.
MAYBE I'D GO FOR A DO-OVER OF OUR TEST.
YOU DORK!
OH, I GET IT. IMAMURA USED THE DO-OVER AS A PLOT POINT IN THAT PLAY,
SO NOW MORE PEOPLE ARE TALKING ABOUT THE IDEA.

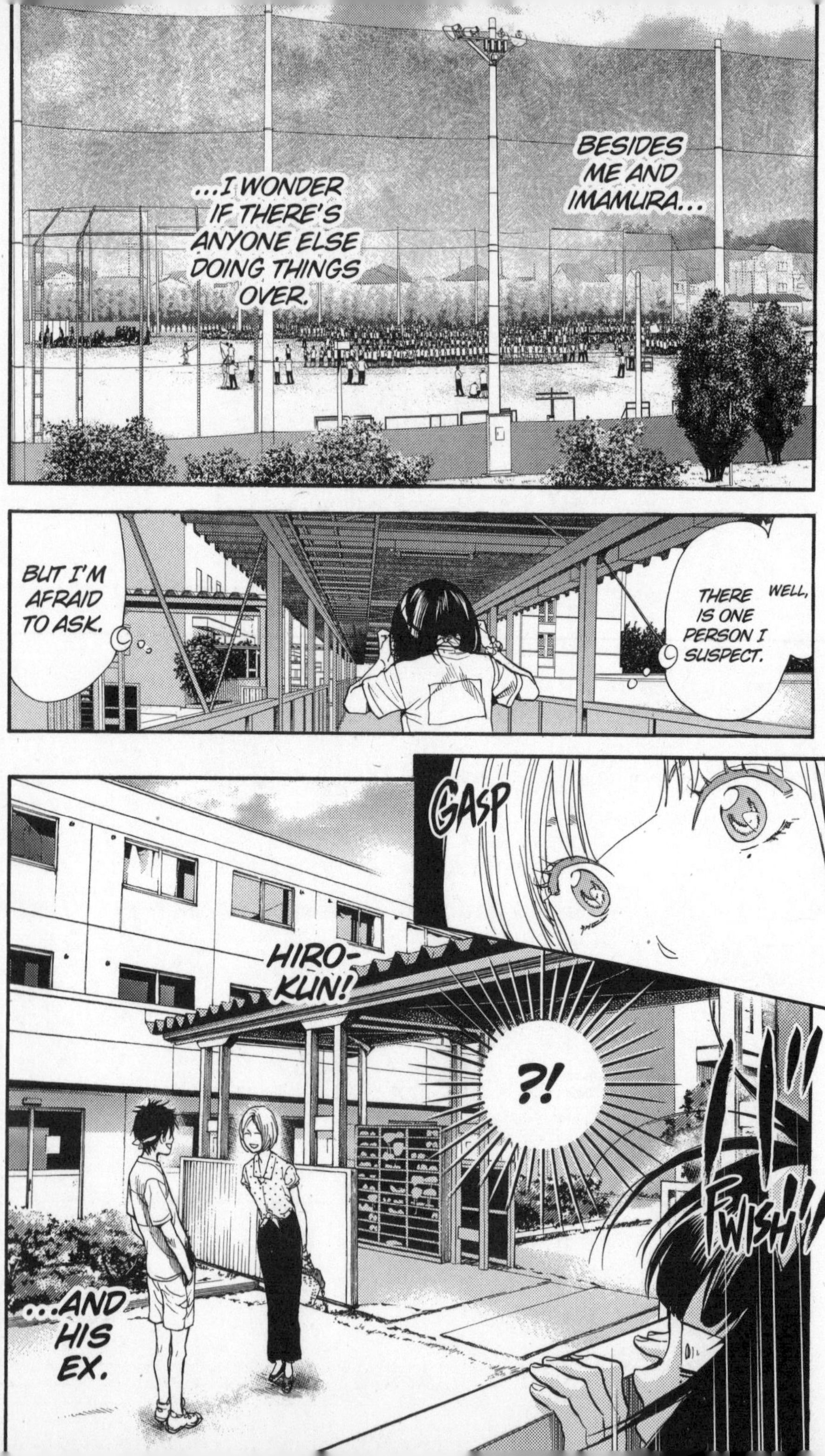
BESIDES ME AND IMAMURA...
...I WONDER IF THERE'S ANYONE ELSE DOING THINGS OVER.
WELL, THERE IS ONE PERSON I SUSPECT.
BUT I'M AFRAID TO ASK.
HIRO-KUN!
GASP
?!
FWISH!!
...AND HIS EX.

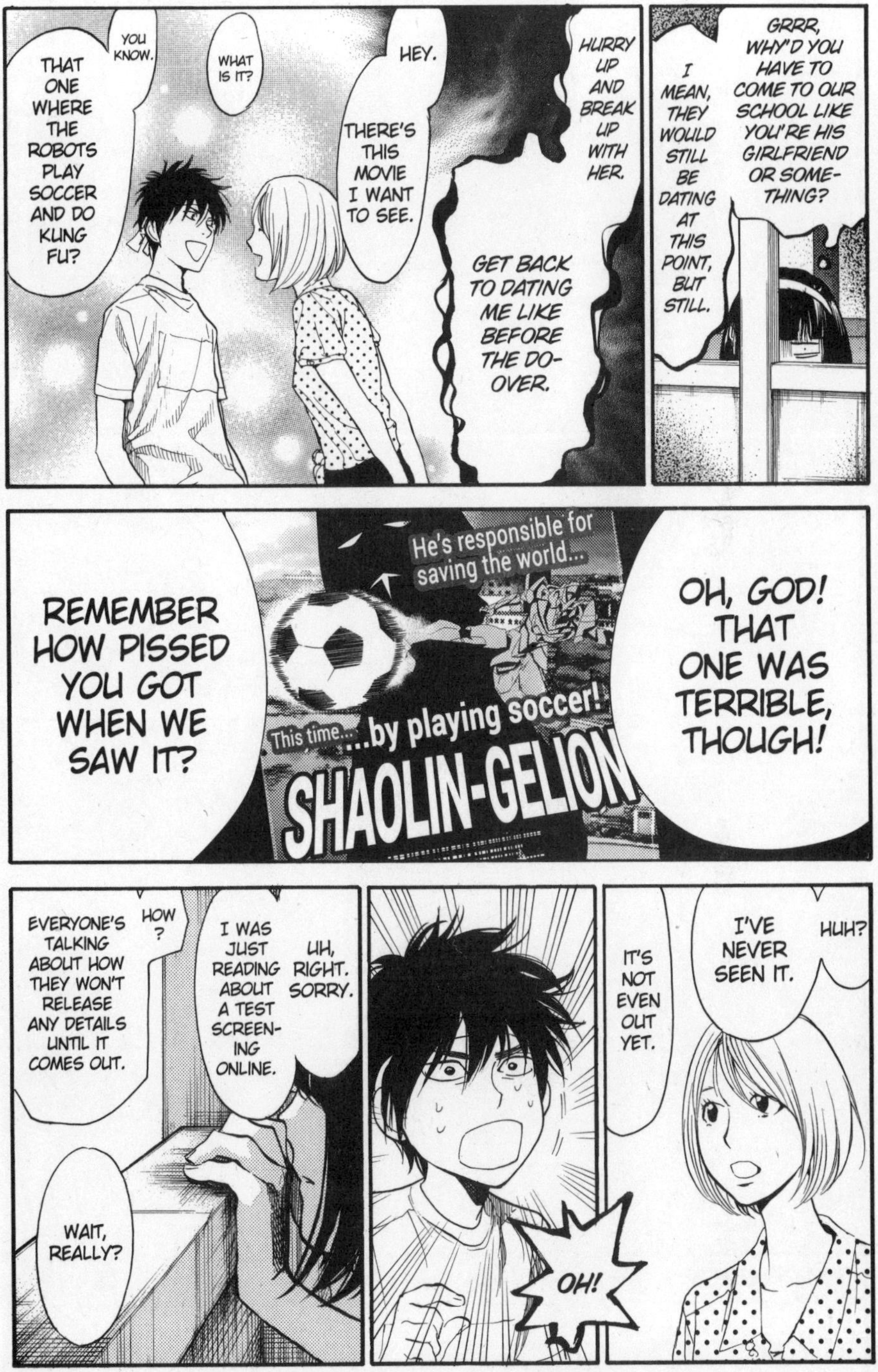
GRRR, WHY'D YOU HAVE TO COME TO OUR SCHOOL LIKE YOU'RE HIS GIRLFRIEND OR SOME-THING?
I MEAN, THEY WOULD STILL BE DATING AT THIS POINT, BUT STILL.
HURRY UP AND BREAK UP WITH HER.
GET BACK TO DATING ME LIKE BEFORE THE DO-OVER.
HEY.
THERE'S THIS MOVIE I WANT TO SEE.
WHAT IS IT?
YOU KNOW.
THAT ONE WHERE THE ROBOTS PLAY SOCCER AND DO KUNG FU?
OH, GOD! THAT ONE WAS TERRIBLE, THOUGH!
He's responsible for saving the world...
This time... ...by playing soccer!
SHAOLIN-GELION
REMEMBER HOW PISSED YOU GOT WHEN WE SAW IT?
HUH?
I'VE NEVER SEEN IT.
IT'S NOT EVEN OUT YET.
OH!
UH, RIGHT. SORRY.
I WAS JUST READING ABOUT A TEST SCREEN-ING ONLINE.
HOW?
EVERYONE'S TALKING ABOUT HOW THEY WON'T RELEASE ANY DETAILS UNTIL IT COMES OUT.
WAIT, REALLY?

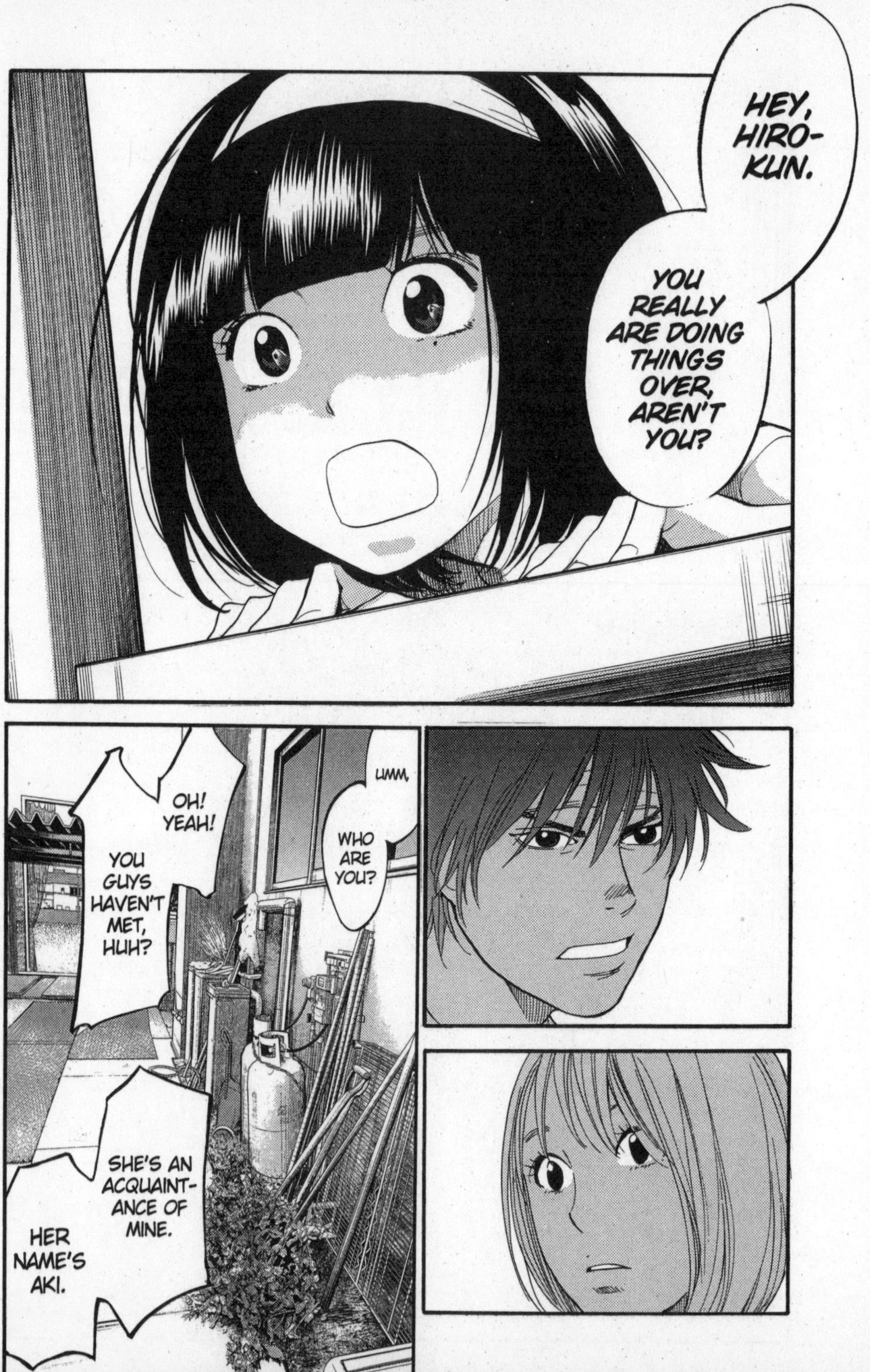
HEY, HIRO-KUN.
YOU REALLY ARE DOING THINGS OVER, AREN'T YOU?
UMM,
WHO ARE YOU?
OH! YEAH!
YOU GUYS HAVEN'T MET, HUH?
SHE'S AN ACQUAINT-ANCE OF MINE.
HER NAME'S AKI.

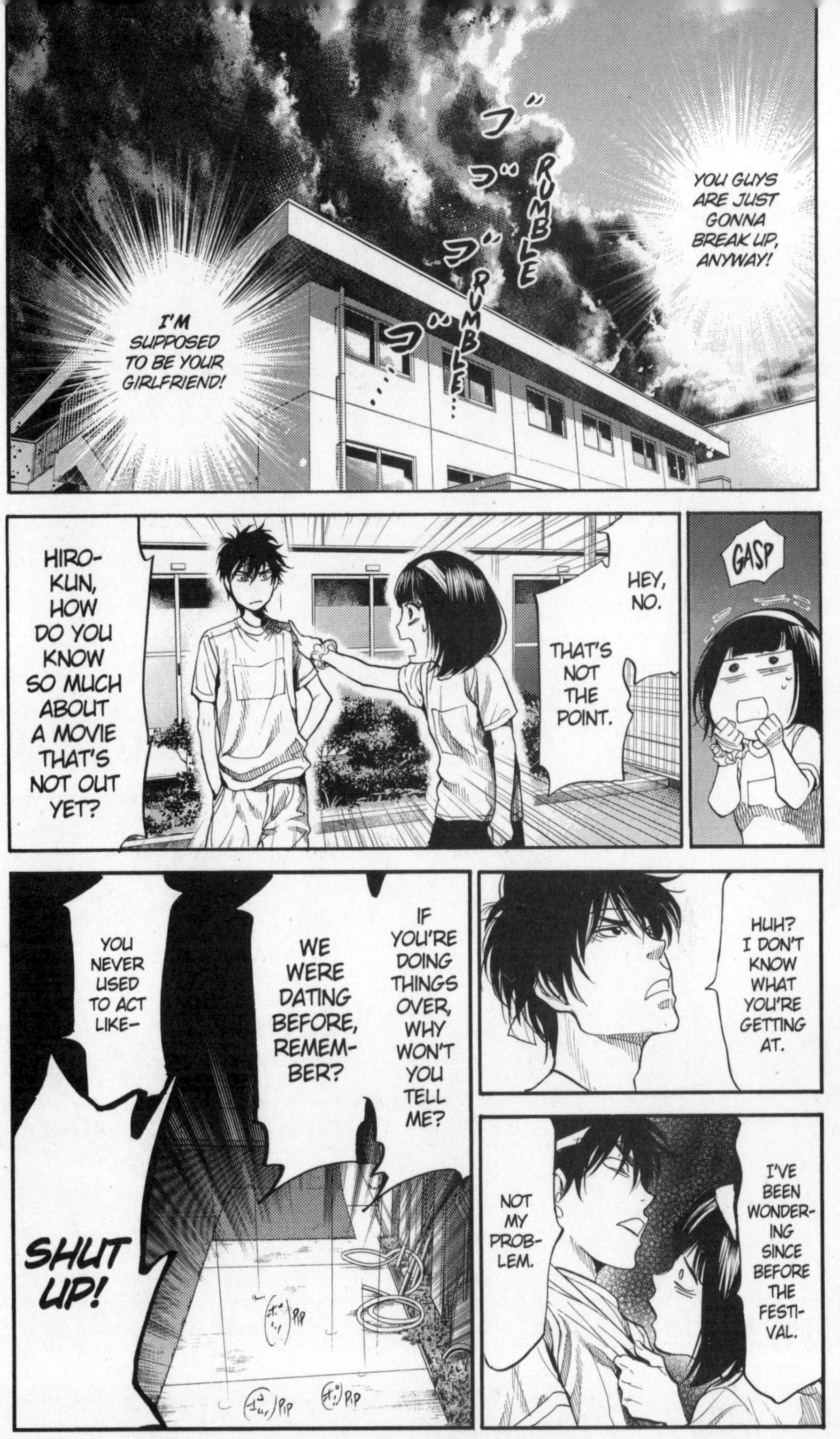
YOU GUYS ARE JUST GONNA BREAK UP, ANYWAY!
RUMBLE
RUMBLE
I'M SUPPOSED TO BE YOUR GIRLFRIEND!
GASP
HEY, NO.
THAT'S NOT THE POINT.
HIRO-KUN, HOW DO YOU KNOW SO MUCH ABOUT A MOVIE THAT'S NOT OUT YET?
HUH? I DON'T KNOW WHAT YOU'RE GETTING AT.
I'VE BEEN WONDER-ING SINCE BEFORE THE FESTI-VAL.
NOT MY PROB-LEM.
IF YOU'RE DOING THINGS OVER, WHY WON'T YOU TELL ME?
WE WERE DATING BEFORE, REMEM-BER?
YOU NEVER USED TO ACT LIKE-
SHUT UP!
PIP
PIP
PIP

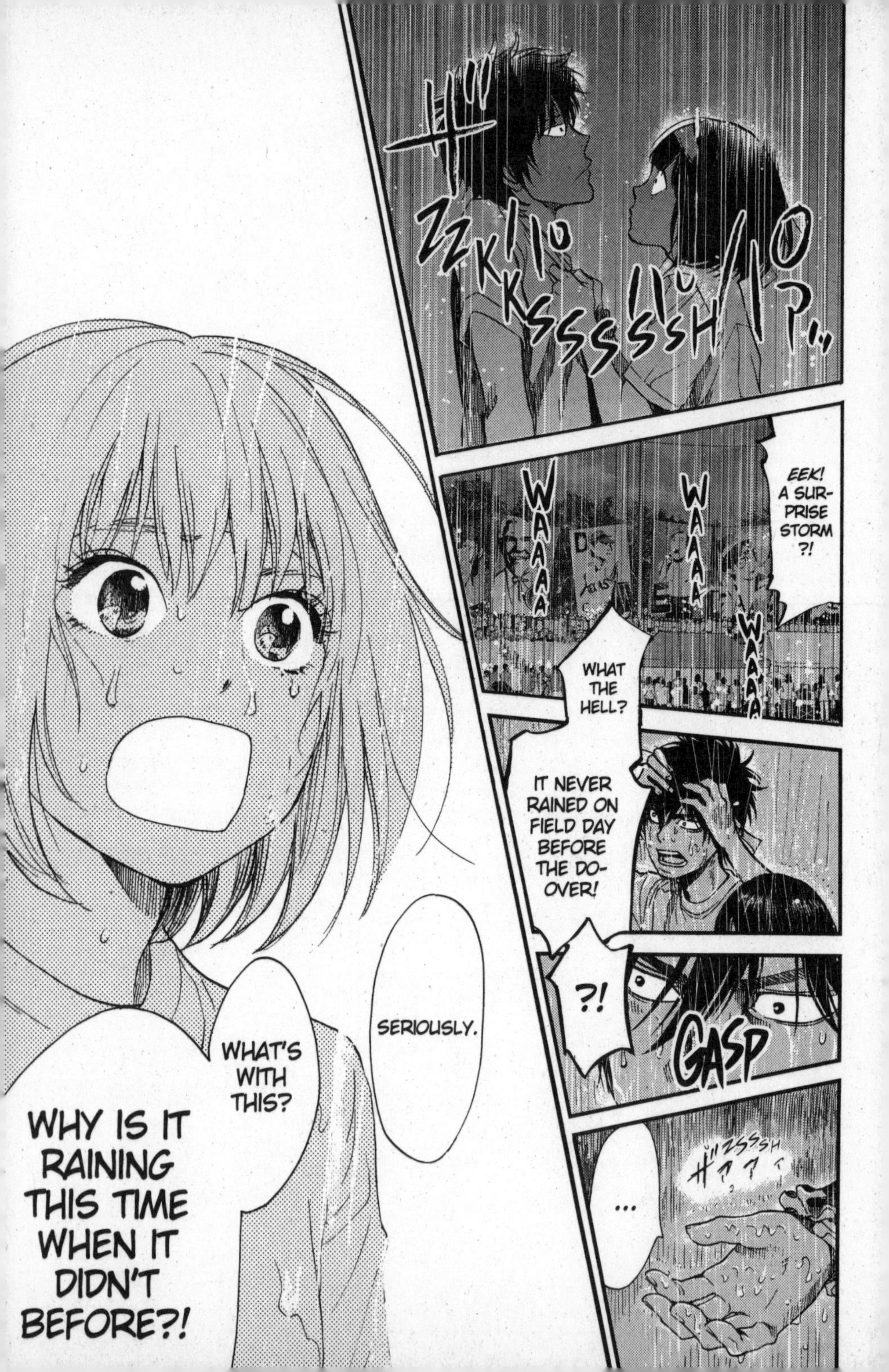
ZZKKSSSSSSH
WAAAA
WAAAA
EEK! A SURPRISE STORM?!
WAAAA
WHAT THE HELL?
IT NEVER RAINED ON FIELD DAY BEFORE THE DO-OVER!
?!
GASP
...
ZSSSSH
SERIOUSLY.
WHAT'S WITH THIS?
WHY IS IT RAINING THIS TIME WHEN IT DIDN'T BEFORE?!

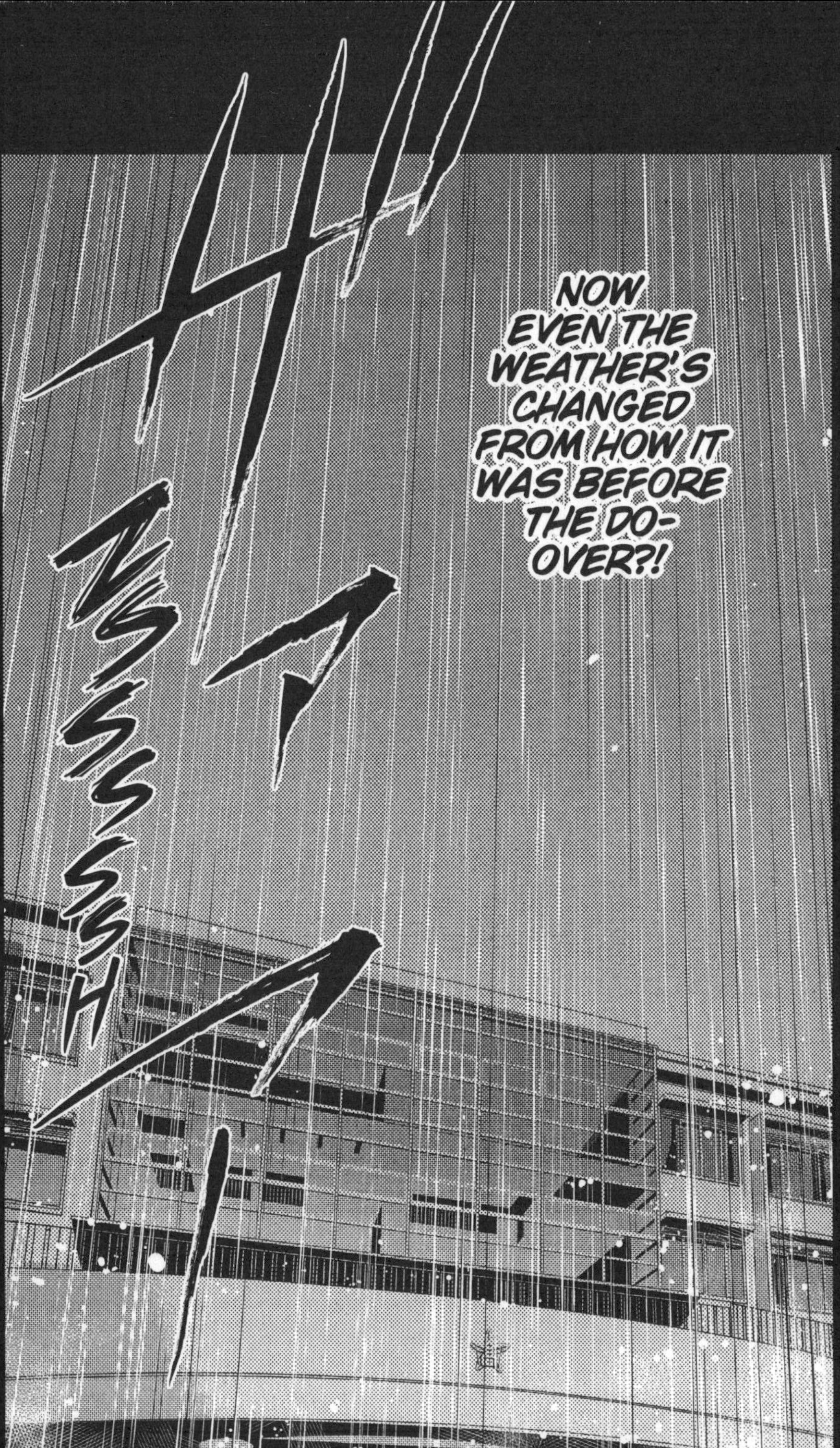
NOW EVEN THE WEATHER'S CHANGED FROM HOW IT WAS BEFORE THE DO-OVER?!

Again!!

アゲイン!!

102. DRAMATIC RAIN

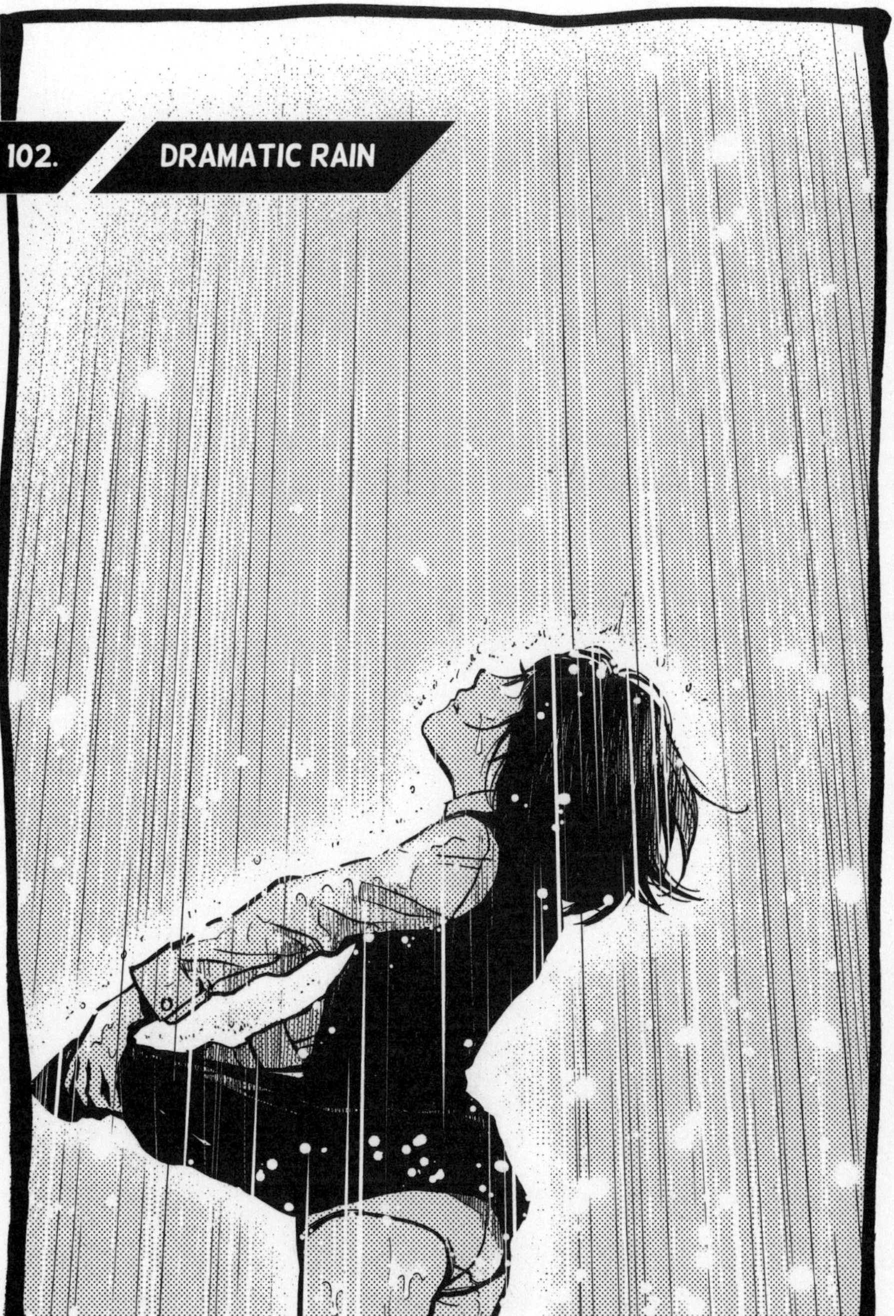

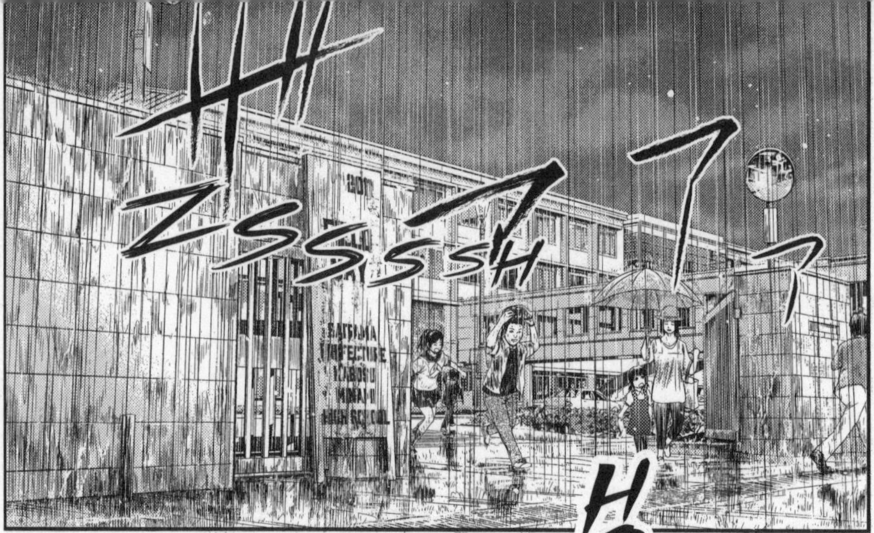
ZSSSSSH
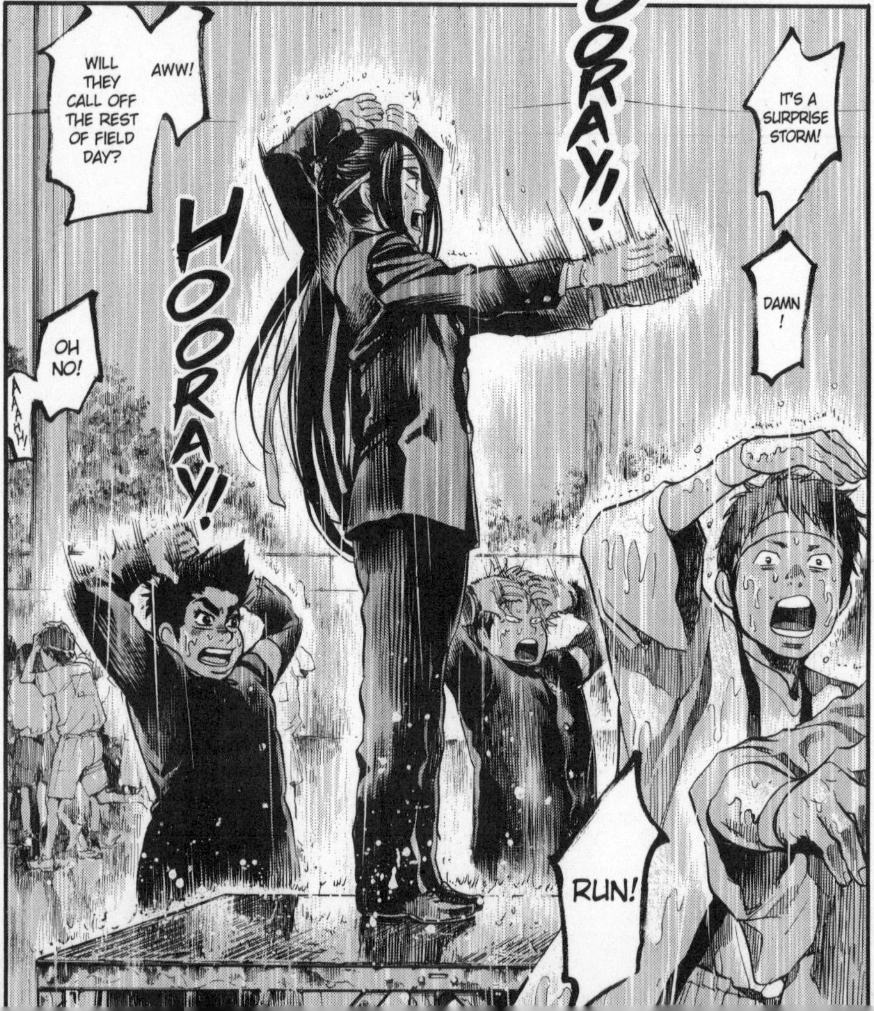
IT'S A SURPRISE STORM!
HOORAY!
DAMN!
AWW!
WILL THEY CALL OFF THE REST OF FIELD DAY?
HOORAY!
OH NO!
AAAACH!
RUN!

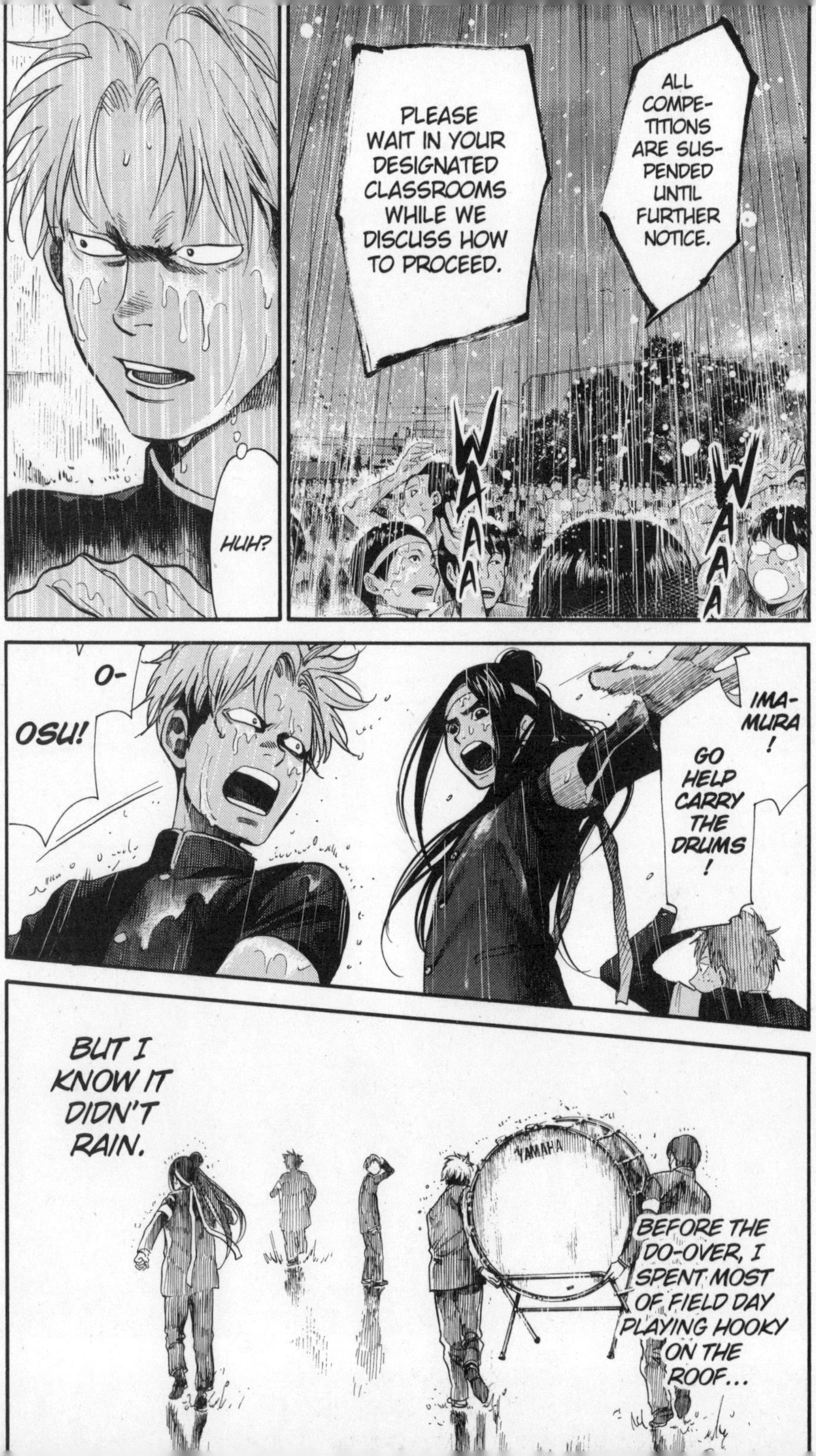
ALL COMPETITIONS ARE SUSPENDED UNTIL FURTHER NOTICE.
PLEASE WAIT IN YOUR DESIGNATED CLASSROOMS WHILE WE DISCUSS HOW TO PROCEED.
WAAAA
WAAA
HUH?
IMAMURA! GO HELP CARRY THE DRUMS!
O- OSU!
BEFORE THE DO-OVER, I SPENT MOST OF FIELD DAY PLAYING HOOKY ON THE ROOF...
BUT I KNOW IT DIDN'T RAIN.
YAMAHA

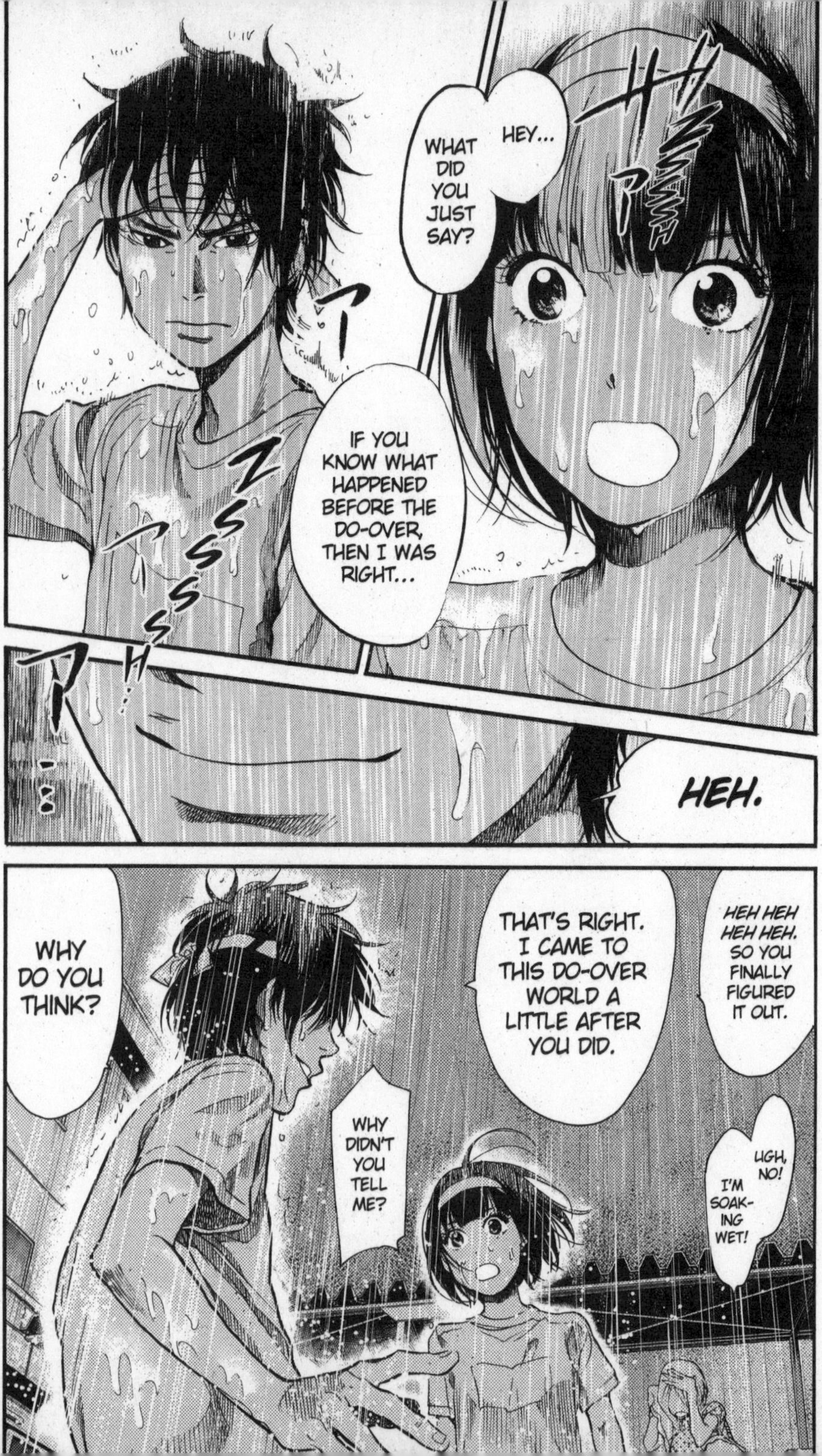
HEY... WHAT DID YOU JUST SAY?
IF YOU KNOW WHAT HAPPENED BEFORE THE DO-OVER, THEN I WAS RIGHT...
ZSSSSSH!!
HEH.
HEH HEH HEH HEH. SO YOU FINALLY FIGURED IT OUT.
THAT'S RIGHT. I CAME TO THIS DO-OVER WORLD A LITTLE AFTER YOU DID.
WHY DO YOU THINK?
UGH, NO! I'M SOAK-ING WET!
WHY DIDN'T YOU TELL ME?

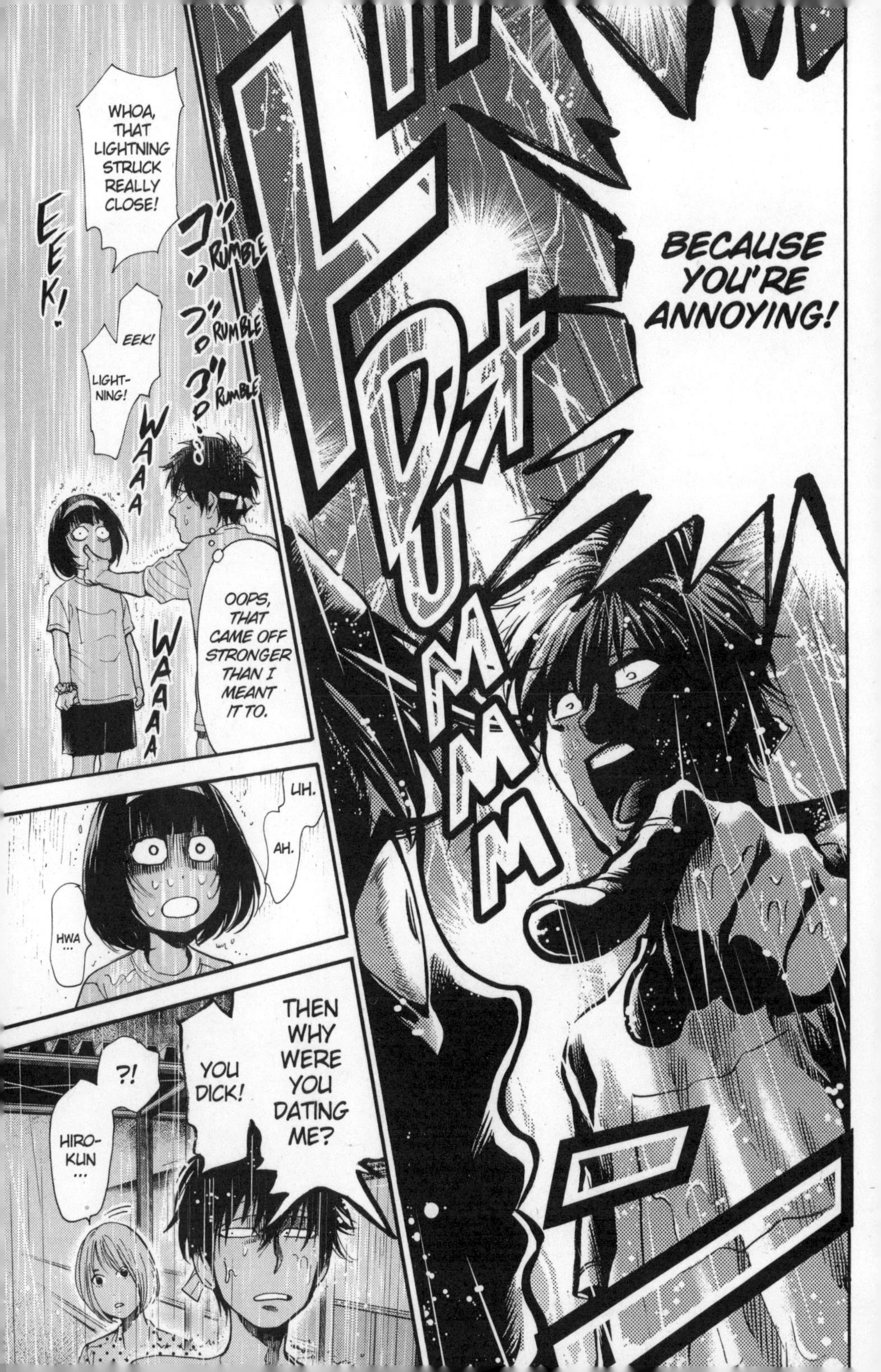
BECAUSE YOU'RE ANNOYING!
WHOA, THAT LIGHTNING STRUCK REALLY CLOSE!
RUMBLE
RUMBLE
RUMBLE
EEK!
EEK!
LIGHT-NING!
WAAAA
OOPS, THAT CAME OFF STRONGER THAN I MEANT IT TO.
WAAAAA
UH.
AH.
HWA...
THEN WHY WERE YOU DATING ME?
YOU DICK!
?!
HIRO-KUN...

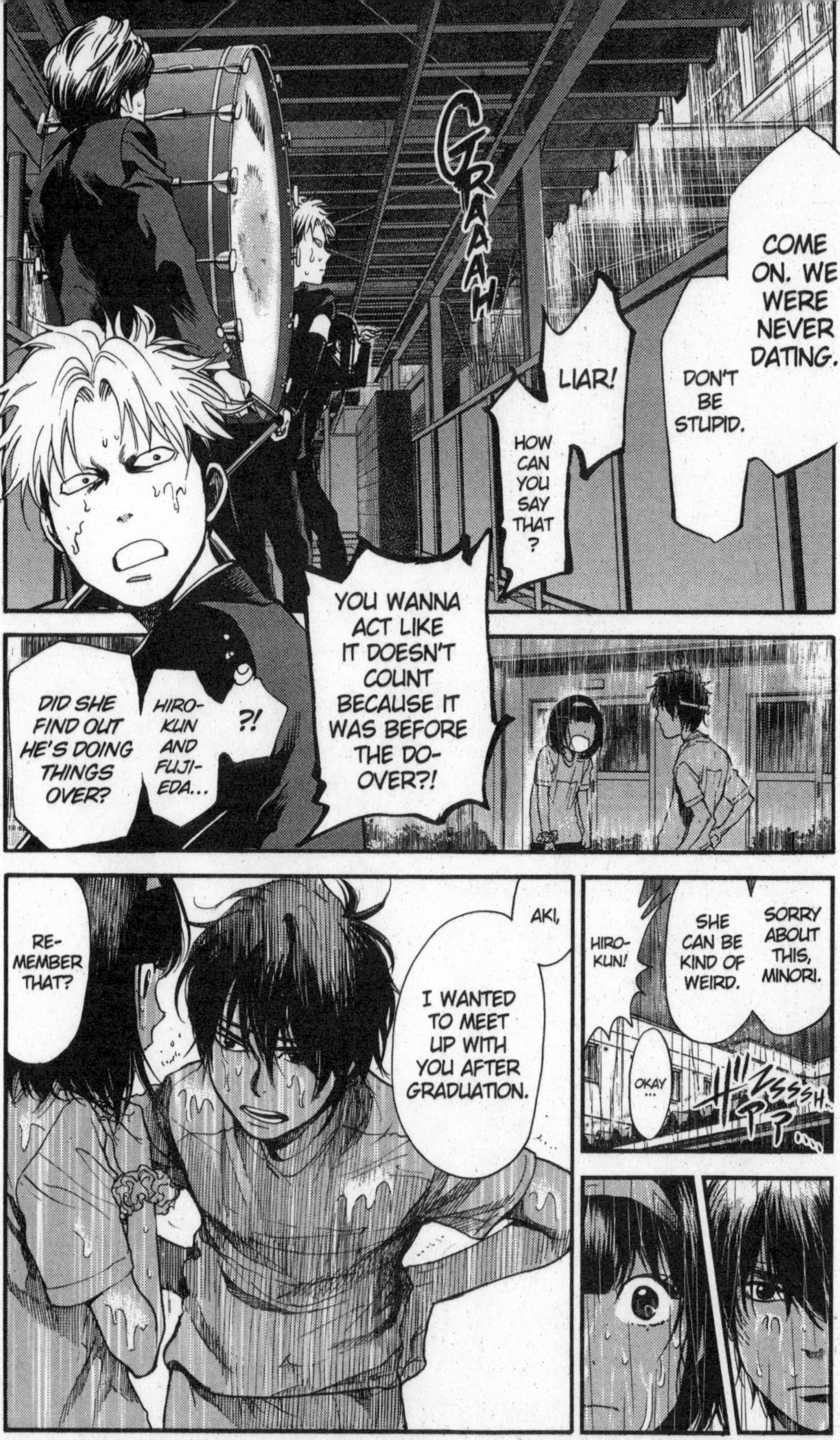
COME ON. WE WERE NEVER DATING.
DON'T BE STUPID.
LIAR!
HOW CAN YOU SAY THAT?
GRAAAAH
YOU WANNA ACT LIKE IT DOESN'T COUNT BECAUSE IT WAS BEFORE THE DO-OVER?!
?!
HIRO-KUN AND FUJI-EDA...
DID SHE FIND OUT HE'S DOING THINGS OVER?
SORRY ABOUT THIS, MINORI.
SHE CAN BE KIND OF WEIRD.
HIRO-KUN!
OKAY...
ZSSSH...
AKI,
I WANTED TO MEET UP WITH YOU AFTER GRADUATION.
RE-MEMBER THAT?

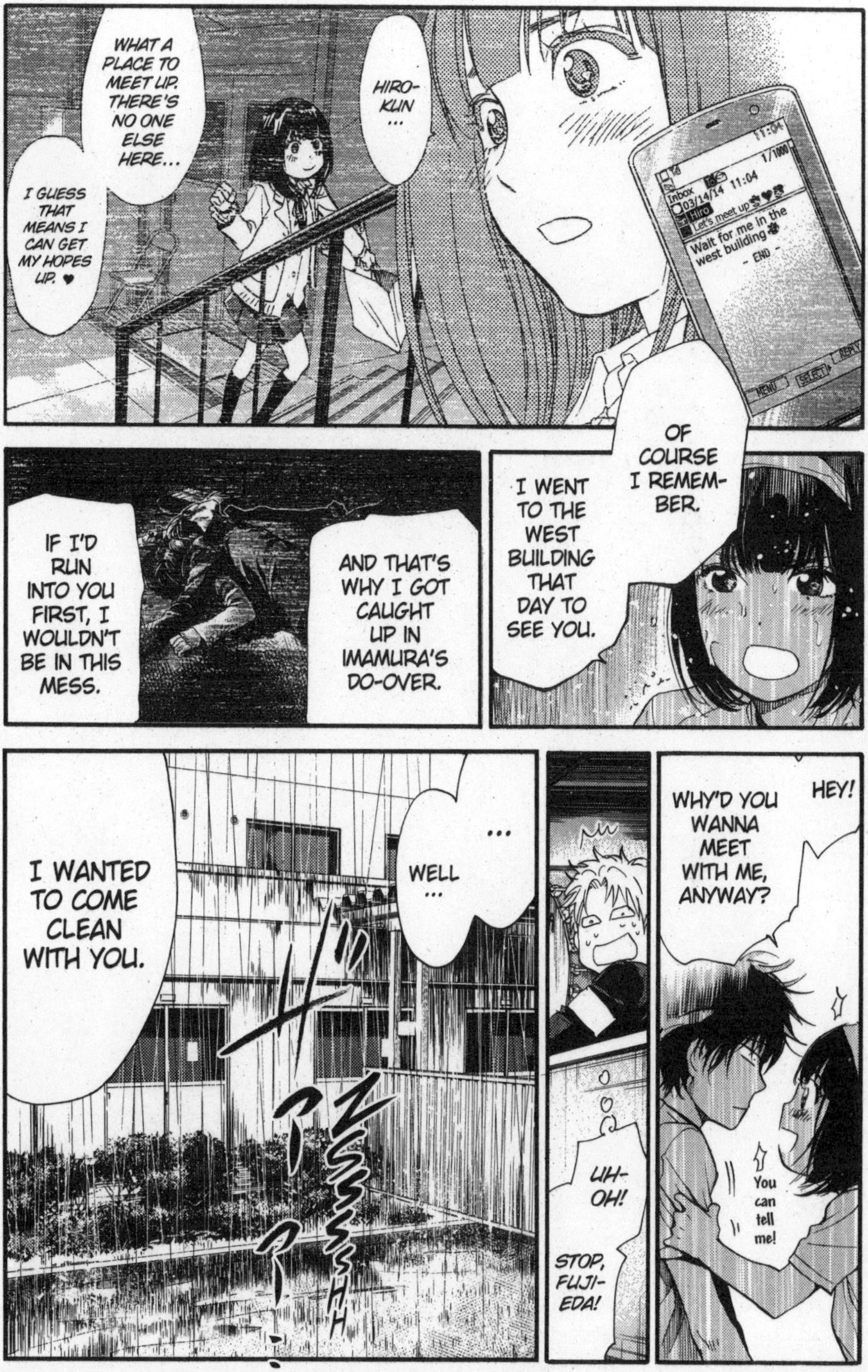
11:04
1/1000
Inbox 03/14/14 11:04
Hiro
Let's meet up
Wait for me in the west building
- END -
MENU
SELECT
REPLY
HIRO-KUN ...
WHAT A PLACE TO MEET UP. THERE'S NO ONE ELSE HERE...
I GUESS THAT MEANS I CAN GET MY HOPES UP. ♥
OF COURSE I REMEMBER.
I WENT TO THE WEST BUILDING THAT DAY TO SEE YOU.
AND THAT'S WHY I GOT CAUGHT UP IN IMAMURA'S DO-OVER.
IF I'D RUN INTO YOU FIRST, I WOULDN'T BE IN THIS MESS.
HEY!
WHY'D YOU WANNA MEET WITH ME, ANYWAY?
You can tell me!
UH-OH!
STOP, FUJIEDA!
...
WELL ...
I WANTED TO COME CLEAN WITH YOU.

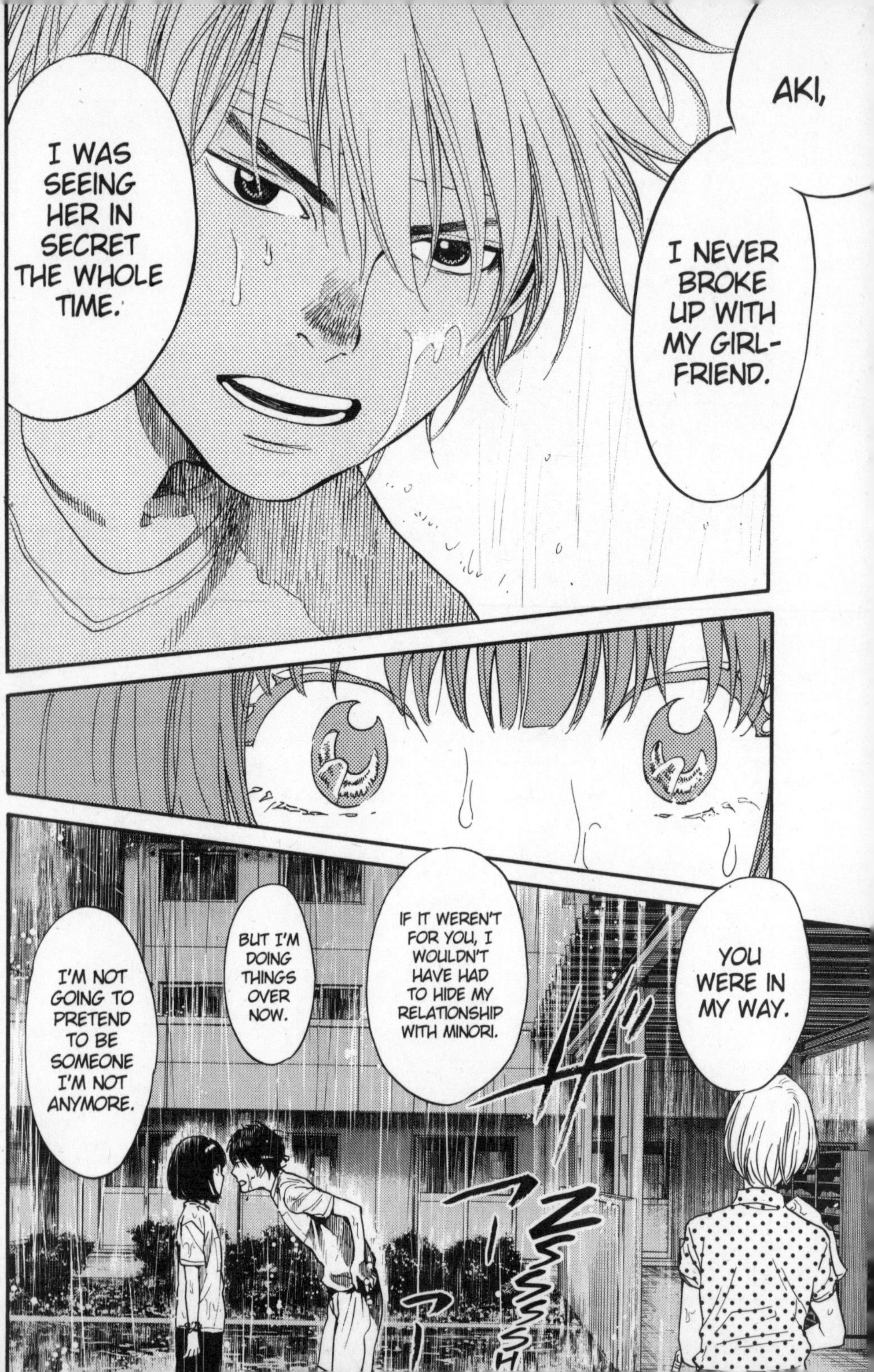
AKI,
I NEVER BROKE UP WITH MY GIRL-FRIEND.
I WAS SEEING HER IN SECRET THE WHOLE TIME.
YOU WERE IN MY WAY.
IF IT WEREN'T FOR YOU, I WOULDN'T HAVE HAD TO HIDE MY RELATIONSHIP WITH MINORI.
BUT I'M DOING THINGS OVER NOW.
I'M NOT GOING TO PRETEND TO BE SOMEONE I'M NOT ANYMORE.

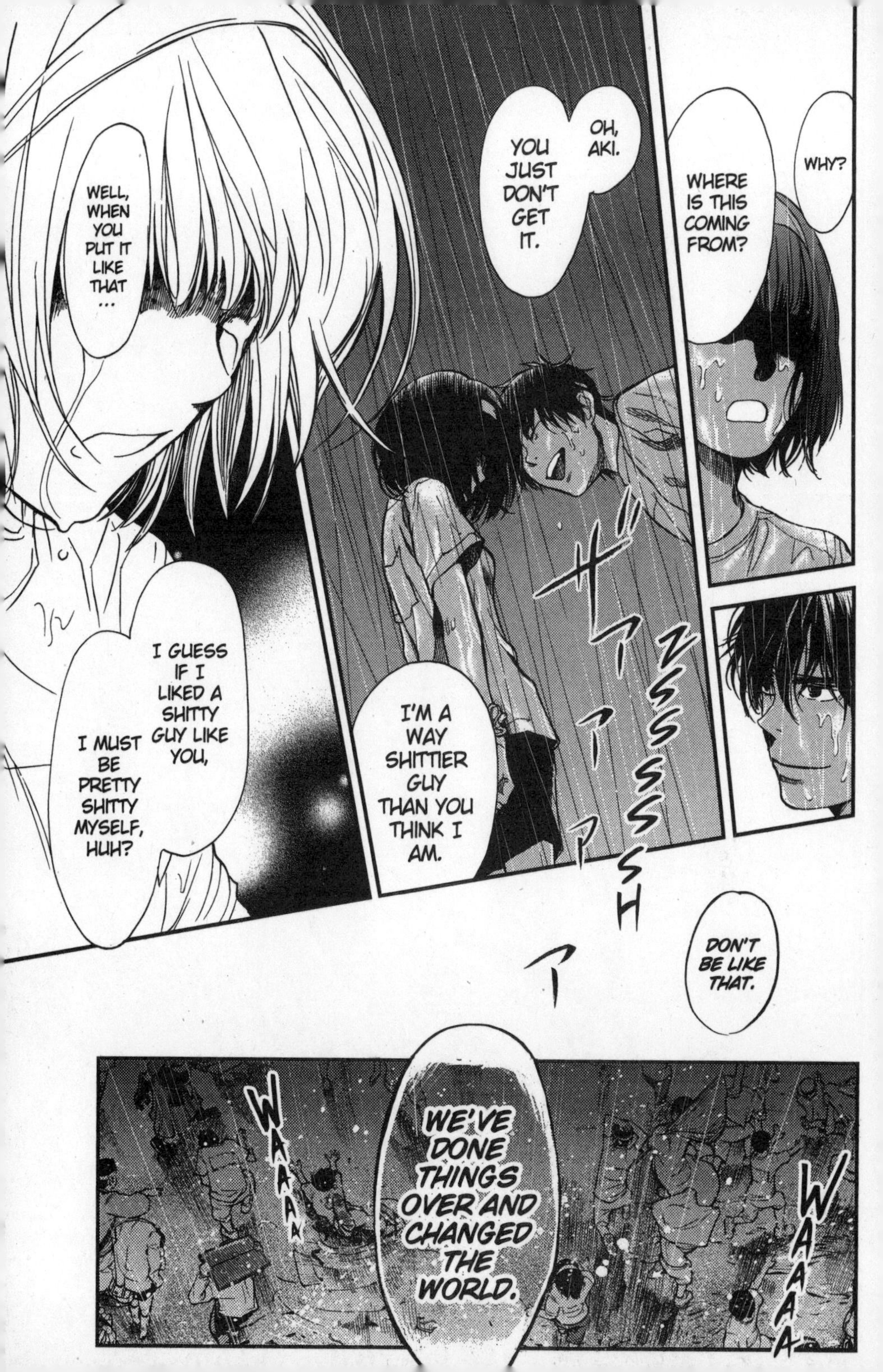
WHY?
WHERE IS THIS COMING FROM?
OH, AKI.
YOU JUST DON'T GET IT.
ZSSSSSH
I'M A WAY SHITTIER GUY THAN YOU THINK I AM.
WELL, WHEN YOU PUT IT LIKE THAT...
I GUESS IF I LIKED A SHITTY GUY LIKE YOU,
I MUST BE PRETTY SHITTY MYSELF, HUH?
DON'T BE LIKE THAT.
WAAAAA
WE'VE DONE THINGS OVER AND CHANGED THE WORLD.
WAAAAA

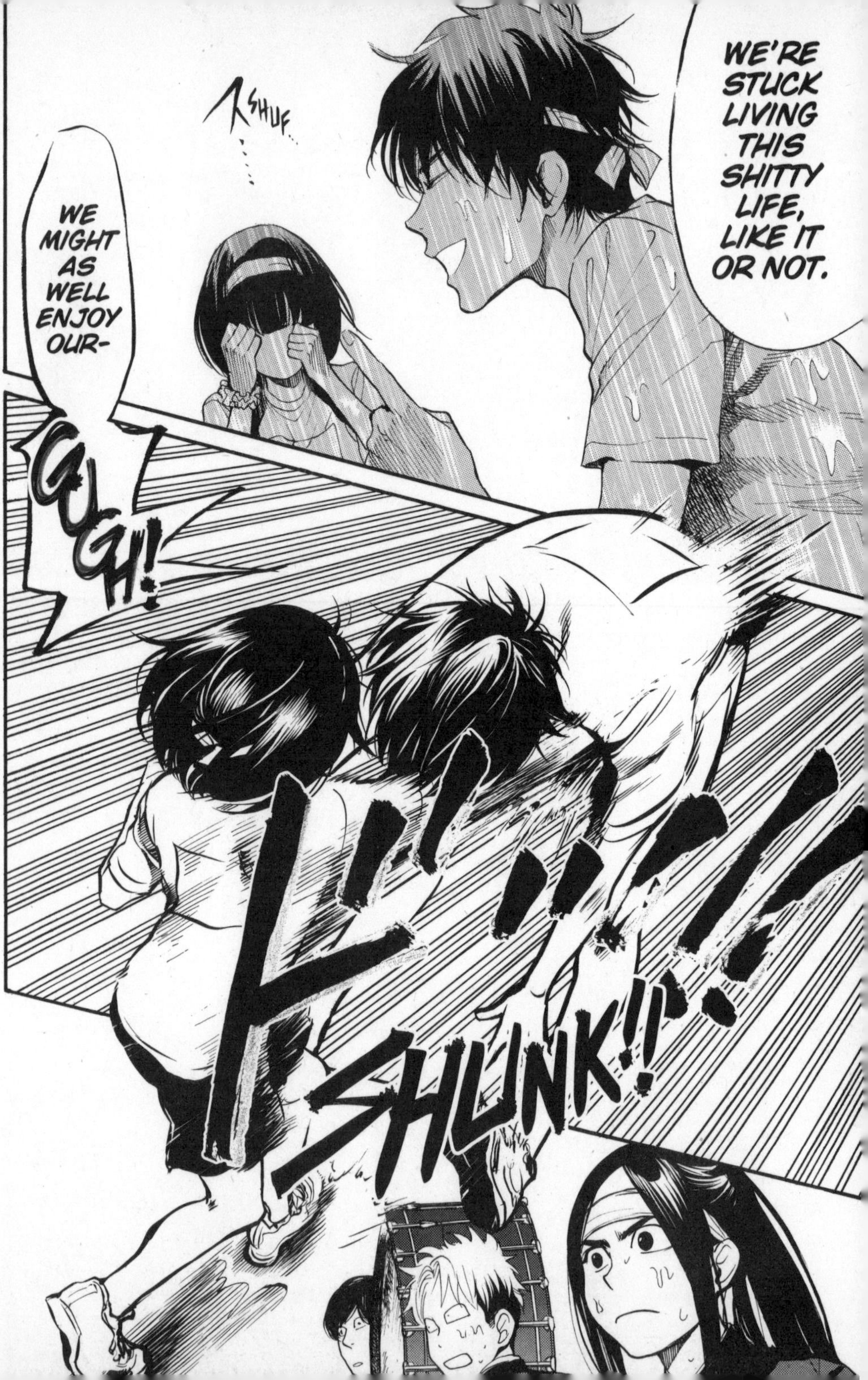
WE'RE STUCK LIVING THIS SHITTY LIFE, LIKE IT OR NOT.
SHUF...
WE MIGHT AS WELL ENJOY OUR-
UUGH!
K!!!!!!
SHUNK!!

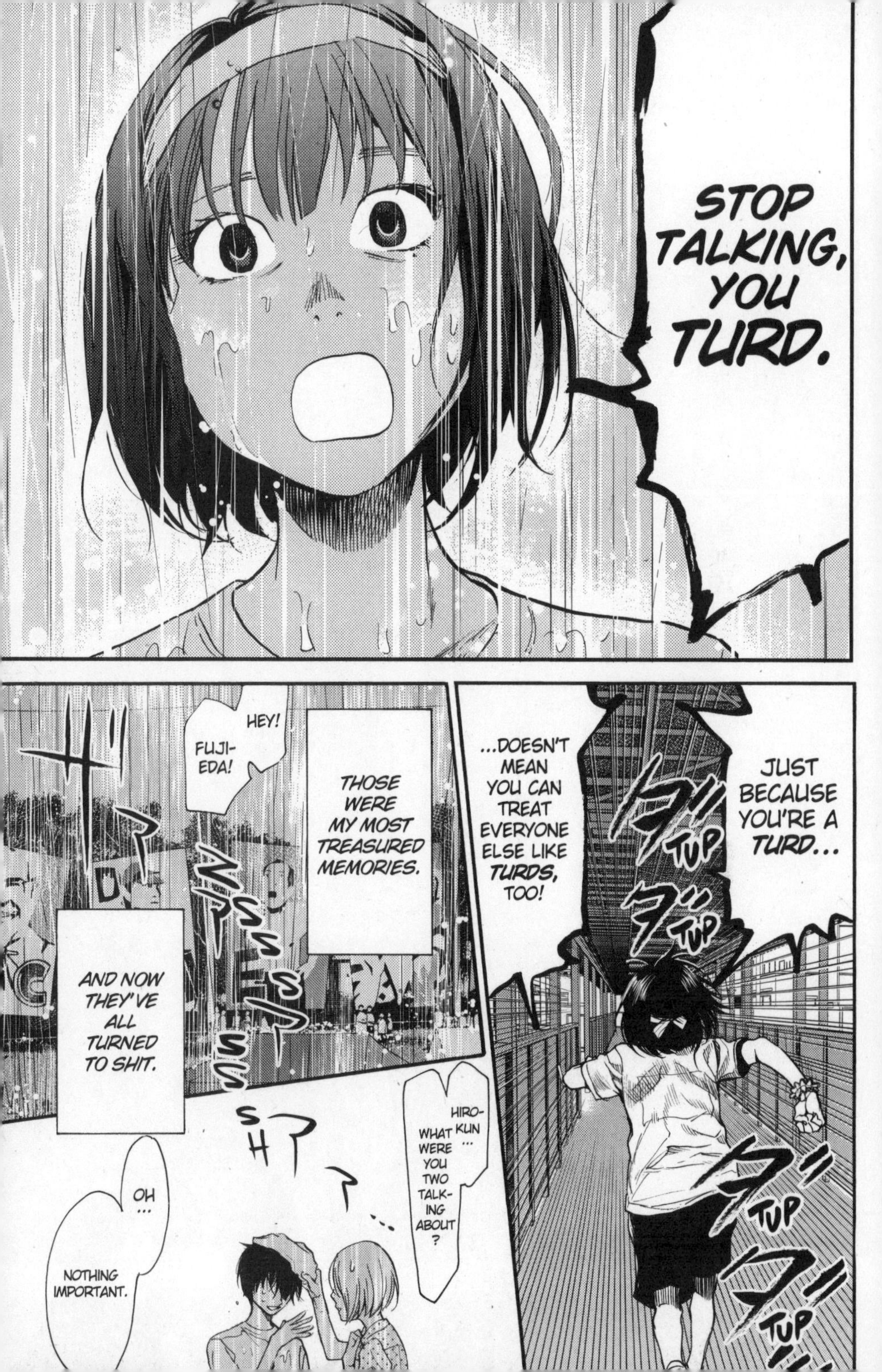
STOP TALKING, YOU TURD.
JUST BECAUSE YOU'RE A TURD...
...DOESN'T MEAN YOU CAN TREAT EVERYONE ELSE LIKE TURDS, TOO!
TUP
TUP
TUP
TUP
THOSE WERE MY MOST TREASURED MEMORIES.
HEY! FUJI-EDA!
AND NOW THEY'VE ALL TURNED TO SHIT.
SH
HIRO-KUN... WHAT WERE YOU TWO TALKING ABOUT?
OH...
NOTHING IMPORTANT.

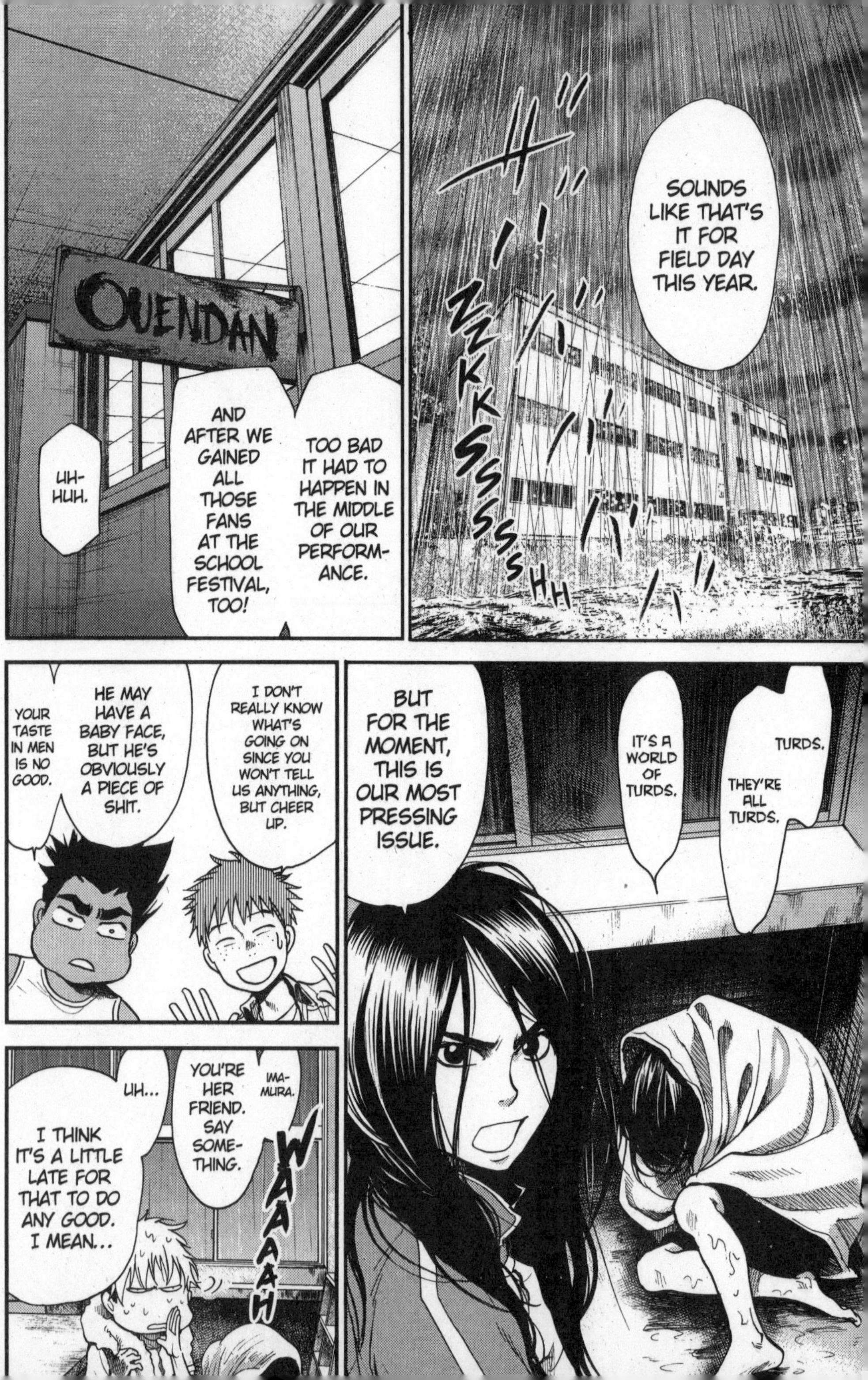
ZZZKKSSSSSHH
SOUNDS LIKE THAT'S IT FOR FIELD DAY THIS YEAR.
OUENDAN
TOO BAD IT HAD TO HAPPEN IN THE MIDDLE OF OUR PERFORM-ANCE.
AND AFTER WE GAINED ALL THOSE FANS AT THE SCHOOL FESTIVAL, TOO!
UH-HUH.
TURDS.
THEY'RE ALL TURDS.
IT'S A WORLD OF TURDS.
BUT FOR THE MOMENT, THIS IS OUR MOST PRESSING ISSUE.
WAAAAAH
I DON'T REALLY KNOW WHAT'S GOING ON SINCE YOU WON'T TELL US ANYTHING, BUT CHEER UP.
HE MAY HAVE A BABY FACE, BUT HE'S OBVIOUSLY A PIECE OF SHIT.
YOUR TASTE IN MEN IS NO GOOD.
IMA-MURA.
YOU'RE HER FRIEND. SAY SOME-THING.
UH...
I THINK IT'S A LITTLE LATE FOR THAT TO DO ANY GOOD. I MEAN...

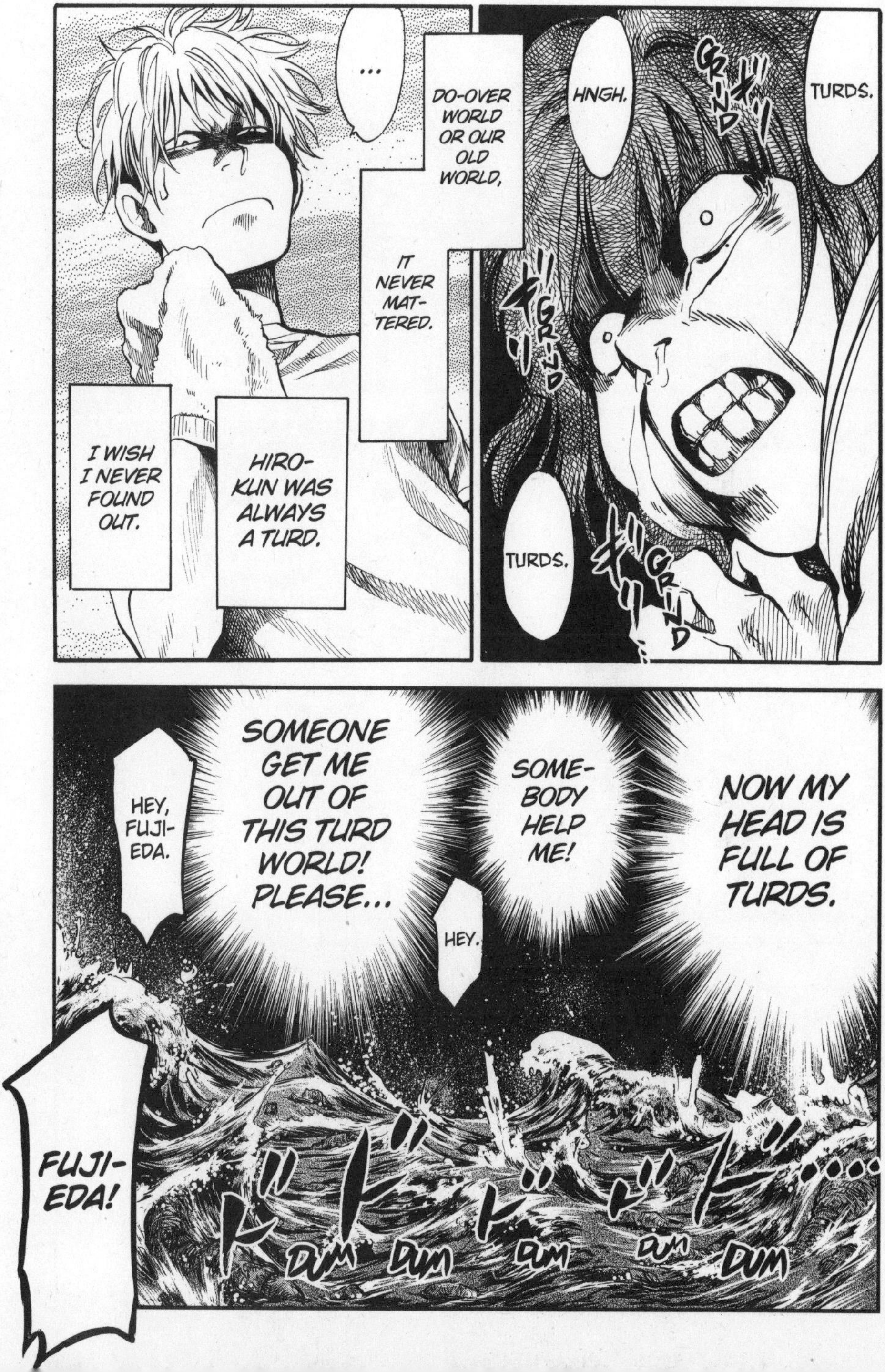
TURDS.
GRIND
HNGH.
GRIND
TURDS.
GRIND
...
DO-OVER WORLD OR OUR OLD WORLD,
IT NEVER MAT-TERED.
HIRO-KUN WAS ALWAYS A TURD.
I WISH I NEVER FOUND OUT.
NOW MY HEAD IS FULL OF TURDS.
SOME-BODY HELP ME!
SOMEONE GET ME OUT OF THIS TURD WORLD! PLEASE...
HEY.
HEY, FUJI-EDA.
FUJI-EDA!
DUM
DUM
DUM
DUM
DUM

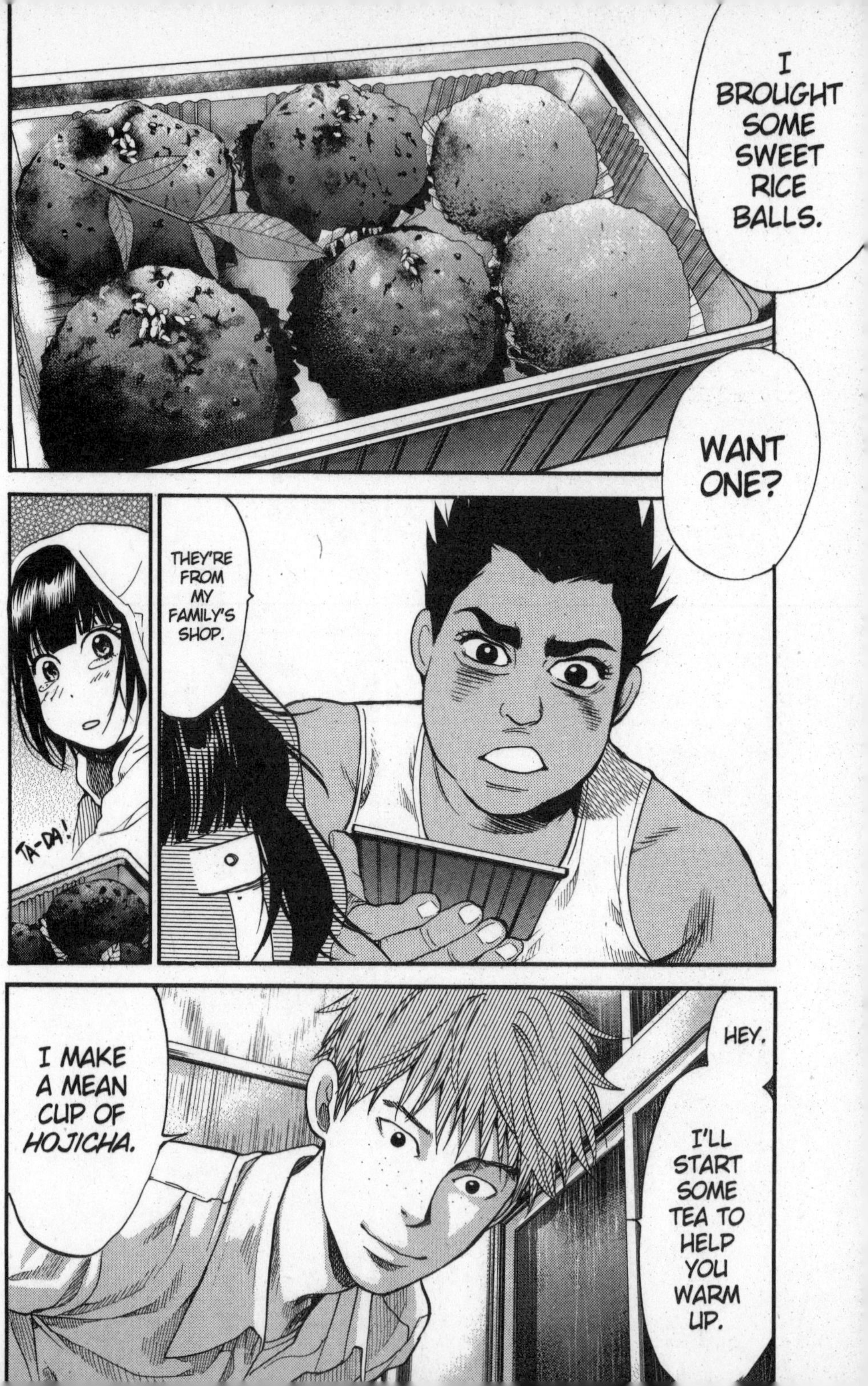
I BROUGHT SOME SWEET RICE BALLS.
WANT ONE?
THEY'RE FROM MY FAMILY'S SHOP.
TA-DA!
HEY.
I'LL START SOME TEA TO HELP YOU WARM UP.
I MAKE A MEAN CUP OF *HOJICHA*.

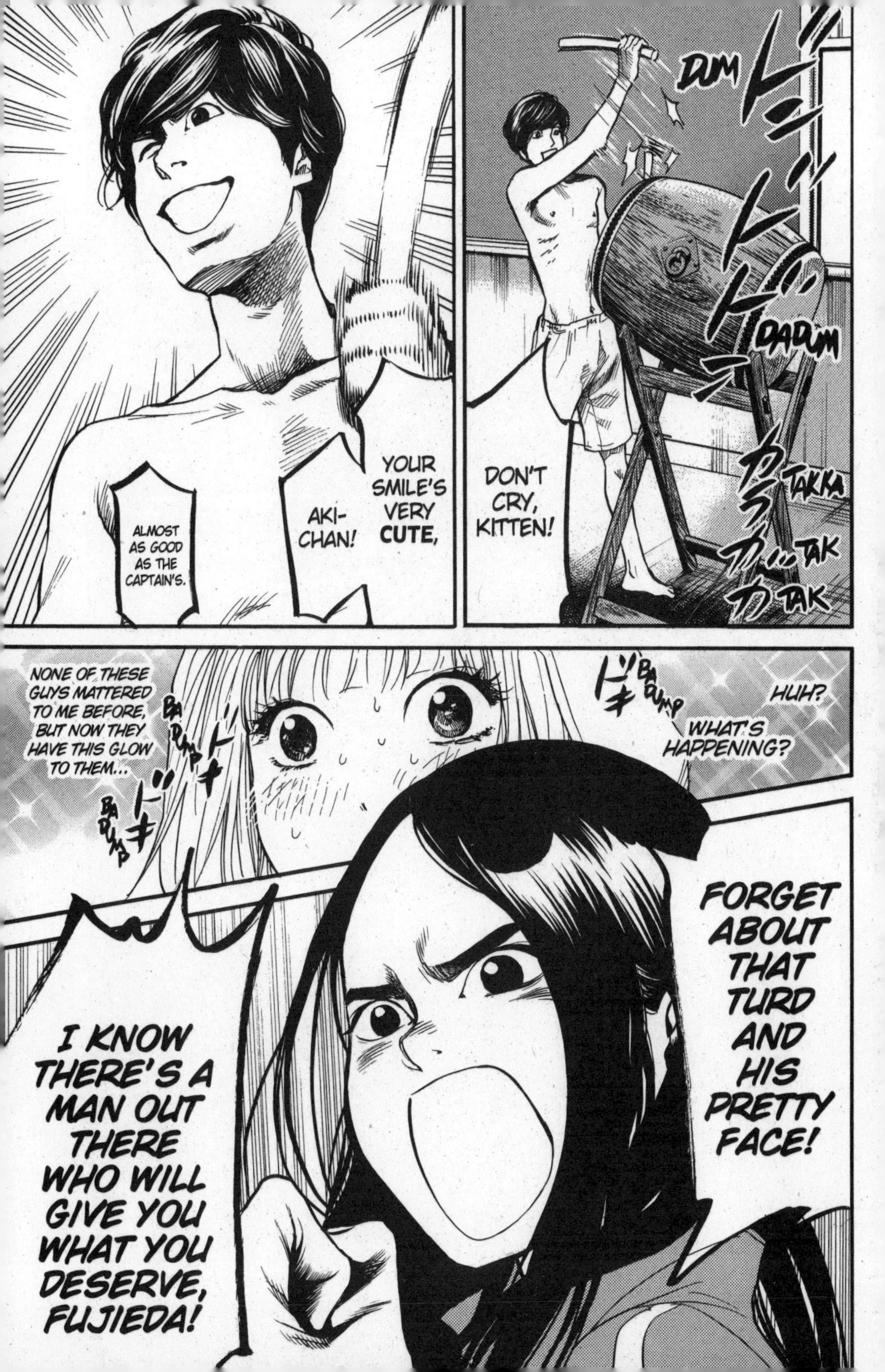
DUM
DADUM
TAKKA
TAK
TAK
DON'T CRY, KITTEN!
YOUR SMILE'S VERY CUTE,
AKI-CHAN!
ALMOST AS GOOD AS THE CAPTAIN'S.
BA DUMP
HUH?
WHAT'S HAPPENING?
BA DUMP
NONE OF THESE GUYS MATTERED TO ME BEFORE, BUT NOW THEY HAVE THIS GLOW TO THEM...
BA DUMP
FORGET ABOUT THAT TURD AND HIS PRETTY FACE!
I KNOW THERE'S A MAN OUT THERE WHO WILL GIVE YOU WHAT YOU DESERVE, FUJIEDA!

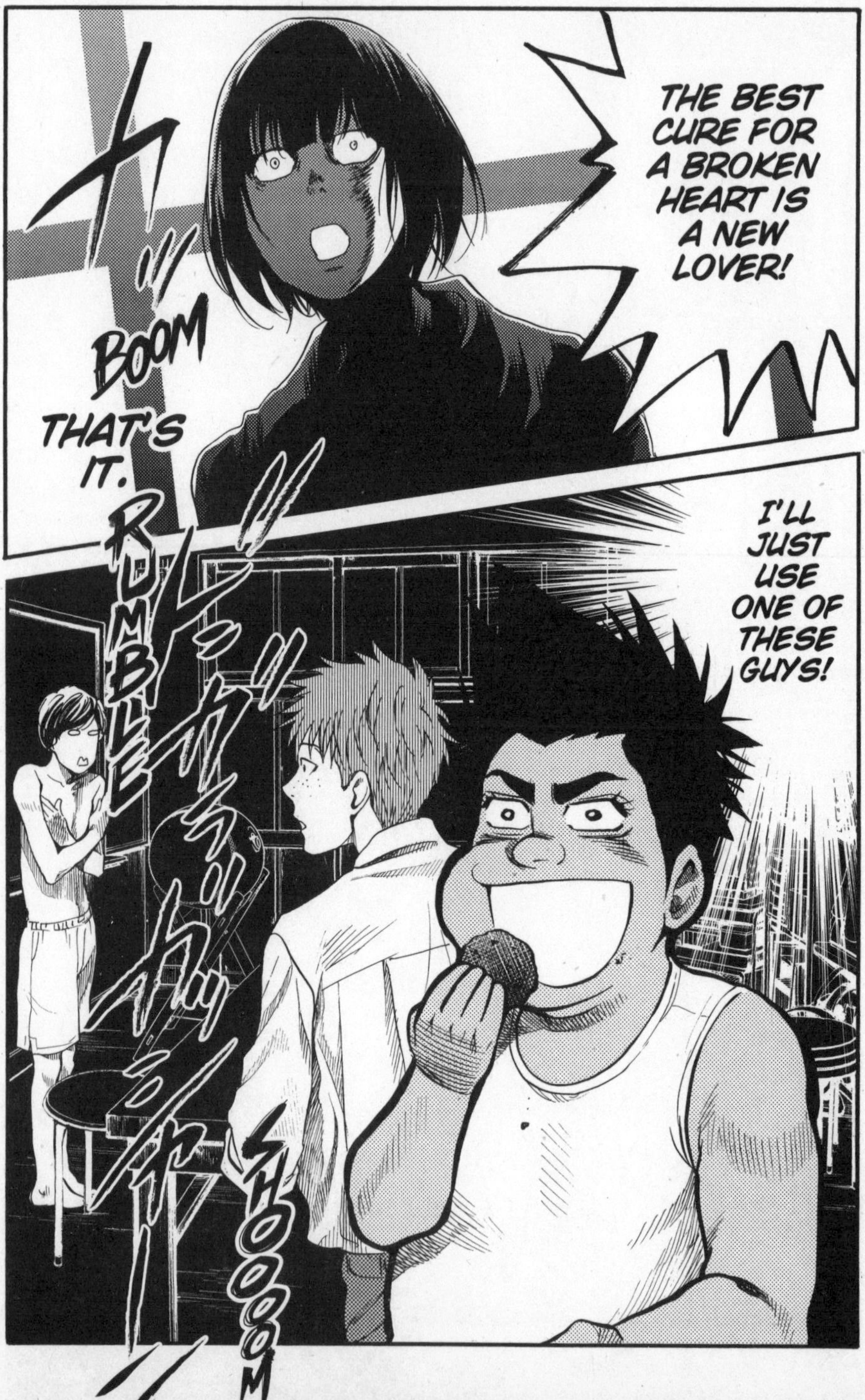
THE BEST CURE FOR A BROKEN HEART IS A NEW LOVER!
BOOM
THAT'S IT.
I'LL JUST USE ONE OF THESE GUYS!
RUMBLE
SHOOOOOM

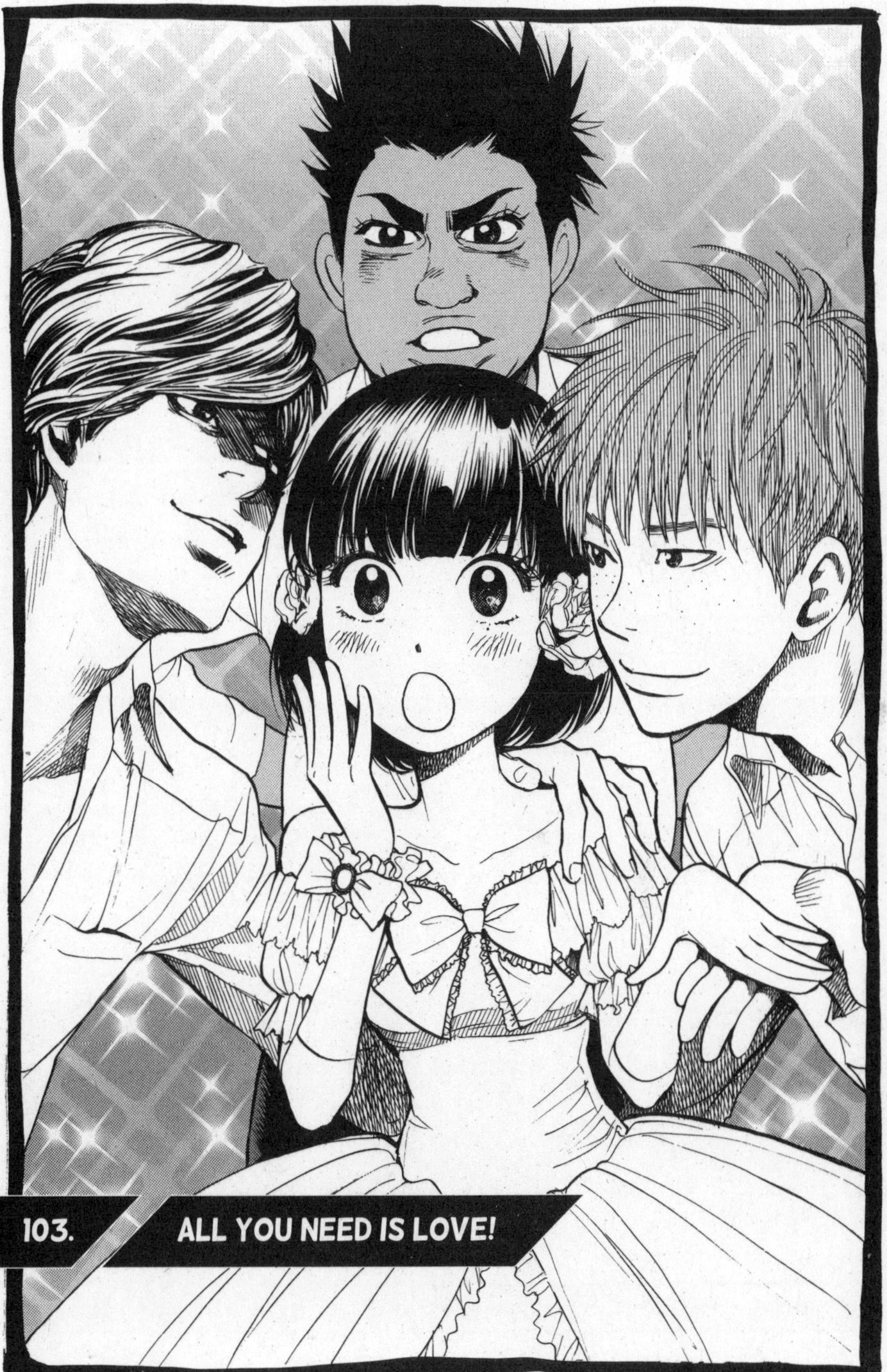

103. ALL YOU NEED IS LOVE!

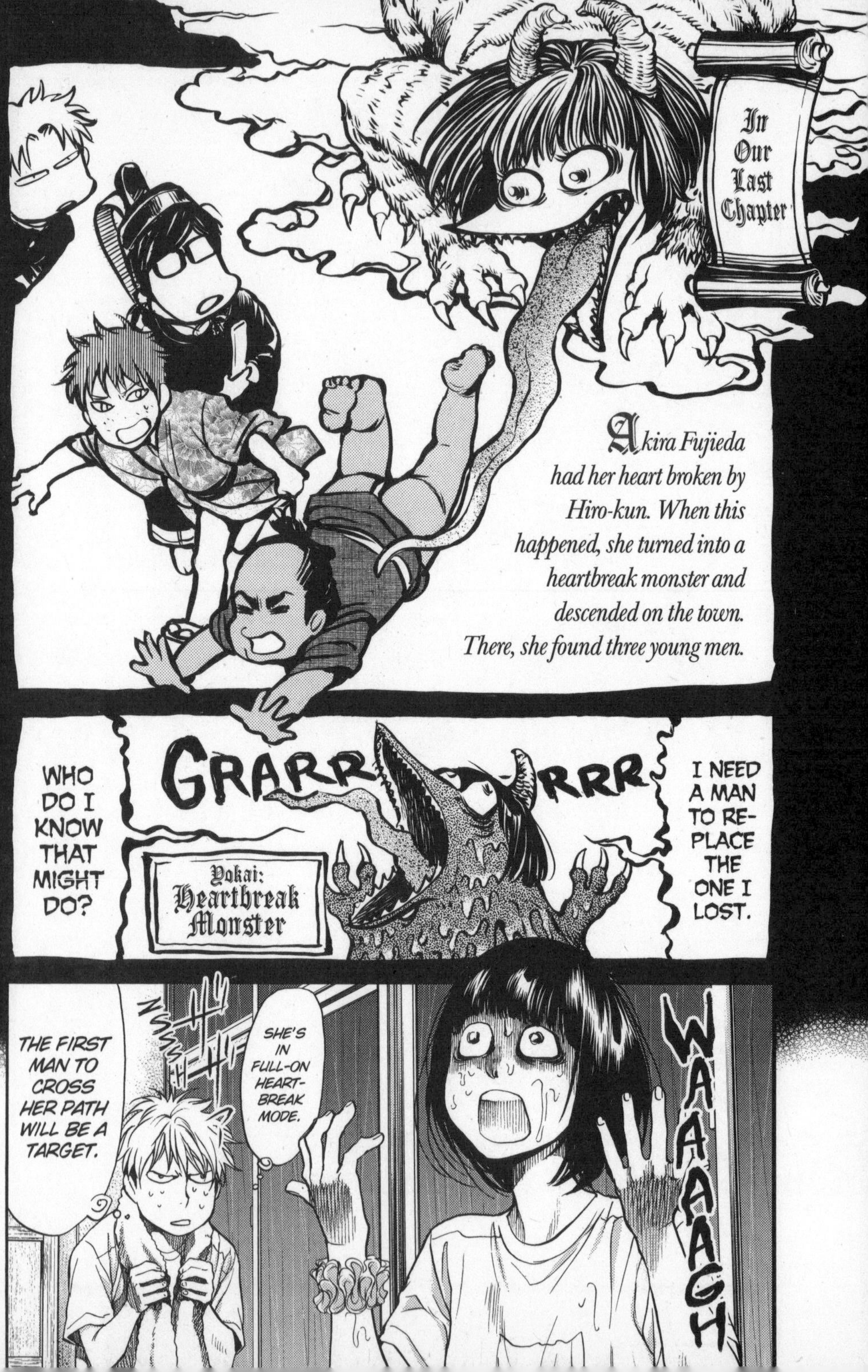
In Our Last Chapter
Akira Fujieda had her heart broken by Hiro-kun. When this happened, she turned into a heartbreak monster and descended on the town. There, she found three young men.
I NEED A MAN TO RE-PLACE THE ONE I LOST.
GRARRRRR
Yokai: Heartbreak Monster
WHO DO I KNOW THAT MIGHT DO?
WAAAAGH
SHE'S IN FULL-ON HEART-BREAK MODE.
THE FIRST MAN TO CROSS HER PATH WILL BE A TARGET.

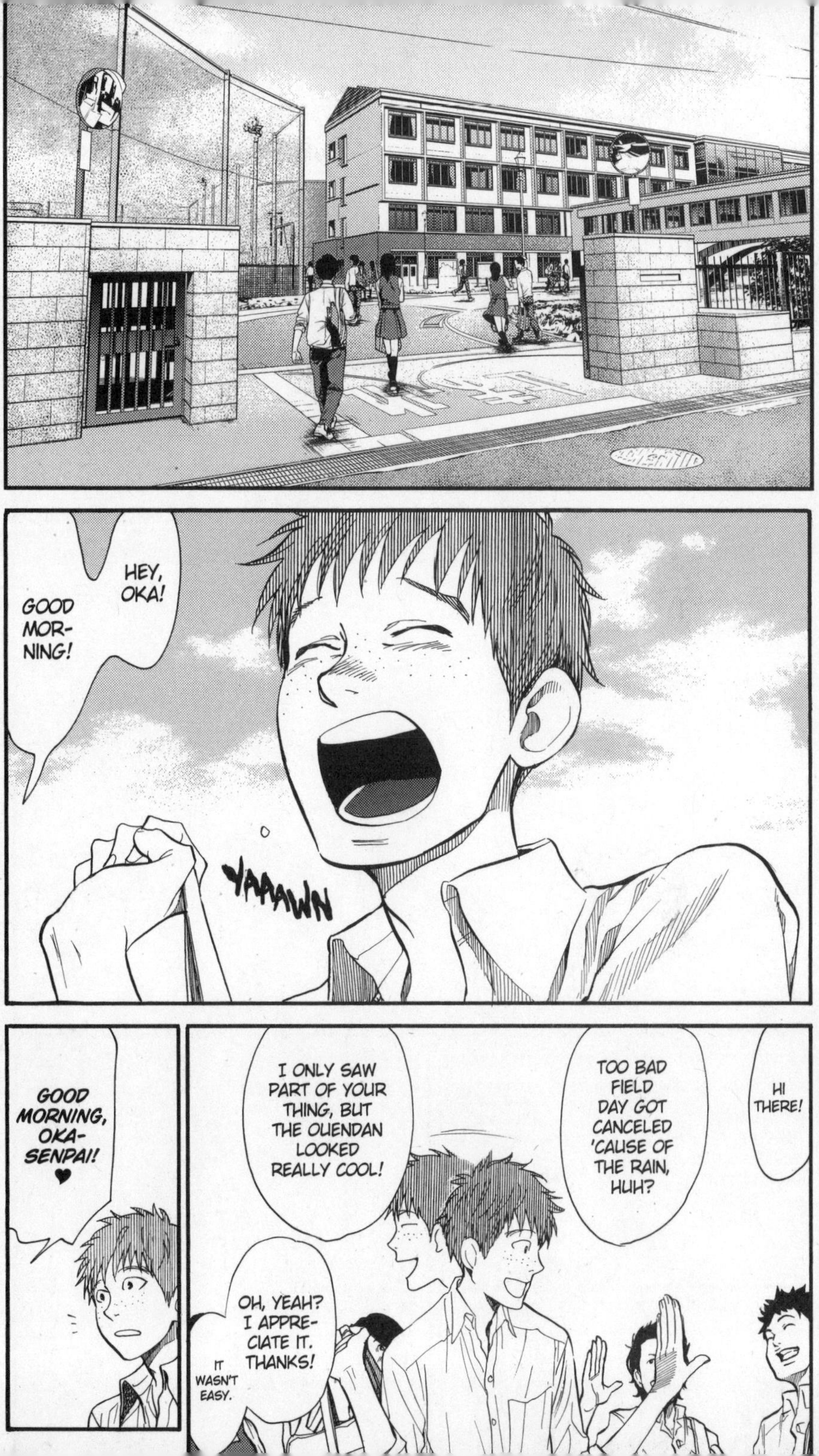
HEY, OKA! GOOD MOR-NING!
YAAAWN
HI THERE!
TOO BAD FIELD DAY GOT CANCELED 'CAUSE OF THE RAIN, HUH?
I ONLY SAW PART OF YOUR THING, BUT THE OUENDAN LOOKED REALLY COOL!
OH, YEAH? I APPRE-CIATE IT. THANKS!
IT WASN'T EASY.
GOOD MORNING, OKA-SENPAI! ♥

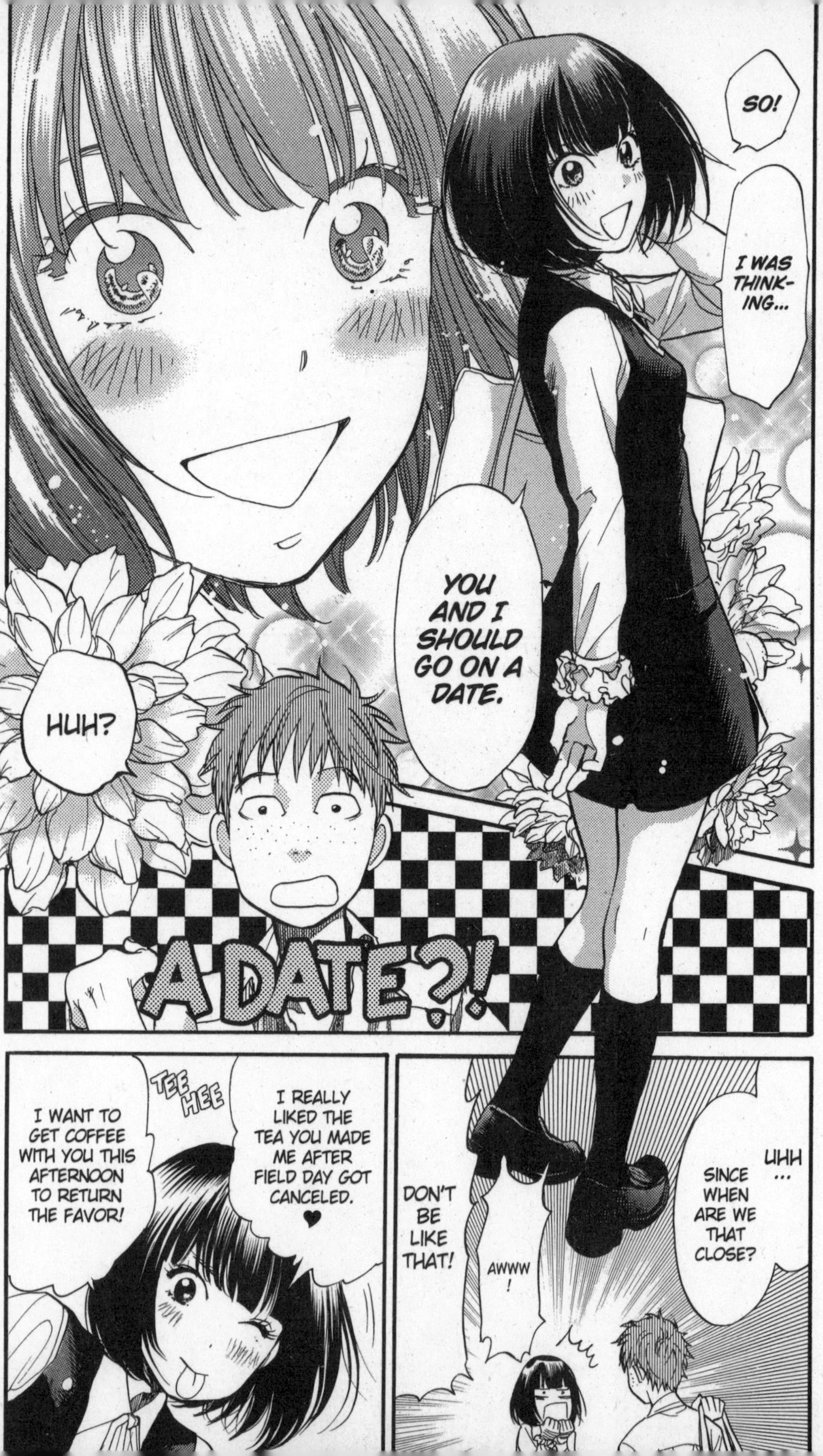
SO!
I WAS THINK-ING...
YOU AND I SHOULD GO ON A DATE.
HUH?
A DATE?!
UHH...
SINCE WHEN ARE WE THAT CLOSE?
DON'T BE LIKE THAT!
AWWW!
I REALLY LIKED THE TEA YOU MADE ME AFTER FIELD DAY GOT CANCELED. ♥
TEE HEE
I WANT TO GET COFFEE WITH YOU THIS AFTERNOON TO RETURN THE FAVOR!

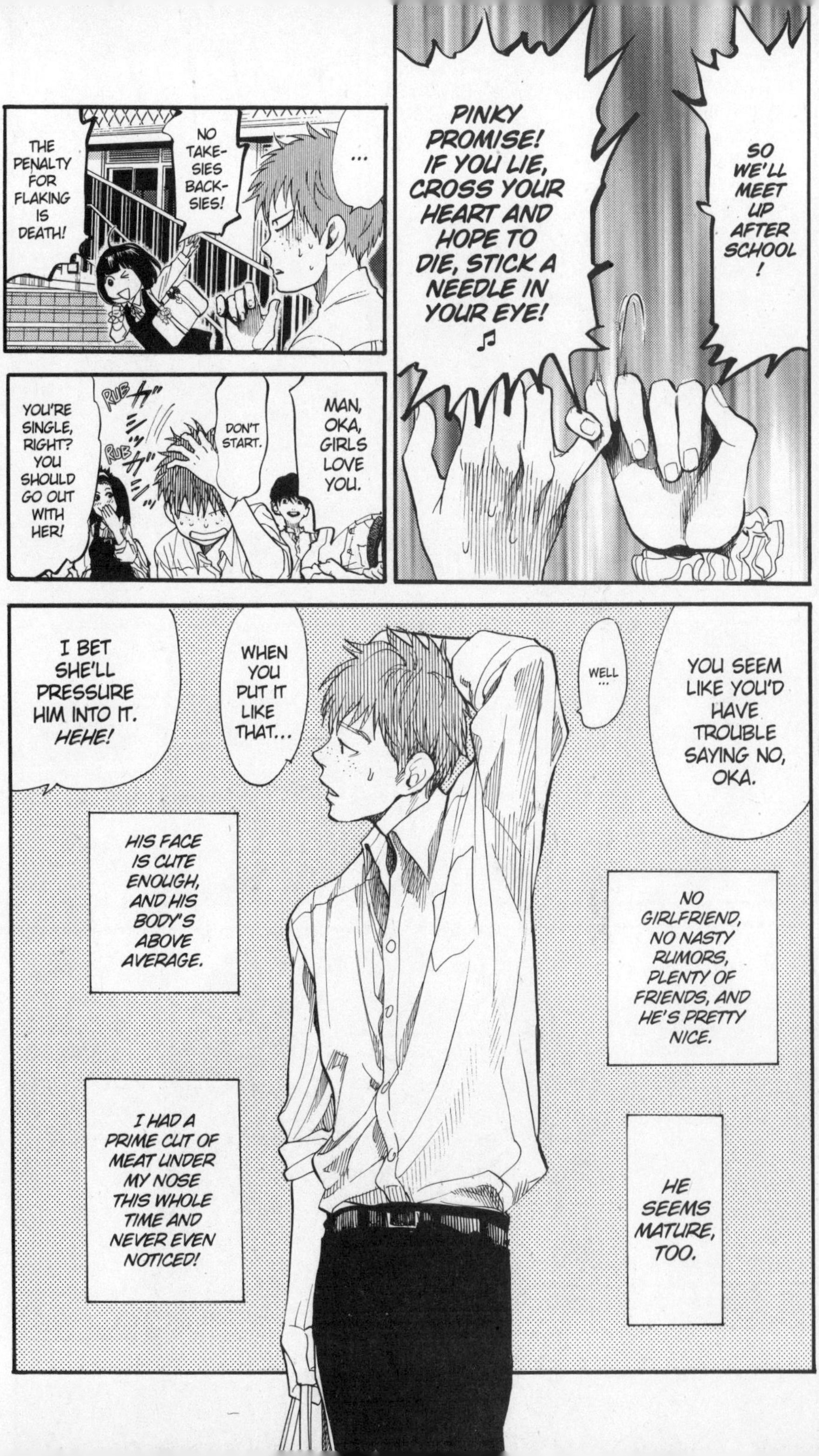
SO WE'LL MEET UP AFTER SCHOOL!
PINKY PROMISE! IF YOU LIE, CROSS YOUR HEART AND HOPE TO DIE, STICK A NEEDLE IN YOUR EYE! ♫
...
NO TAKESIES BACKSIES!
THE PENALTY FOR FLAKING IS DEATH!
MAN, OKA, GIRLS LOVE YOU.
DON'T START.
RUB
RUB
YOU'RE SINGLE, RIGHT? YOU SHOULD GO OUT WITH HER!
YOU SEEM LIKE YOU'D HAVE TROUBLE SAYING NO, OKA.
WELL...
WHEN YOU PUT IT LIKE THAT...
I BET SHE'LL PRESSURE HIM INTO IT. HEHE!
NO GIRLFRIEND, NO NASTY RUMORS, PLENTY OF FRIENDS, AND HE'S PRETTY NICE.
HIS FACE IS CUTE ENOUGH, AND HIS BODY'S ABOVE AVERAGE.
HE SEEMS MATURE, TOO.
I HAD A PRIME CUT OF MEAT UNDER MY NOSE THIS WHOLE TIME AND NEVER EVEN NOTICED!

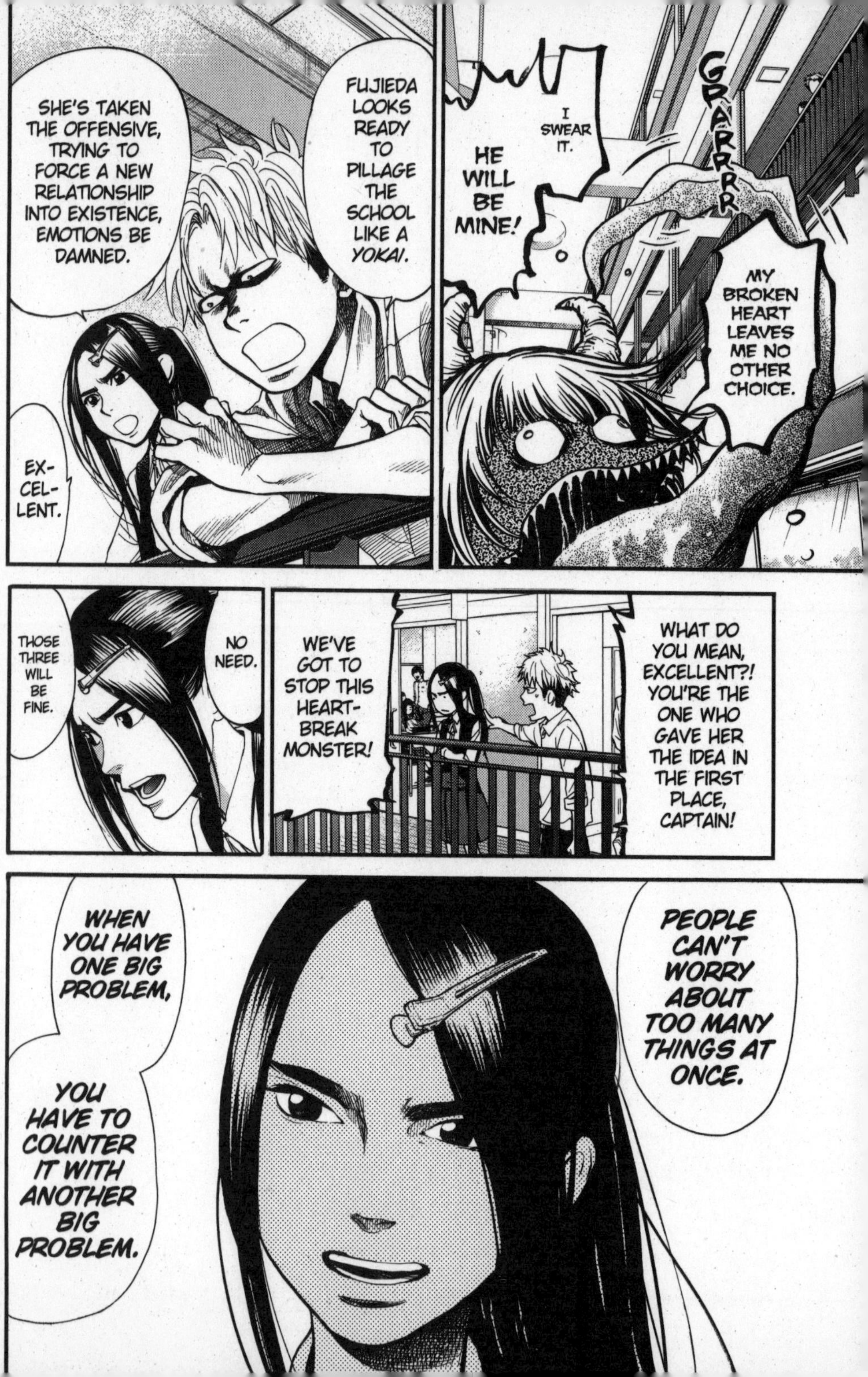
GRARRRR
I SWEAR IT.
HE WILL BE MINE!
MY BROKEN HEART LEAVES ME NO OTHER CHOICE.
FUJIEDA LOOKS READY TO PILLAGE THE SCHOOL LIKE A *YOKAI*.
SHE'S TAKEN THE OFFENSIVE, TRYING TO FORCE A NEW RELATIONSHIP INTO EXISTENCE, EMOTIONS BE DAMNED.
EX-CEL-LENT.
WHAT DO YOU MEAN, EXCELLENT?! YOU'RE THE ONE WHO GAVE HER THE IDEA IN THE FIRST PLACE, CAPTAIN!
WE'VE GOT TO STOP THIS HEART-BREAK MONSTER!
NO NEED.
THOSE THREE WILL BE FINE.
PEOPLE CAN'T WORRY ABOUT TOO MANY THINGS AT ONCE.
WHEN YOU HAVE ONE BIG PROBLEM,
YOU HAVE TO COUNTER IT WITH ANOTHER BIG PROBLEM.

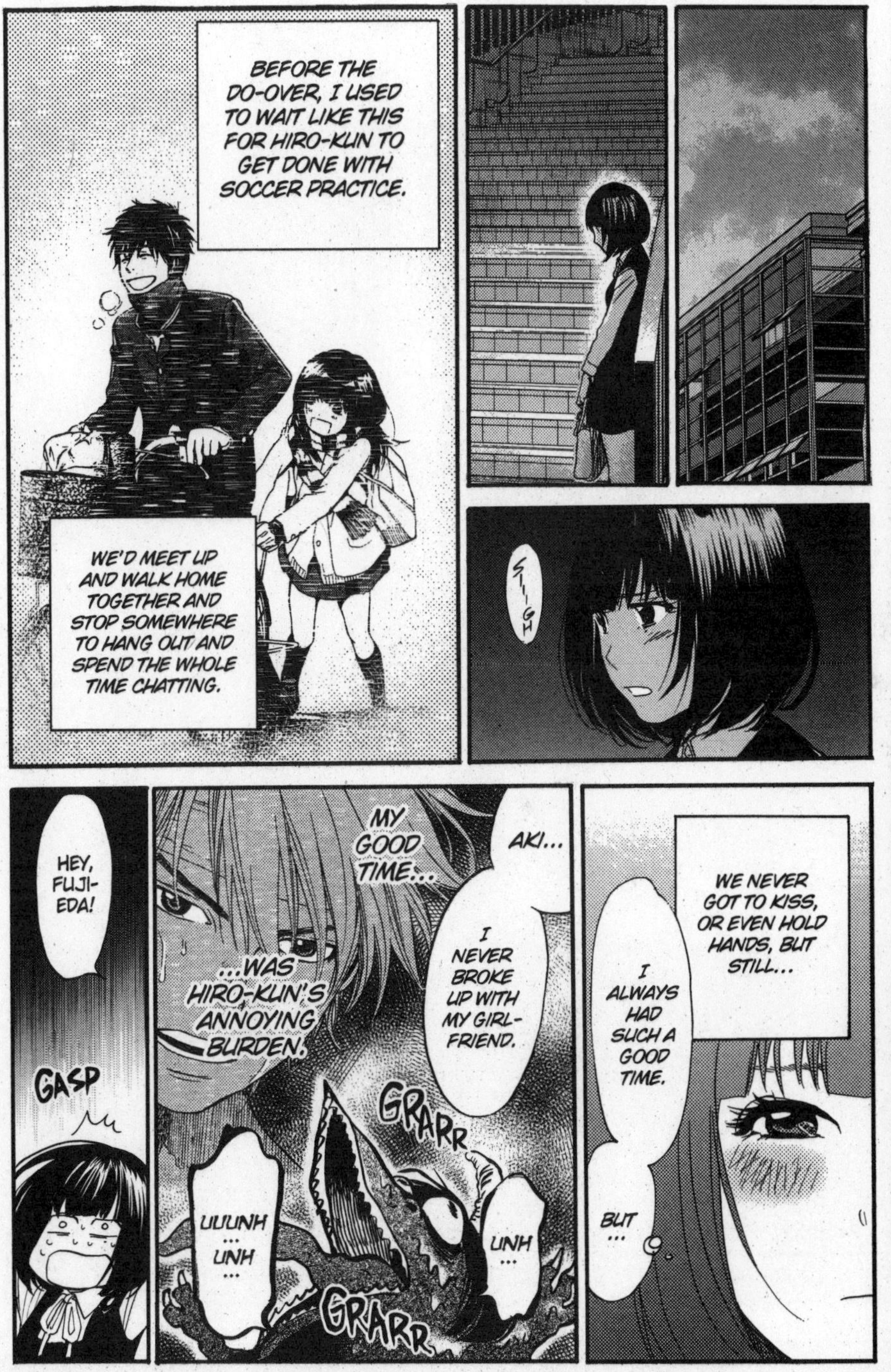
SIIIGH
BEFORE THE DO-OVER, I USED TO WAIT LIKE THIS FOR HIRO-KUN TO GET DONE WITH SOCCER PRACTICE.
WE'D MEET UP AND WALK HOME TOGETHER AND STOP SOMEWHERE TO HANG OUT AND SPEND THE WHOLE TIME CHATTING.
WE NEVER GOT TO KISS, OR EVEN HOLD HANDS, BUT STILL...
I ALWAYS HAD SUCH A GOOD TIME.
BUT...
AKI...
I NEVER BROKE UP WITH MY GIRL-FRIEND.
MY GOOD TIME...
...WAS HIRO-KUN'S ANNOYING BURDEN.
GRARR
UNH...
UUUNH... UNH...
GRARR
HEY, FUJI-EDA!
GASP

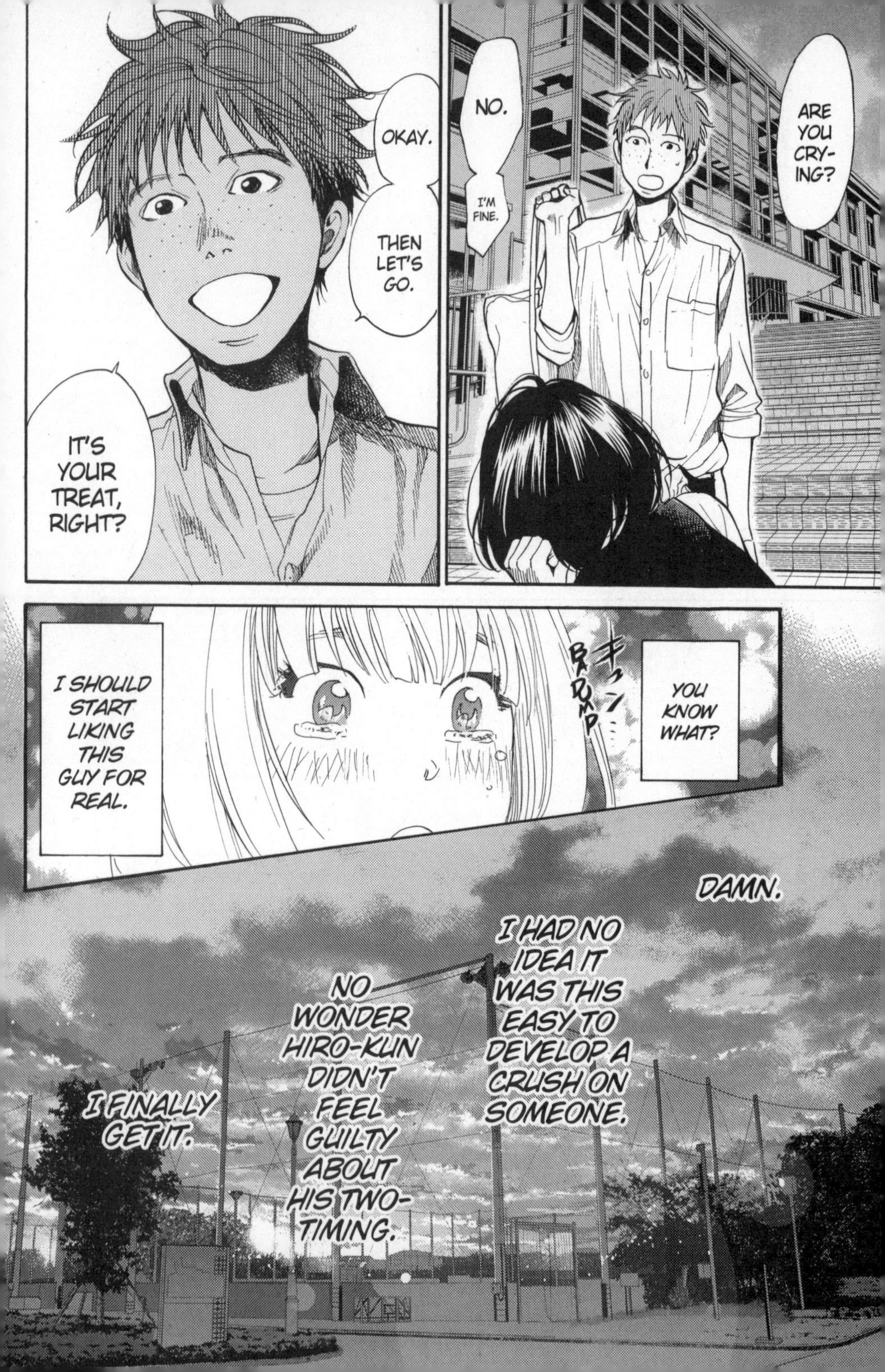
ARE YOU CRY-ING?
NO.
I'M FINE.
OKAY.
THEN LET'S GO.
IT'S YOUR TREAT, RIGHT?
YOU KNOW WHAT?
BADUMP
I SHOULD START LIKING THIS GUY FOR REAL.
DAMN.
I HAD NO IDEA IT WAS THIS EASY TO DEVELOP A CRUSH ON SOMEONE.
NO WONDER HIRO-KUN DIDN'T FEEL GUILTY ABOUT HIS TWO-TIMING.
I FINALLY GET IT.

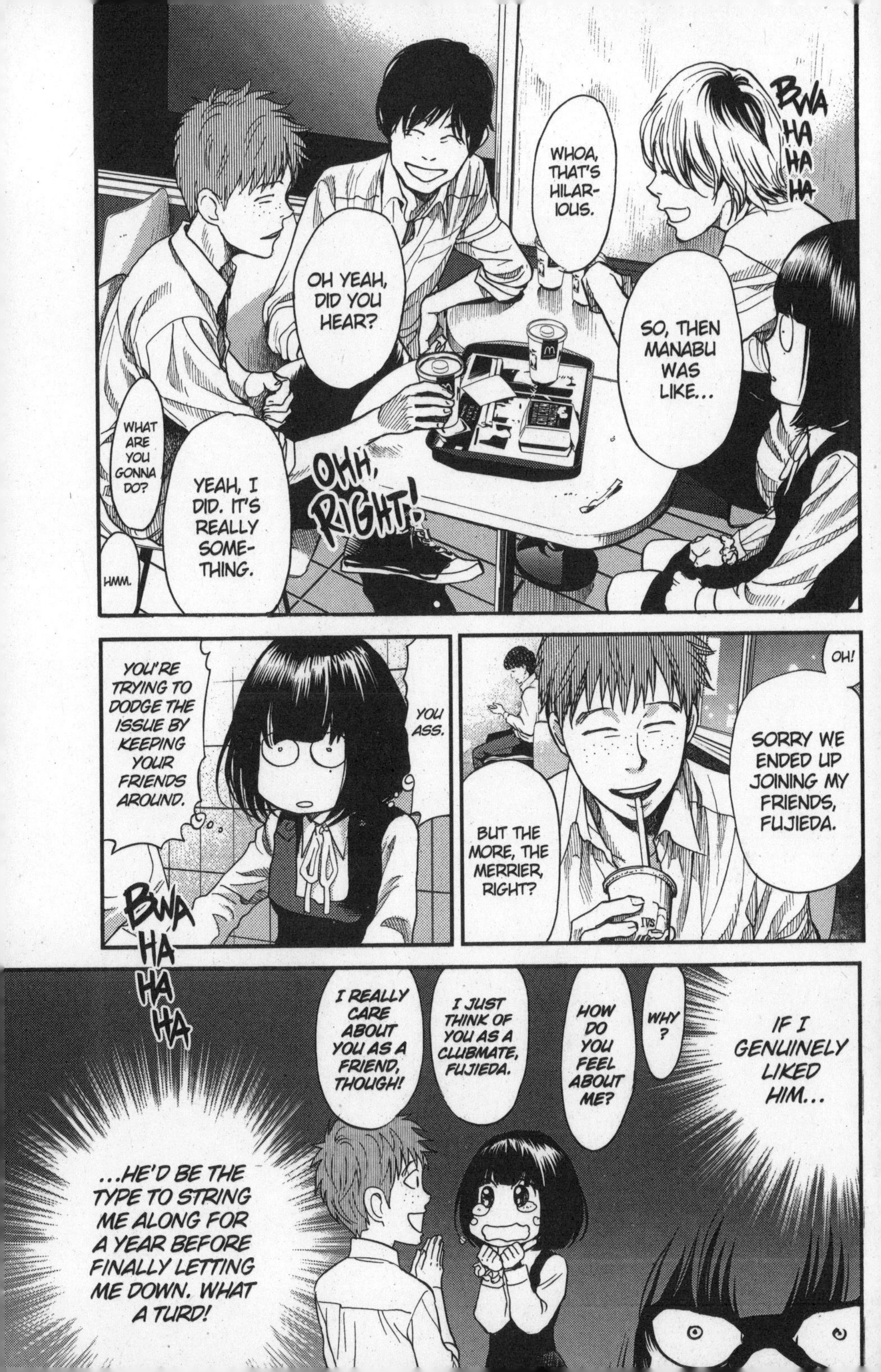
BWA HA HA HA
WHOA, THAT'S HILAR-IOUS.
SO, THEN MANABU WAS LIKE...
OH YEAH, DID YOU HEAR?
OHH, RIGHT!
YEAH, I DID. IT'S REALLY SOME-THING.
WHAT ARE YOU GONNA DO?
HMM.
OH!
SORRY WE ENDED UP JOINING MY FRIENDS, FUJIEDA.
BUT THE MORE, THE MERRIER, RIGHT?
YOU ASS.
YOU'RE TRYING TO DODGE THE ISSUE BY KEEPING YOUR FRIENDS AROUND.
BWA HA HA HA
IF I GENUINELY LIKED HIM...
WHY?
HOW DO YOU FEEL ABOUT ME?
I JUST THINK OF YOU AS A CLUBMATE, FUJIEDA.
I REALLY CARE ABOUT YOU AS A FRIEND, THOUGH!
...HE'D BE THE TYPE TO STRING ME ALONG FOR A YEAR BEFORE FINALLY LETTING ME DOWN. WHAT A TURD!

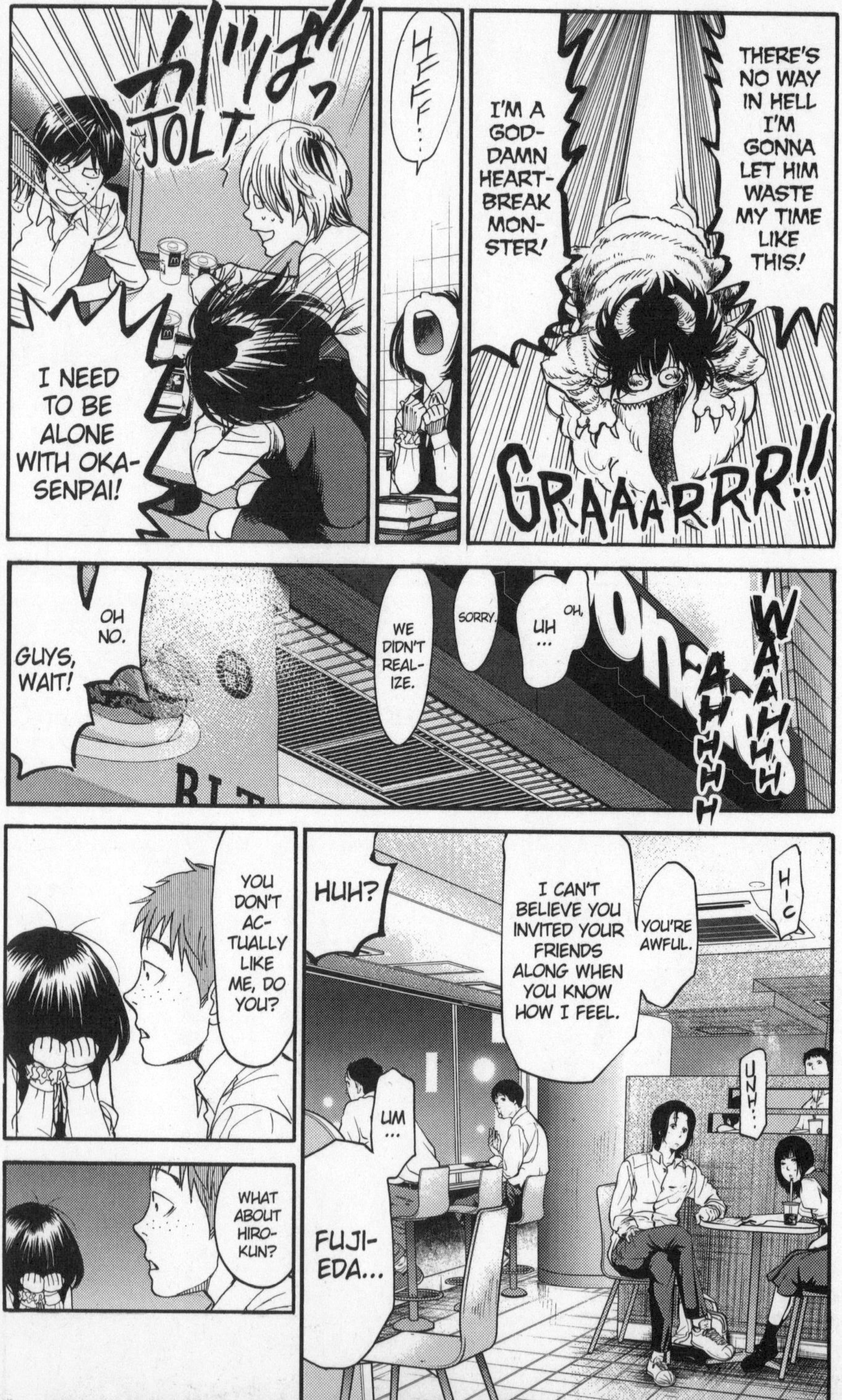
THERE'S NO WAY IN HELL I'M GONNA LET HIM WASTE MY TIME LIKE THIS!
I'M A GOD-DAMN HEART-BREAK MON-STER!
GRAAARRR!!
HEFF...
JOLT
I NEED TO BE ALONE WITH OKA-SENPAI!
WAAAHHHH
AHHHHHH
OH, UH...
SORRY.
WE DIDN'T REAL-IZE.
OH NO.
GUYS, WAIT!
HIC
YOU'RE AWFUL.
I CAN'T BELIEVE YOU INVITED YOUR FRIENDS ALONG WHEN YOU KNOW HOW I FEEL.
HUH?
UNH...
UM...
FUJI-EDA...
YOU DON'T AC-TUALLY LIKE ME, DO YOU?
WHAT ABOUT HIRO-KUN?

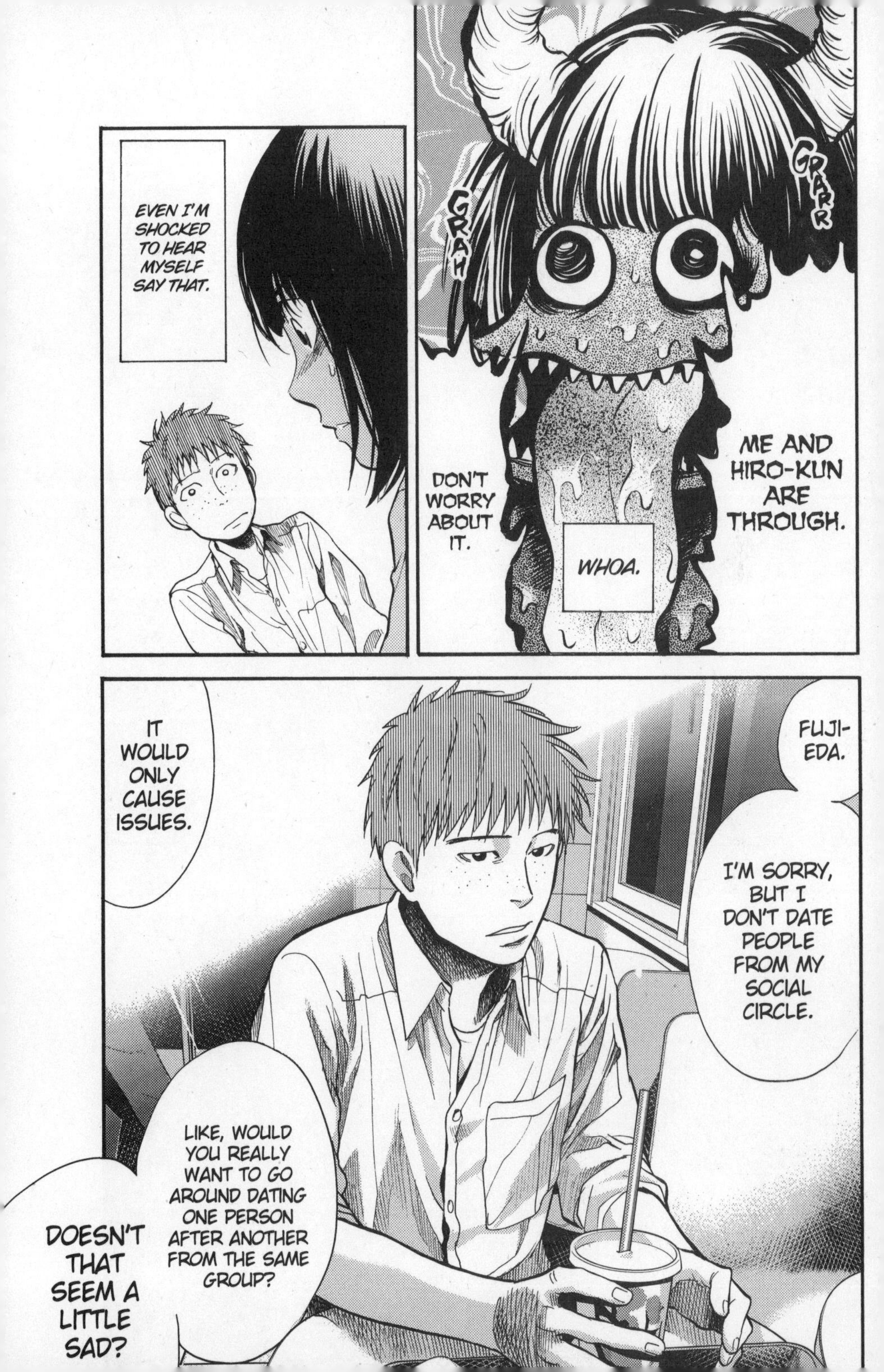
GRARR
GRAH
ME AND HIRO-KUN ARE THROUGH.
DON'T WORRY ABOUT IT.
WHOA.
EVEN I'M SHOCKED TO HEAR MYSELF SAY THAT.
FUJI-EDA.
I'M SORRY, BUT I DON'T DATE PEOPLE FROM MY SOCIAL CIRCLE.
IT WOULD ONLY CAUSE ISSUES.
LIKE, WOULD YOU REALLY WANT TO GO AROUND DATING ONE PERSON AFTER ANOTHER FROM THE SAME GROUP?
DOESN'T THAT SEEM A LITTLE SAD?

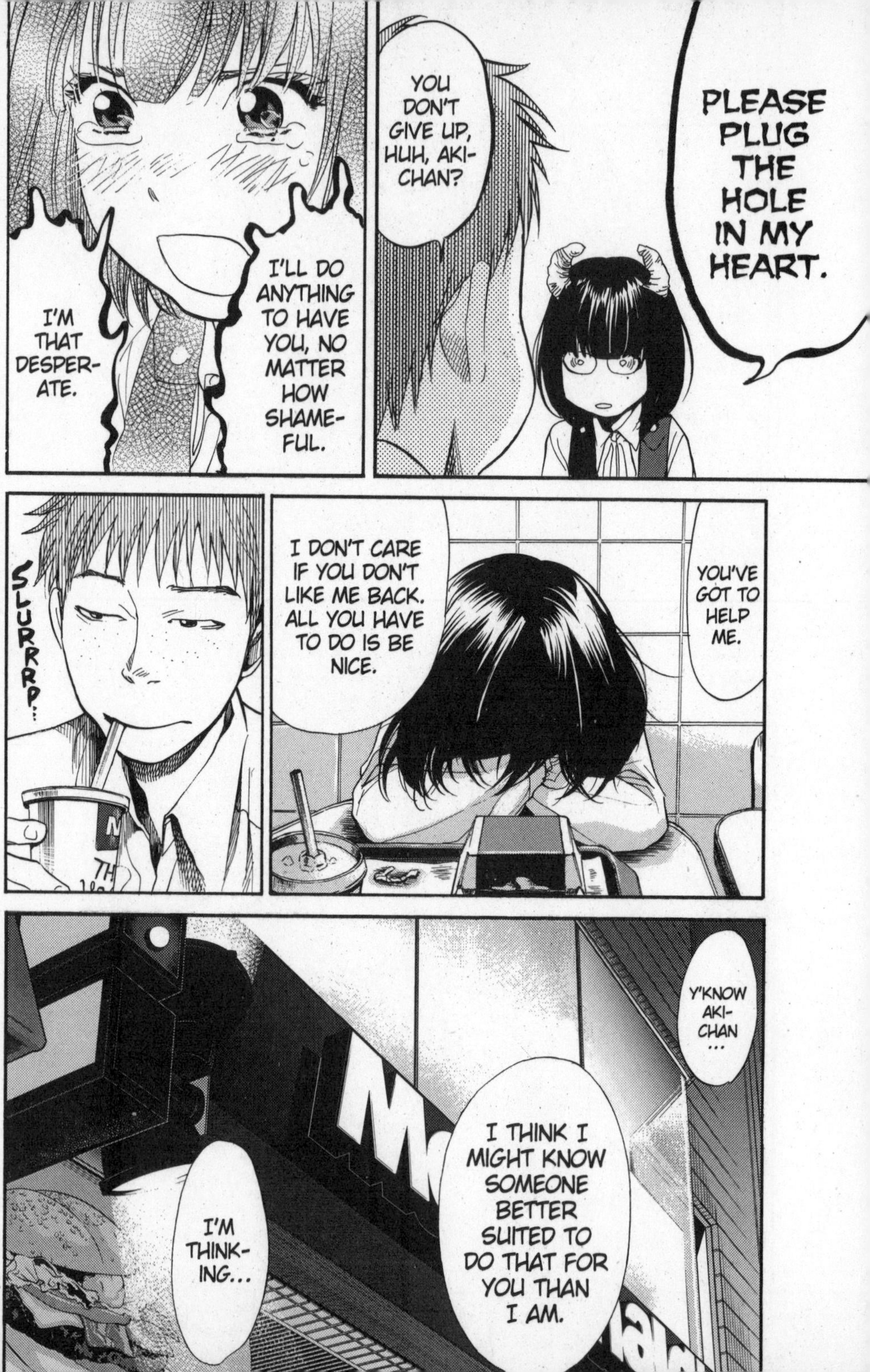
PLEASE PLUG THE HOLE IN MY HEART.
YOU DON'T GIVE UP, HUH, AKI-CHAN?
I'LL DO ANYTHING TO HAVE YOU, NO MATTER HOW SHAME-FUL.
I'M THAT DESPER-ATE.
YOU'VE GOT TO HELP ME.
I DON'T CARE IF YOU DON'T LIKE ME BACK. ALL YOU HAVE TO DO IS BE NICE.
SLURRRP..
Y'KNOW AKI-CHAN...
I THINK I MIGHT KNOW SOMEONE BETTER SUITED TO DO THAT FOR YOU THAN I AM.
I'M THINK-ING...

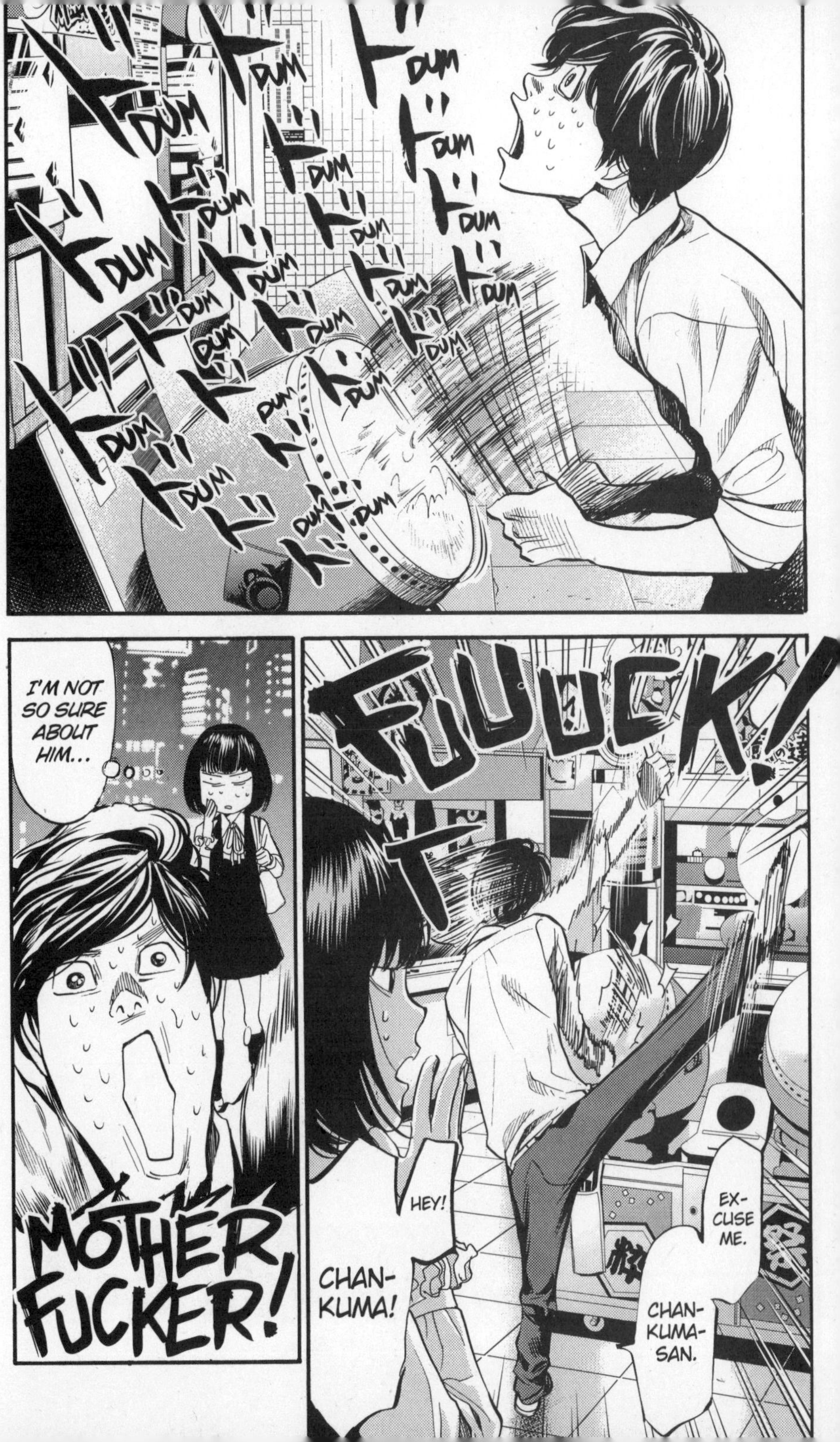
ドドドドドドドドドド
DUM DUM DUM DUM DUM DUM DUM DUM DUM DUM DUM DUM DUM DUM DUM DUM DUM DUM DUM DUM DUM
FUUUUCK!
EX-CUSE ME.
CHAN-KUMA-SAN.
HEY!
CHAN-KUMA!
I'M NOT SO SURE ABOUT HIM...
MOTHER FUCKER!

Again!!
アゲイン!!

104. WOMAN, SUCH A FICKLE CREATURE

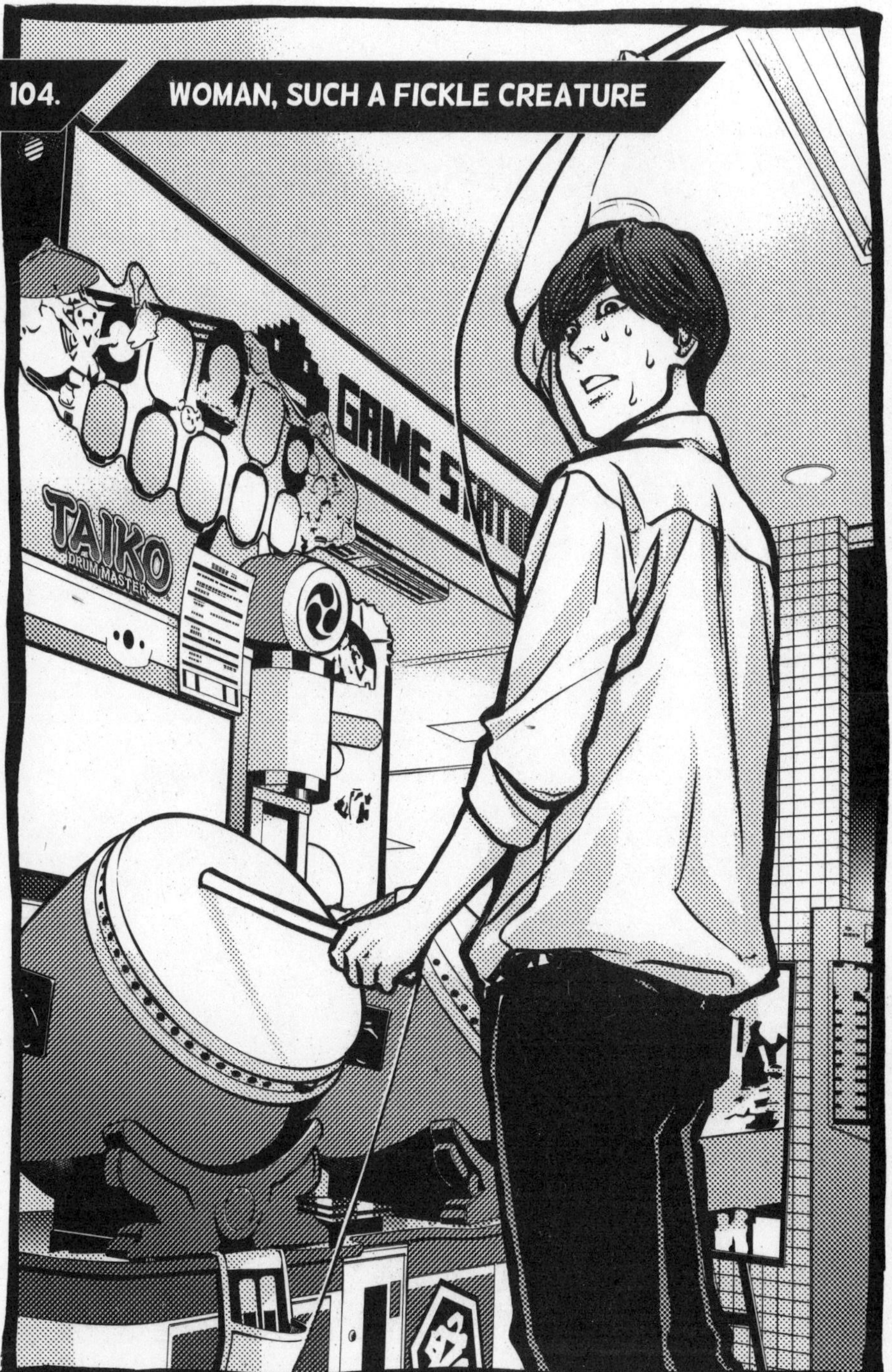
TAIKO
DRUM MASTER
GAME

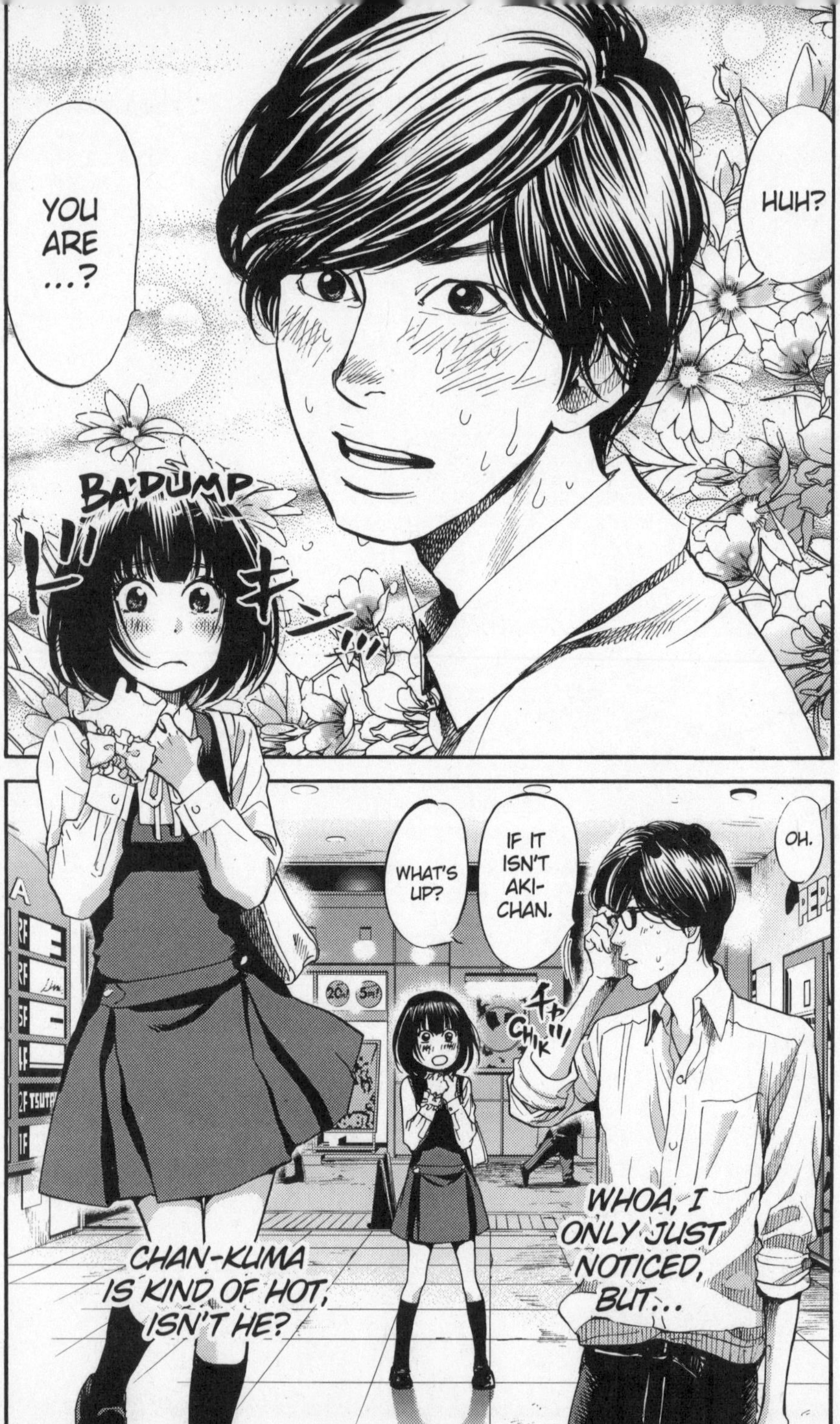
HUH?
YOU ARE ...?
BA-DUMP
OH.
IF IT ISN'T AKI-CHAN.
WHAT'S UP?
CHIK
WHOA, I ONLY JUST NOTICED, BUT...
CHAN-KUMA IS KIND OF HOT, ISN'T HE?

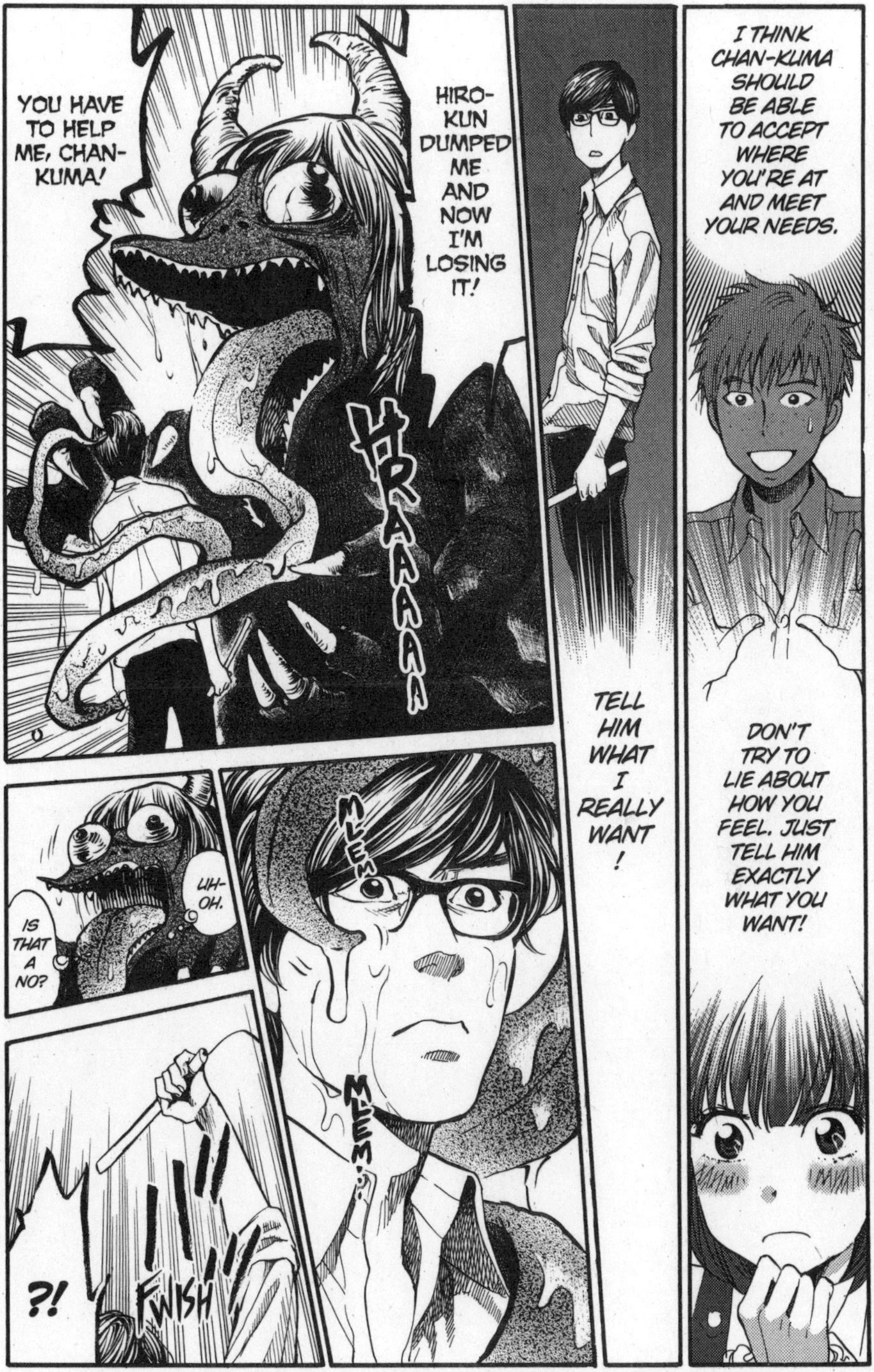
I THINK CHAN-KUMA SHOULD BE ABLE TO ACCEPT WHERE YOU'RE AT AND MEET YOUR NEEDS.
DON'T TRY TO LIE ABOUT HOW YOU FEEL. JUST TELL HIM EXACTLY WHAT YOU WANT!
TELL HIM WHAT I REALLY WANT!
HIRO-KUN DUMPED ME AND NOW I'M LOSING IT!
YOU HAVE TO HELP ME, CHAN-KUMA!
HRAAAAAAA
MLEM
MLEM...
UH-OH.
IS THAT A NO?
?!
FWISH

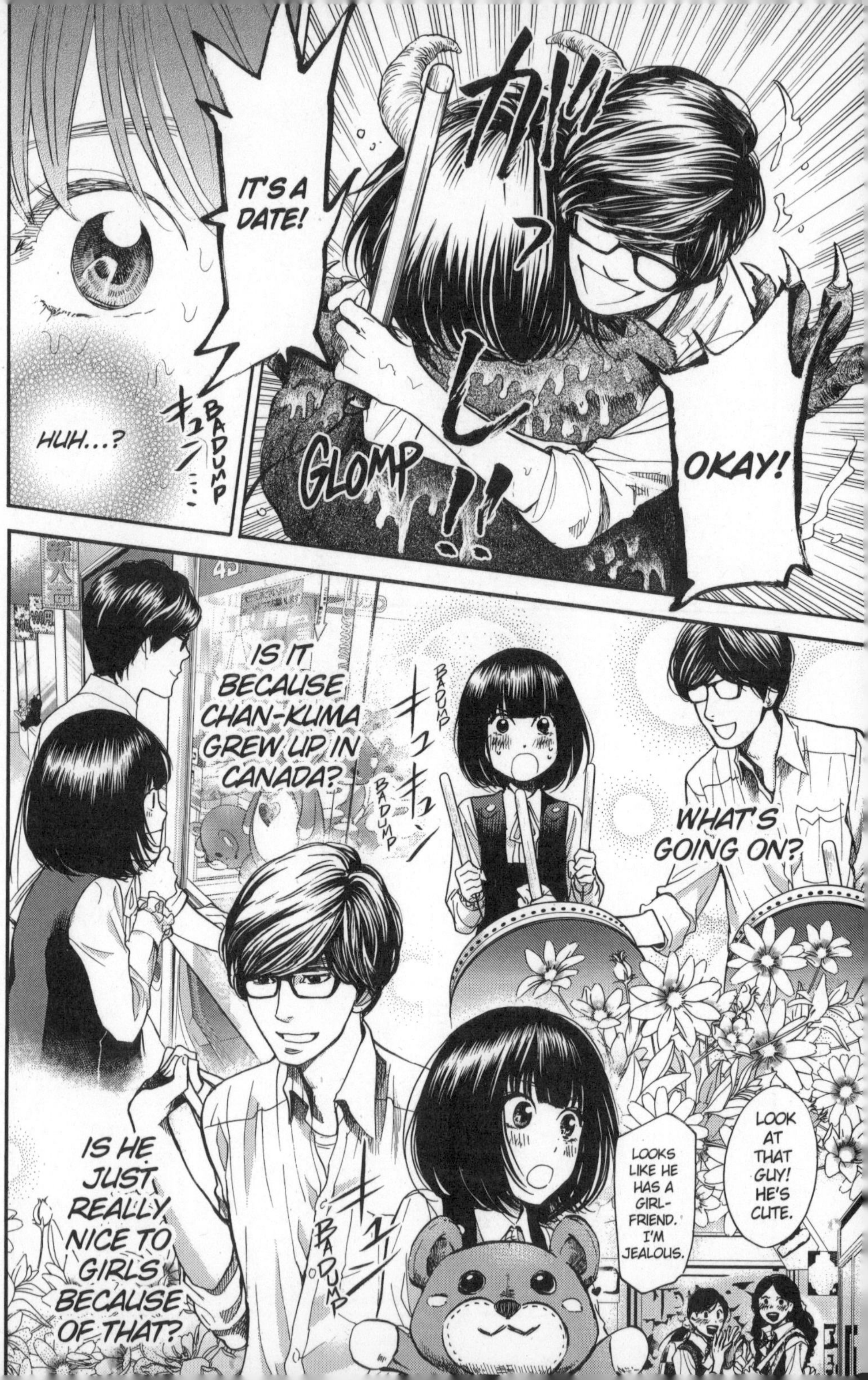
OKAY!
IT'S A DATE!
GLOMP
BADUMP
HUH...?
WHAT'S GOING ON?
BADUMP
BADUMP
IS IT BECAUSE CHAN-KUMA GREW UP IN CANADA?
LOOK AT THAT GUY! HE'S CUTE.
LOOKS LIKE HE HAS A GIRL-FRIEND. I'M JEALOUS.
BADUMP
IS HE JUST REALLY NICE TO GIRLS BECAUSE OF THAT?

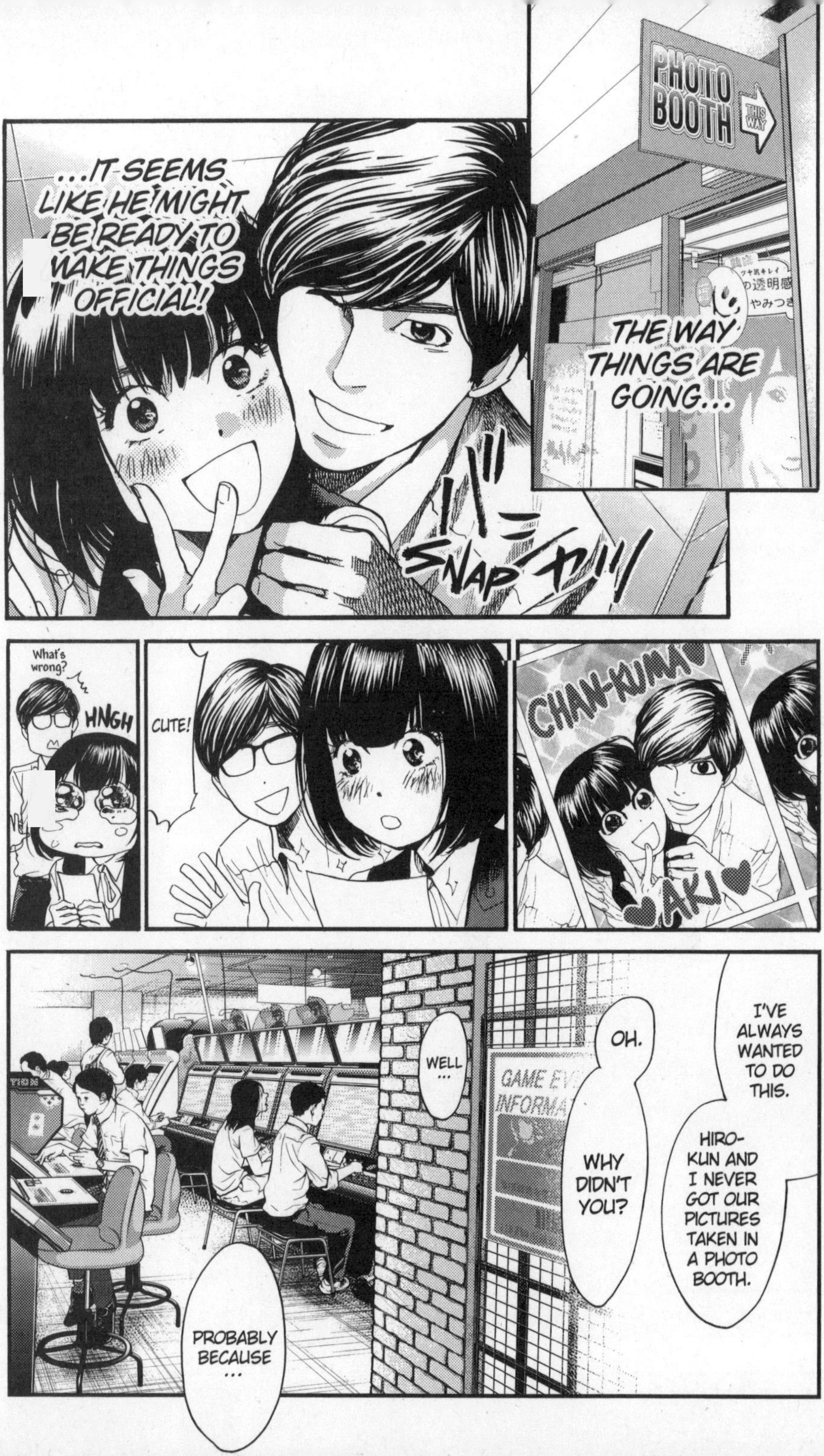

PHOTO BOOTH
THIS WAY
THE WAY THINGS ARE GOING...
...IT SEEMS LIKE HE MIGHT BE READY TO MAKE THINGS OFFICIAL!
SNAP
CHAN-KUMA
AKI
CUTE!
What's wrong?
HNGH
I'VE ALWAYS WANTED TO DO THIS.
HIRO-KUN AND I NEVER GOT OUR PICTURES TAKEN IN A PHOTO BOOTH.
OH.
WHY DIDN'T YOU?
WELL...
PROBABLY BECAUSE...

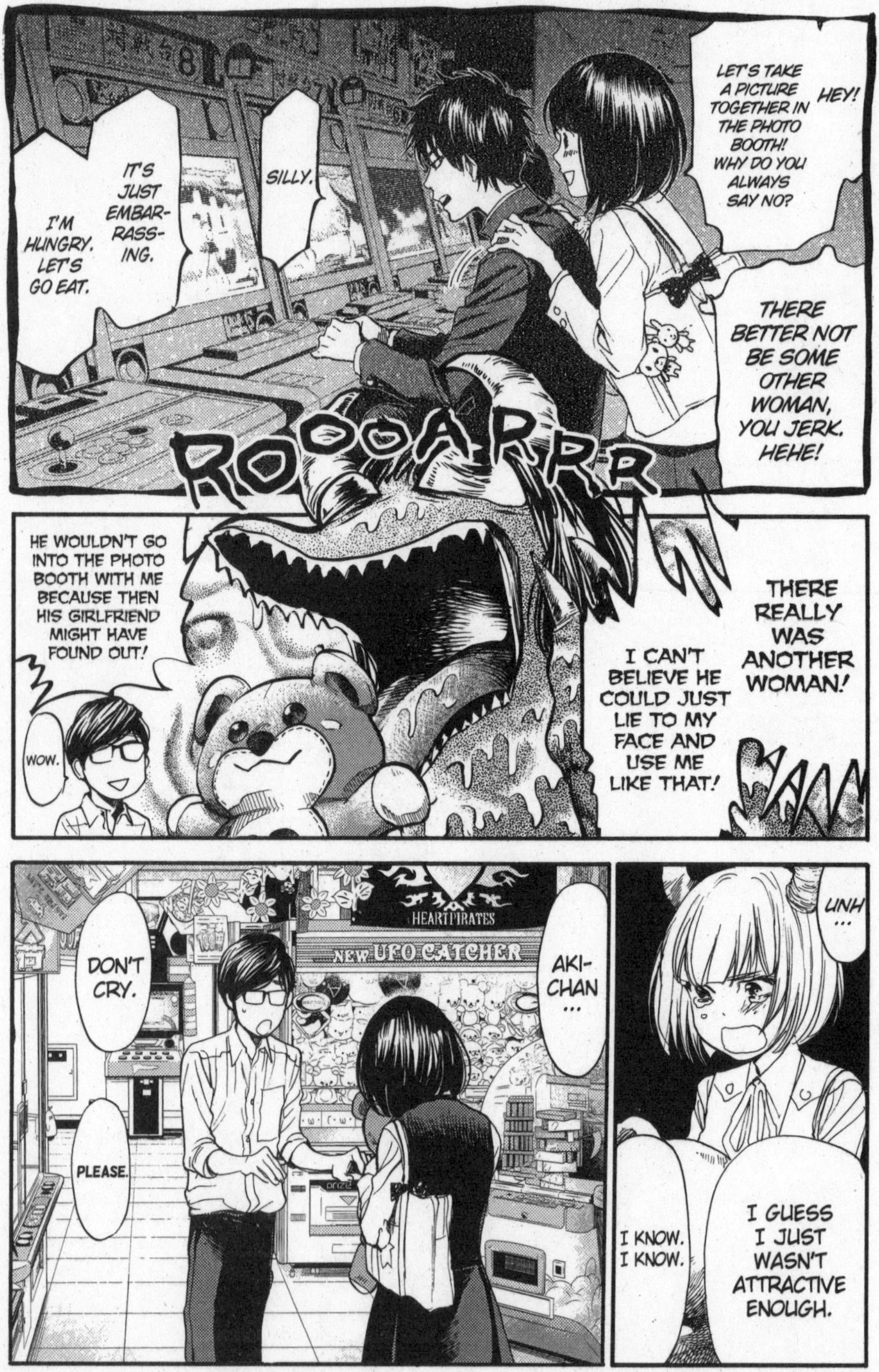
HEY!
LET'S TAKE A PICTURE TOGETHER IN THE PHOTO BOOTH! WHY DO YOU ALWAYS SAY NO?
SILLY.
IT'S JUST EMBARRASSING.
I'M HUNGRY. LET'S GO EAT.
THERE BETTER NOT BE SOME OTHER WOMAN, YOU JERK. HEHE!
ROOOARRR
THERE REALLY WAS ANOTHER WOMAN!
I CAN'T BELIEVE HE COULD JUST LIE TO MY FACE AND USE ME LIKE THAT!
HE WOULDN'T GO INTO THE PHOTO BOOTH WITH ME BECAUSE THEN HIS GIRLFRIEND MIGHT HAVE FOUND OUT!
WOW.
UNH...
I GUESS I JUST WASN'T ATTRACTIVE ENOUGH.
I KNOW. I KNOW.
HEARTPIRATES
NEW UFO CATCHER
AKI-CHAN...
DON'T CRY.
PLEASE.

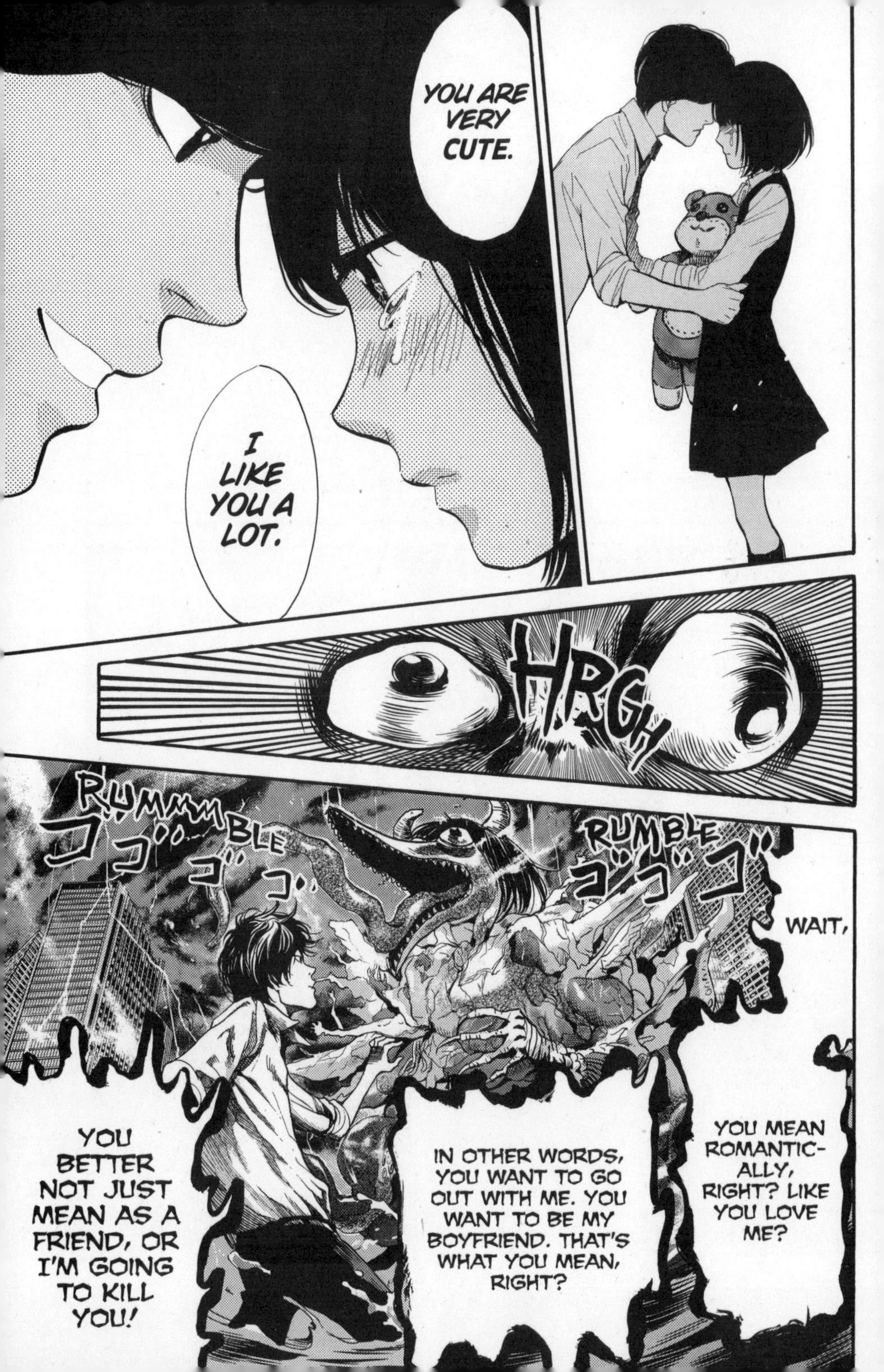
YOU ARE VERY CUTE.
I LIKE YOU A LOT.
HRGH
RUMMMMBLE
RUMBLE
WAIT,
YOU MEAN ROMANTIC-ALLY, RIGHT? LIKE YOU LOVE ME?
IN OTHER WORDS, YOU WANT TO GO OUT WITH ME. YOU WANT TO BE MY BOYFRIEND. THAT'S WHAT YOU MEAN, RIGHT?
YOU BETTER NOT JUST MEAN AS A FRIEND, OR I'M GOING TO KILL YOU!

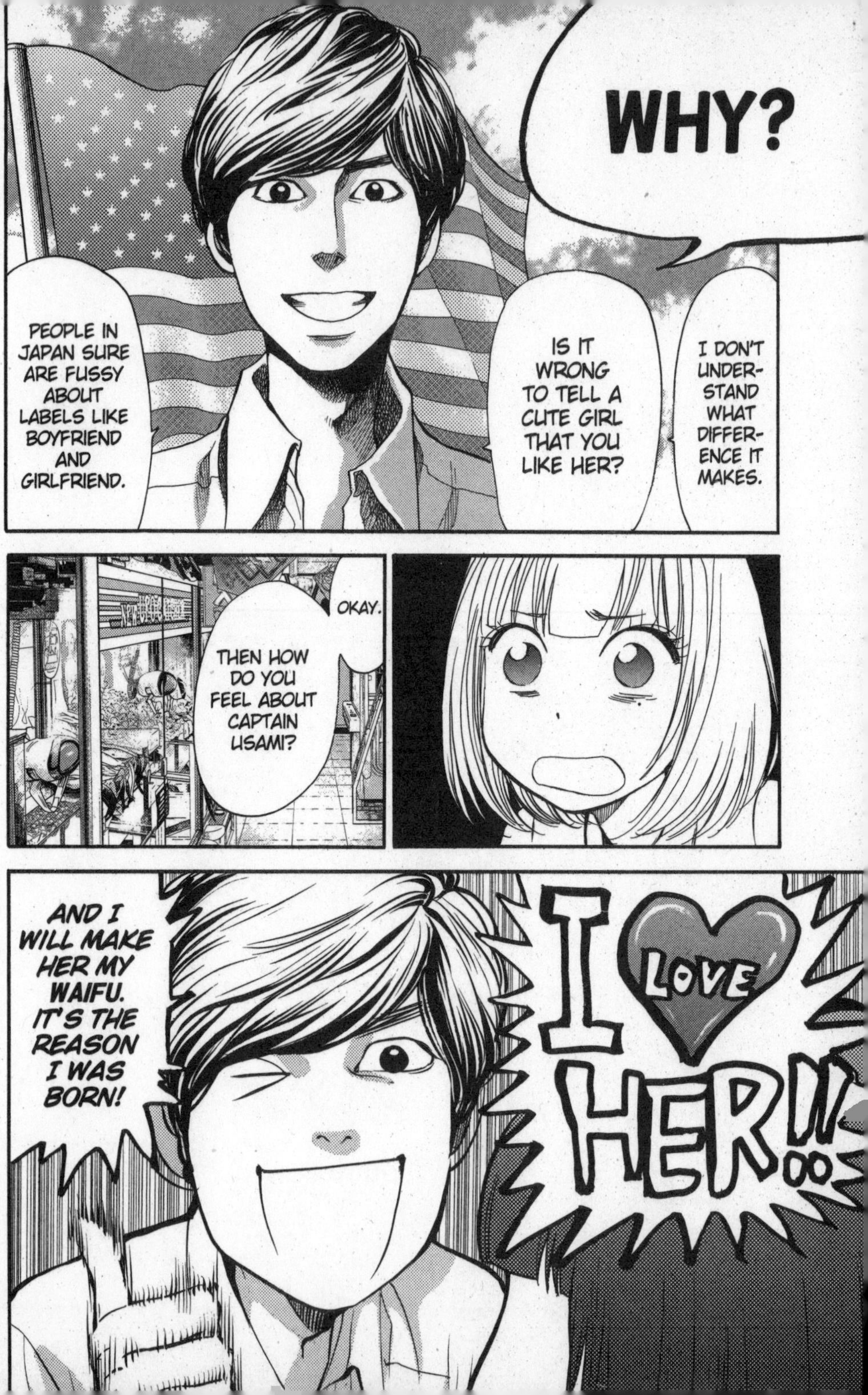
WHY?
I DON'T UNDER-STAND WHAT DIFFER-ENCE IT MAKES.
IS IT WRONG TO TELL A CUTE GIRL THAT YOU LIKE HER?
PEOPLE IN JAPAN SURE ARE FUSSY ABOUT LABELS LIKE BOYFRIEND AND GIRLFRIEND.
OKAY.
THEN HOW DO YOU FEEL ABOUT CAPTAIN USAMI?
I LOVE HER!!
AND I WILL MAKE HER MY WAIFU. IT'S THE REASON I WAS BORN!

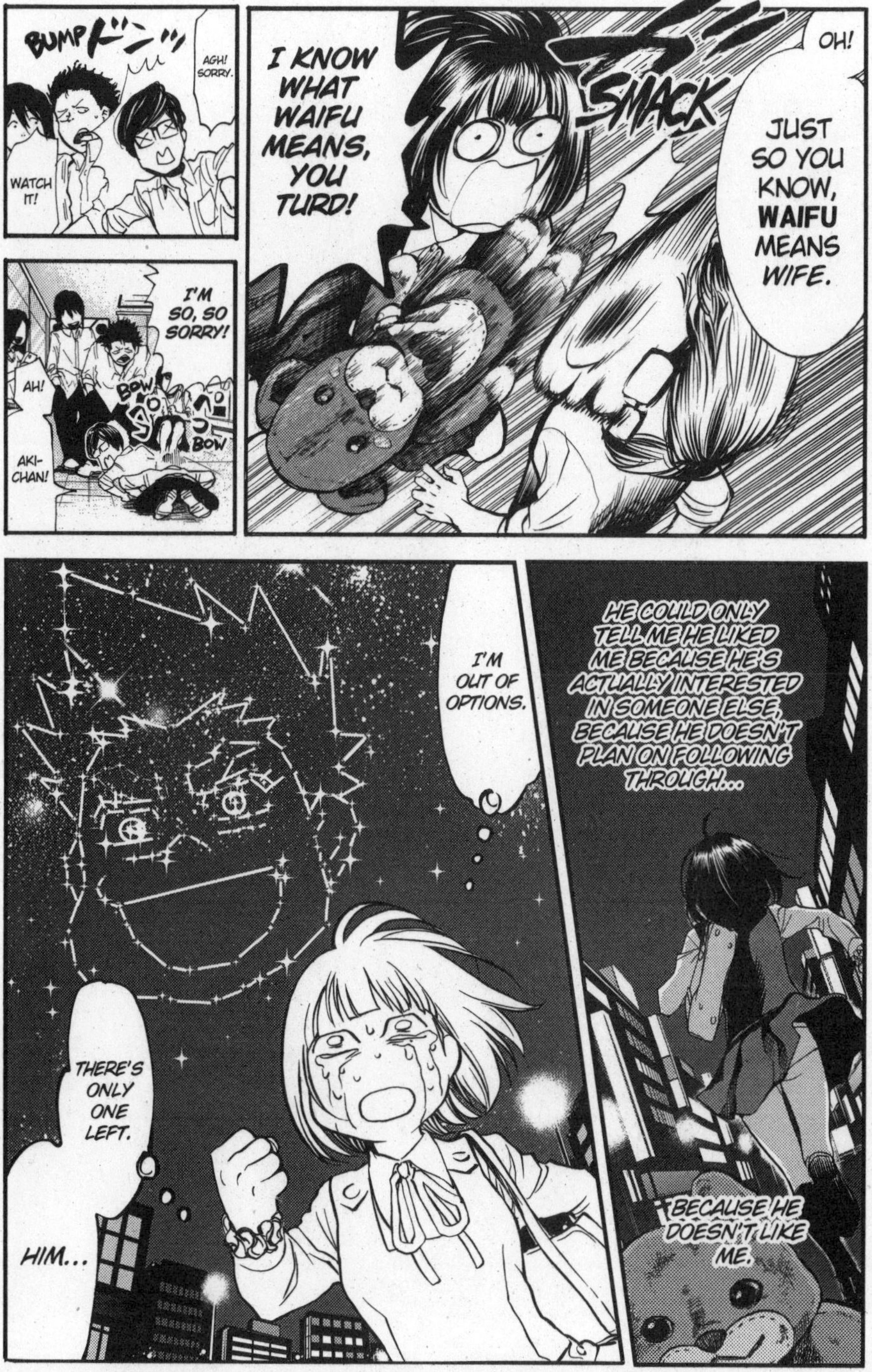
OH!
JUST SO YOU KNOW, **WAIFU** MEANS **WIFE.**
SMACK
I KNOW WHAT WAIFU MEANS, YOU TURD!
BUMP ドンッ
AGH! SORRY.
WATCH IT!
I'M SO, SO SORRY!
BOW
BOW
AH!
AKI-CHAN!
HE COULD ONLY TELL ME HE LIKED ME BECAUSE HE'S ACTUALLY INTERESTED IN SOMEONE ELSE, BECAUSE HE DOESN'T PLAN ON FOLLOWING THROUGH...
BECAUSE HE DOESN'T LIKE ME.
I'M OUT OF OPTIONS.
THERE'S ONLY ONE LEFT.
HIM...

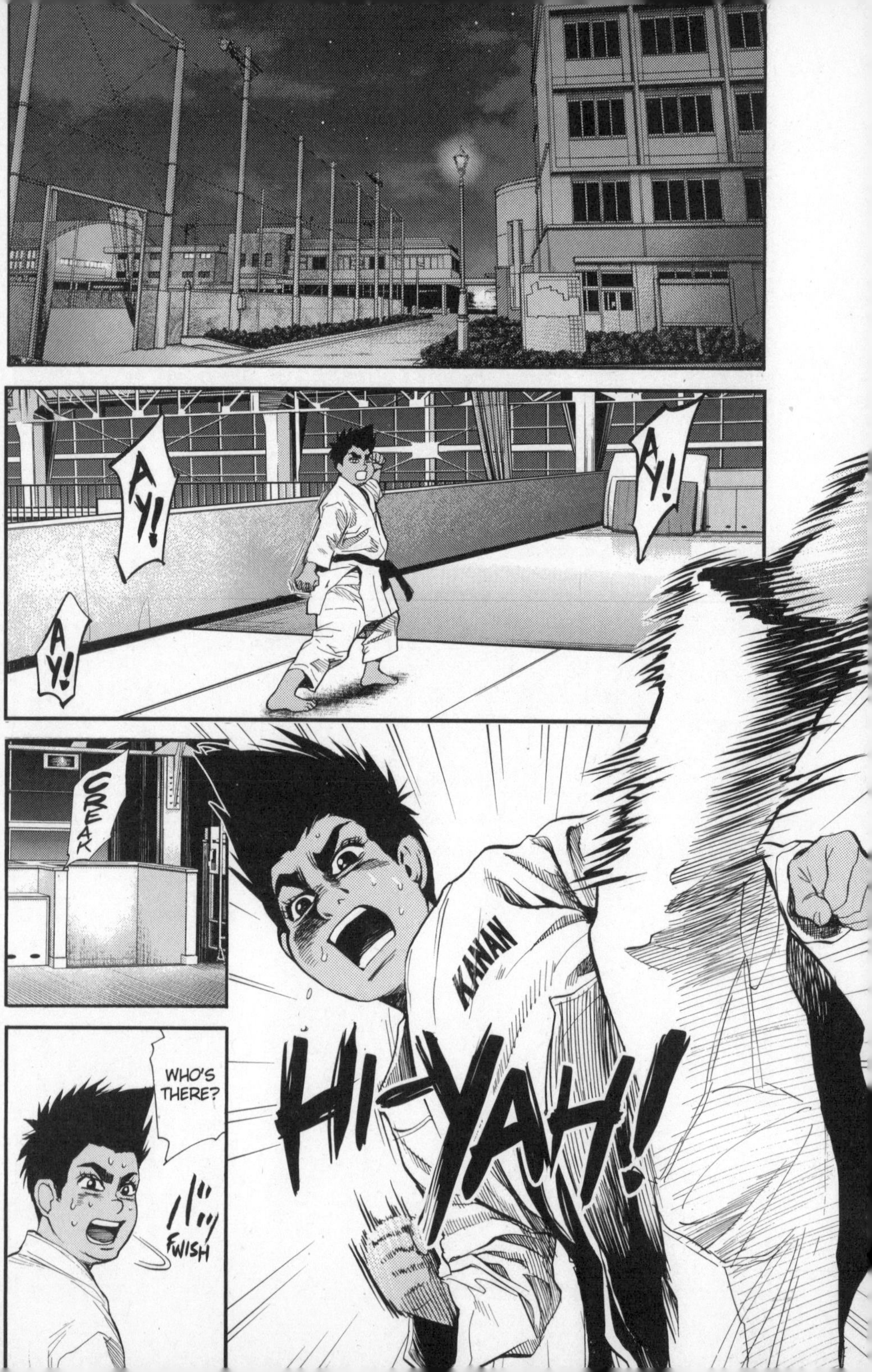
AY!
AY!
AY!
KANAN
HI-YAH!
CREAK
WHO'S THERE?
バッ
FWISH

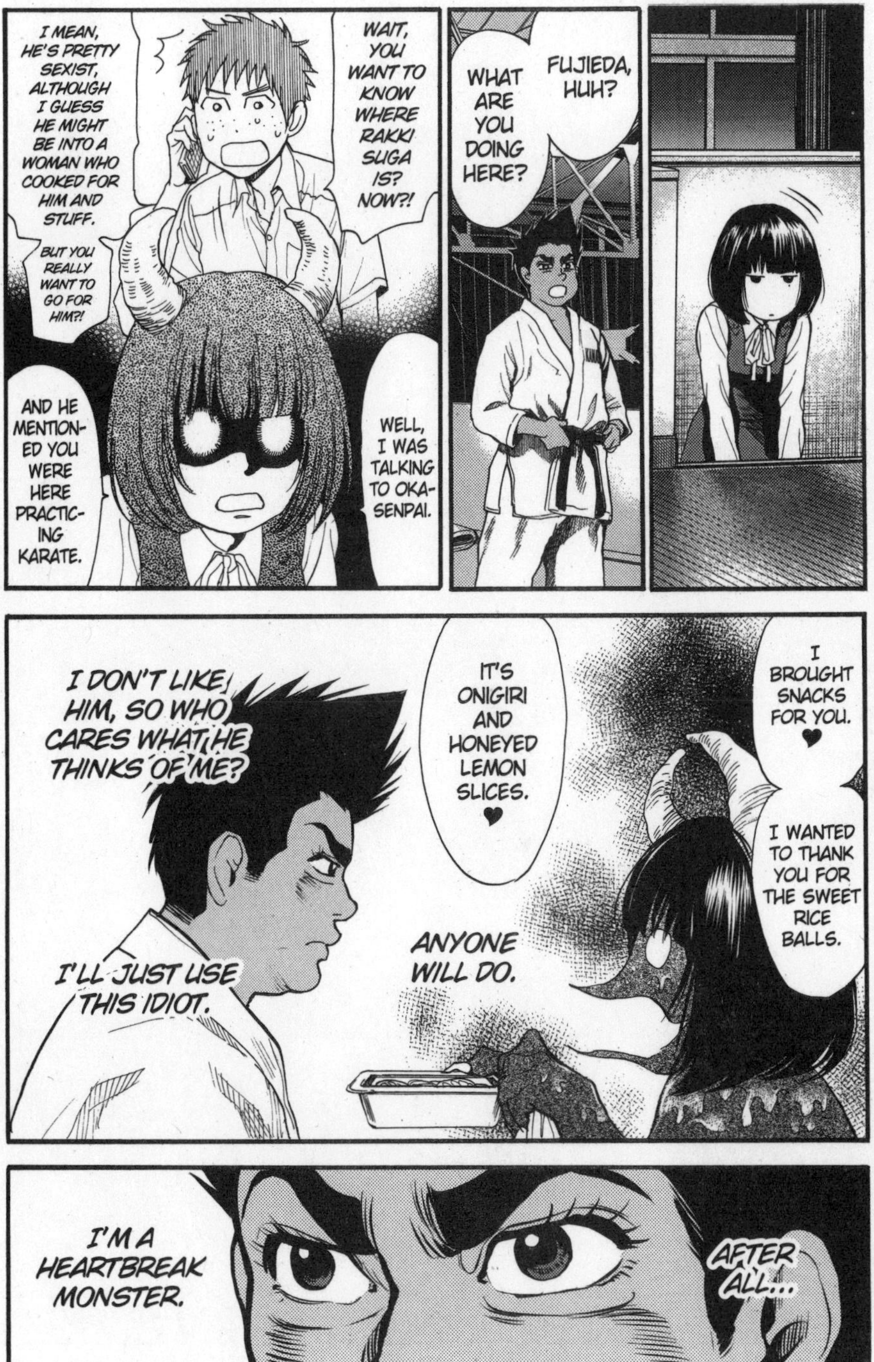
FUJIEDA, HUH?
WHAT ARE YOU DOING HERE?
WAIT, YOU WANT TO KNOW WHERE RAKKI SUGA IS? NOW?!
I MEAN, HE'S PRETTY SEXIST, ALTHOUGH I GUESS HE MIGHT BE INTO A WOMAN WHO COOKED FOR HIM AND STUFF.
BUT YOU REALLY WANT TO GO FOR HIM?!
WELL, I WAS TALKING TO OKA-SENPAI.
AND HE MENTIONED YOU WERE HERE PRACTICING KARATE.
I BROUGHT SNACKS FOR YOU. ♥
IT'S ONIGIRI AND HONEYED LEMON SLICES. ♥
I WANTED TO THANK YOU FOR THE SWEET RICE BALLS.
ANYONE WILL DO.
I DON'T LIKE HIM, SO WHO CARES WHAT HE THINKS OF ME?
I'LL JUST USE THIS IDIOT.
AFTER ALL...
I'M A HEARTBREAK MONSTER.

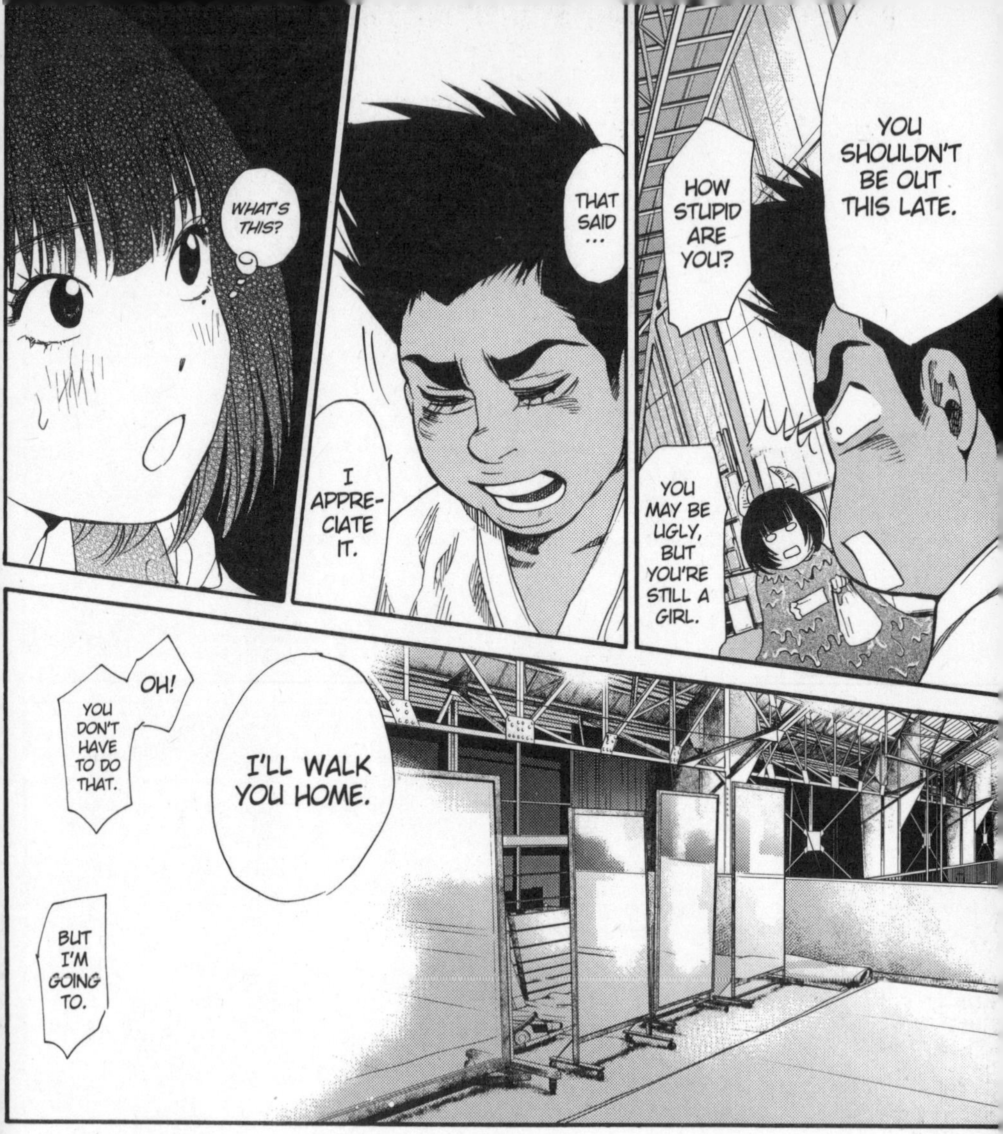
YOU SHOULDN'T BE OUT THIS LATE.
HOW STUPID ARE YOU?
YOU MAY BE UGLY, BUT YOU'RE STILL A GIRL.
THAT SAID ...
I APPRE-CIATE IT.
WHAT'S THIS?
I'LL WALK YOU HOME.
OH!
YOU DON'T HAVE TO DO THAT.
BUT I'M GOING TO.

WHAT'S WITH THIS PIG?

HE'S NOT ACTING LIKE HIS USUAL SELF.

HEH HEH HEH! COULD IT BE THAT I ALREADY HAVE HIM WRAPPED AROUND MY LITTLE FINGER?

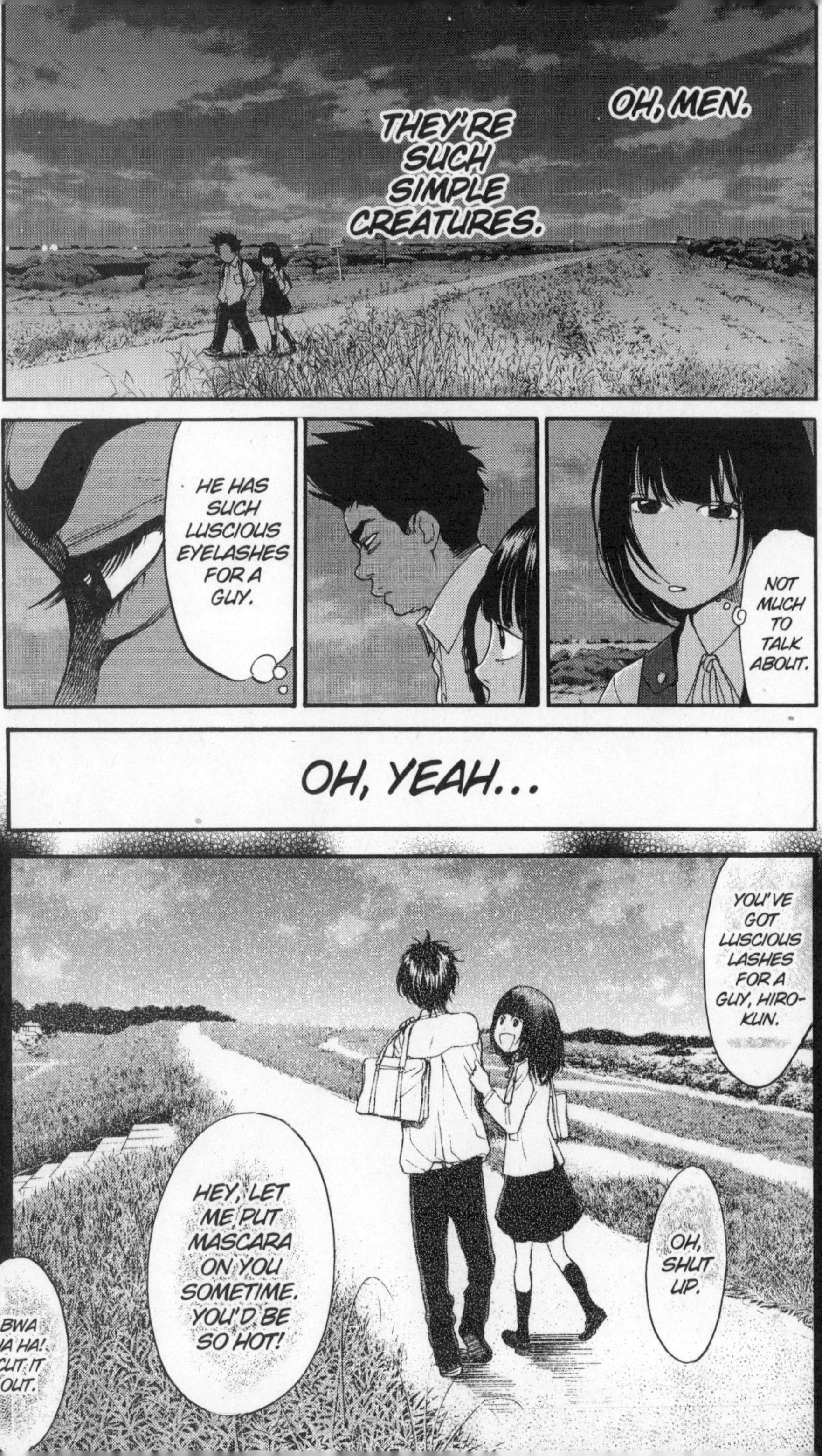
OH, MEN.
THEY'RE SUCH SIMPLE CREATURES.
NOT MUCH TO TALK ABOUT.
HE HAS SUCH LUSCIOUS EYELASHES FOR A GUY.
OH, YEAH...
YOU'VE GOT LUSCIOUS LASHES FOR A GUY, HIRO-KUN.
OH, SHUT UP.
HEY, LET ME PUT MASCARA ON YOU SOMETIME. YOU'D BE SO HOT!
BWA HA HA! CUT IT OUT.

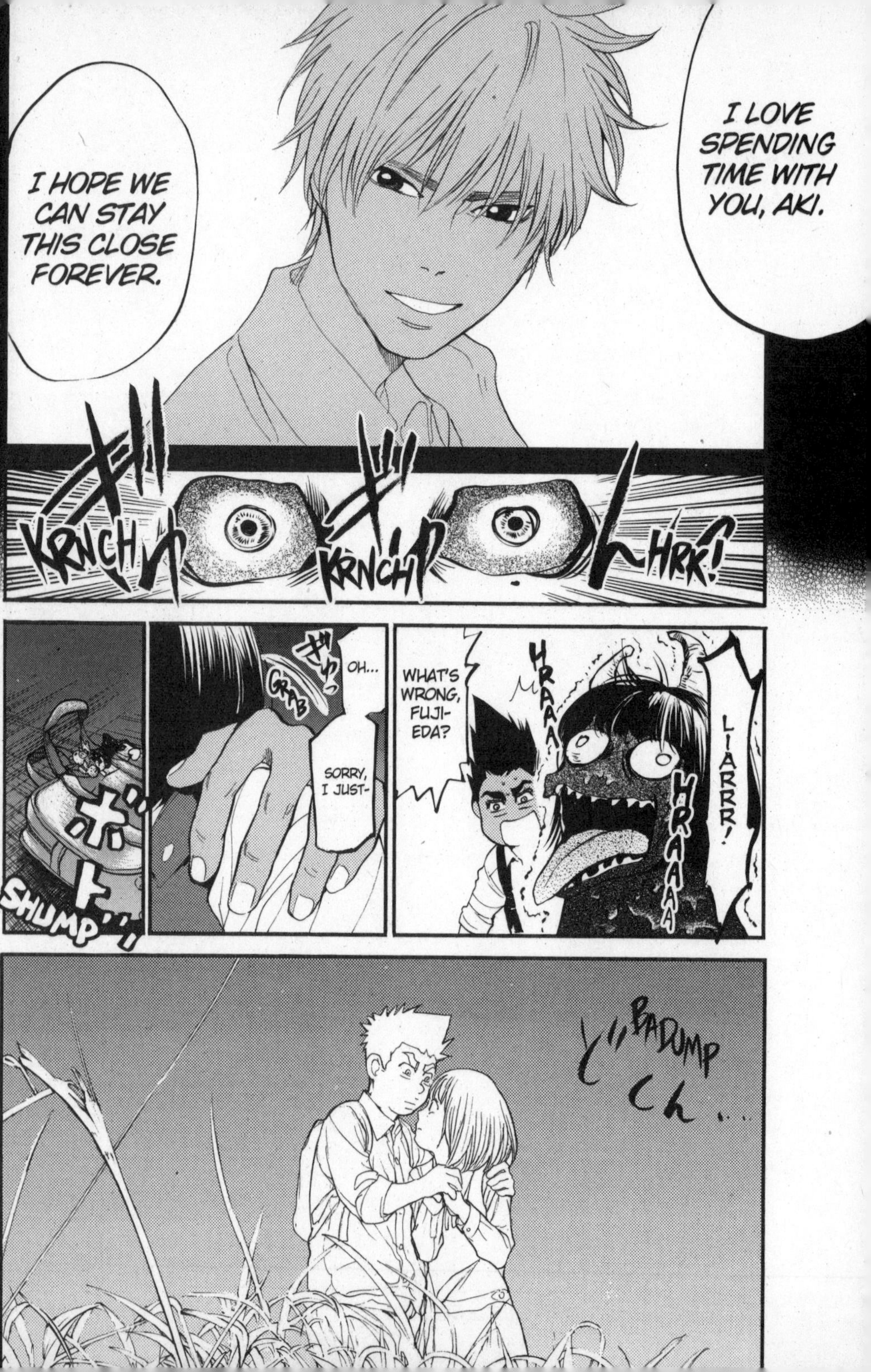
I LOVE SPENDING TIME WITH YOU, AKI.
I HOPE WE CAN STAY THIS CLOSE FOREVER.
HRK!
KRNCH
KRNCH
LIARRR!
HRAAAA
HRAAAAAAA
WHAT'S WRONG, FUJI-EDA?
OH...
SORRY, I JUST-
GRAB
SHUMP
BADUMP
Ch...

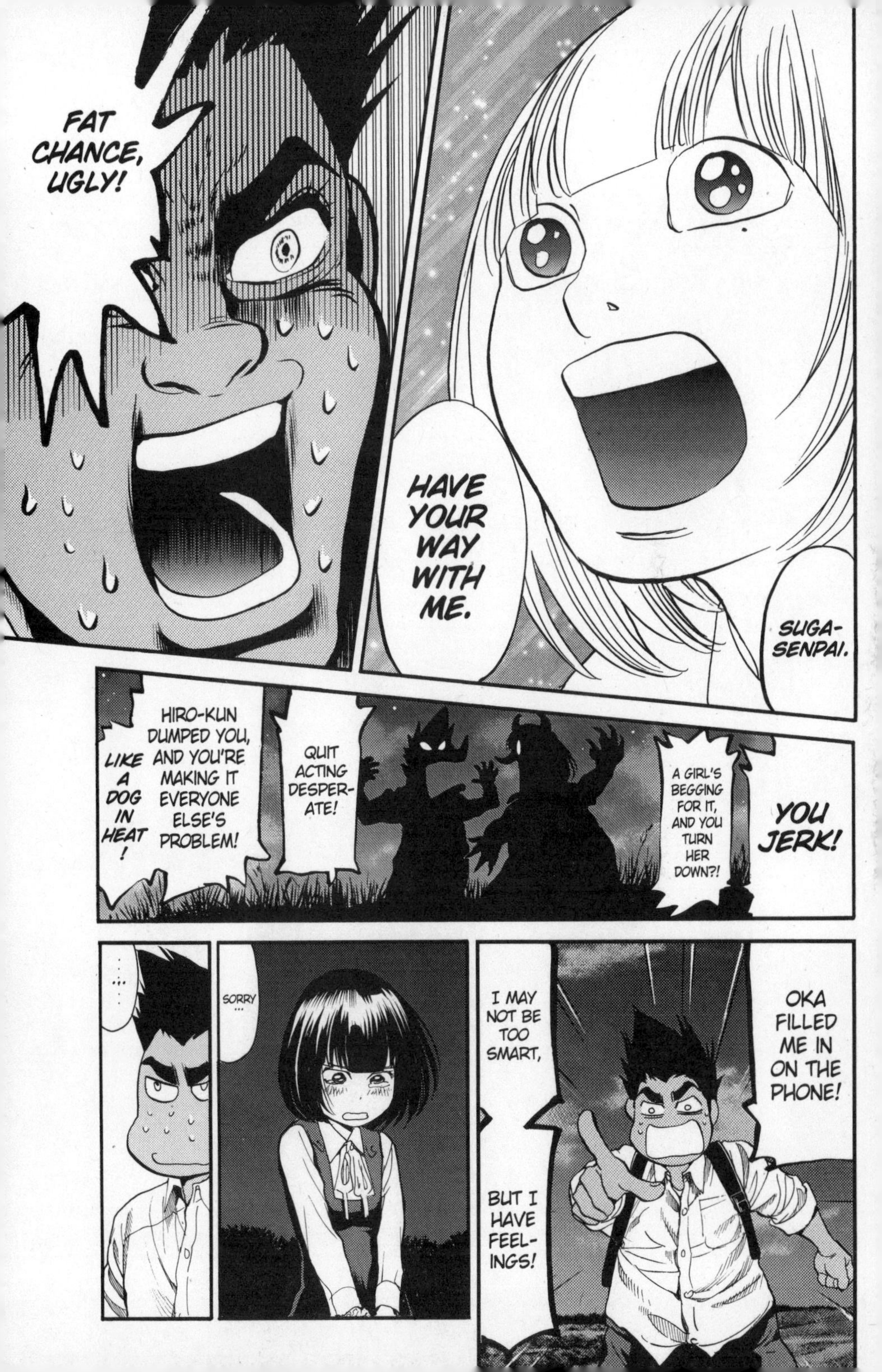
SUGA-SENPAI.
HAVE YOUR WAY WITH ME.
FAT CHANCE, UGLY!
YOU JERK!
A GIRL'S BEGGING FOR IT, AND YOU TURN HER DOWN?!
QUIT ACTING DESPERATE!
HIRO-KUN DUMPED YOU, AND YOU'RE MAKING IT EVERYONE ELSE'S PROBLEM!
LIKE A DOG IN HEAT!
OKA FILLED ME IN ON THE PHONE!
I MAY NOT BE TOO SMART,
BUT I HAVE FEEL-INGS!
SORRY...
...

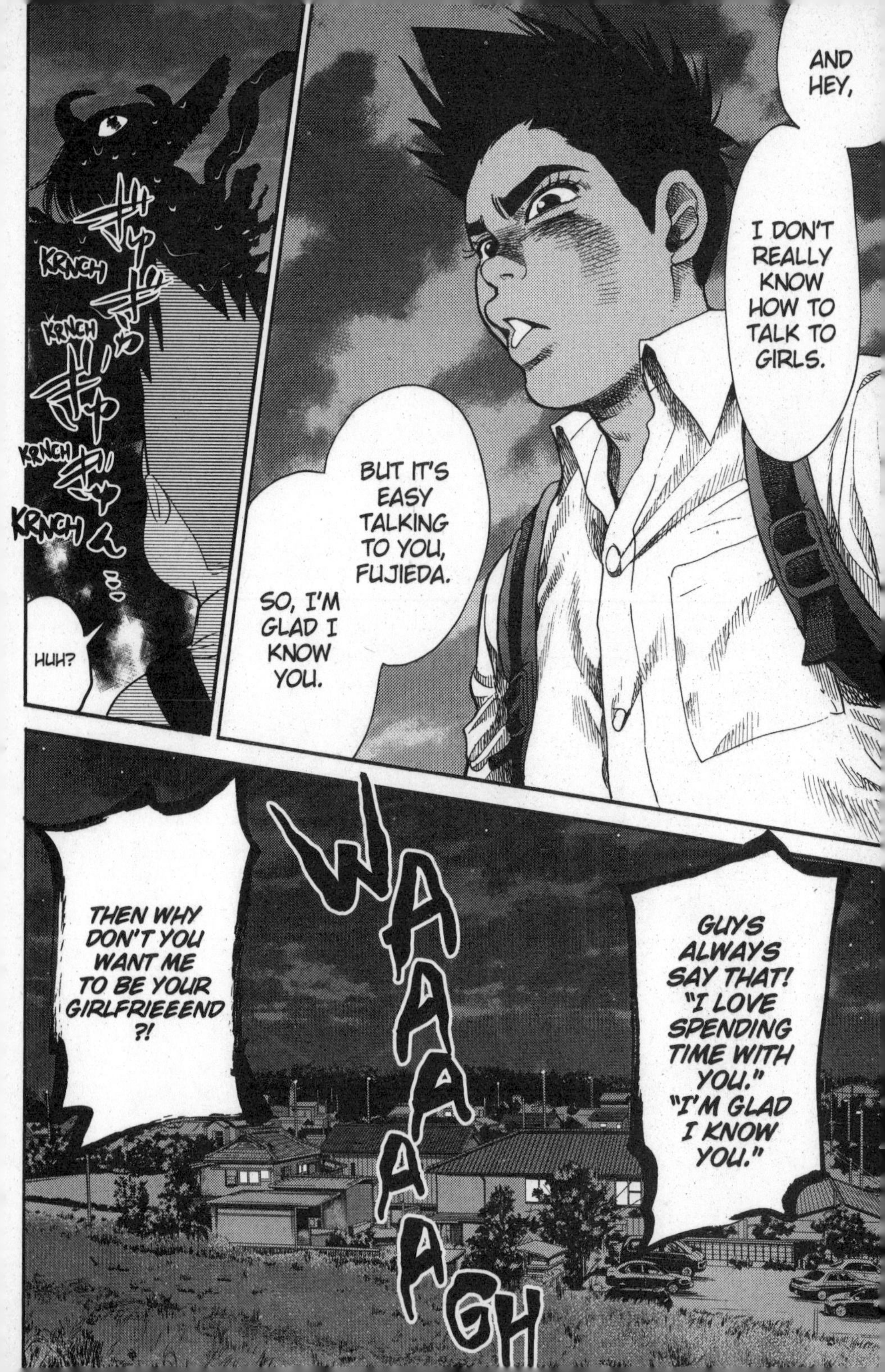
AND HEY,
I DON'T REALLY KNOW HOW TO TALK TO GIRLS.
BUT IT'S EASY TALKING TO YOU, FUJIEDA.
SO, I'M GLAD I KNOW YOU.
KRNCH
KRNCH
KRNCH
KRNCH
HUH?
GUYS ALWAYS SAY THAT! "I LOVE SPENDING TIME WITH YOU." "I'M GLAD I KNOW YOU."
WAAAAAGH
THEN WHY DON'T YOU WANT ME TO BE YOUR GIRLFRIEEEND ?!

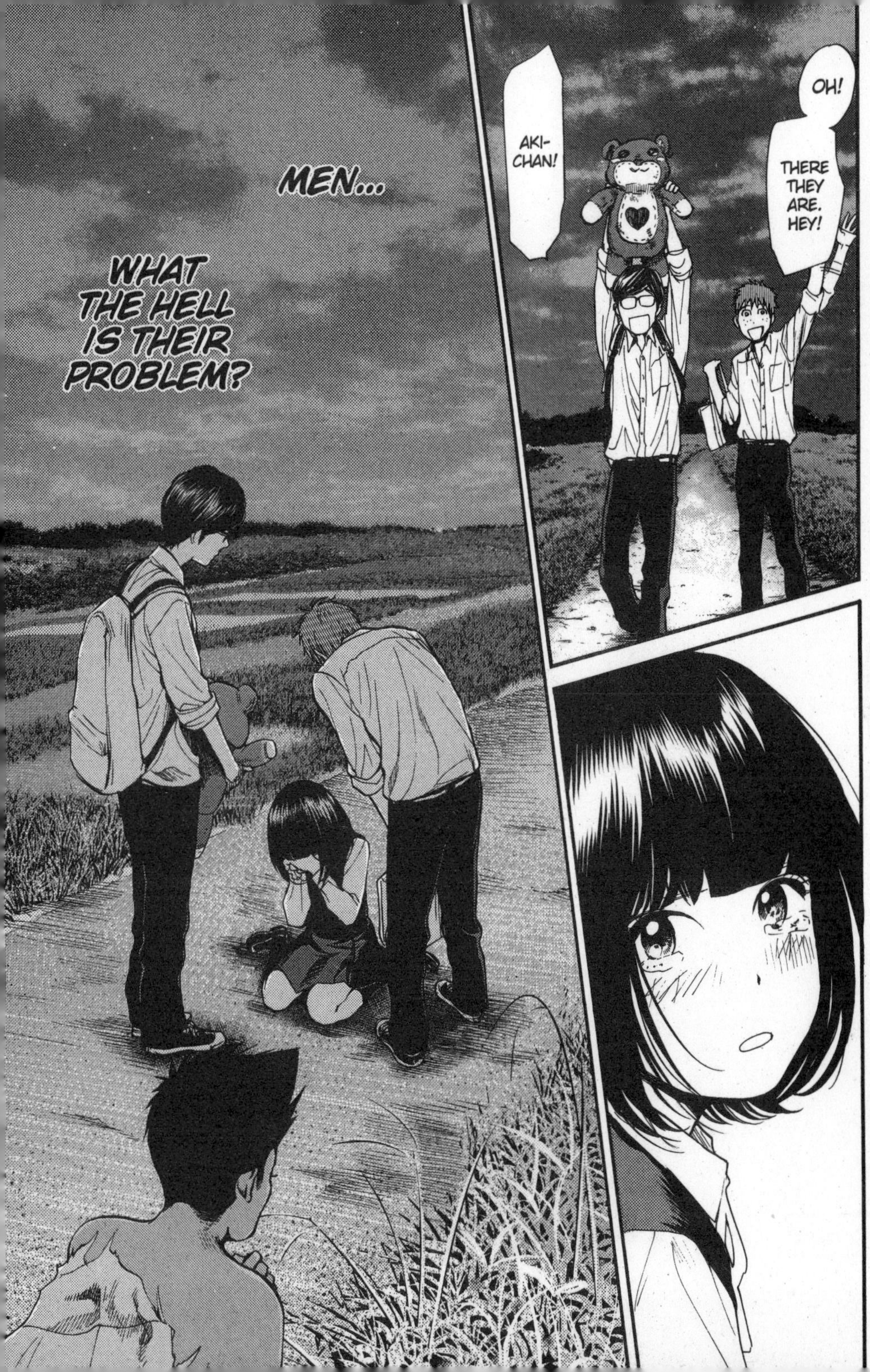
OH!
THERE THEY ARE. HEY!
AKI-CHAN!
MEN...
WHAT THE HELL IS THEIR PROBLEM?

Again!!

アゲイン!!

105. FALLING DOWN

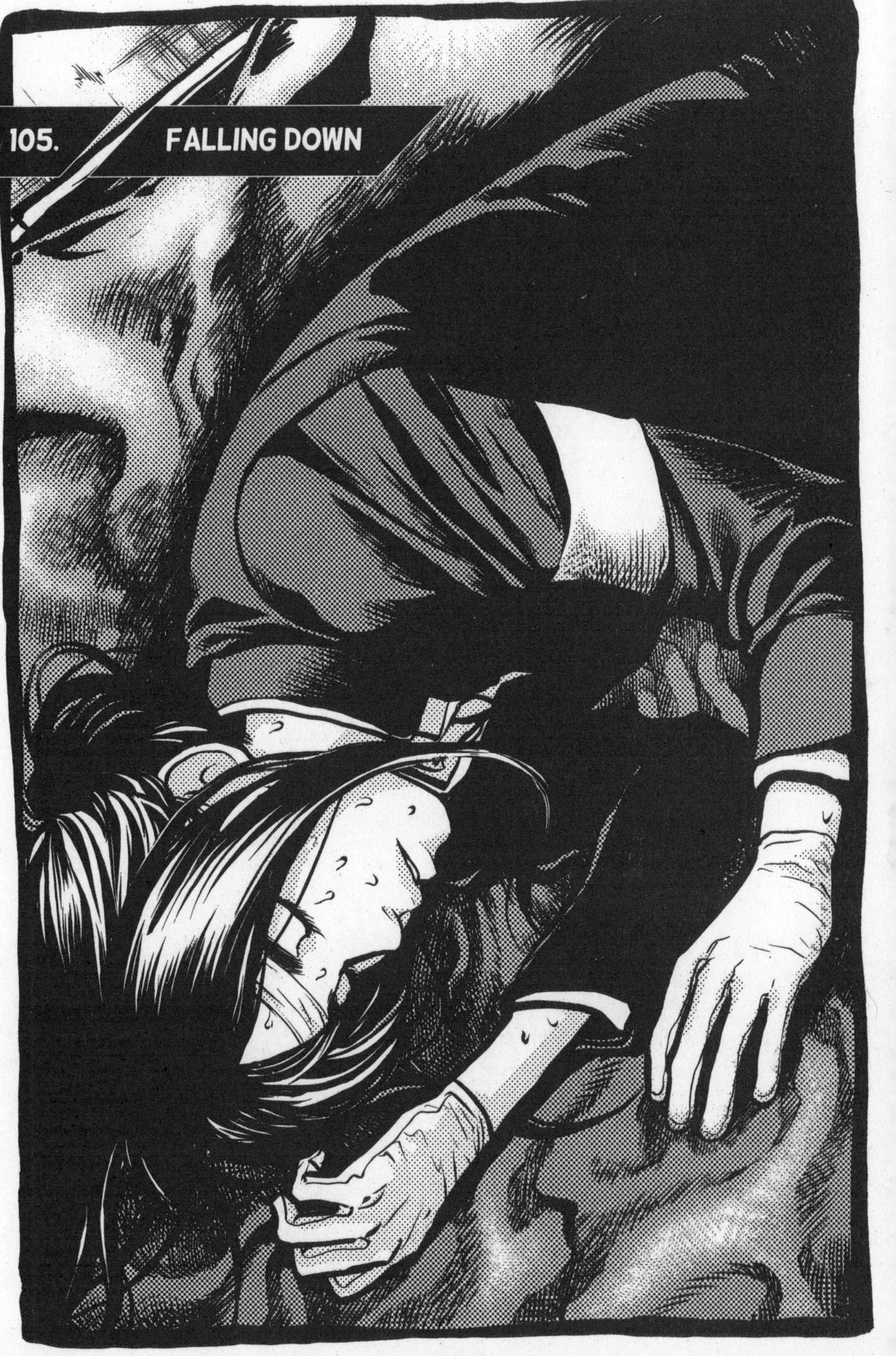

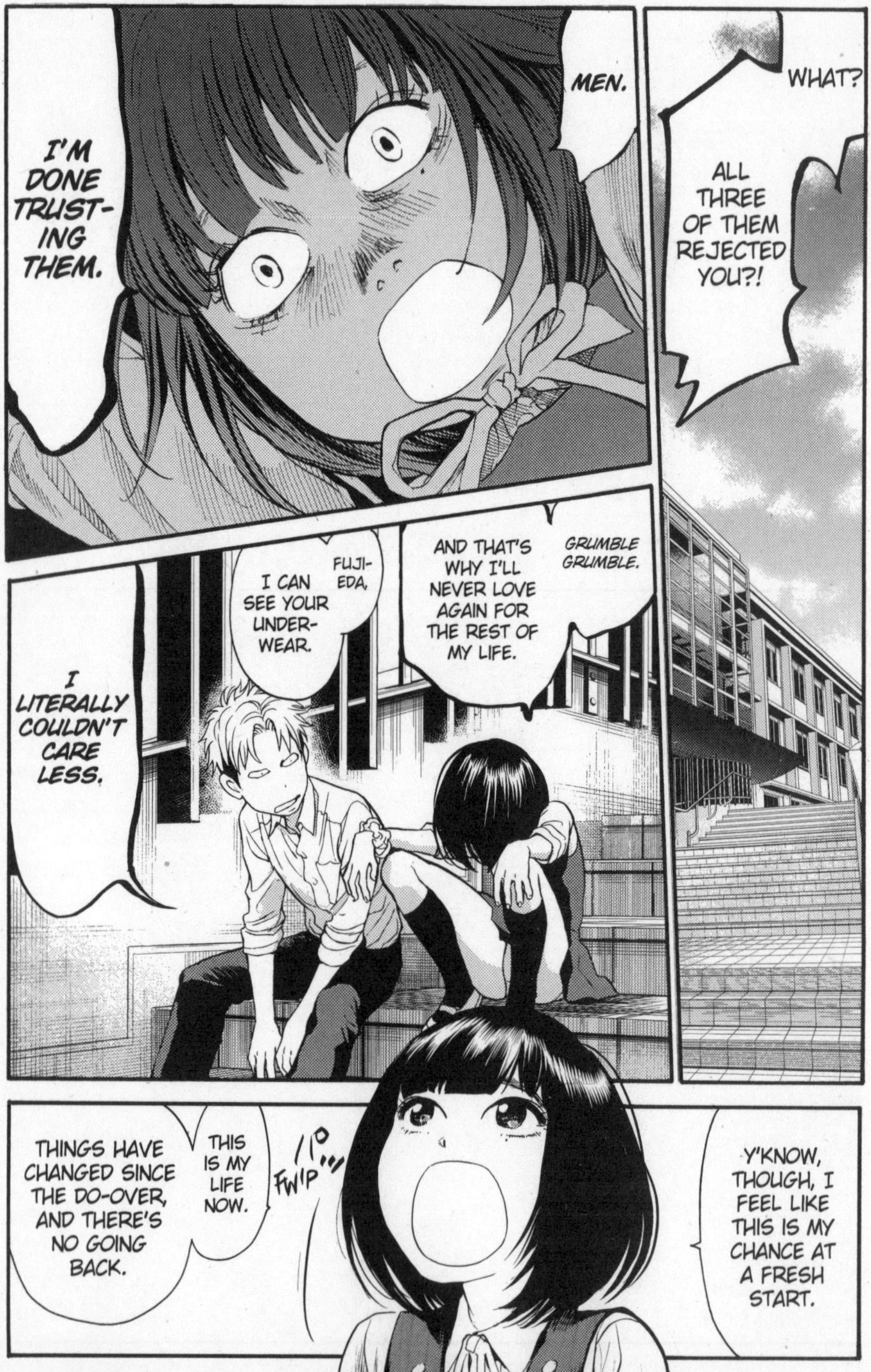
WHAT?
ALL THREE OF THEM REJECTED YOU?!
MEN.
I'M DONE TRUSTING THEM.
GRUMBLE GRUMBLE.
AND THAT'S WHY I'LL NEVER LOVE AGAIN FOR THE REST OF MY LIFE.
FUJI-EDA,
I CAN SEE YOUR UNDER-WEAR.
I LITERALLY COULDN'T CARE LESS.
Y'KNOW, THOUGH, I FEEL LIKE THIS IS MY CHANCE AT A FRESH START.
FWIP
THIS IS MY LIFE NOW.
THINGS HAVE CHANGED SINCE THE DO-OVER, AND THERE'S NO GOING BACK.

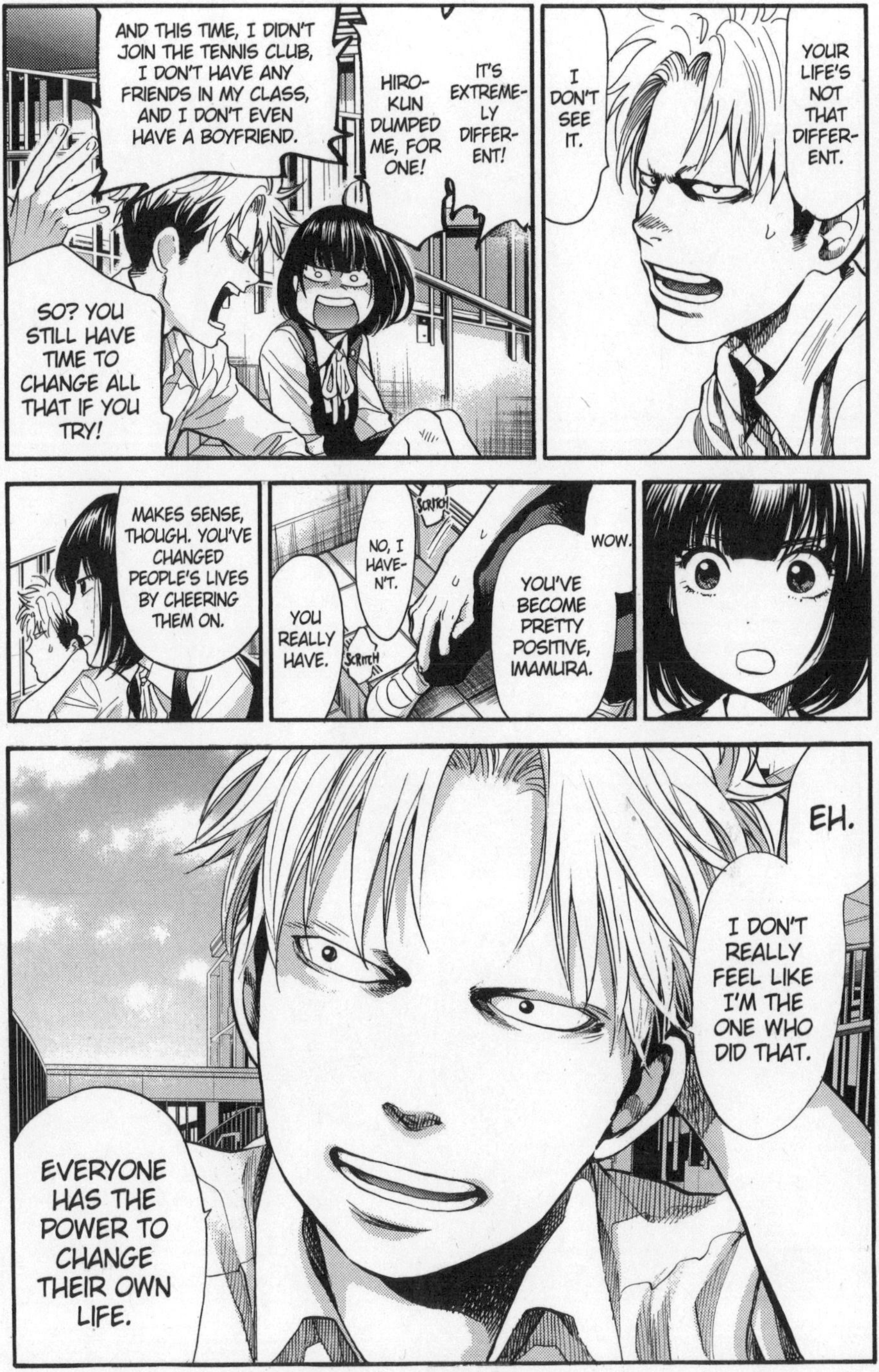
YOUR LIFE'S NOT THAT DIFFERENT.
I DON'T SEE IT.
IT'S EXTREMELY DIFFERENT!
HIRO-KUN DUMPED ME, FOR ONE!
AND THIS TIME, I DIDN'T JOIN THE TENNIS CLUB, I DON'T HAVE ANY FRIENDS IN MY CLASS, AND I DON'T EVEN HAVE A BOYFRIEND.
SO? YOU STILL HAVE TIME TO CHANGE ALL THAT IF YOU TRY!
WOW.
YOU'VE BECOME PRETTY POSITIVE, IMAMURA.
SCRITCH
NO, I HAVEN'T.
YOU REALLY HAVE.
SCRITCH
MAKES SENSE, THOUGH. YOU'VE CHANGED PEOPLE'S LIVES BY CHEERING THEM ON.
EH.
I DON'T REALLY FEEL LIKE I'M THE ONE WHO DID THAT.
EVERYONE HAS THE POWER TO CHANGE THEIR OWN LIFE.

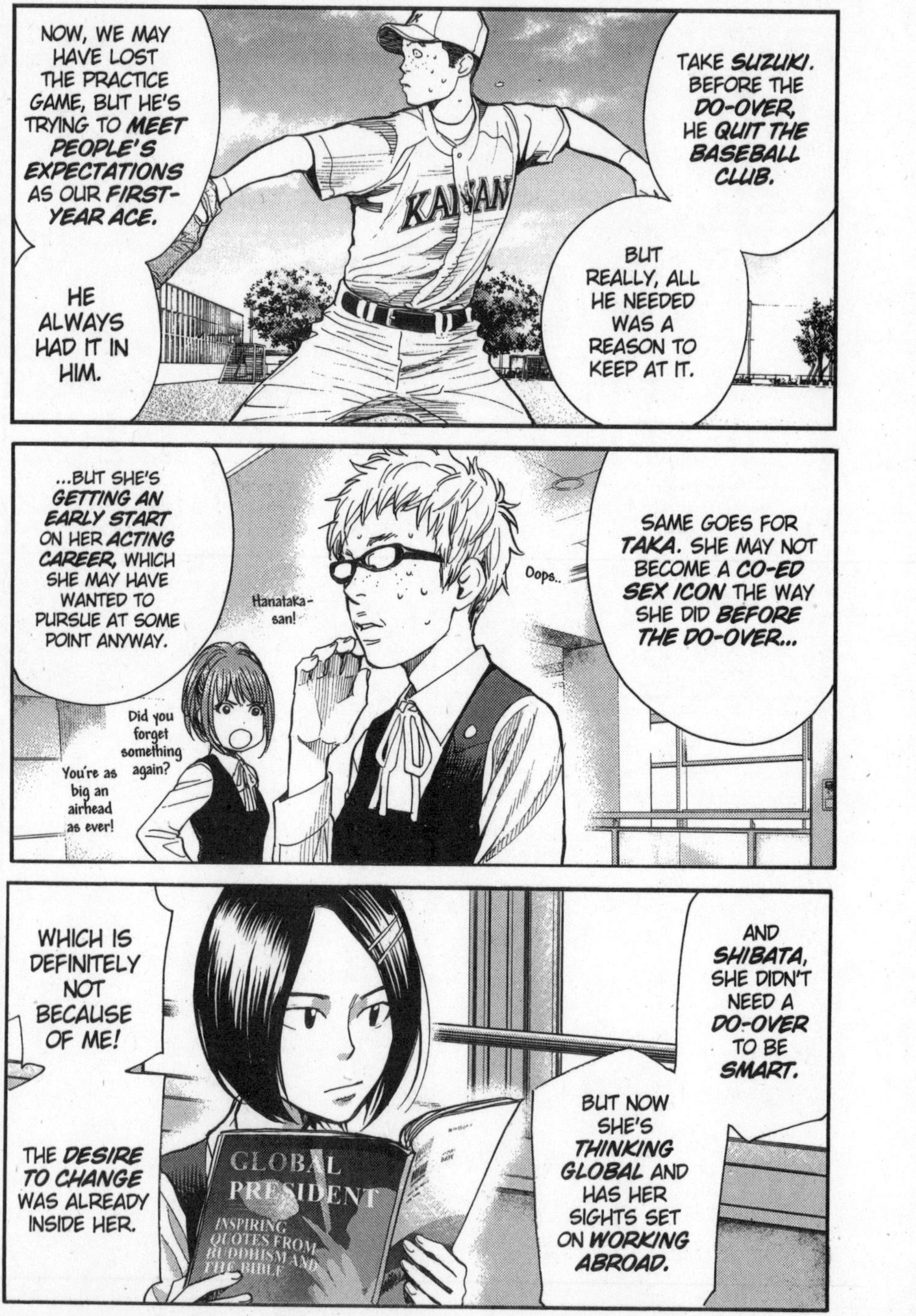
TAKE SUZUKI. BEFORE THE DO-OVER, HE QUIT THE BASEBALL CLUB.
BUT REALLY, ALL HE NEEDED WAS A REASON TO KEEP AT IT.
NOW, WE MAY HAVE LOST THE PRACTICE GAME, BUT HE'S TRYING TO MEET PEOPLE'S EXPECTATIONS AS OUR FIRST-YEAR ACE.
HE ALWAYS HAD IT IN HIM.
KANSAN
SAME GOES FOR TAKA. SHE MAY NOT BECOME A CO-ED SEX ICON THE WAY SHE DID BEFORE THE DO-OVER...
Oops..
Hanataka-san!
...BUT SHE'S GETTING AN EARLY START ON HER ACTING CAREER, WHICH SHE MAY HAVE WANTED TO PURSUE AT SOME POINT ANYWAY.
Did you forget something again?
You're as big an airhead as ever!
AND SHIBATA, SHE DIDN'T NEED A DO-OVER TO BE SMART.
BUT NOW SHE'S THINKING GLOBAL AND HAS HER SIGHTS SET ON WORKING ABROAD.
WHICH IS DEFINITELY NOT BECAUSE OF ME!
THE DESIRE TO CHANGE WAS ALREADY INSIDE HER.
GLOBAL PRESIDENT
INSPIRING QUOTES FROM BUDDHISM AND THE BIBLE

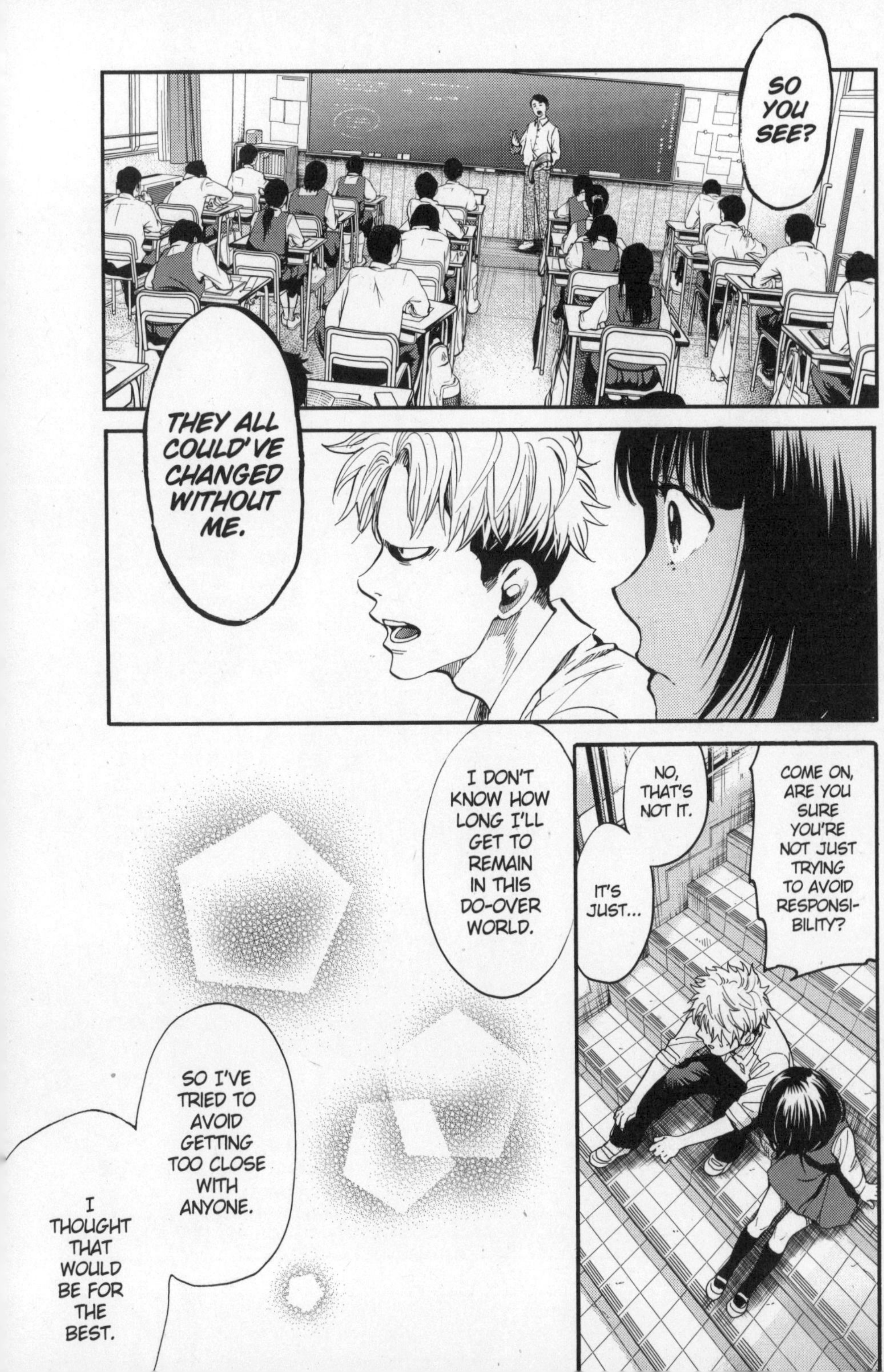
SO YOU SEE?
THEY ALL COULD'VE CHANGED WITHOUT ME.
COME ON, ARE YOU SURE YOU'RE NOT JUST TRYING TO AVOID RESPONSI-BILITY?
NO, THAT'S NOT IT.
IT'S JUST...
I DON'T KNOW HOW LONG I'LL GET TO REMAIN IN THIS DO-OVER WORLD.
SO I'VE TRIED TO AVOID GETTING TOO CLOSE WITH ANYONE.
I THOUGHT THAT WOULD BE FOR THE BEST.

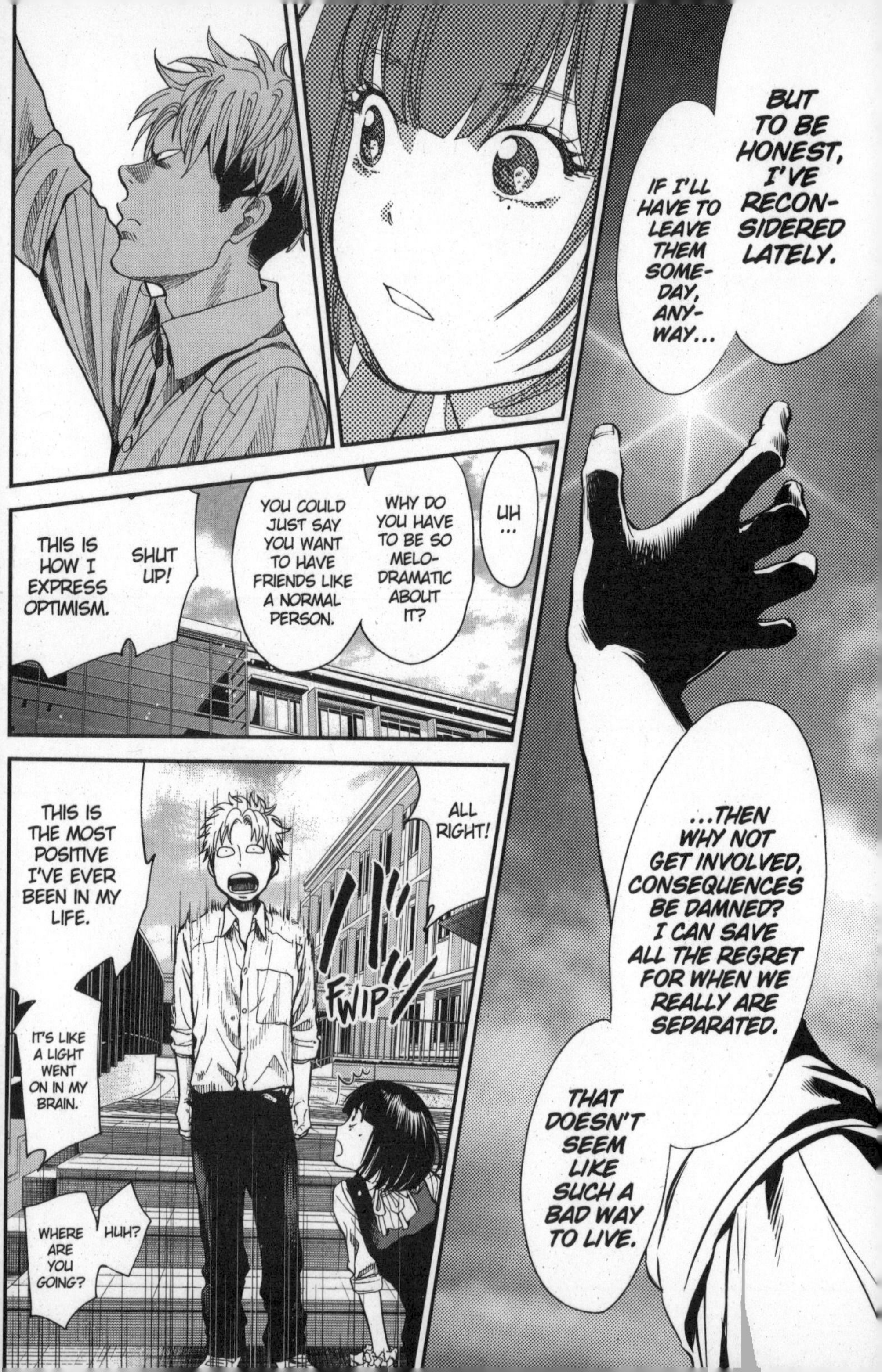
BUT TO BE HONEST, I'VE RECONSIDERED LATELY.
IF I'LL HAVE TO LEAVE THEM SOMEDAY, ANYWAY...
...THEN WHY NOT GET INVOLVED, CONSEQUENCES BE DAMNED? I CAN SAVE ALL THE REGRET FOR WHEN WE REALLY ARE SEPARATED.
THAT DOESN'T SEEM LIKE SUCH A BAD WAY TO LIVE.
UH...
WHY DO YOU HAVE TO BE SO MELODRAMATIC ABOUT IT?
YOU COULD JUST SAY YOU WANT TO HAVE FRIENDS LIKE A NORMAL PERSON.
SHUT UP!
THIS IS HOW I EXPRESS OPTIMISM.
ALL RIGHT!
THIS IS THE MOST POSITIVE I'VE EVER BEEN IN MY LIFE.
FWIP
IT'S LIKE A LIGHT WENT ON IN MY BRAIN.
HUH?
WHERE ARE YOU GOING?

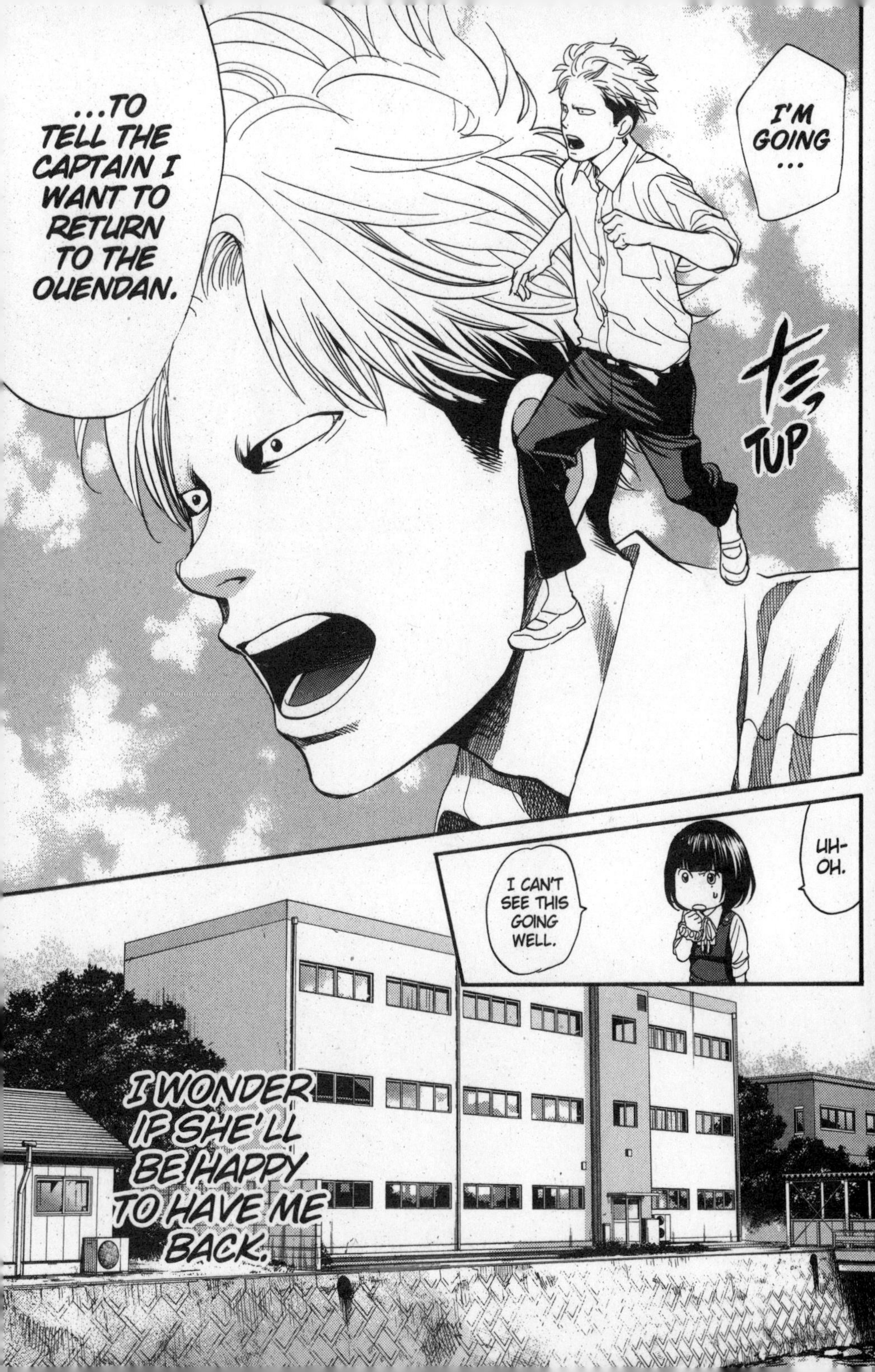
I'M GOING ...
...TO TELL THE CAPTAIN I WANT TO RETURN TO THE OUENDAN.
TUP
UH-OH.
I CAN'T SEE THIS GOING WELL.
I WONDER IF SHE'LL BE HAPPY TO HAVE ME BACK.

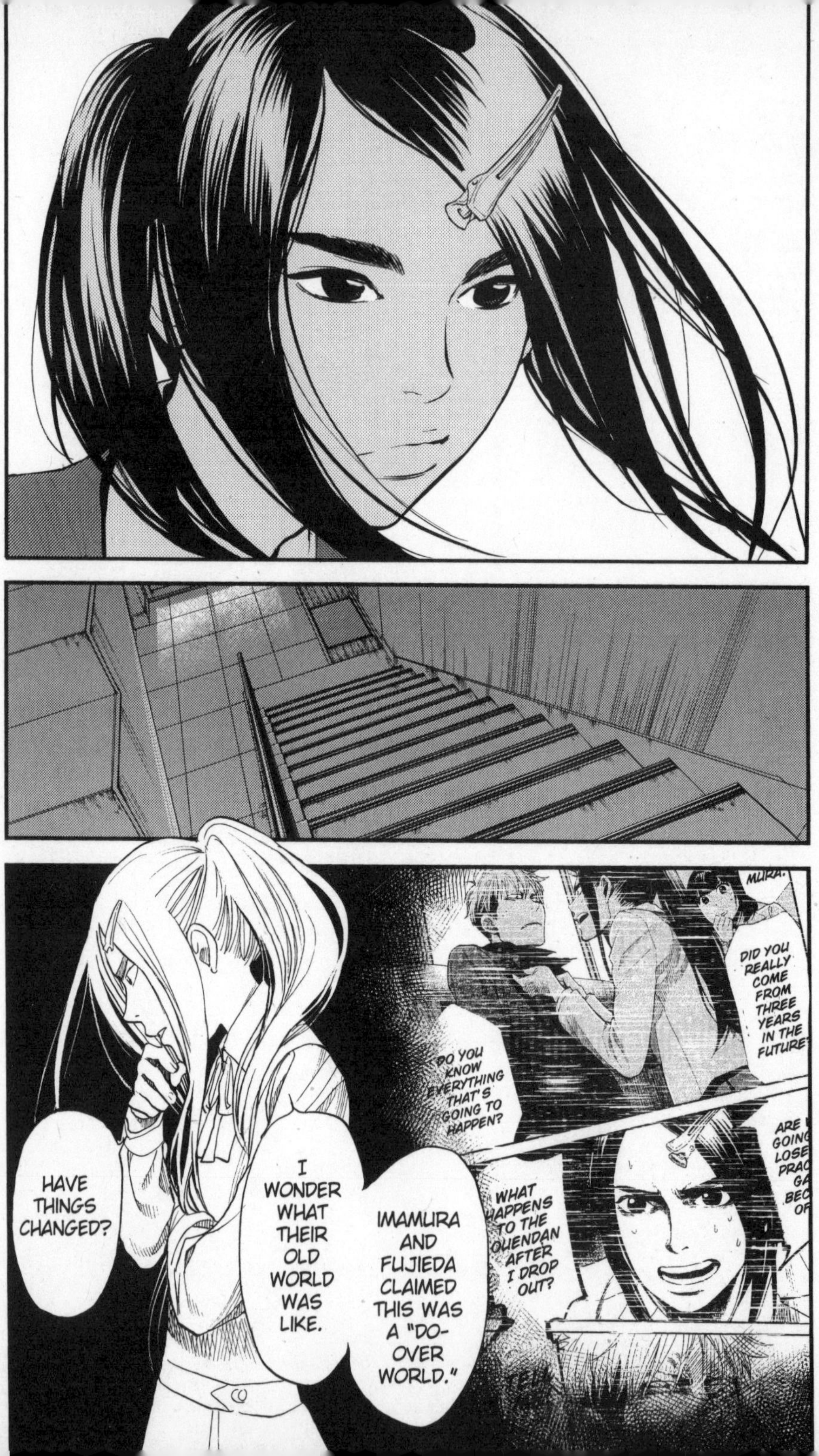
DID YOU REALLY COME FROM THREE YEARS IN THE FUTURE?
DO YOU KNOW EVERYTHING THAT'S GOING TO HAPPEN?
WHAT HAPPENS TO THE OUENDAN AFTER I DROP OUT?
IMAMURA AND FUJIEDA CLAIMED THIS WAS A "DO-OVER WORLD."
I WONDER WHAT THEIR OLD WORLD WAS LIKE.
HAVE THINGS CHANGED?

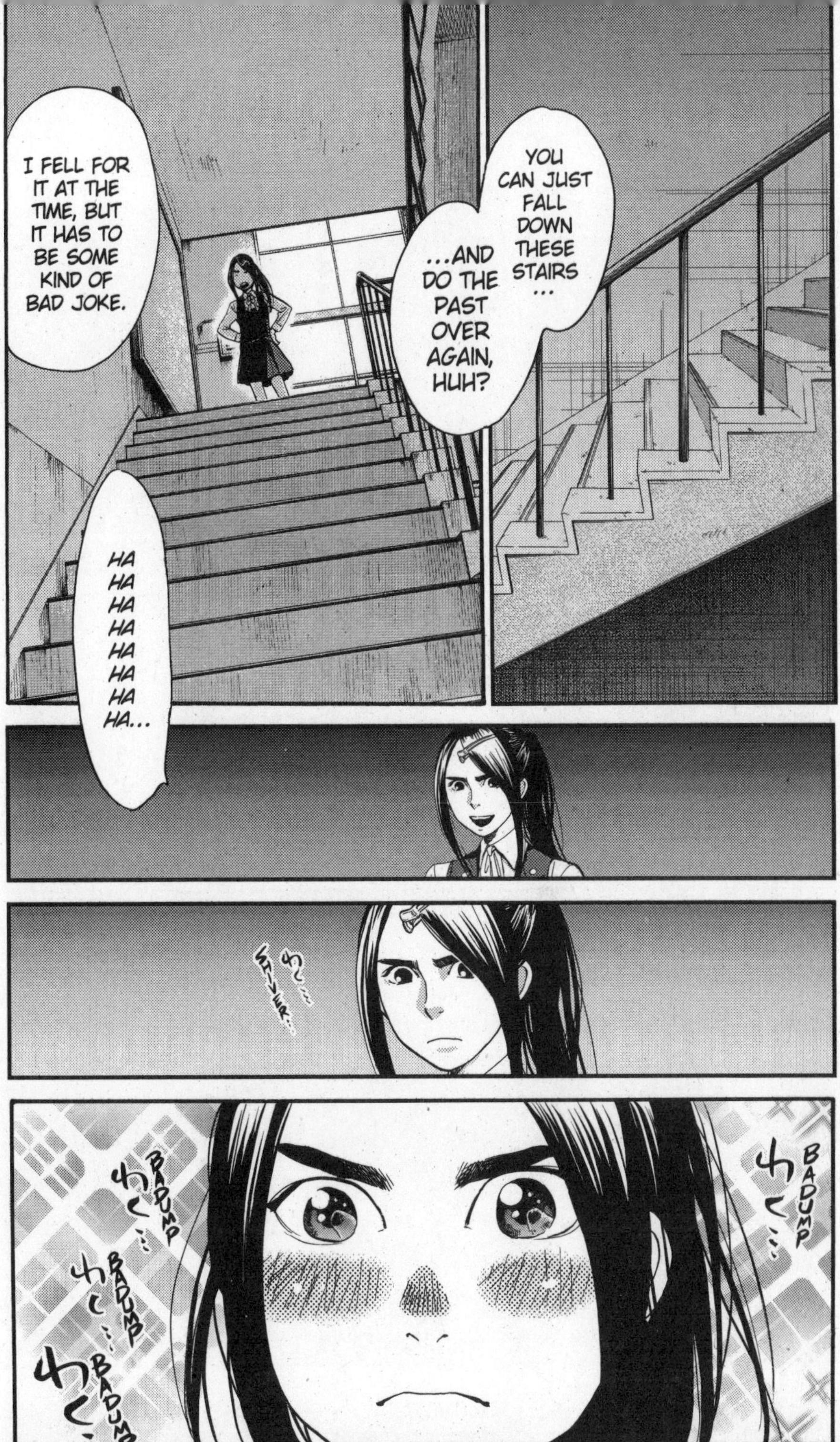
YOU CAN JUST FALL DOWN THESE STAIRS ...
...AND DO THE PAST OVER AGAIN, HUH?
I FELL FOR IT AT THE TIME, BUT IT HAS TO BE SOME KIND OF BAD JOKE.
HA HA HA HA HA HA HA HA...
SHIVER...
BADUMP
BADUMP
BADUMP
BADUMP...

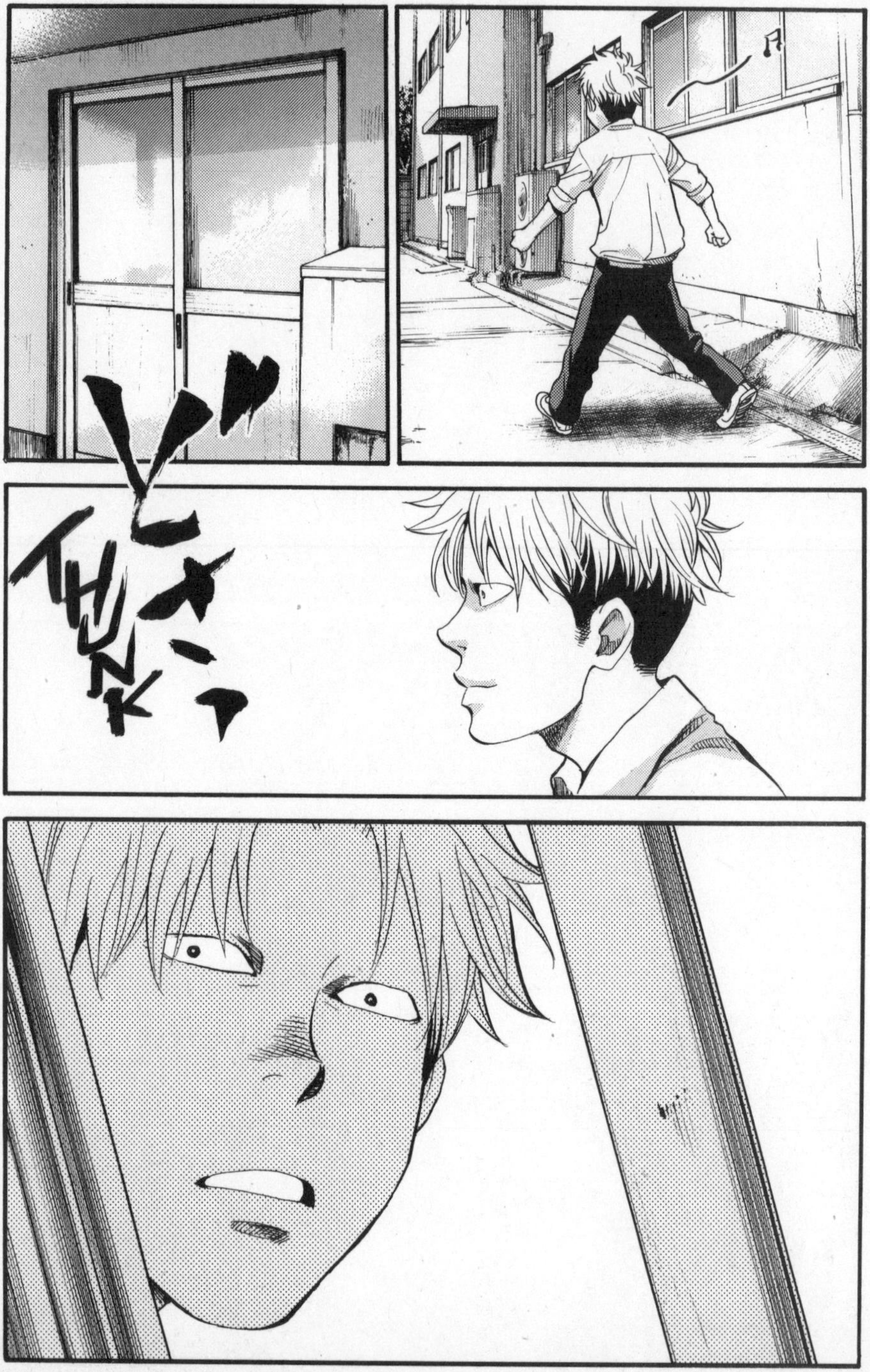
THUNK

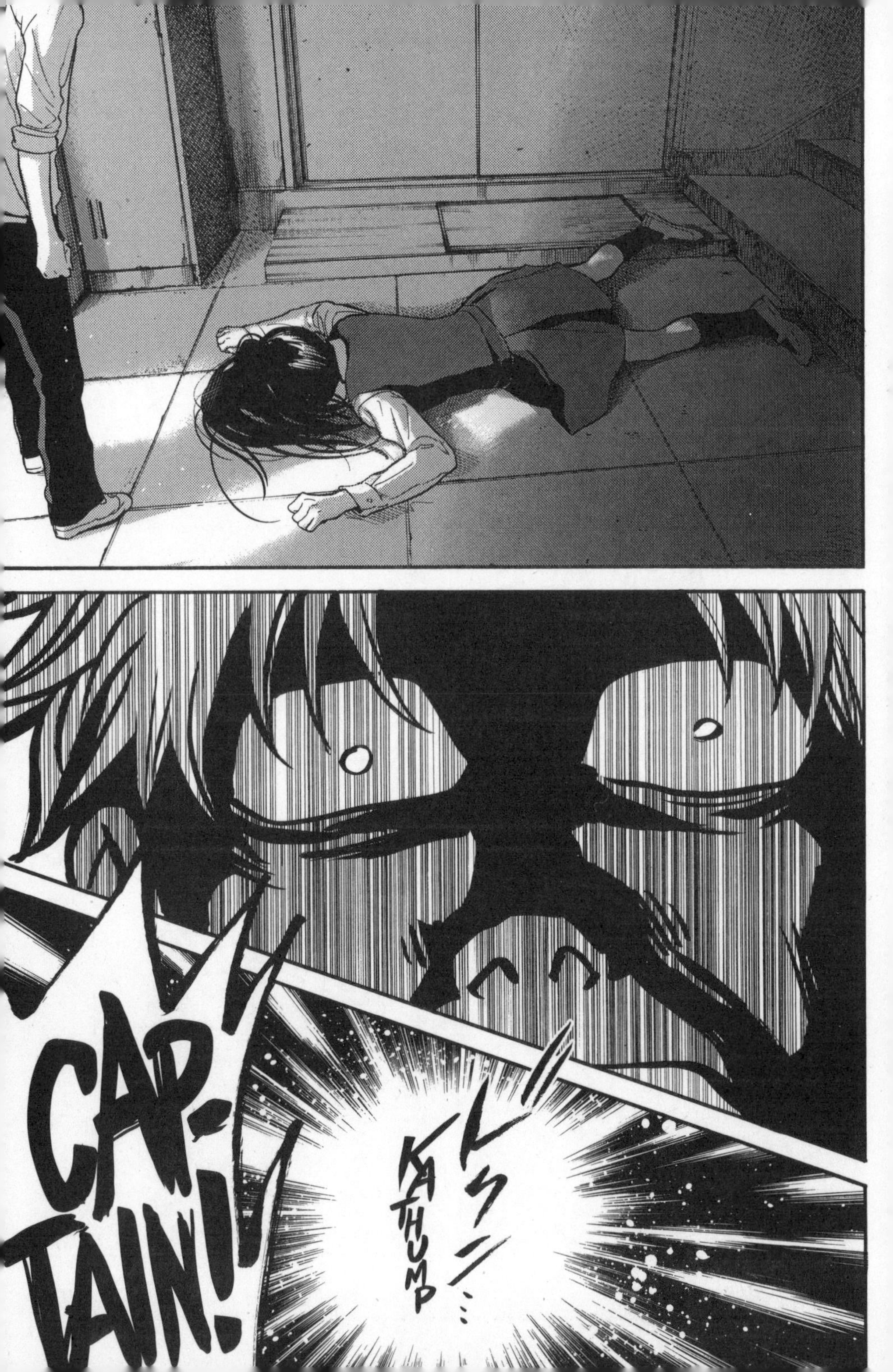
CAP-TAIN!!
KATHUMP

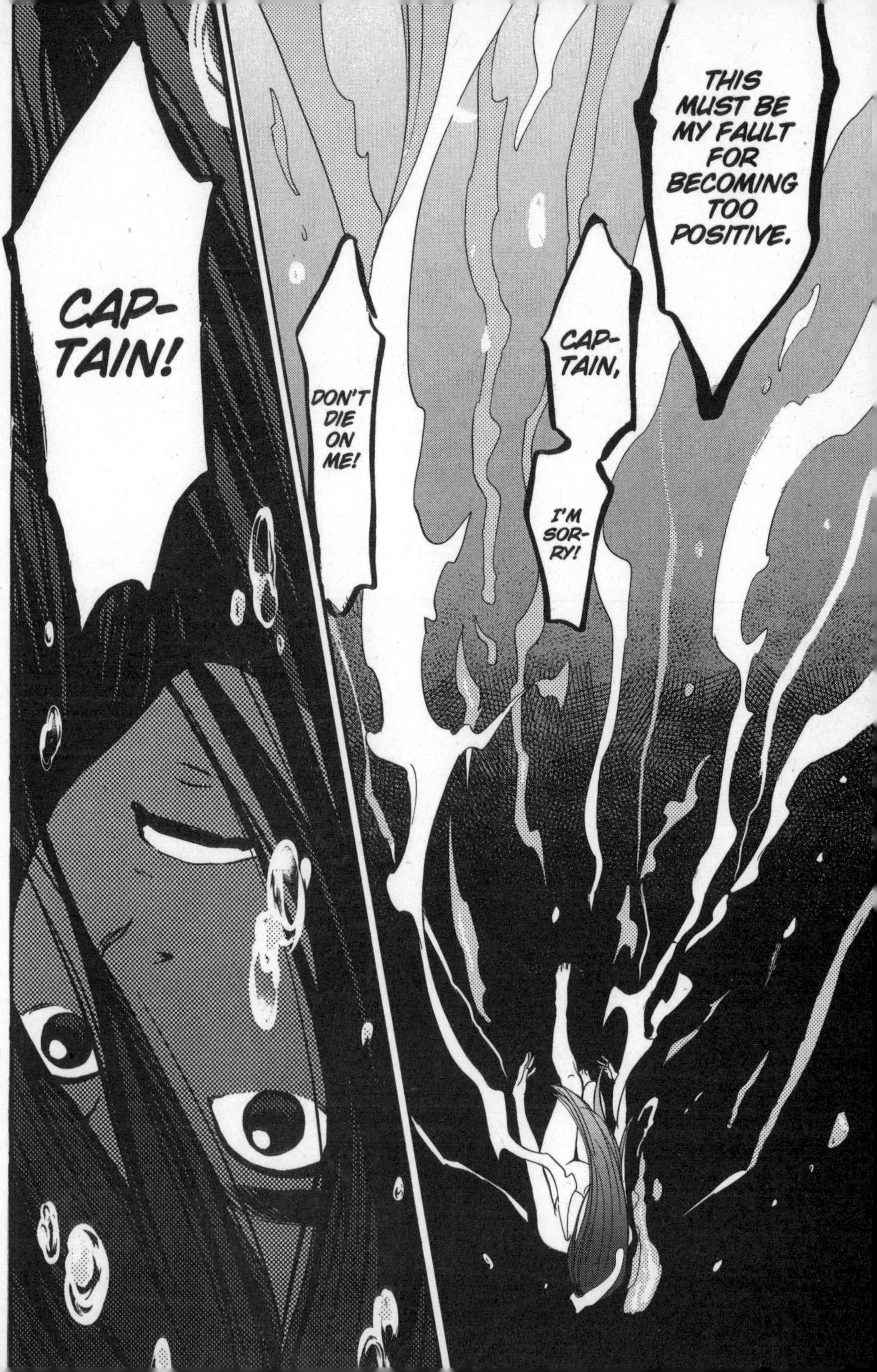
THIS MUST BE MY FAULT FOR BECOMING TOO POSITIVE.
CAP-TAIN,
I'M SOR-RY!
DON'T DIE ON ME!
CAP-TAIN!

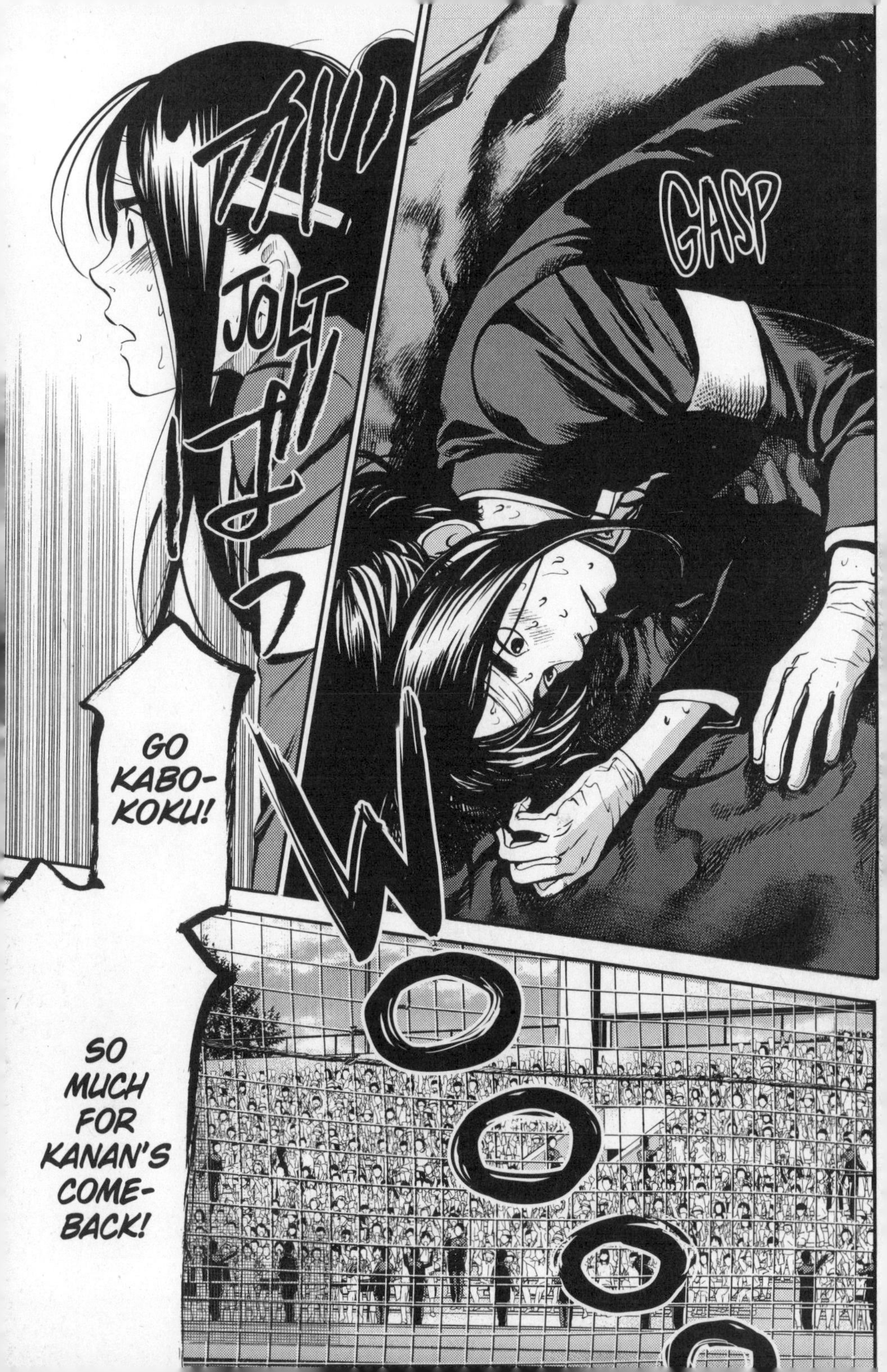
GASP
JOLT
WOOOO
GO KABO-KOKU!
SO MUCH FOR KANAN'S COME-BACK!

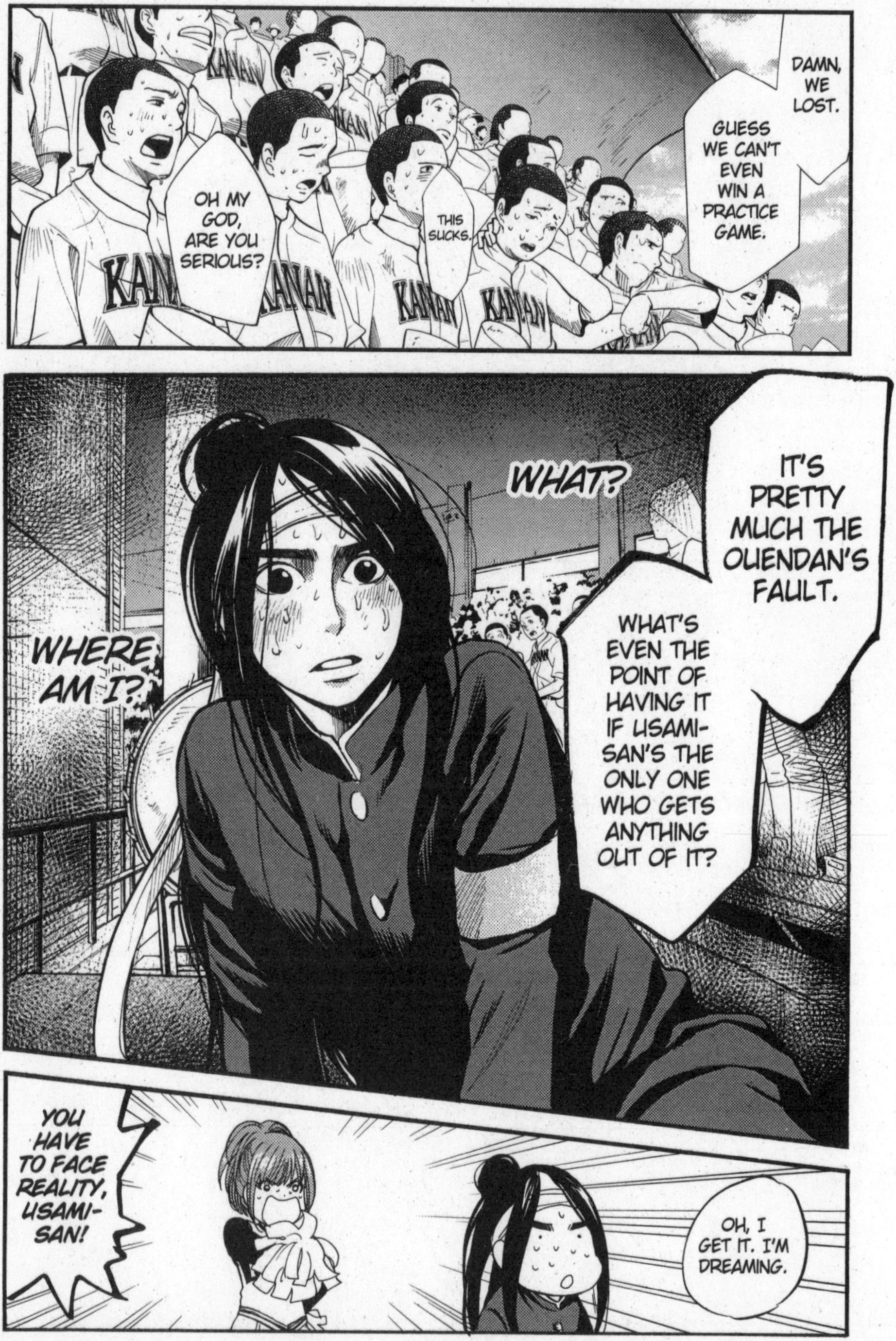
DAMN, WE LOST.
GUESS WE CAN'T EVEN WIN A PRACTICE GAME.
THIS SUCKS.
OH MY GOD, ARE YOU SERIOUS?
KANAN
IT'S PRETTY MUCH THE OUENDAN'S FAULT.
WHAT'S EVEN THE POINT OF HAVING IT IF USAMI-SAN'S THE ONLY ONE WHO GETS ANYTHING OUT OF IT?
WHAT?
WHERE AM I?
OH, I GET IT. I'M DREAMING.
YOU HAVE TO FACE REALITY, USAMI-SAN!

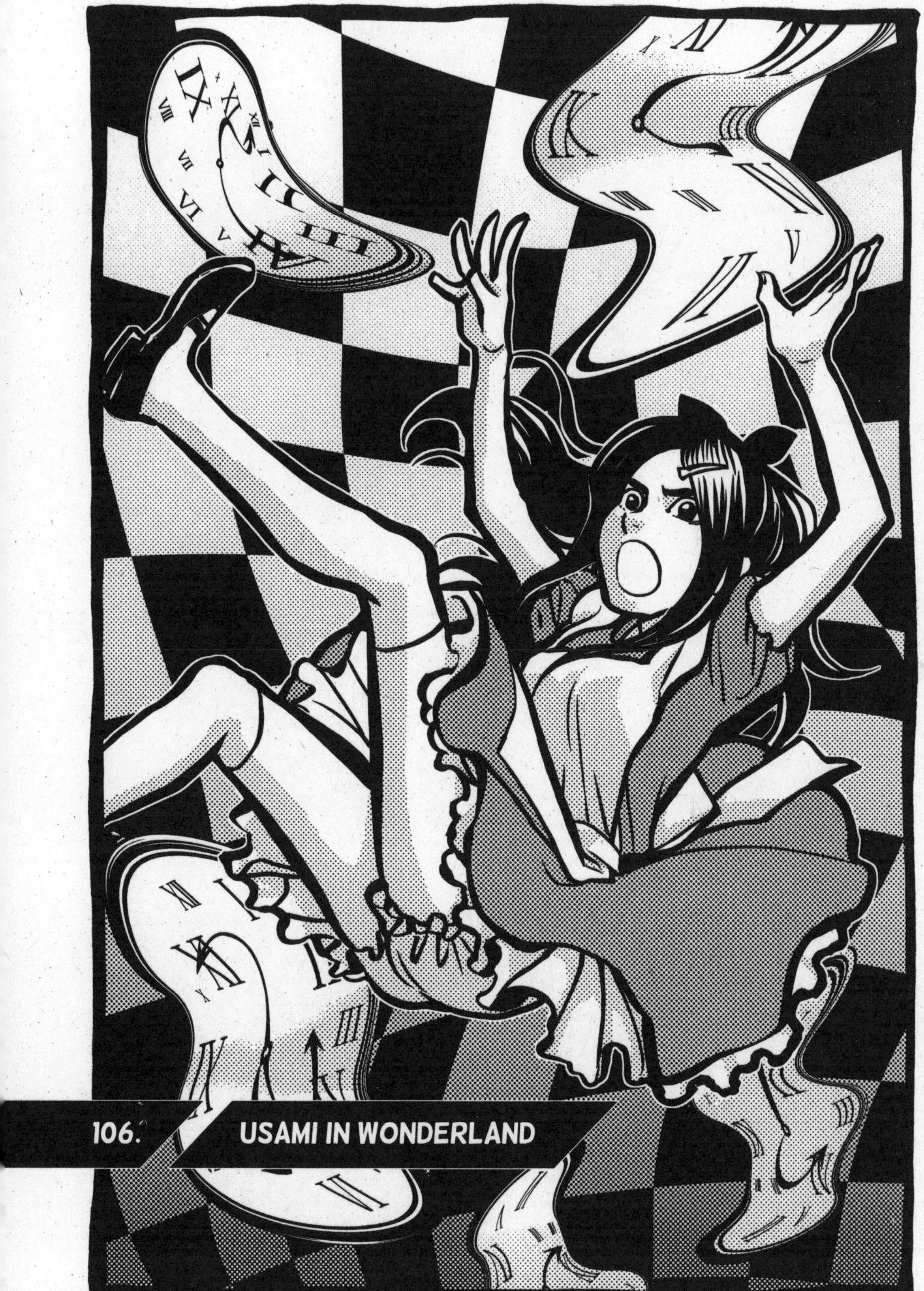
106.
USAMI IN WONDERLAND

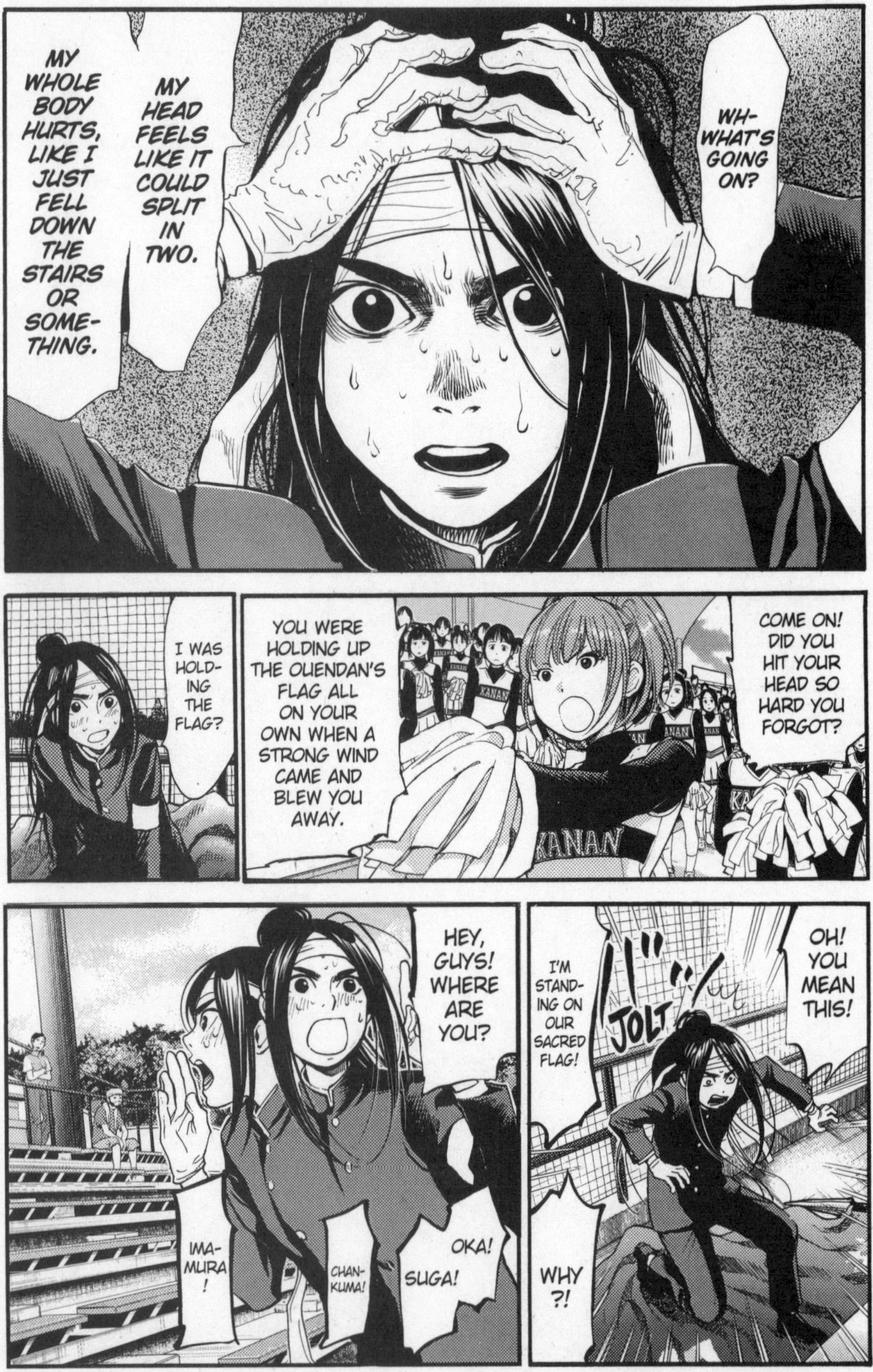
WH-WHAT'S GOING ON?
MY HEAD FEELS LIKE IT COULD SPLIT IN TWO.
MY WHOLE BODY HURTS, LIKE I JUST FELL DOWN THE STAIRS OR SOME-THING.
COME ON! DID YOU HIT YOUR HEAD SO HARD YOU FORGOT?
YOU WERE HOLDING UP THE OUENDAN'S FLAG ALL ON YOUR OWN WHEN A STRONG WIND CAME AND BLEW YOU AWAY.
KANAN
I WAS HOLD-ING THE FLAG?
OH! YOU MEAN THIS!
JOLT
I'M STAND-ING ON OUR SACRED FLAG!
WHY ?!
HEY, GUYS! WHERE ARE YOU?
OKA!
SUGA!
CHAN-KUMA!
IMA-MURA !

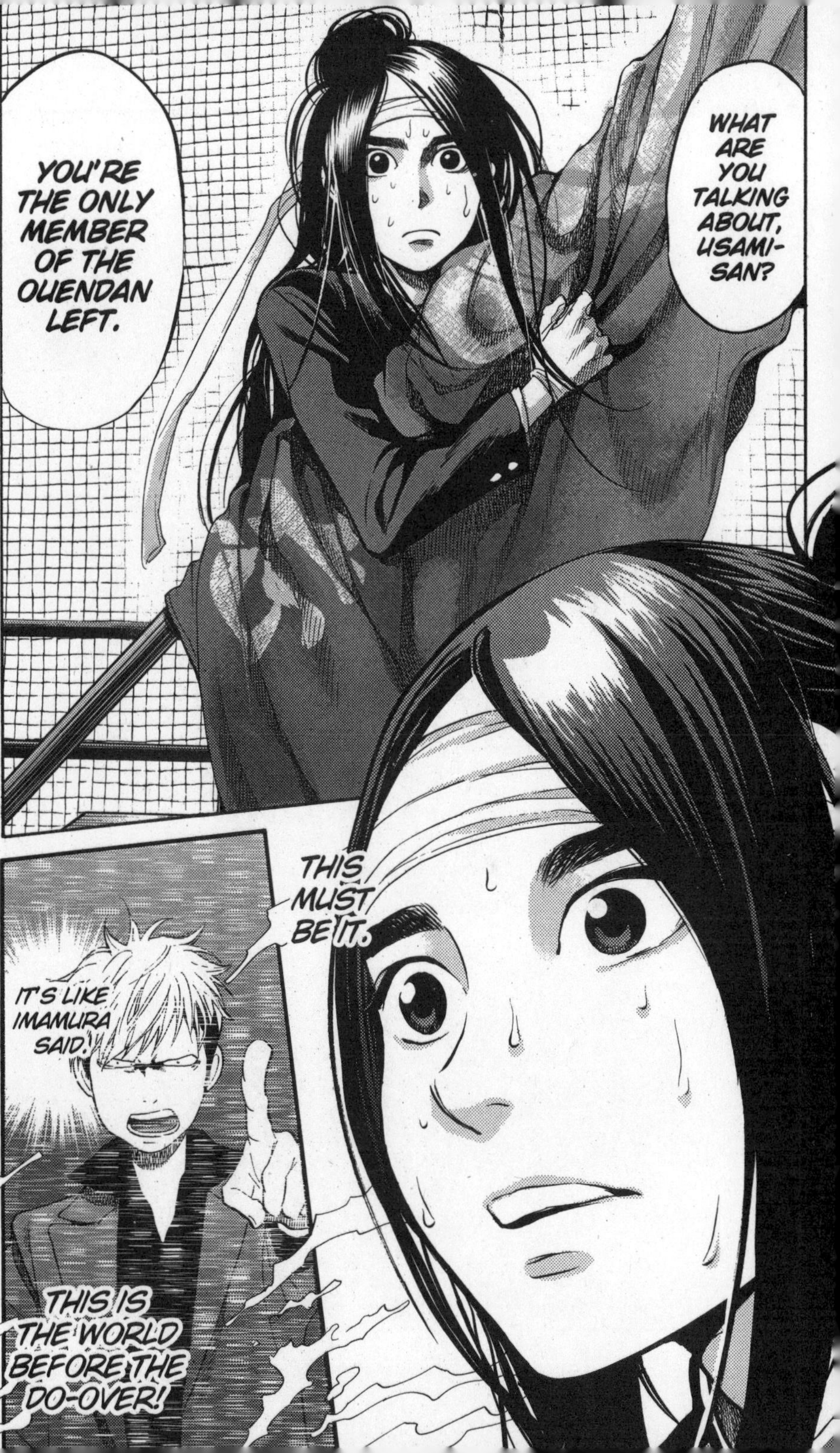
WHAT ARE YOU TALKING ABOUT, USAMI-SAN?
YOU'RE THE ONLY MEMBER OF THE OUENDAN LEFT.
THIS MUST BE IT.
IT'S LIKE IMAMURA SAID!
THIS IS THE WORLD BEFORE THE DO-OVER!

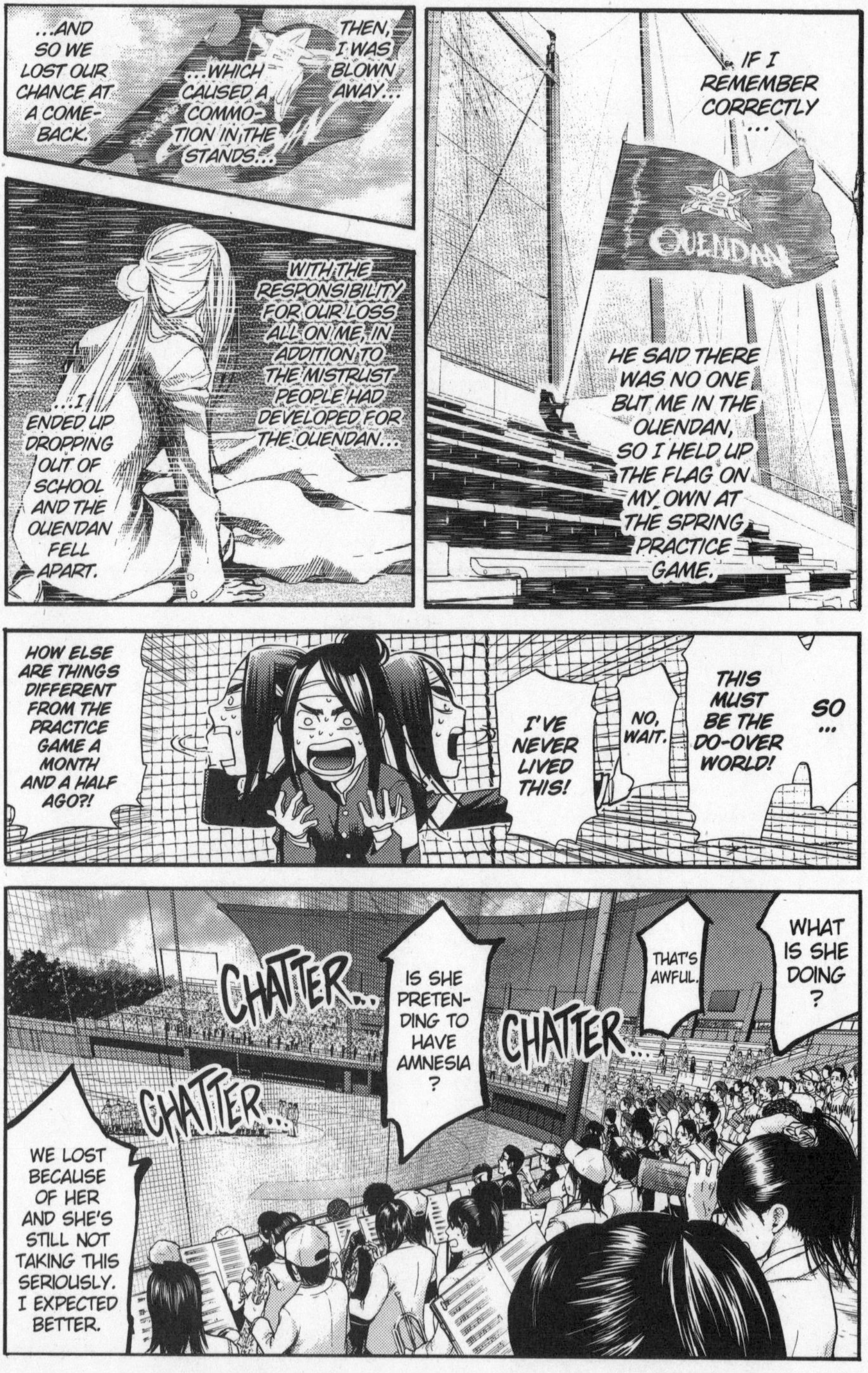
IF I REMEMBER CORRECTLY...
HE SAID THERE WAS NO ONE BUT ME IN THE OUENDAN, SO I HELD UP THE FLAG ON MY OWN AT THE SPRING PRACTICE GAME.
OUENDAN
THEN, I WAS BLOWN AWAY...
...WHICH CAUSED A COMMOTION IN THE STANDS...
...AND SO WE LOST OUR CHANCE AT A COMEBACK.
WITH THE RESPONSIBILITY FOR OUR LOSS ALL ON ME, IN ADDITION TO THE MISTRUST PEOPLE HAD DEVELOPED FOR THE OUENDAN...
...I ENDED UP DROPPING OUT OF SCHOOL AND THE OUENDAN FELL APART.
SO...
THIS MUST BE THE DO-OVER WORLD!
NO, WAIT.
I'VE NEVER LIVED THIS!
HOW ELSE ARE THINGS DIFFERENT FROM THE PRACTICE GAME A MONTH AND A HALF AGO?!
WHAT IS SHE DOING?
THAT'S AWFUL.
CHATTER...
IS SHE PRETENDING TO HAVE AMNESIA?
CHATTER...
CHATTER...
WE LOST BECAUSE OF HER AND SHE'S STILL NOT TAKING THIS SERIOUSLY. I EXPECTED BETTER.

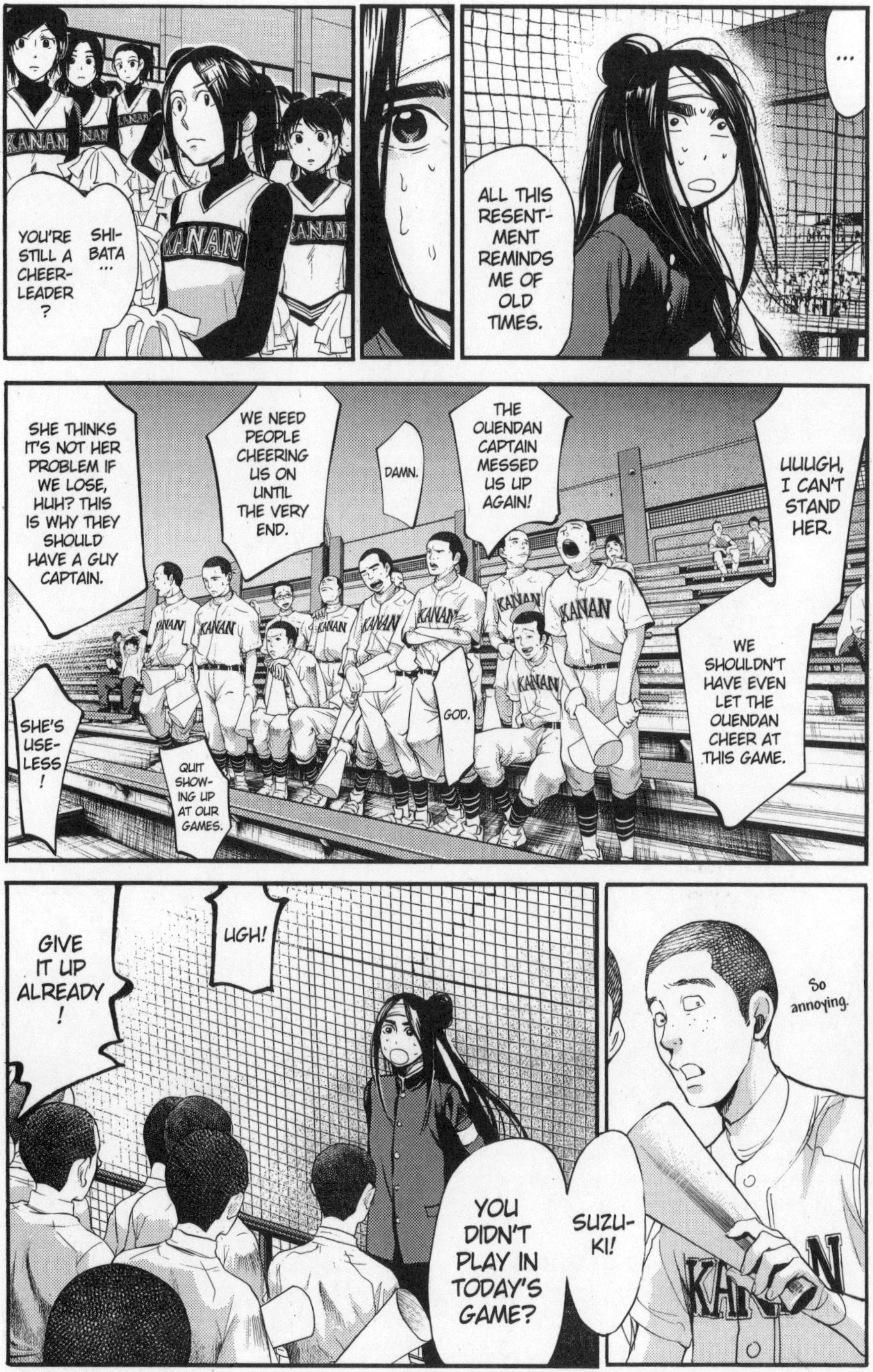
...
ALL THIS RESENTMENT REMINDS ME OF OLD TIMES.
SHIBATA...
YOU'RE STILL A CHEERLEADER?
UUUGH, I CAN'T STAND HER.
THE OUENDAN CAPTAIN MESSED US UP AGAIN!
DAMN.
WE NEED PEOPLE CHEERING US ON UNTIL THE VERY END.
SHE THINKS IT'S NOT HER PROBLEM IF WE LOSE, HUH? THIS IS WHY THEY SHOULD HAVE A GUY CAPTAIN.
WE SHOULDN'T HAVE EVEN LET THE OUENDAN CHEER AT THIS GAME.
GOD.
QUIT SHOWING UP AT OUR GAMES.
SHE'S USELESS!
So annoying.
SUZUKI!
YOU DIDN'T PLAY IN TODAY'S GAME?
UGH!
GIVE IT UP ALREADY!

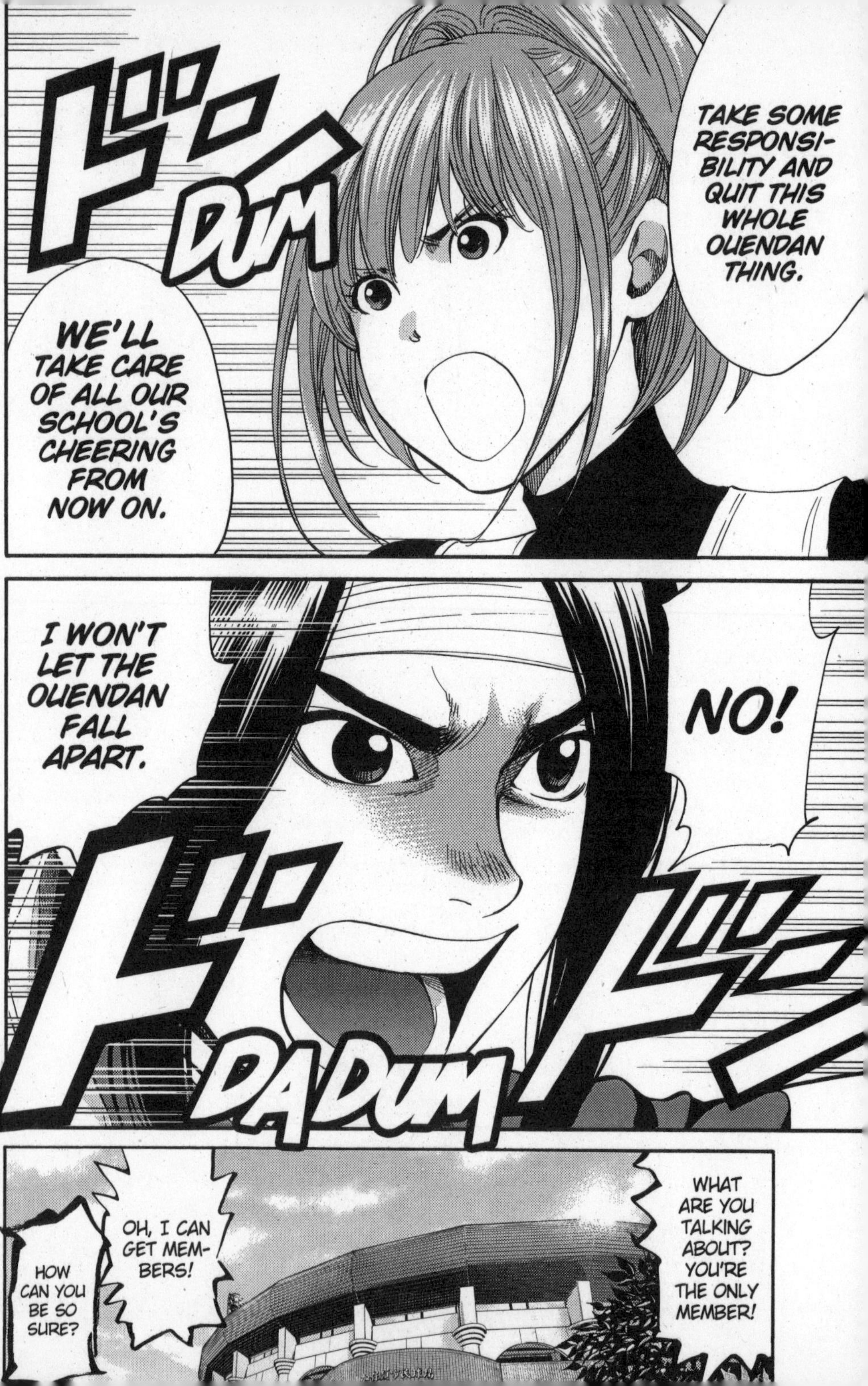
TAKE SOME RESPONSIBILITY AND QUIT THIS WHOLE OUENDAN THING.
DUM
WE'LL TAKE CARE OF ALL OUR SCHOOL'S CHEERING FROM NOW ON.
NO!
I WON'T LET THE OUENDAN FALL APART.
DA DUM
WHAT ARE YOU TALKING ABOUT? YOU'RE THE ONLY MEMBER!
OH, I CAN GET MEMBERS!
HOW CAN YOU BE SO SURE?

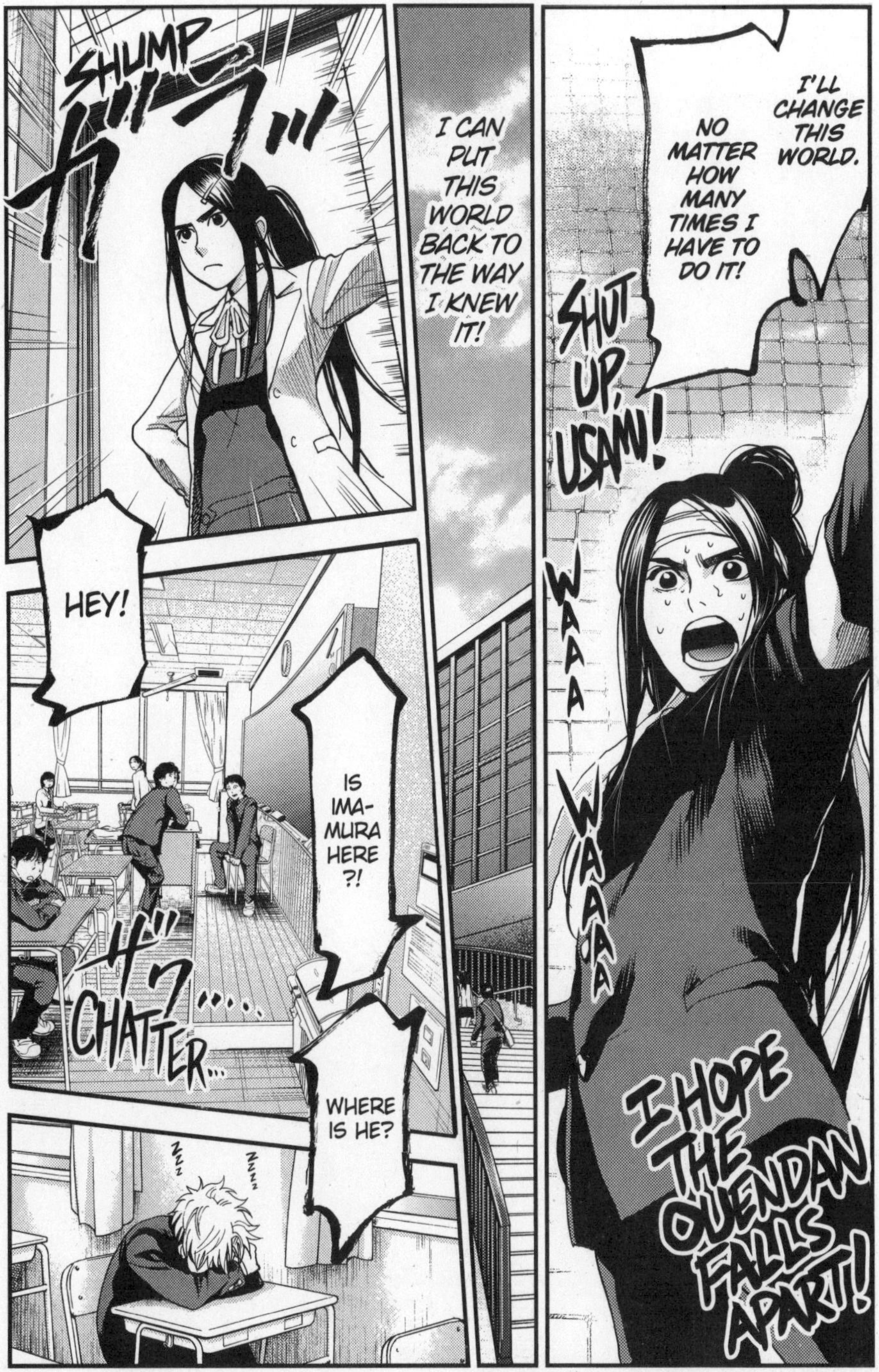
I'LL CHANGE THIS WORLD.
NO MATTER HOW MANY TIMES I HAVE TO DO IT!
SHUT UP, USAMI!
WAAA
WAAAA
I HOPE THE OUENDAN FALLS APART!
I CAN PUT THIS WORLD BACK TO THE WAY I KNEW IT!
SHUMP
HEY!
IS IMAMURA HERE?!
CHATTER...
WHERE IS HE?
ZZZ
ZZZ

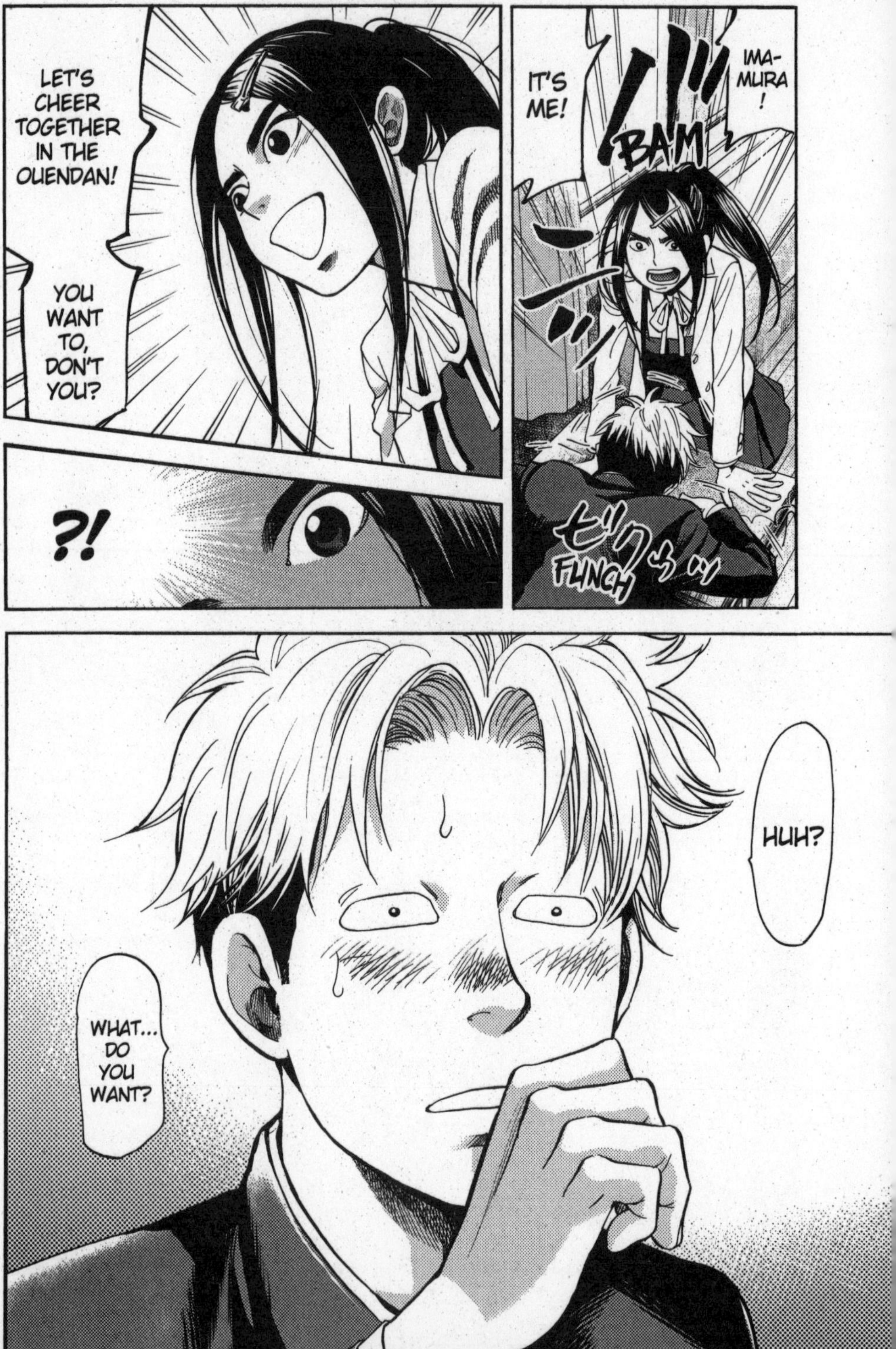
IMA-MURA!
IT'S ME!
BAM
FLINCH
LET'S CHEER TOGETHER IN THE OUENDAN!
YOU WANT TO, DON'T YOU?
?!
HUH?
WHAT... DO YOU WANT?

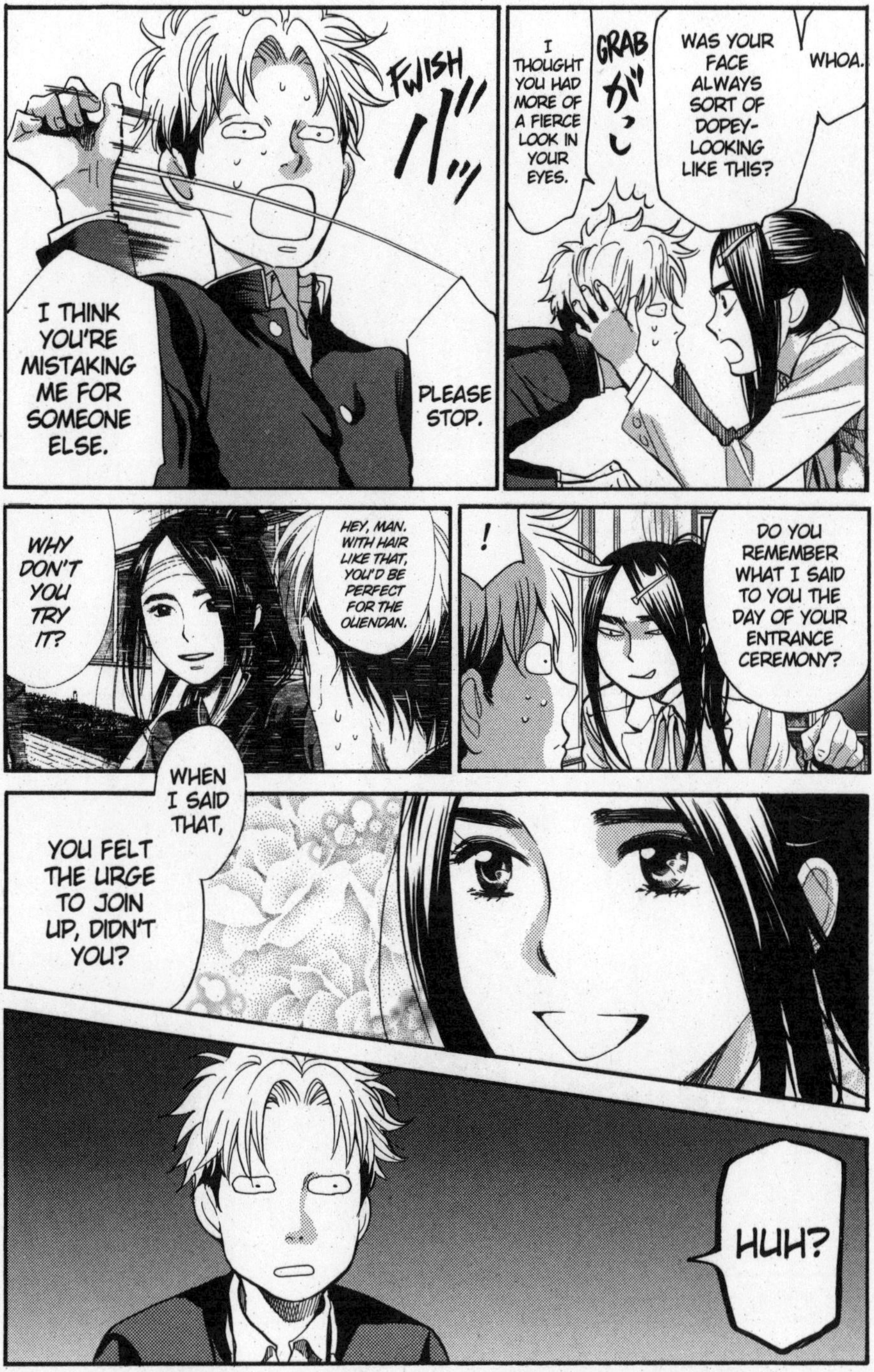
WHOA.
WAS YOUR FACE ALWAYS SORT OF DOPEY-LOOKING LIKE THIS?
GRAB がっし
I THOUGHT YOU HAD MORE OF A FIERCE LOOK IN YOUR EYES.
FWISH バッ
PLEASE STOP.
I THINK YOU'RE MISTAKING ME FOR SOMEONE ELSE.
!
DO YOU REMEMBER WHAT I SAID TO YOU THE DAY OF YOUR ENTRANCE CEREMONY?
HEY, MAN. WITH HAIR LIKE THAT, YOU'D BE PERFECT FOR THE OUENDAN.
WHY DON'T YOU TRY IT?
WHEN I SAID THAT,
YOU FELT THE URGE TO JOIN UP, DIDN'T YOU?
HUH?

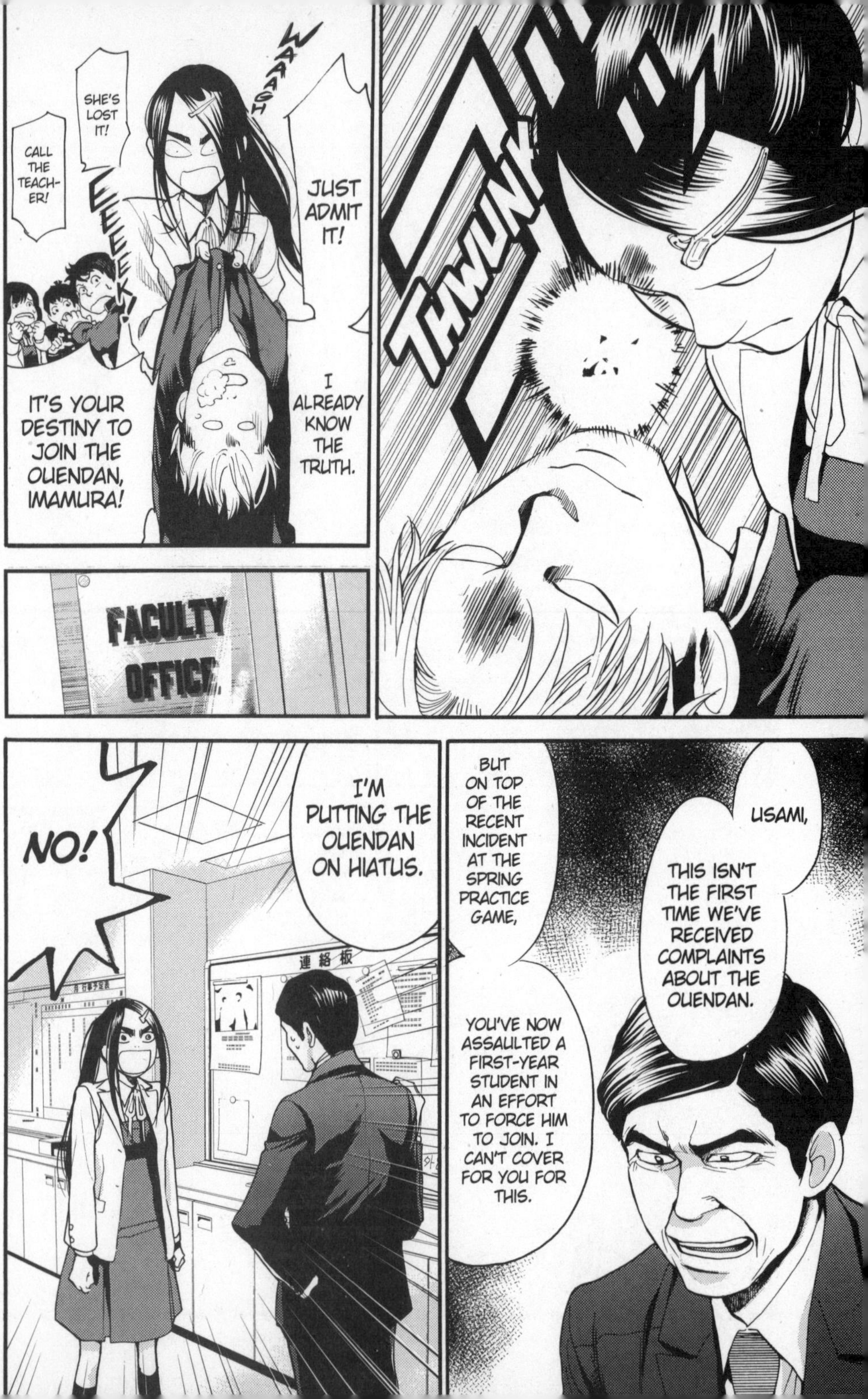
THWUNK!
WAAAGH
JUST ADMIT IT!
SHE'S LOST IT!
CALL THE TEACHER!
EEEEK!
I ALREADY KNOW THE TRUTH.
IT'S YOUR DESTINY TO JOIN THE OUENDAN, IMAMURA!
FACULTY OFFICE
USAMI,
THIS ISN'T THE FIRST TIME WE'VE RECEIVED COMPLAINTS ABOUT THE OUENDAN.
BUT ON TOP OF THE RECENT INCIDENT AT THE SPRING PRACTICE GAME,
YOU'VE NOW ASSAULTED A FIRST-YEAR STUDENT IN AN EFFORT TO FORCE HIM TO JOIN. I CAN'T COVER FOR YOU FOR THIS.
I'M PUTTING THE OUENDAN ON HIATUS.
NO!
連絡板

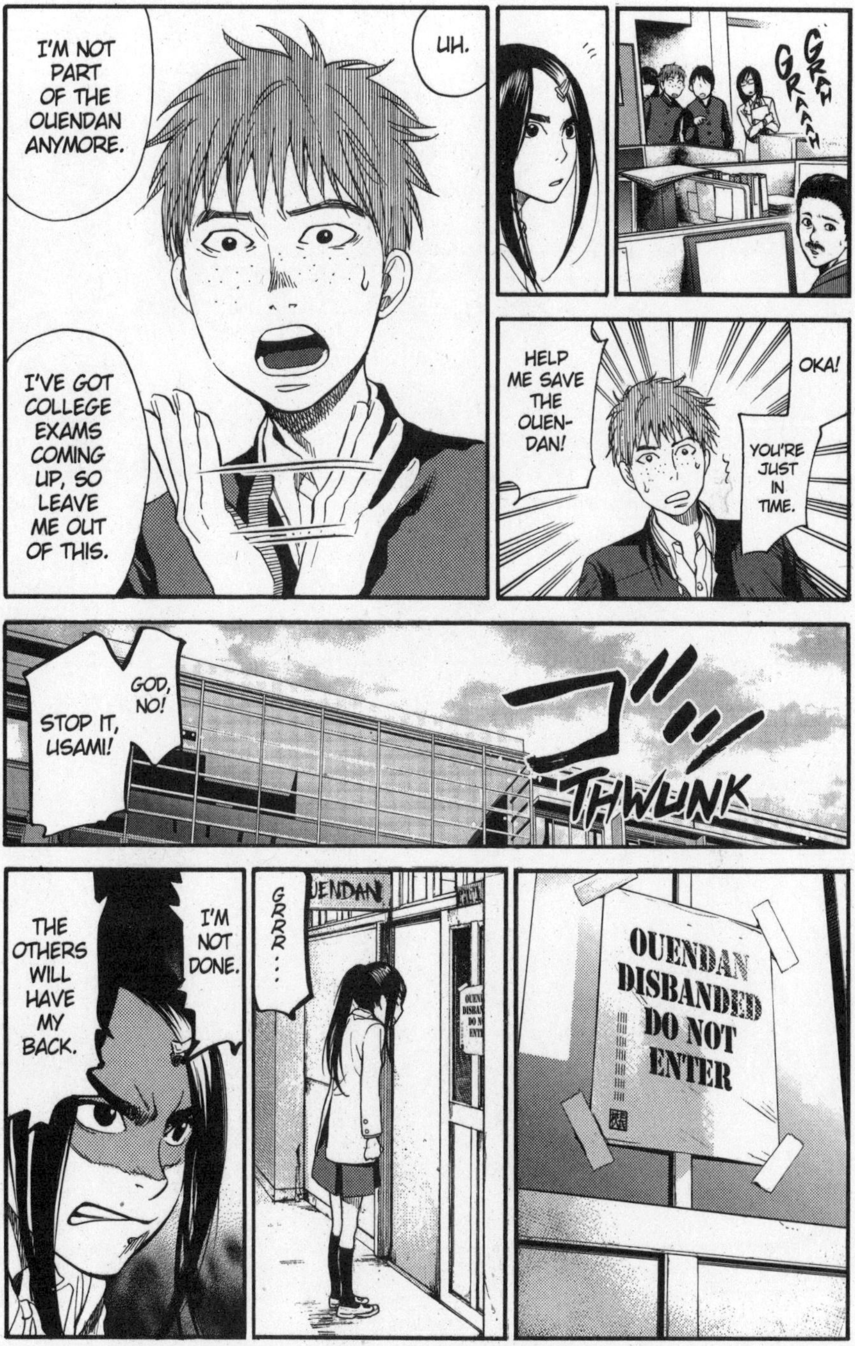
GRAAAH
GRAH
OKA!
YOU'RE JUST IN TIME.
HELP ME SAVE THE OUEN-DAN!
UH.
I'M NOT PART OF THE OUENDAN ANYMORE.
I'VE GOT COLLEGE EXAMS COMING UP, SO LEAVE ME OUT OF THIS.
THWUNK
GOD, NO!
STOP IT, USAMI!
OUENDAN DISBANDED DO NOT ENTER
OUENDAN
GRRR...
I'M NOT DONE.
THE OTHERS WILL HAVE MY BACK.

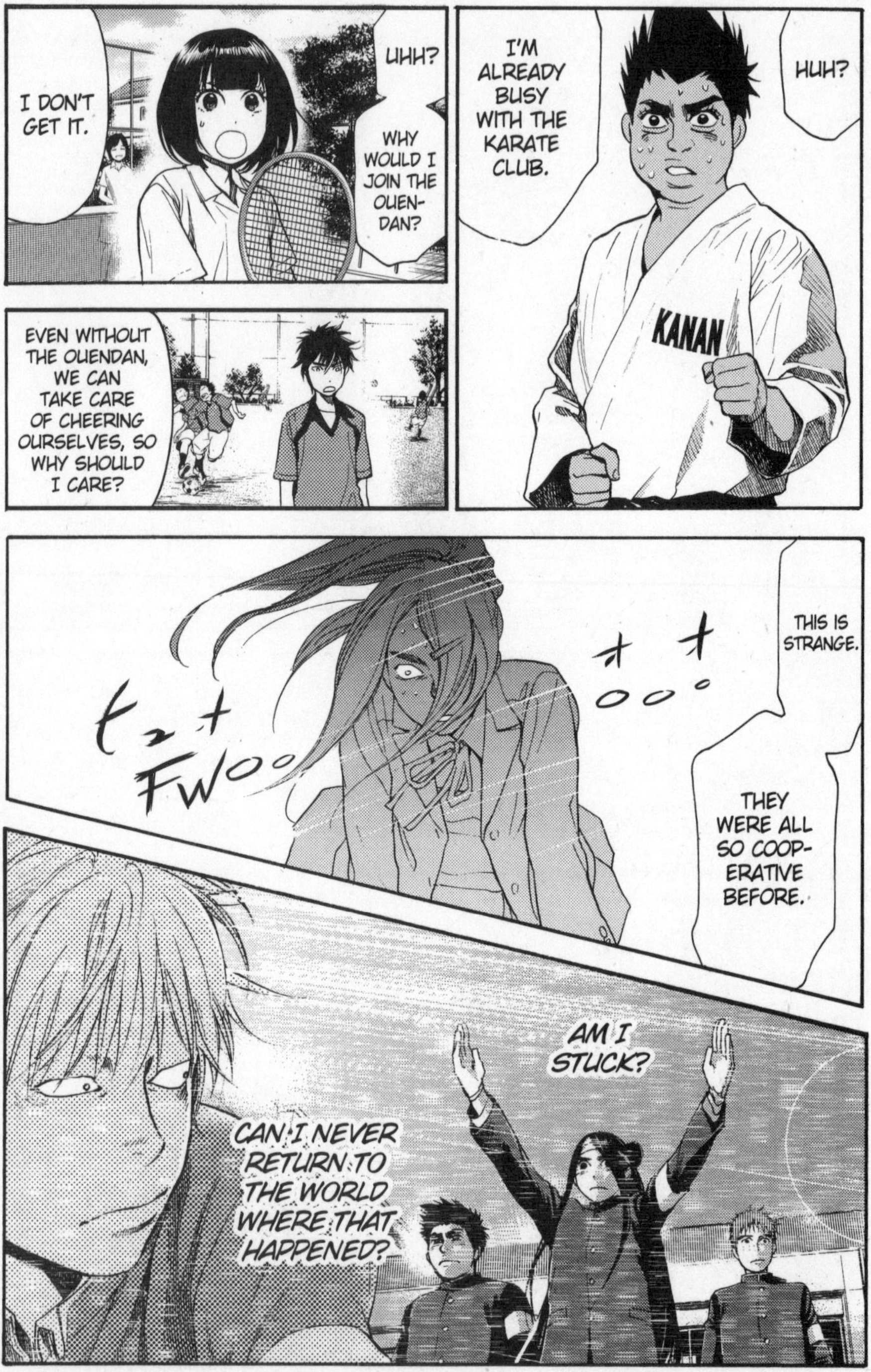

HUH?
I'M ALREADY BUSY WITH THE KARATE CLUB.
KANAN
UHH?
WHY WOULD I JOIN THE OUENDAN?
I DON'T GET IT.
EVEN WITHOUT THE OUENDAN, WE CAN TAKE CARE OF CHEERING OURSELVES, SO WHY SHOULD I CARE?
THIS IS STRANGE.
THEY WERE ALL SO COOPERATIVE BEFORE.
FWOO
AM I STUCK?
CAN I NEVER RETURN TO THE WORLD WHERE THAT HAPPENED?

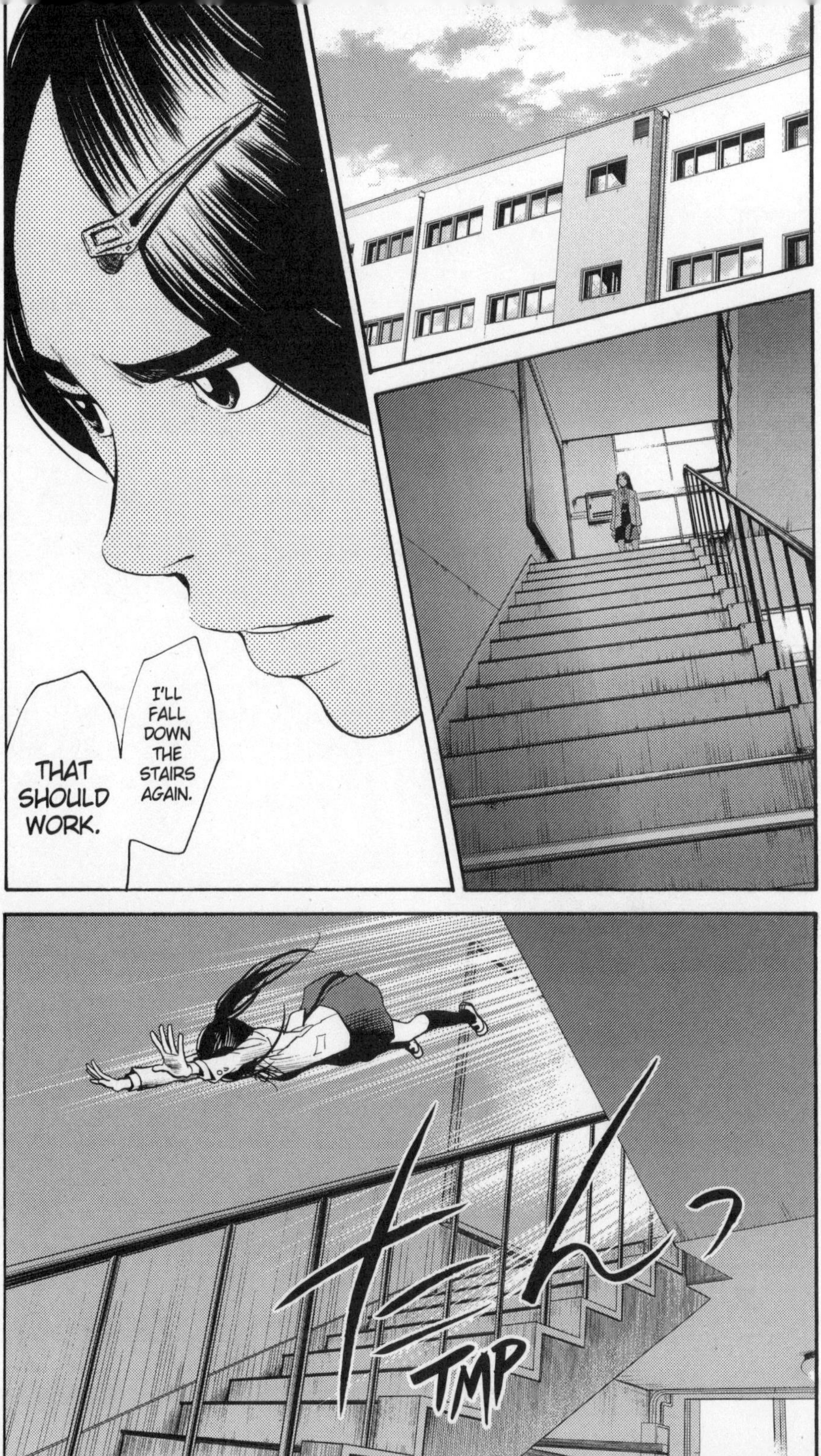
I'LL FALL DOWN THE STAIRS AGAIN.
THAT SHOULD WORK.
TMP

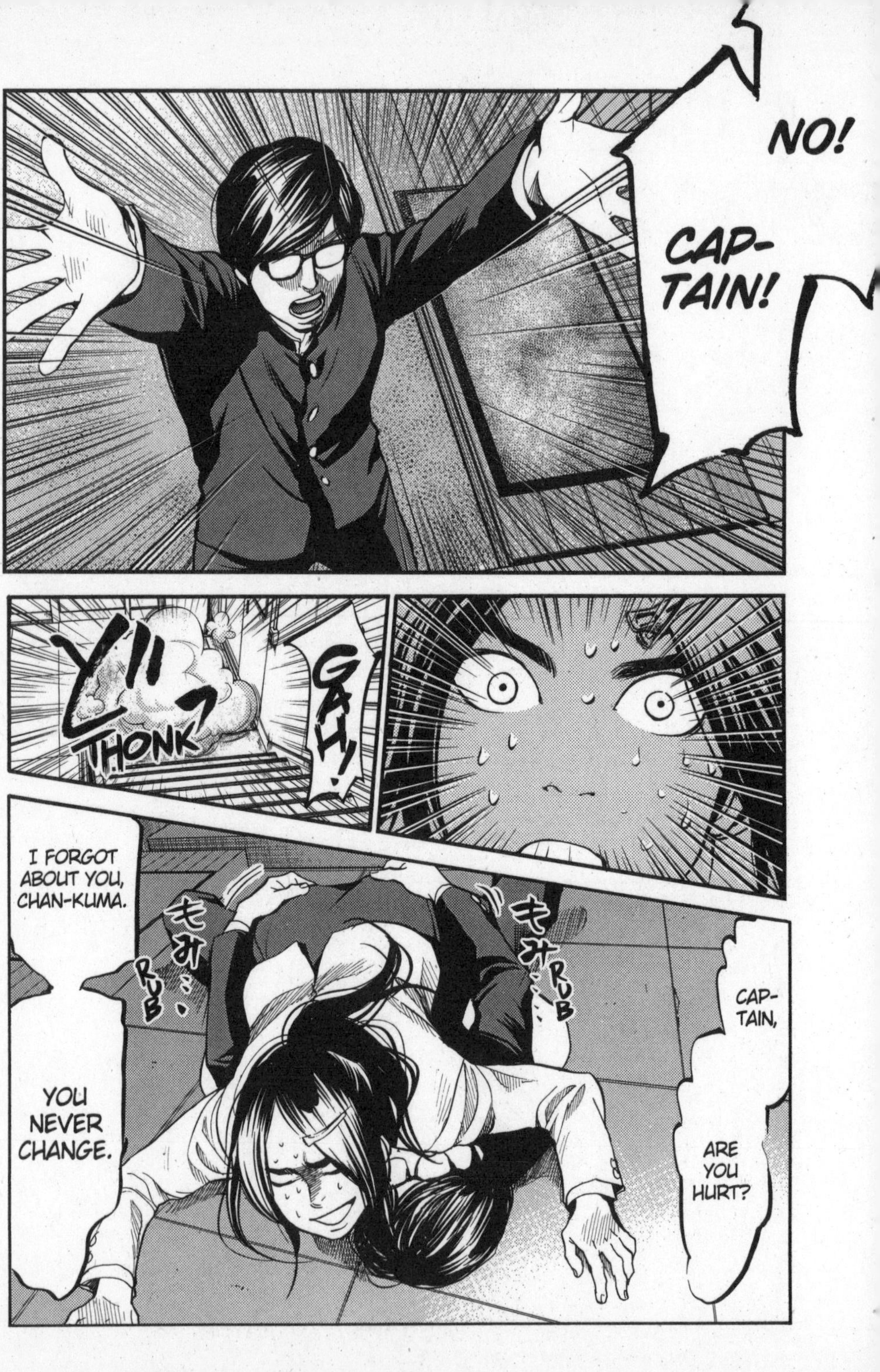
NO!
CAP-TAIN!
GAH!
THONK
CAP-TAIN,
ARE YOU HURT?
もみ RUB
もみ RUB
I FORGOT ABOUT YOU, CHAN-KUMA.
YOU NEVER CHANGE.

107. THE UNBEARABLE LONELINESS OF BEING

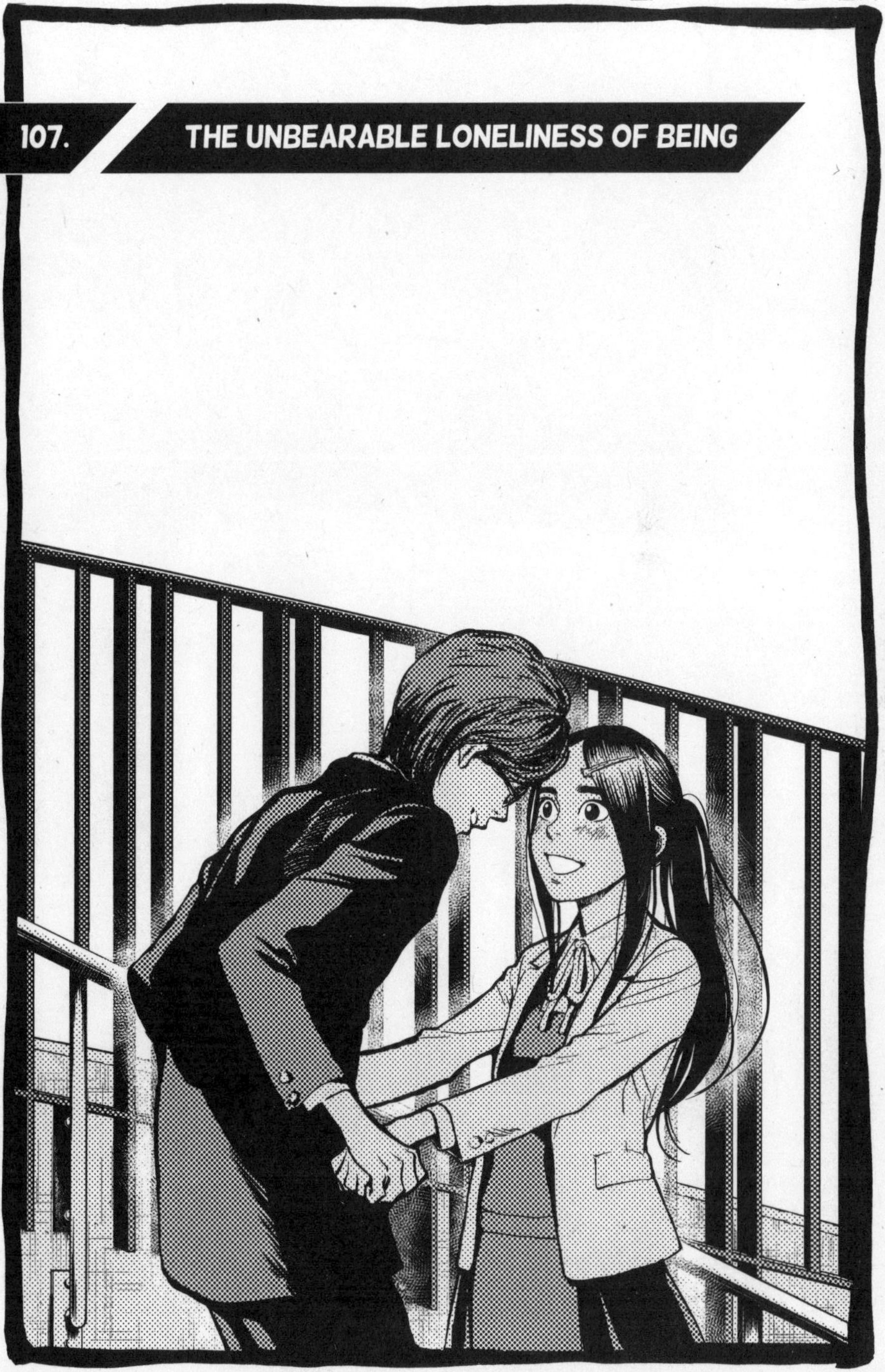

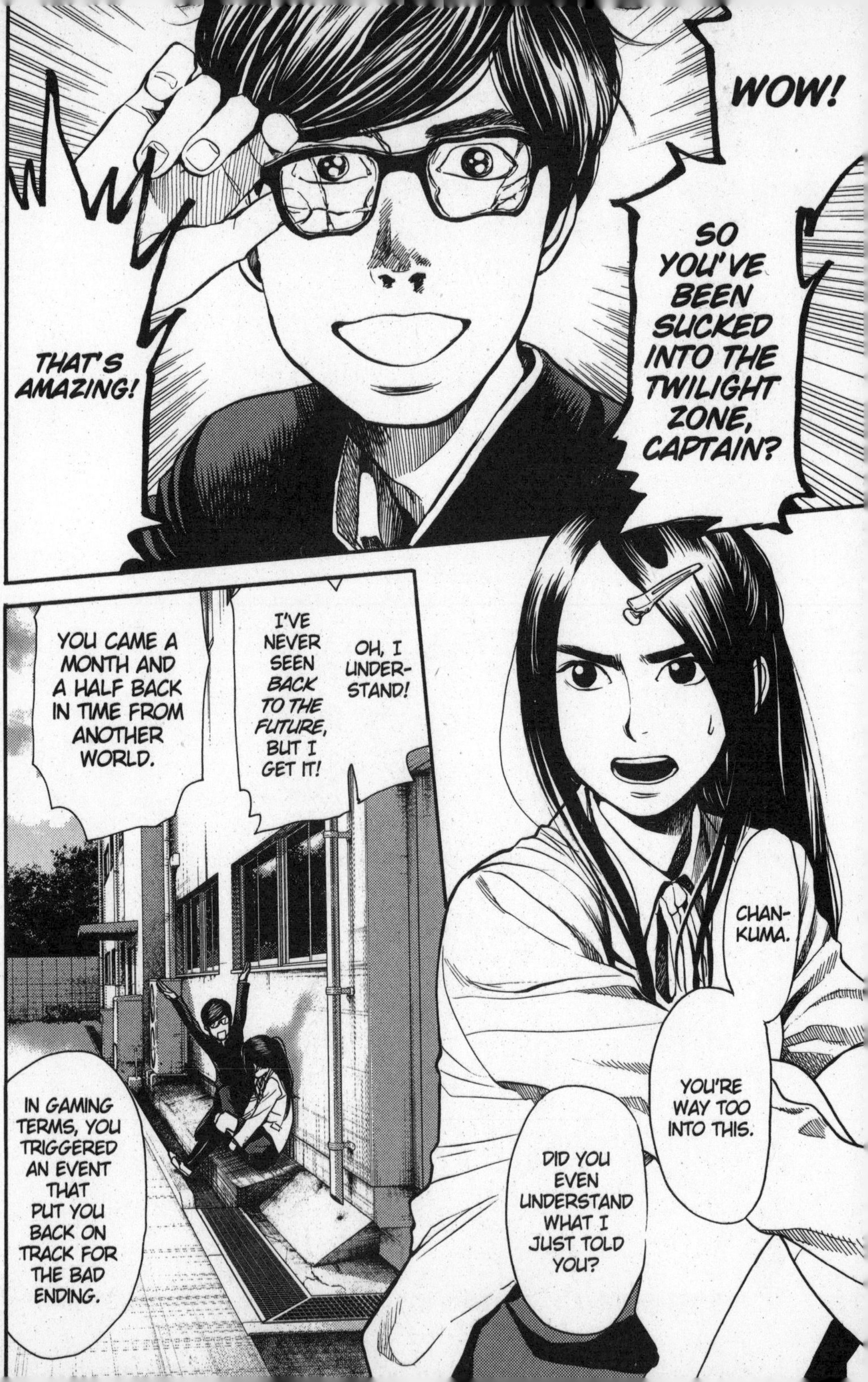
WOW!
SO YOU'VE BEEN SUCKED INTO THE TWILIGHT ZONE, CAPTAIN?
THAT'S AMAZING!
CHAN-KUMA.
YOU'RE WAY TOO INTO THIS.
DID YOU EVEN UNDERSTAND WHAT I JUST TOLD YOU?
OH, I UNDERSTAND!
I'VE NEVER SEEN BACK TO THE FUTURE, BUT I GET IT!
YOU CAME A MONTH AND A HALF BACK IN TIME FROM ANOTHER WORLD.
IN GAMING TERMS, YOU TRIGGERED AN EVENT THAT PUT YOU BACK ON TRACK FOR THE BAD ENDING.

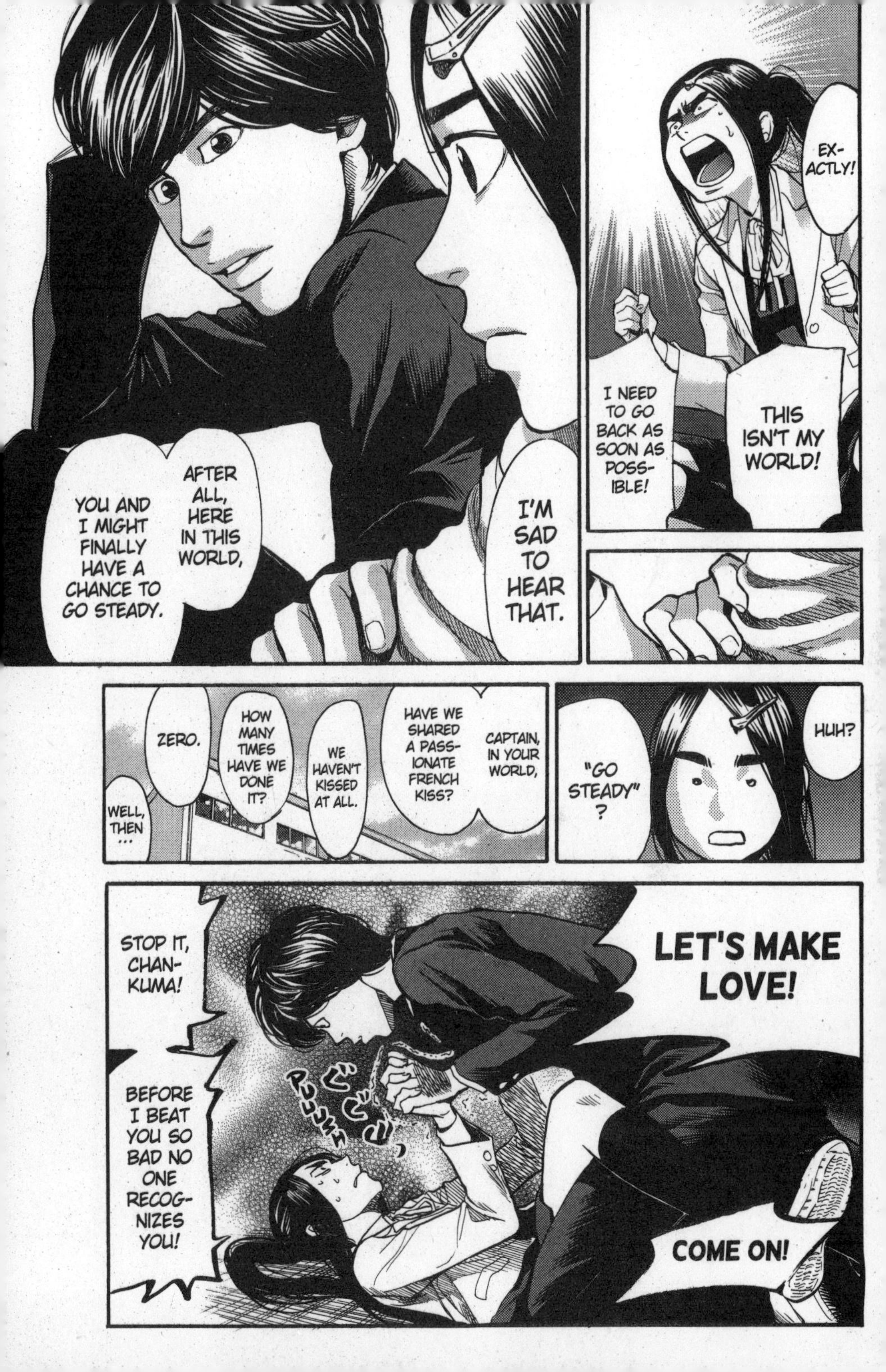
EX-ACTLY!
THIS ISN'T MY WORLD!
I NEED TO GO BACK AS SOON AS POSS-IBLE!
I'M SAD TO HEAR THAT.
AFTER ALL, HERE IN THIS WORLD,
YOU AND I MIGHT FINALLY HAVE A CHANCE TO GO STEADY.
HUH?
"GO STEADY"?
CAPTAIN, IN YOUR WORLD,
HAVE WE SHARED A PASS-IONATE FRENCH KISS?
WE HAVEN'T KISSED AT ALL.
HOW MANY TIMES HAVE WE DONE IT?
ZERO.
WELL, THEN...
LET'S MAKE LOVE!
COME ON!
STOP IT, CHAN-KUMA!
BEFORE I BEAT YOU SO BAD NO ONE RECOG-NIZES YOU!

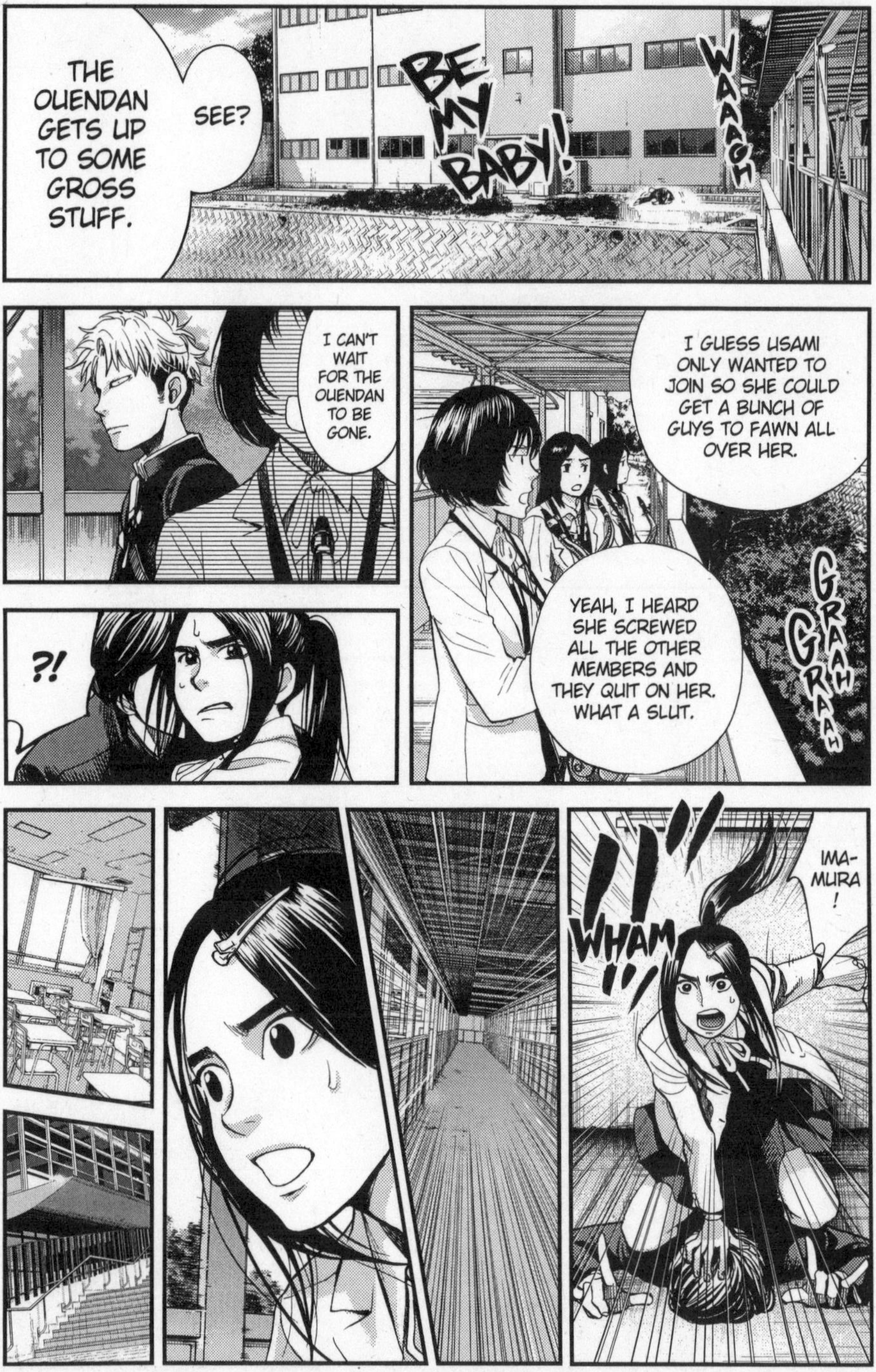
WAAAGH
BE MY BABY!
SEE?
THE OUENDAN GETS UP TO SOME GROSS STUFF.
I GUESS USAMI ONLY WANTED TO JOIN SO SHE COULD GET A BUNCH OF GUYS TO FAWN ALL OVER HER.
GRAAH GRAAH
YEAH, I HEARD SHE SCREWED ALL THE OTHER MEMBERS AND THEY QUIT ON HER. WHAT A SLUT.
I CAN'T WAIT FOR THE OUENDAN TO BE GONE.
?!
IMA-MURA!
WHAM

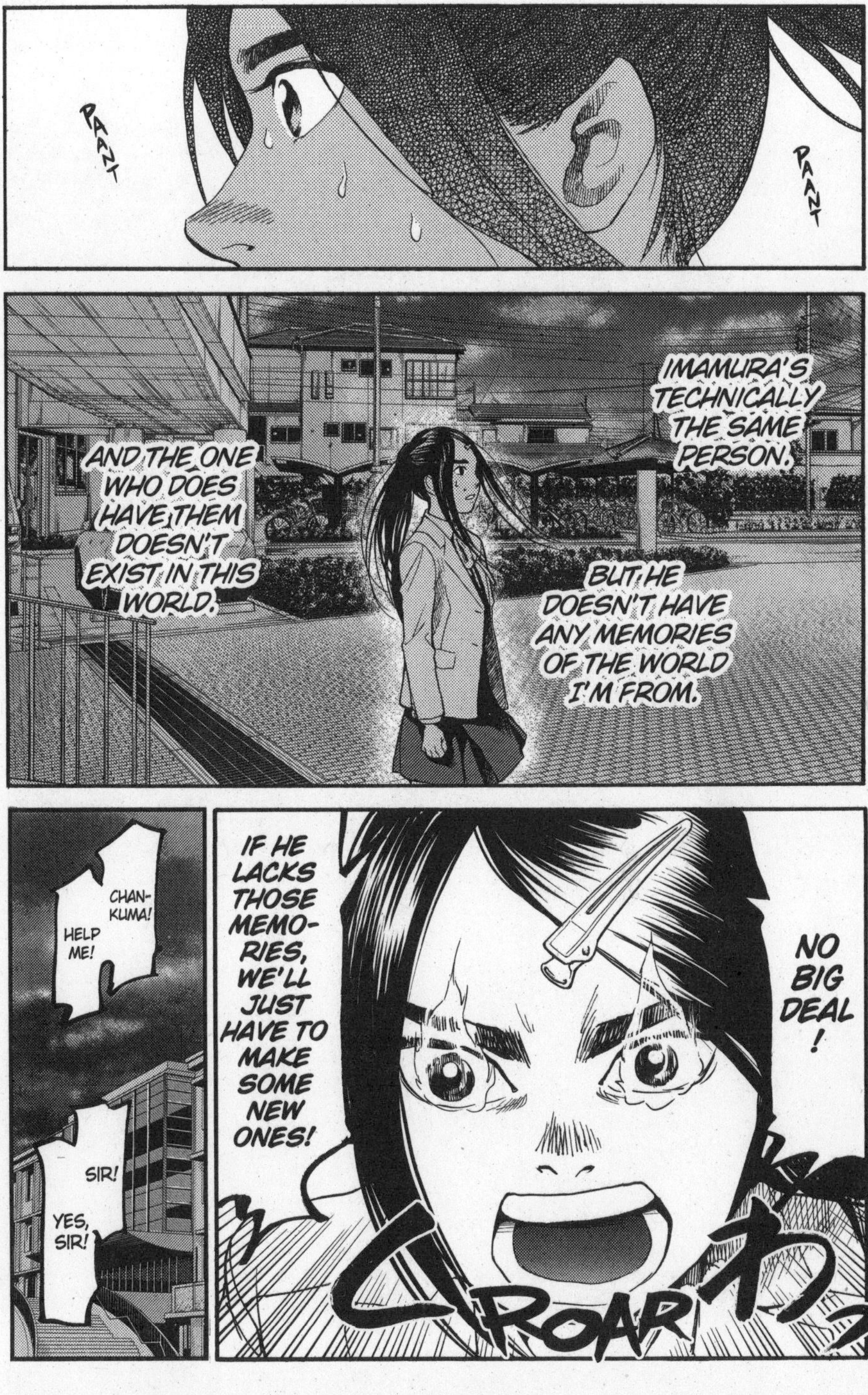
PAANT
PAANT
IMAMURA'S TECHNICALLY THE SAME PERSON.
BUT HE DOESN'T HAVE ANY MEMORIES OF THE WORLD I'M FROM.
AND THE ONE WHO DOES HAVE THEM DOESN'T EXIST IN THIS WORLD.
NO BIG DEAL!
IF HE LACKS THOSE MEMO-RIES, WE'LL JUST HAVE TO MAKE SOME NEW ONES!
ROAR
CHAN-KUMA!
HELP ME!
SIR!
YES, SIR!

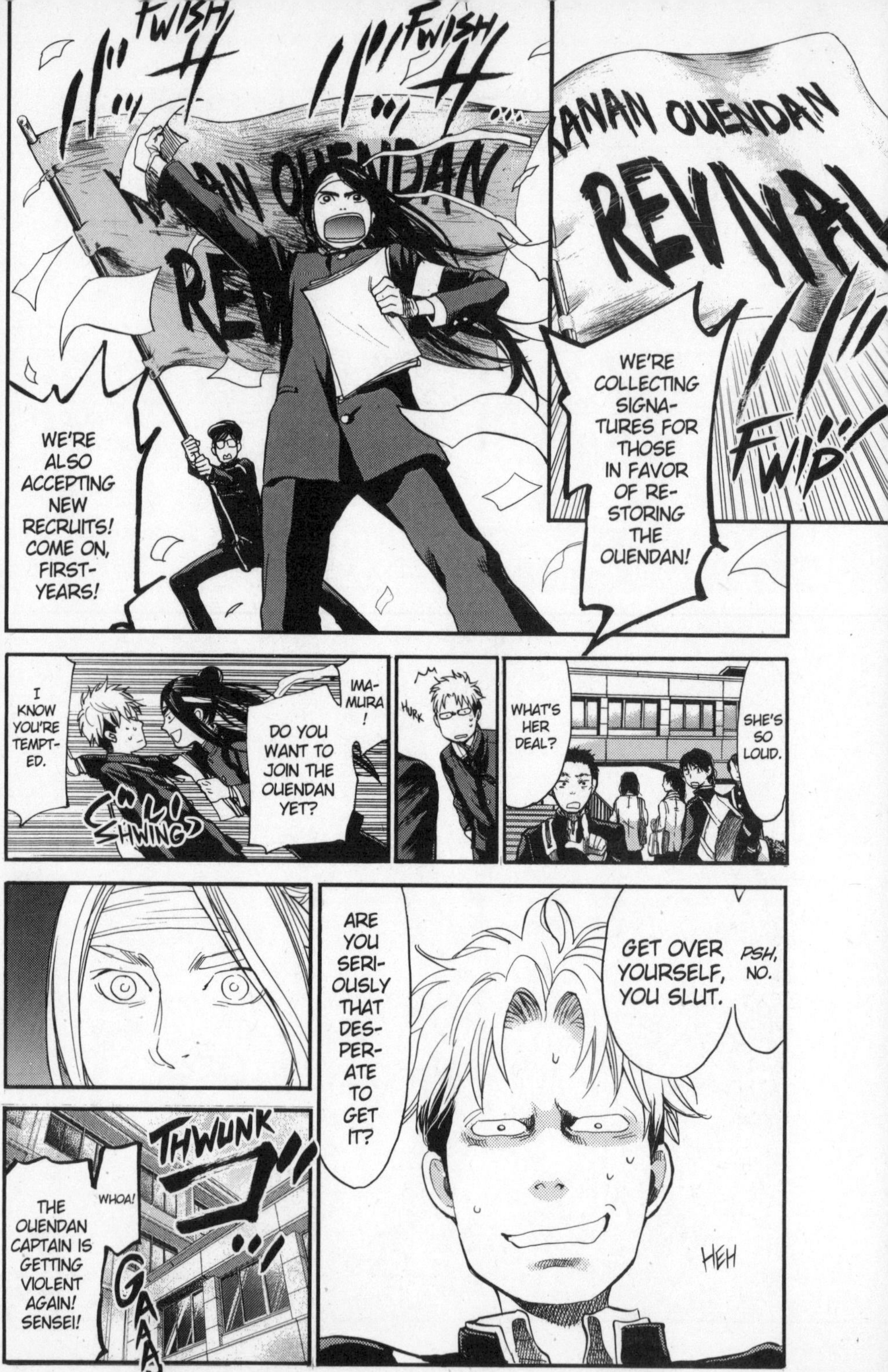
KANAN OUENDAN REVIVAL
FWIP
WE'RE COLLECTING SIGNATURES FOR THOSE IN FAVOR OF RESTORING THE OUENDAN!
FWISH
FWISH
WE'RE ALSO ACCEPTING NEW RECRUITS! COME ON, FIRST-YEARS!
SHE'S SO LOUD.
WHAT'S HER DEAL?
HURK
IMAMURA!
DO YOU WANT TO JOIN THE OUENDAN YET?
I KNOW YOU'RE TEMPTED.
SHWING
PSH, NO.
GET OVER YOURSELF, YOU SLUT.
ARE YOU SERIOUSLY THAT DESPERATE TO GET IT?
HEH
THWUNK
GAAAH!
WHOA!
THE OUENDAN CAPTAIN IS GETTING VIOLENT AGAIN! SENSEI!

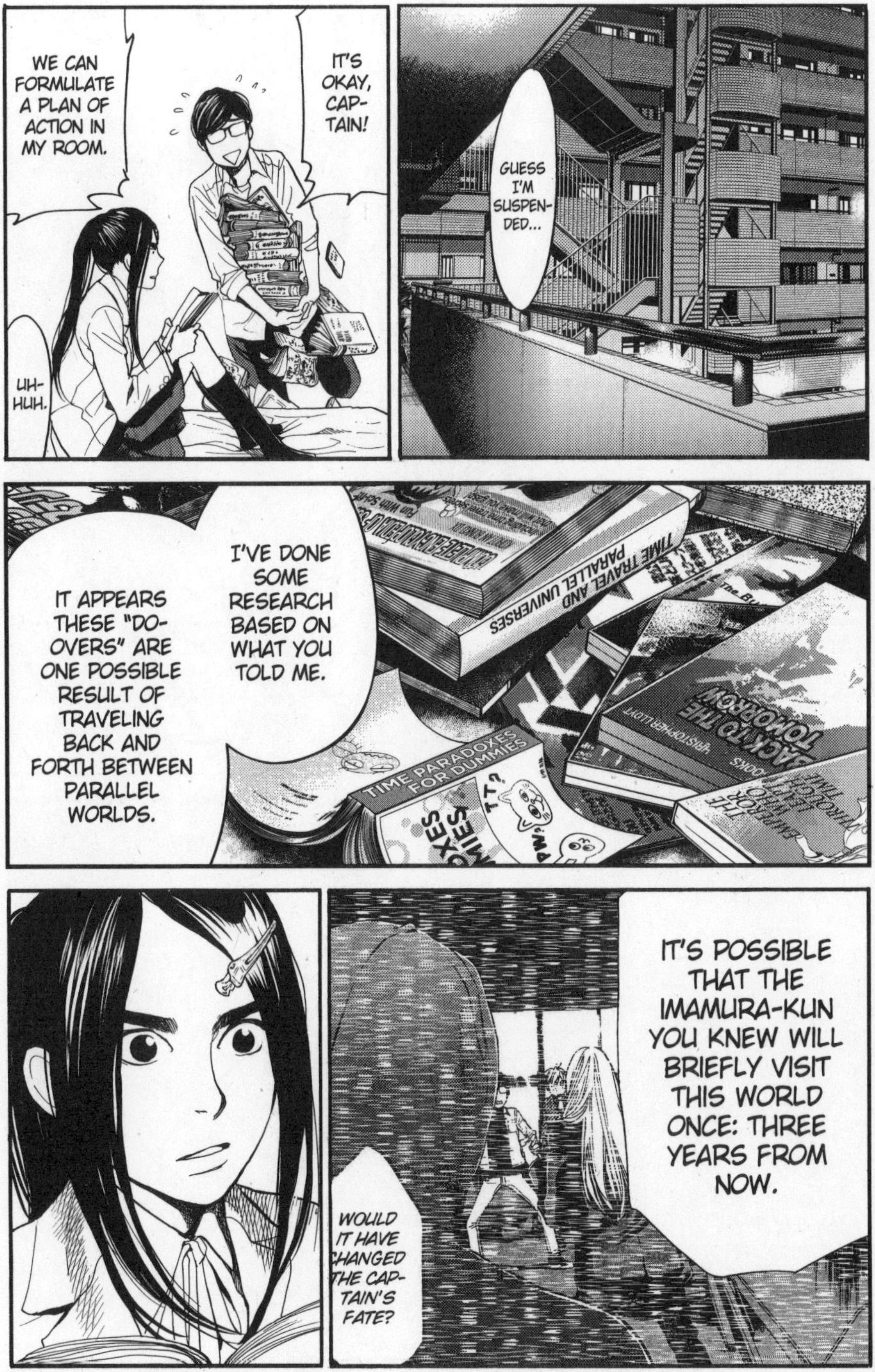
GUESS I'M SUSPENDED...
IT'S OKAY, CAPTAIN!
WE CAN FORMULATE A PLAN OF ACTION IN MY ROOM.
UH-HUH.
TIME TRAVEL AND PARALLEL UNIVERSES
TIME PARADOXES FOR DUMMIES
I'VE DONE SOME RESEARCH BASED ON WHAT YOU TOLD ME.
IT APPEARS THESE "DO-OVERS" ARE ONE POSSIBLE RESULT OF TRAVELING BACK AND FORTH BETWEEN PARALLEL WORLDS.
IT'S POSSIBLE THAT THE IMAMURA-KUN YOU KNEW WILL BRIEFLY VISIT THIS WORLD ONCE: THREE YEARS FROM NOW.
WOULD IT HAVE CHANGED THE CAPTAIN'S FATE?

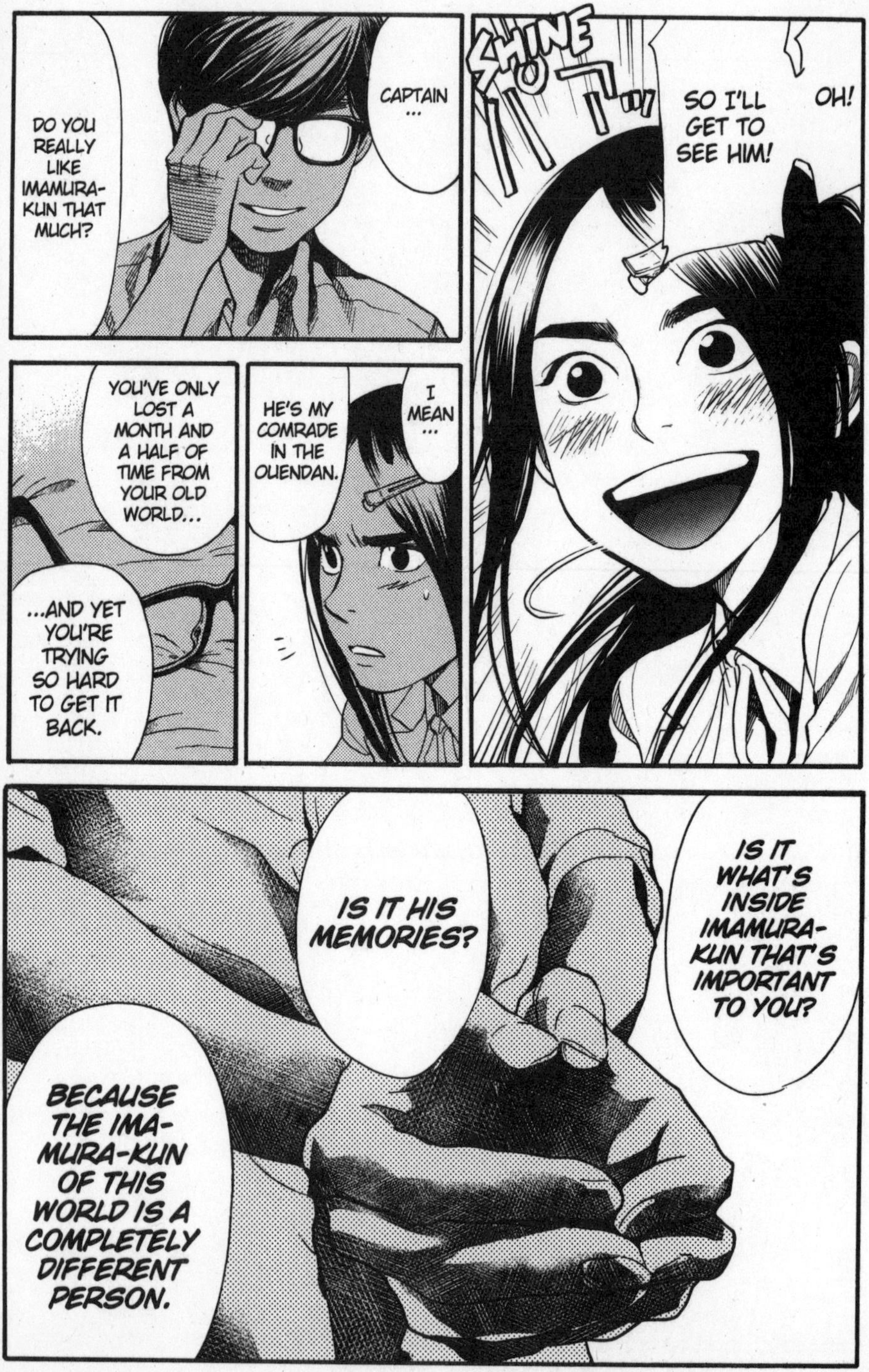
OH!
SO I'LL GET TO SEE HIM!
SHINE
CAPTAIN...
DO YOU REALLY LIKE IMAMURA-KUN THAT MUCH?
I MEAN...
HE'S MY COMRADE IN THE OUENDAN.
YOU'VE ONLY LOST A MONTH AND A HALF OF TIME FROM YOUR OLD WORLD...
...AND YET YOU'RE TRYING SO HARD TO GET IT BACK.
IS IT WHAT'S INSIDE IMAMURA-KUN THAT'S IMPORTANT TO YOU?
IS IT HIS MEMORIES?
BECAUSE THE IMA-MURA-KUN OF THIS WORLD IS A COMPLETELY DIFFERENT PERSON.

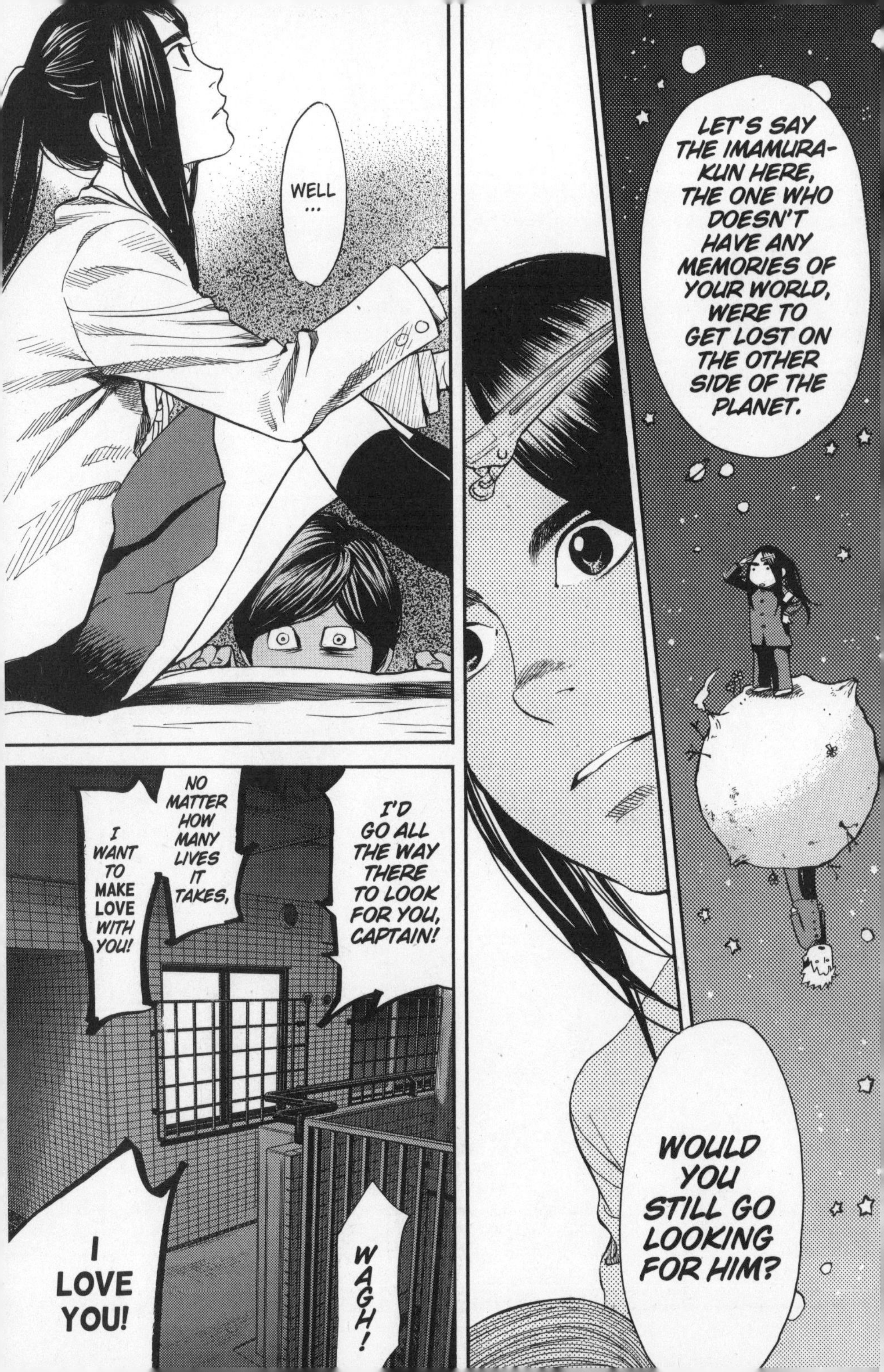
LET'S SAY THE IMAMURA-KUN HERE, THE ONE WHO DOESN'T HAVE ANY MEMORIES OF YOUR WORLD, WERE TO GET LOST ON THE OTHER SIDE OF THE PLANET.
WOULD YOU STILL GO LOOKING FOR HIM?
WELL ...
I'D GO ALL THE WAY THERE TO LOOK FOR YOU, CAPTAIN!
NO MATTER HOW MANY LIVES IT TAKES,
I WANT TO MAKE LOVE WITH YOU!
WAGH!
I LOVE YOU!

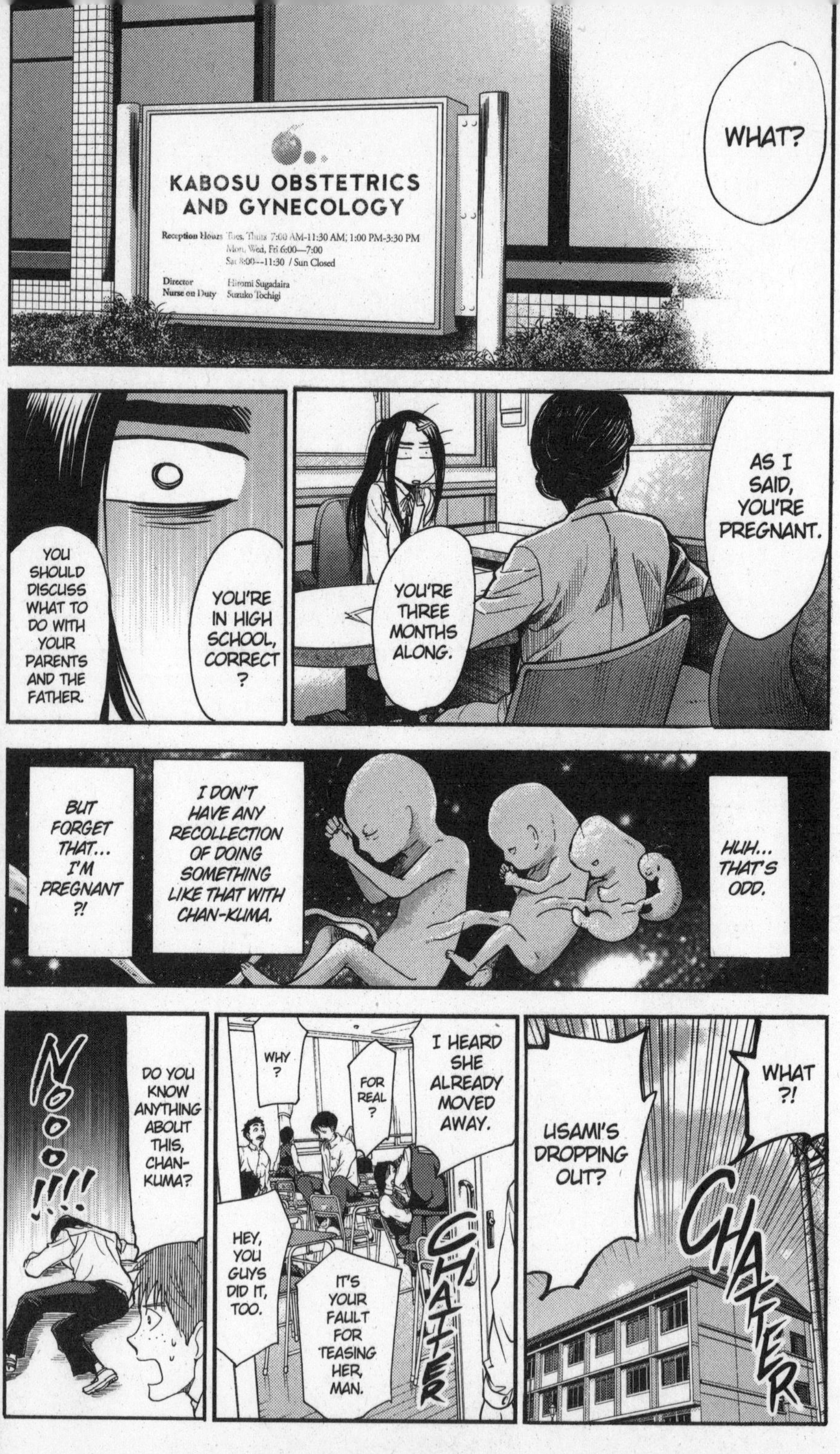
WHAT?
KABOSU OBSTETRICS AND GYNECOLOGY
Reception Hours Tues, Thurs 7:00 AM-11:30 AM, 1:00 PM-3:30 PM
Mon, Wed, Fri 6:00—7:00
Sat 8:00--11:30 / Sun Closed
Director Hiromi Sugadaira
Nurse on Duty Suzuko Tochigi
AS I SAID, YOU'RE PREGNANT.
YOU'RE THREE MONTHS ALONG.
YOU'RE IN HIGH SCHOOL, CORRECT?
YOU SHOULD DISCUSS WHAT TO DO WITH YOUR PARENTS AND THE FATHER.
HUH... THAT'S ODD.
I DON'T HAVE ANY RECOLLECTION OF DOING SOMETHING LIKE THAT WITH CHAN-KUMA.
BUT FORGET THAT... I'M PREGNANT?!
WHAT?!
USAMI'S DROPPING OUT?
CHATTER
I HEARD SHE ALREADY MOVED AWAY.
FOR REAL?
WHY?
CHATTER
IT'S YOUR FAULT FOR TEASING HER, MAN.
HEY, YOU GUYS DID IT, TOO.
DO YOU KNOW ANYTHING ABOUT THIS, CHAN-KUMA?
NOOO!!!

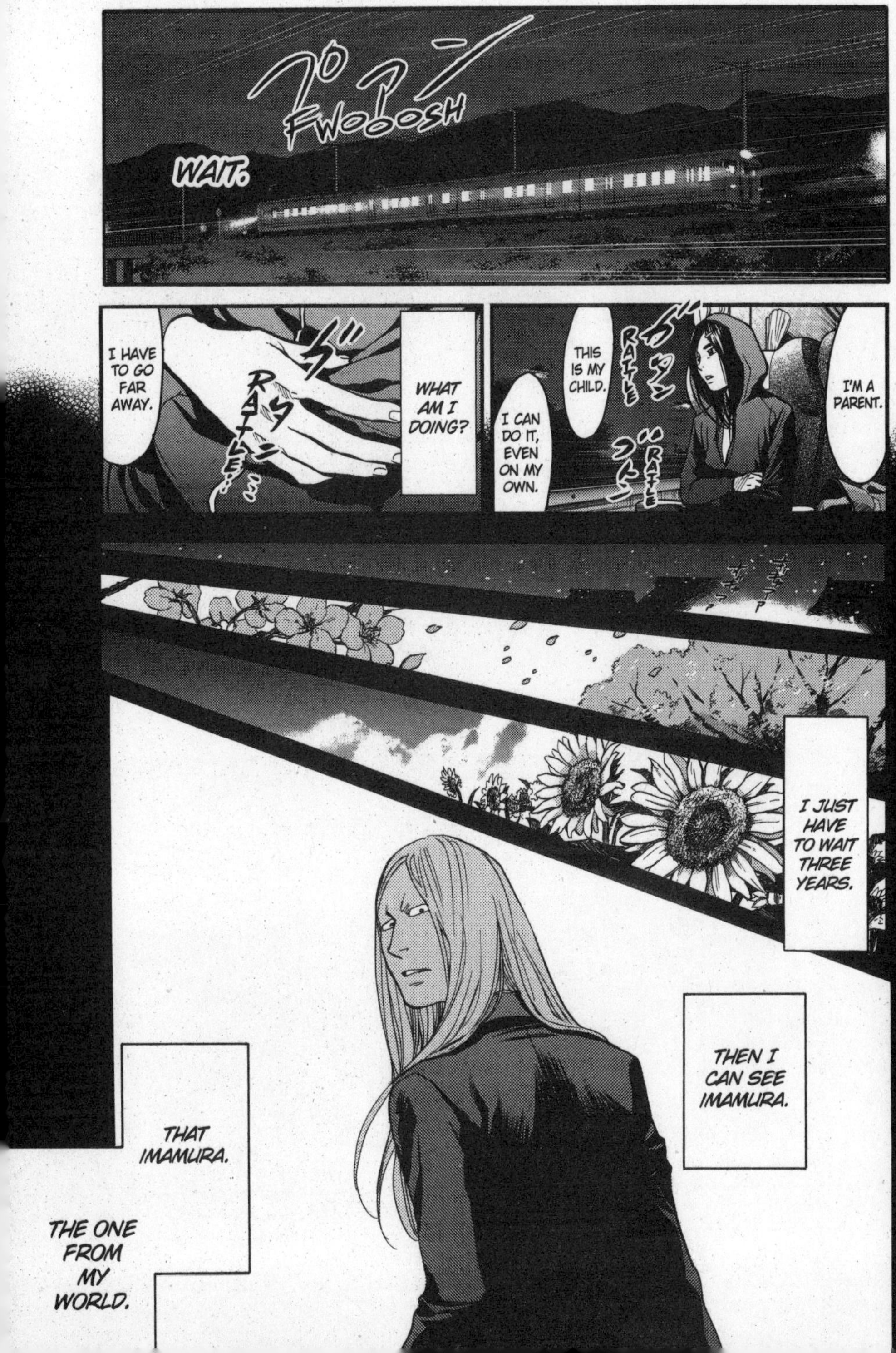
FWOOOSH
WAIT.
I'M A PARENT.
RATTLE
THIS IS MY CHILD.
RATTLE
I CAN DO IT, EVEN ON MY OWN.
WHAT AM I DOING?
RATTLE...
I HAVE TO GO FAR AWAY.
I JUST HAVE TO WAIT THREE YEARS.
THEN I CAN SEE IMAMURA.
THAT IMAMURA.
THE ONE FROM MY WORLD.

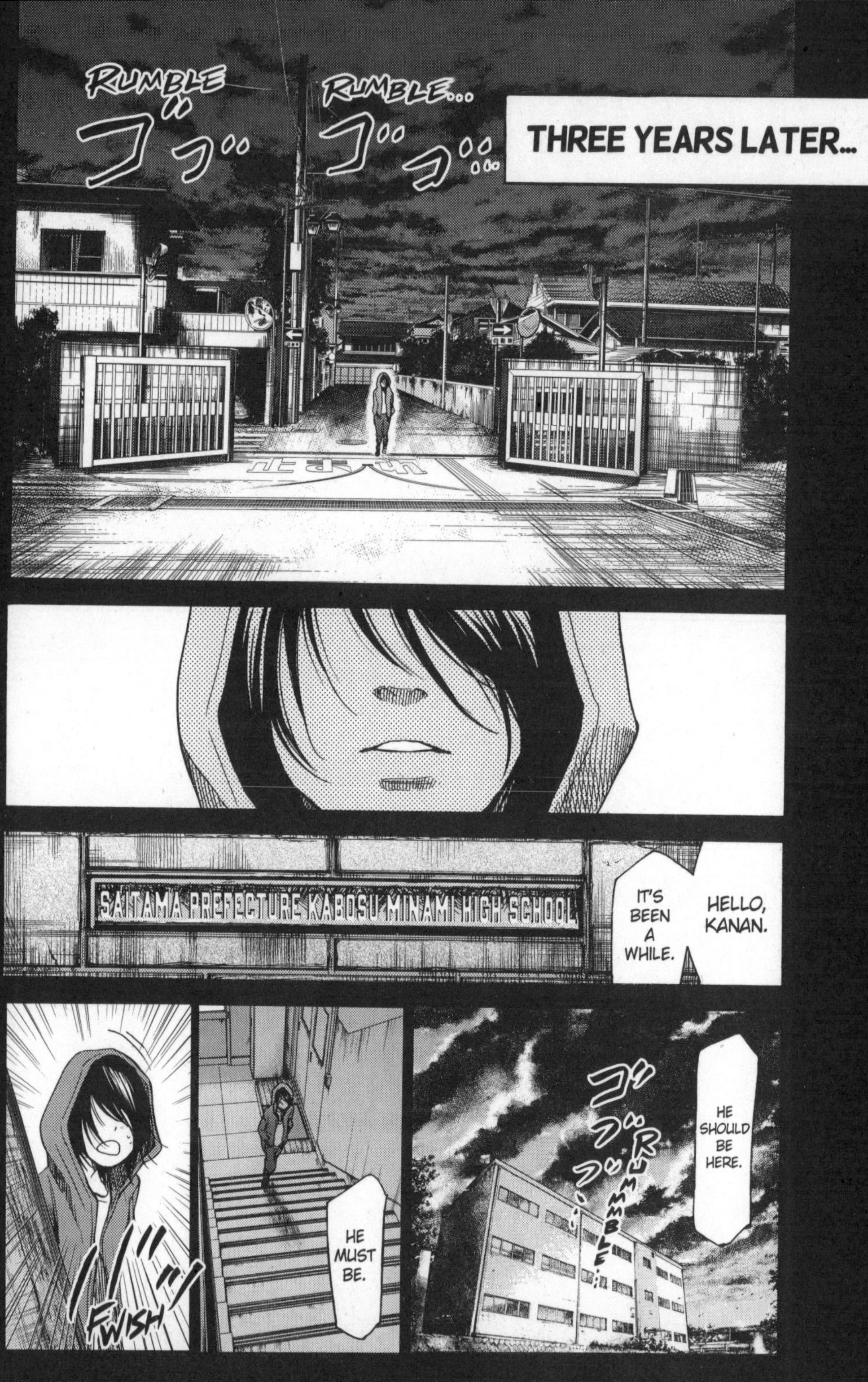
THREE YEARS LATER...
RUMBLE...
RUMBLE
HELLO, KANAN.
IT'S BEEN A WHILE.
SAITAMA PREFECTURE KABOSU MINAMI HIGH SCHOOL
HE SHOULD BE HERE.
RUMMMBLE...
HE MUST BE.
FWISH

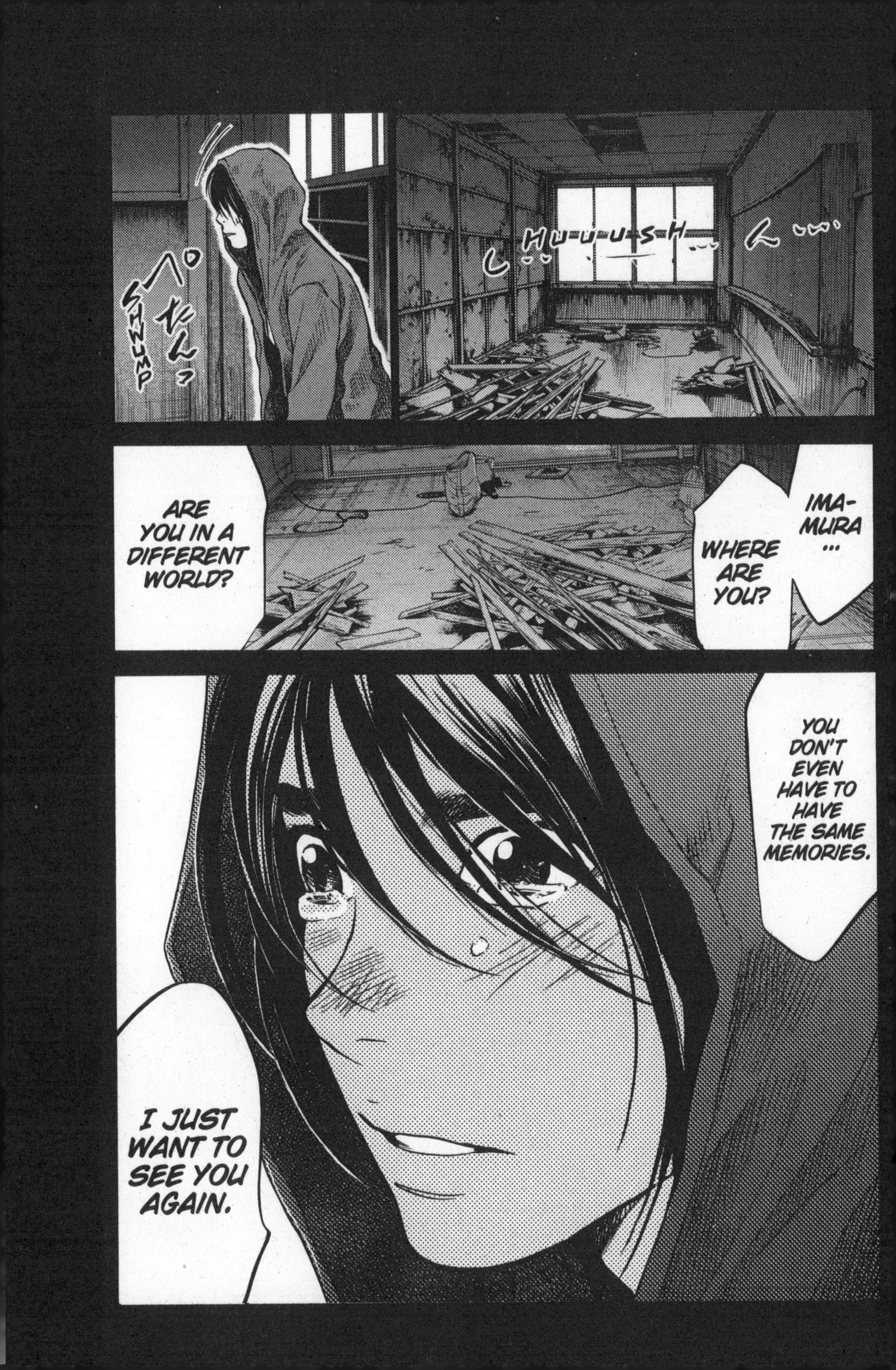
HUUUUSH...
SHWUMP
IMAMURA...
WHERE ARE YOU?
ARE YOU IN A DIFFERENT WORLD?
YOU DON'T EVEN HAVE TO HAVE THE SAME MEMORIES.
I JUST WANT TO SEE YOU AGAIN.

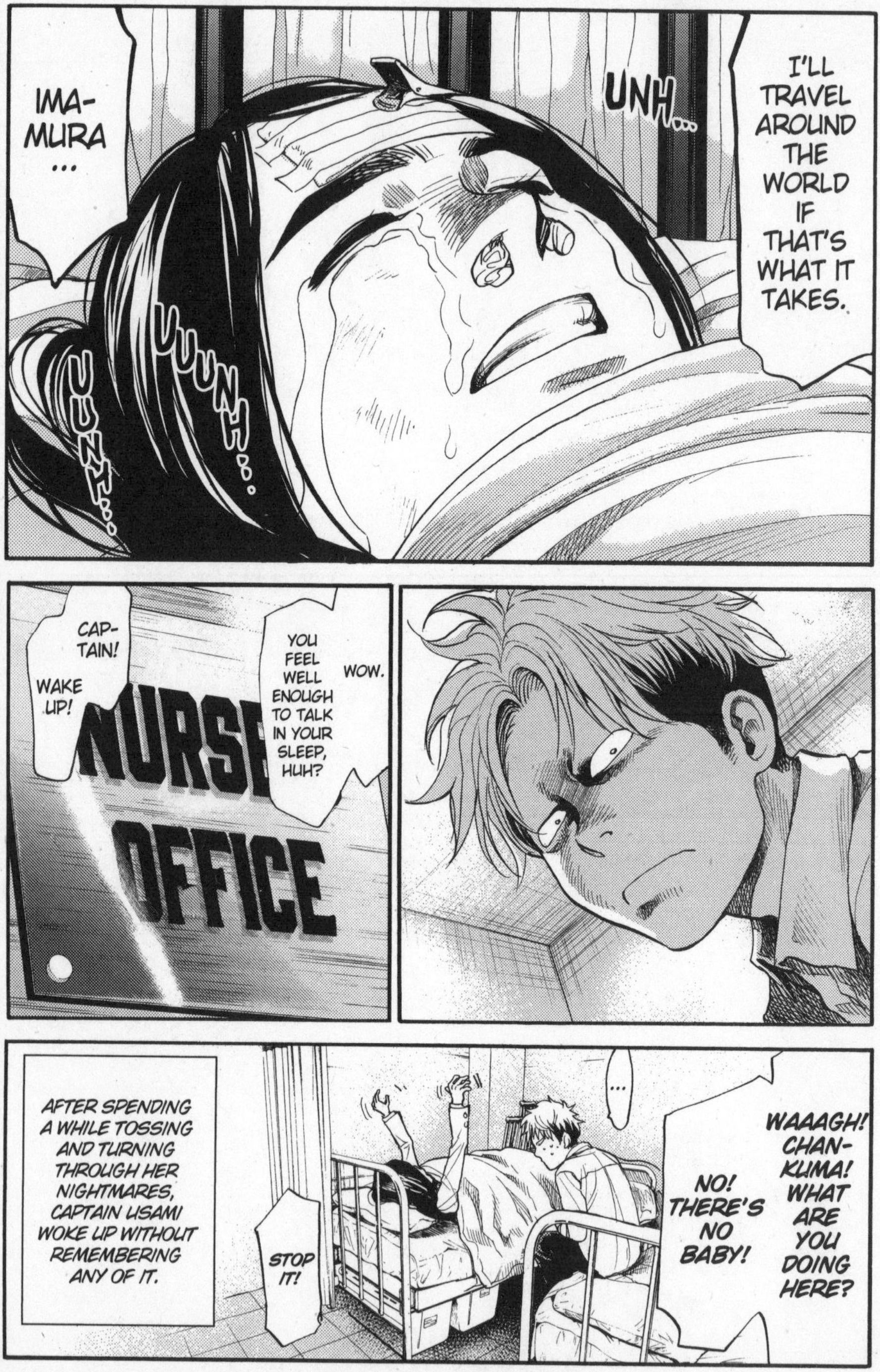
I'LL TRAVEL AROUND THE WORLD IF THAT'S WHAT IT TAKES.
UNH...
UUUNH...
UUNH...
IMA-MURA...
WOW.
YOU FEEL WELL ENOUGH TO TALK IN YOUR SLEEP, HUH?
CAP-TAIN!
WAKE UP!
NURSE OFFICE
WAAAGH! CHAN-KUMA! WHAT ARE YOU DOING HERE?
...
NO! THERE'S NO BABY!
STOP IT!
AFTER SPENDING A WHILE TOSSING AND TURNING THROUGH HER NIGHTMARES, CAPTAIN USAMI WOKE UP WITHOUT REMEMBERING ANY OF IT.

Again!!

アゲイン!!

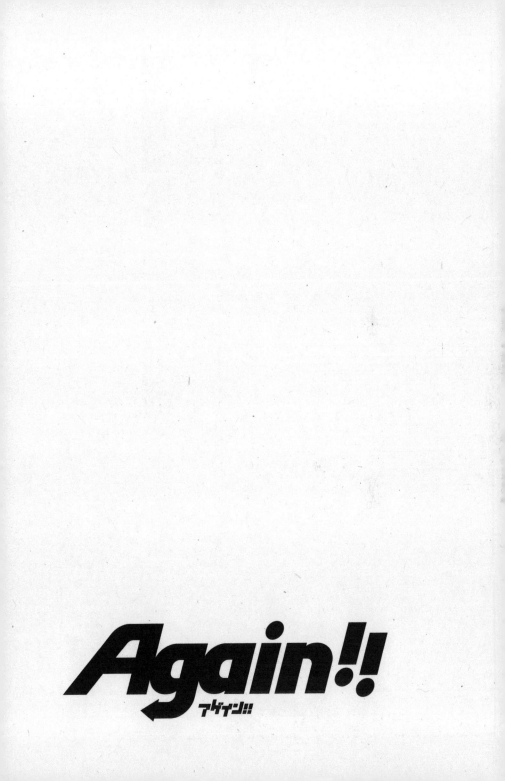

Again!!

アゲイン!!

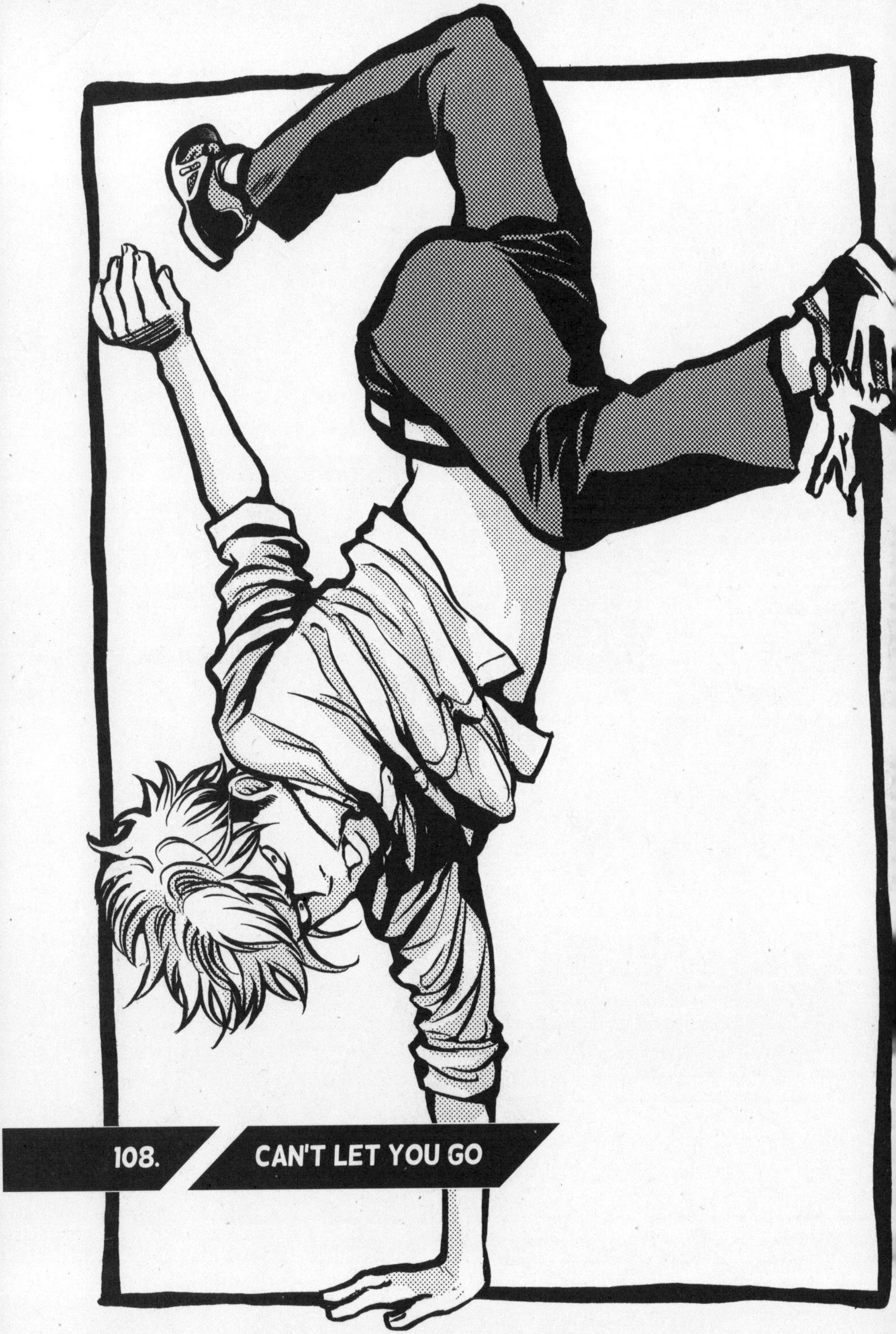

108.
CAN'T LET YOU GO

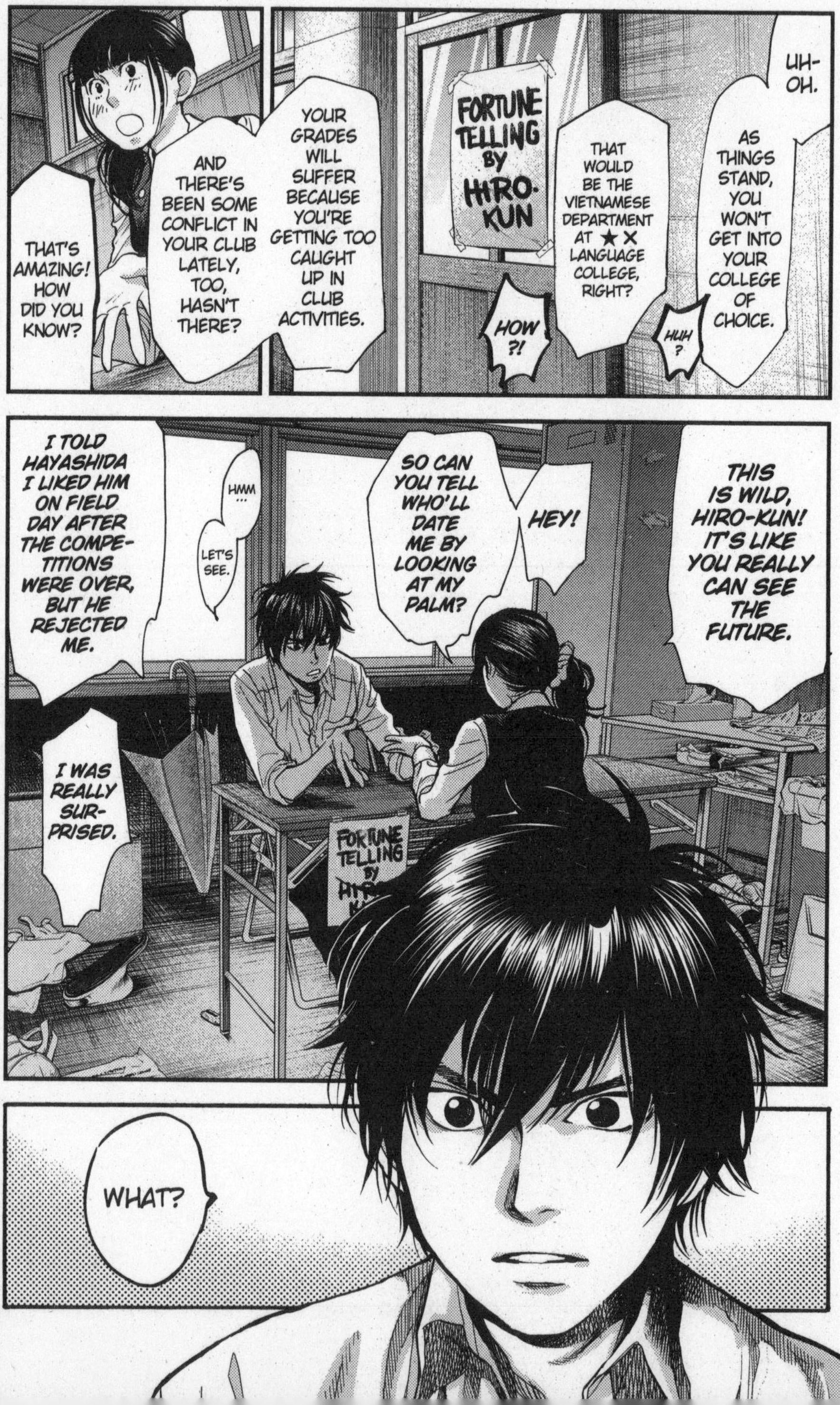
UH-OH.
AS THINGS STAND, YOU WON'T GET INTO YOUR COLLEGE OF CHOICE.
HUH?
THAT WOULD BE THE VIETNAMESE DEPARTMENT AT ★✕ LANGUAGE COLLEGE, RIGHT?
HOW?!
FORTUNE TELLING BY HIRO-KUN
YOUR GRADES WILL SUFFER BECAUSE YOU'RE GETTING TOO CAUGHT UP IN CLUB ACTIVITIES.
AND THERE'S BEEN SOME CONFLICT IN YOUR CLUB LATELY, TOO, HASN'T THERE?
THAT'S AMAZING! HOW DID YOU KNOW?
THIS IS WILD, HIRO-KUN! IT'S LIKE YOU REALLY CAN SEE THE FUTURE.
HEY!
SO CAN YOU TELL WHO'LL DATE ME BY LOOKING AT MY PALM?
HMM...
LET'S SEE.
I TOLD HAYASHIDA I LIKED HIM ON FIELD DAY AFTER THE COMPETITIONS WERE OVER, BUT HE REJECTED ME.
I WAS REALLY SURPRISED.
WHAT?

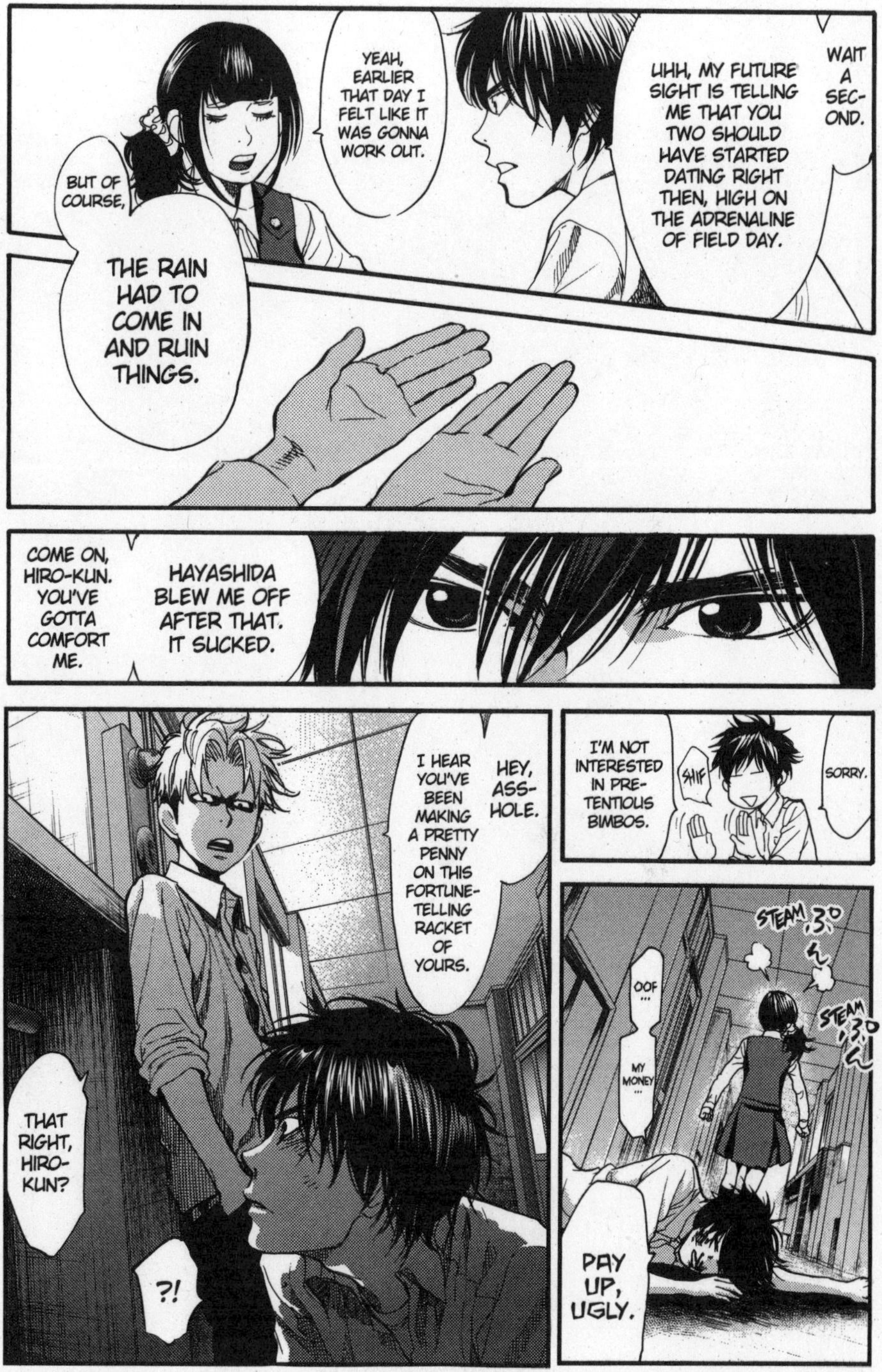
WAIT A SEC-OND.
UHH, MY FUTURE SIGHT IS TELLING ME THAT YOU TWO SHOULD HAVE STARTED DATING RIGHT THEN, HIGH ON THE ADRENALINE OF FIELD DAY.
YEAH, EARLIER THAT DAY I FELT LIKE IT WAS GONNA WORK OUT.
BUT OF COURSE,
THE RAIN HAD TO COME IN AND RUIN THINGS.
HAYASHIDA BLEW ME OFF AFTER THAT. IT SUCKED.
COME ON, HIRO-KUN. YOU'VE GOTTA COMFORT ME.
SORRY.
SHIF
I'M NOT INTERESTED IN PRE-TENTIOUS BIMBOS.
STEAM
STEAM
OOF...
MY MONEY...
PAY UP, UGLY.
HEY, ASS-HOLE.
I HEAR YOU'VE BEEN MAKING A PRETTY PENNY ON THIS FORTUNE-TELLING RACKET OF YOURS.
THAT RIGHT, HIRO-KUN?
?!

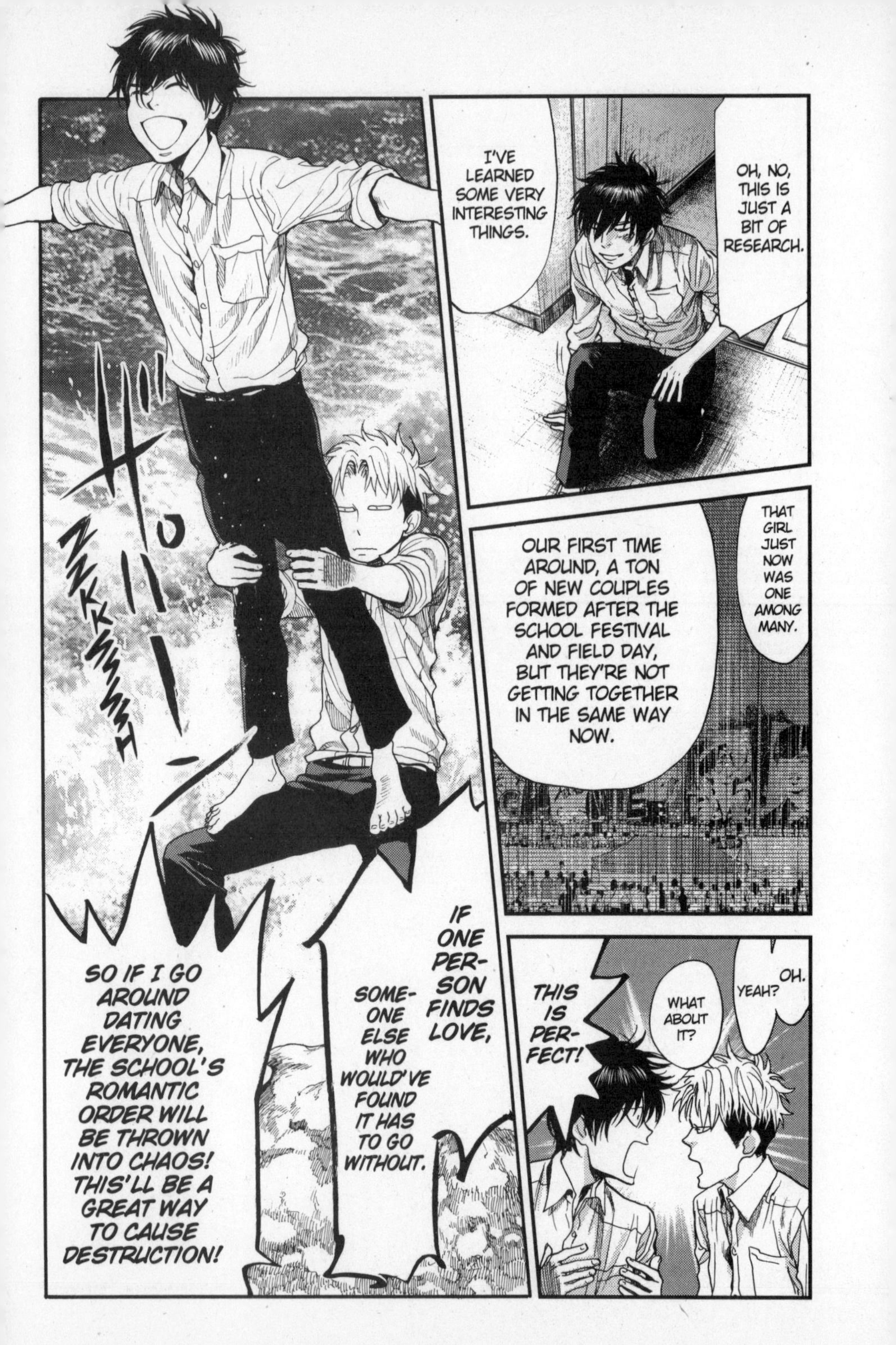
OH, NO, THIS IS JUST A BIT OF RESEARCH.
I'VE LEARNED SOME VERY INTERESTING THINGS.
THAT GIRL JUST NOW WAS ONE AMONG MANY.
OUR FIRST TIME AROUND, A TON OF NEW COUPLES FORMED AFTER THE SCHOOL FESTIVAL AND FIELD DAY, BUT THEY'RE NOT GETTING TOGETHER IN THE SAME WAY NOW.
OH. YEAH?
WHAT ABOUT IT?
THIS IS PERFECT!
IF ONE PERSON FINDS LOVE,
SOMEONE ELSE WHO WOULD'VE FOUND IT HAS TO GO WITHOUT.
SO IF I GO AROUND DATING EVERYONE, THE SCHOOL'S ROMANTIC ORDER WILL BE THROWN INTO CHAOS! THIS'LL BE A GREAT WAY TO CAUSE DESTRUCTION!

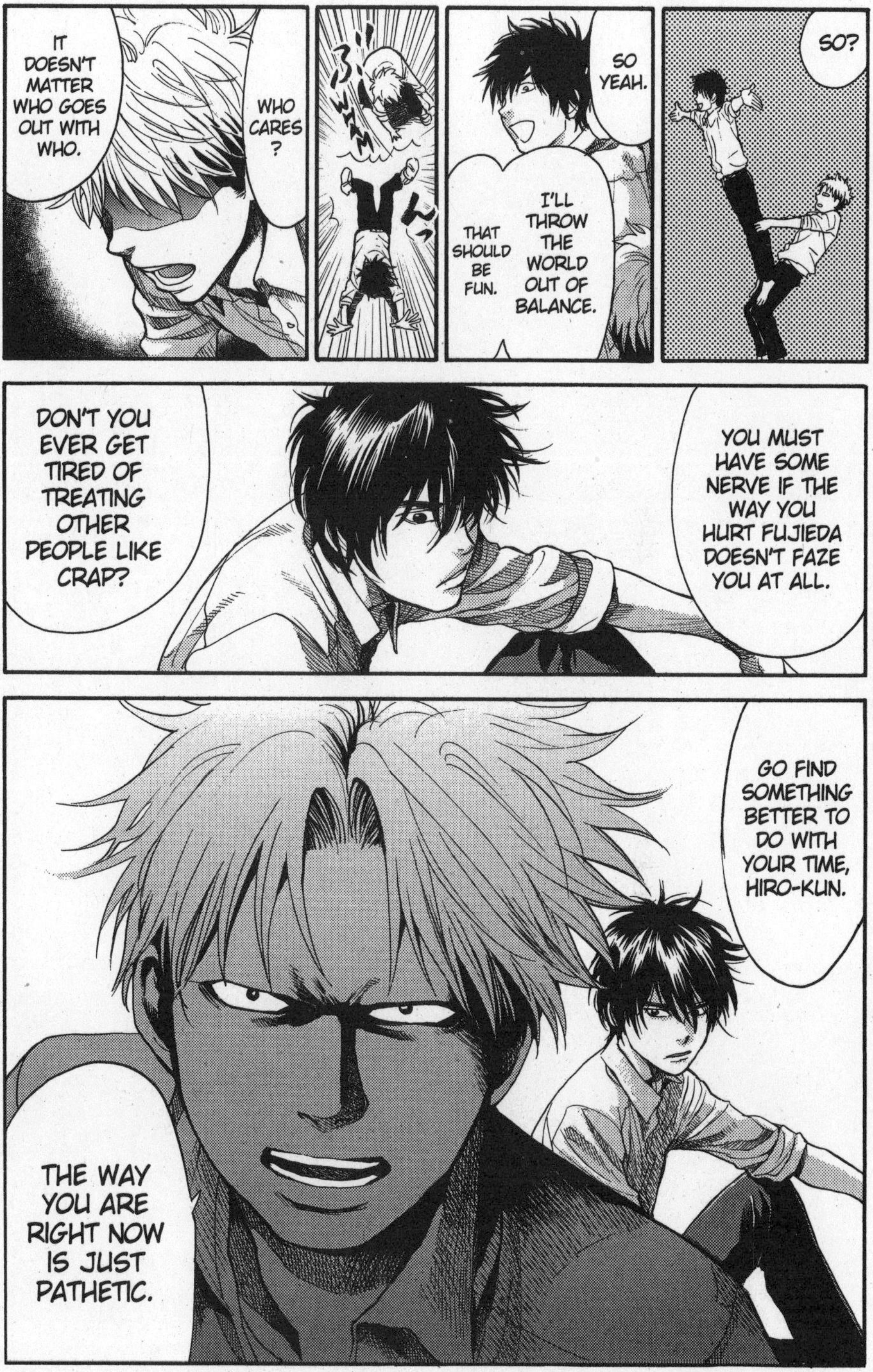
SO?
SO YEAH.
I'LL THROW THE WORLD OUT OF BALANCE.
THAT SHOULD BE FUN.
WHO CARES?
WHAM
IT DOESN'T MATTER WHO GOES OUT WITH WHO.
YOU MUST HAVE SOME NERVE IF THE WAY YOU HURT FUJIEDA DOESN'T FAZE YOU AT ALL.
DON'T YOU EVER GET TIRED OF TREATING OTHER PEOPLE LIKE CRAP?
GO FIND SOMETHING BETTER TO DO WITH YOUR TIME, HIRO-KUN.
THE WAY YOU ARE RIGHT NOW IS JUST PATHETIC.

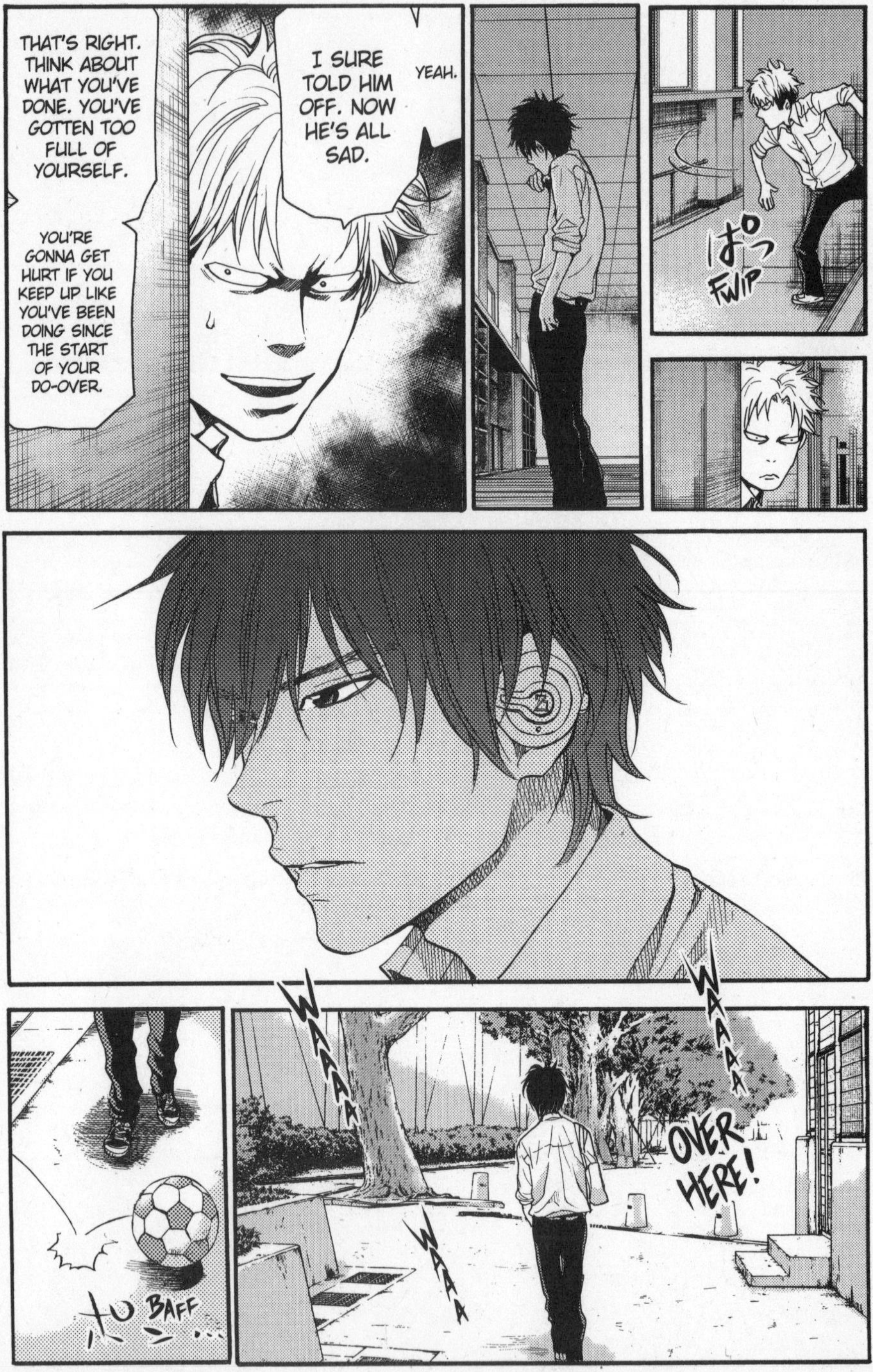
ぱっ
FWIP
YEAH.
I SURE TOLD HIM OFF. NOW HE'S ALL SAD.
THAT'S RIGHT. THINK ABOUT WHAT YOU'VE DONE. YOU'VE GOTTEN TOO FULL OF YOURSELF.
YOU'RE GONNA GET HURT IF YOU KEEP UP LIKE YOU'VE BEEN DOING SINCE THE START OF YOUR DO-OVER.
WAAAAA
OVER HERE!
WAAAA
WAAAA
BAFF

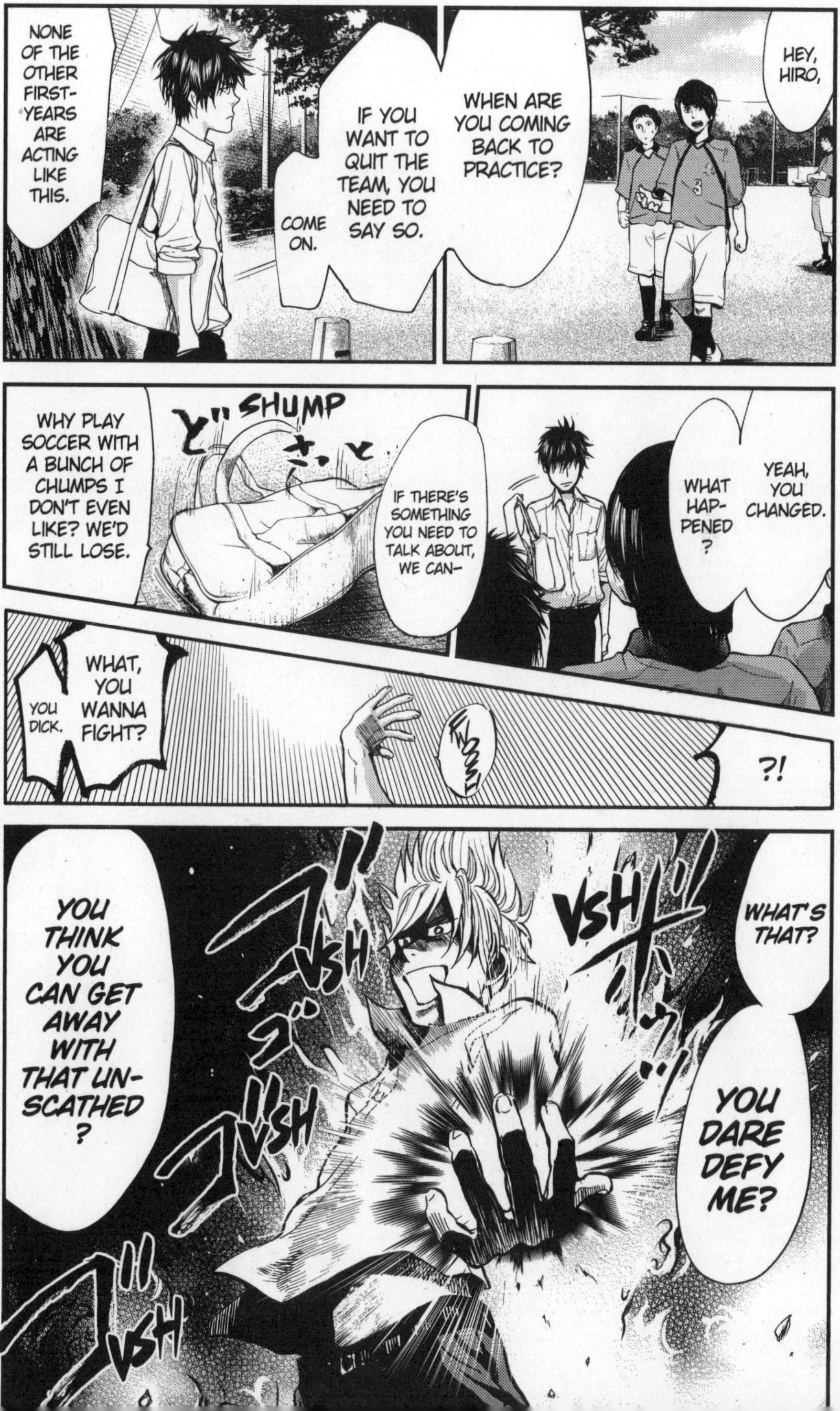
HEY, HIRO,
WHEN ARE YOU COMING BACK TO PRACTICE?
IF YOU WANT TO QUIT THE TEAM, YOU NEED TO SAY SO.
COME ON.
NONE OF THE OTHER FIRST-YEARS ARE ACTING LIKE THIS.
YEAH, YOU CHANGED.
WHAT HAPPENED?
IF THERE'S SOMETHING YOU NEED TO TALK ABOUT, WE CAN-
SHUMP
WHY PLAY SOCCER WITH A BUNCH OF CHUMPS I DON'T EVEN LIKE? WE'D STILL LOSE.
?!
FWOOSH
WHAT, YOU WANNA FIGHT?
YOU DICK.
WHAT'S THAT?
YOU DARE DEFY ME?
VSH
VSH
VSH
VSH
YOU THINK YOU CAN GET AWAY WITH THAT UN-SCATHED?

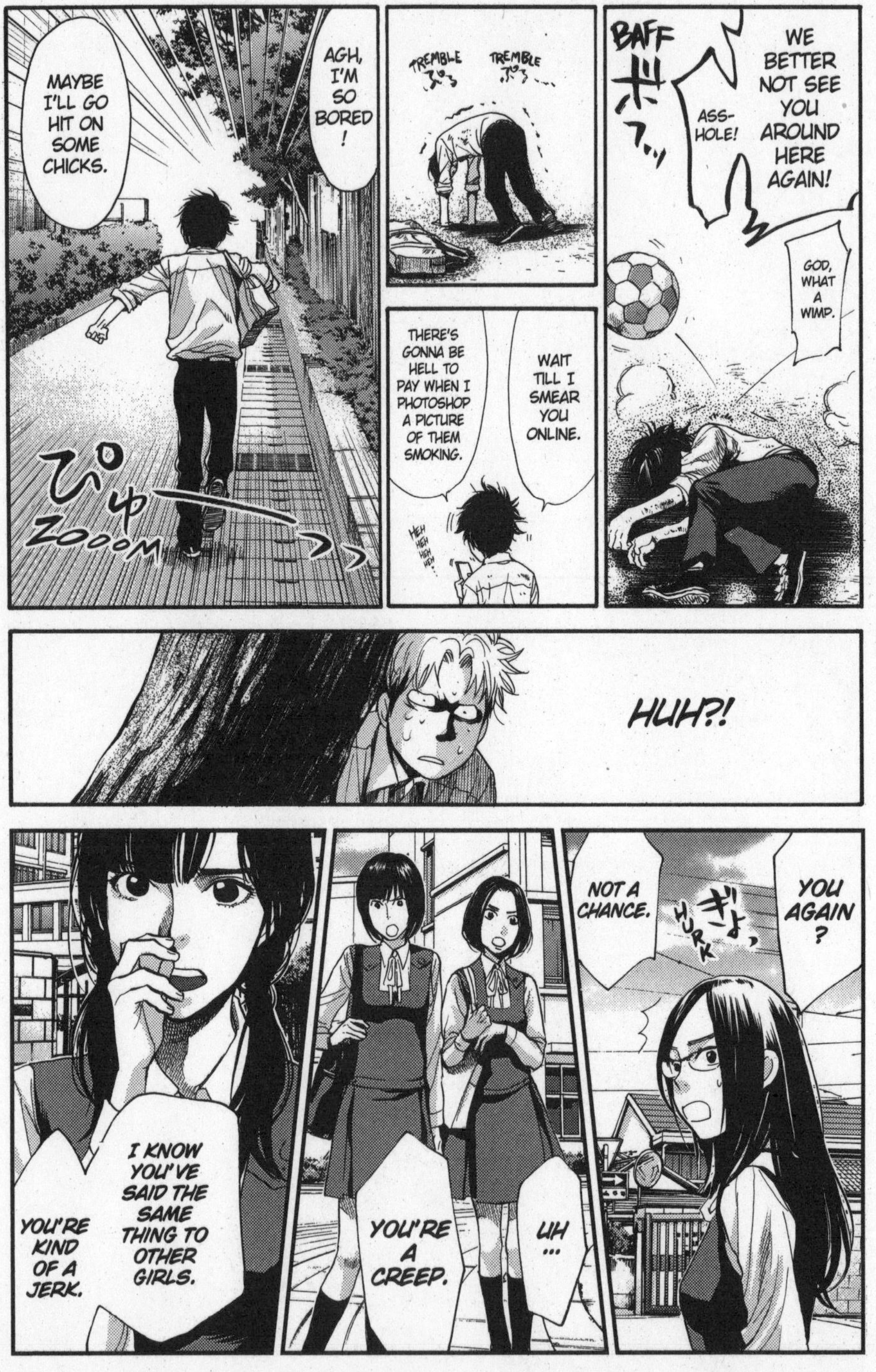
BAFF
WE BETTER NOT SEE YOU AROUND HERE AGAIN!
ASS-HOLE!
GOD, WHAT A WIMP.
TREMBLE
TREMBLE
WAIT TILL I SMEAR YOU ONLINE.
THERE'S GONNA BE HELL TO PAY WHEN I PHOTOSHOP A PICTURE OF THEM SMOKING.
HEH HEH HEH HEH
AGH, I'M SO BORED!
MAYBE I'LL GO HIT ON SOME CHICKS.
ZOOOM
HUH?!
YOU AGAIN?
HURK
NOT A CHANCE.
UH...
YOU'RE A CREEP.
I KNOW YOU'VE SAID THE SAME THING TO OTHER GIRLS.
YOU'RE KIND OF A JERK.

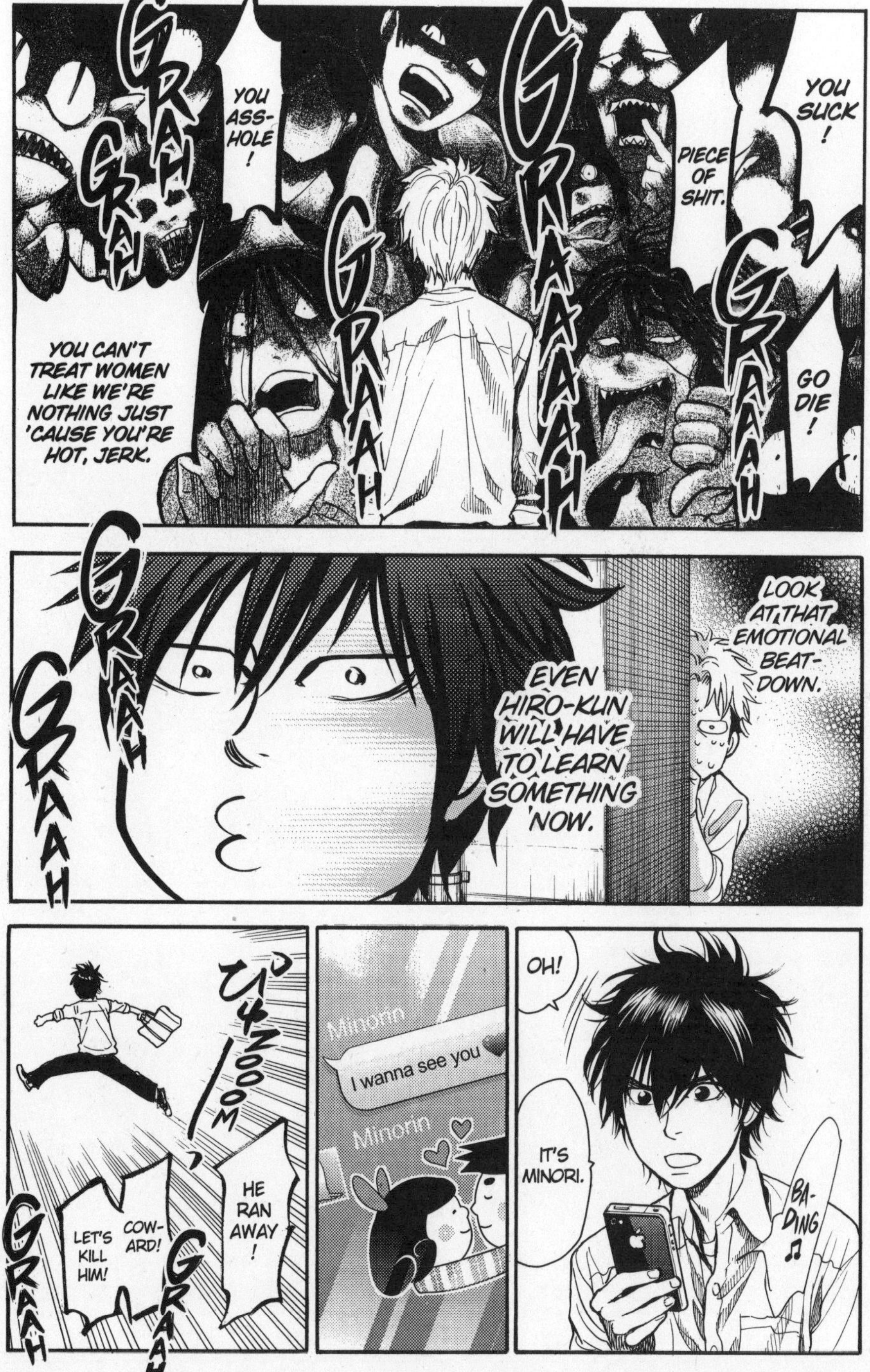
YOU SUCK!
PIECE OF SHIT.
GRAAAAAH
GRAAAH
GO DIE!
YOU ASSHOLE!
GRAAH
GRAAH
GRAAAH
YOU CAN'T TREAT WOMEN LIKE WE'RE NOTHING JUST 'CAUSE YOU'RE HOT, JERK.
LOOK AT THAT EMOTIONAL BEAT-DOWN.
EVEN HIRO-KUN WILL HAVE TO LEARN SOMETHING NOW.
GRAAH
GRAAAH
OH!
IT'S MINORI.
BA-DING ♪
Minorin
I wanna see you
Minorin
ZOOOOM
HE RAN AWAY!
COW-ARD!
LET'S KILL HIM!
GRAAH
GRAAH

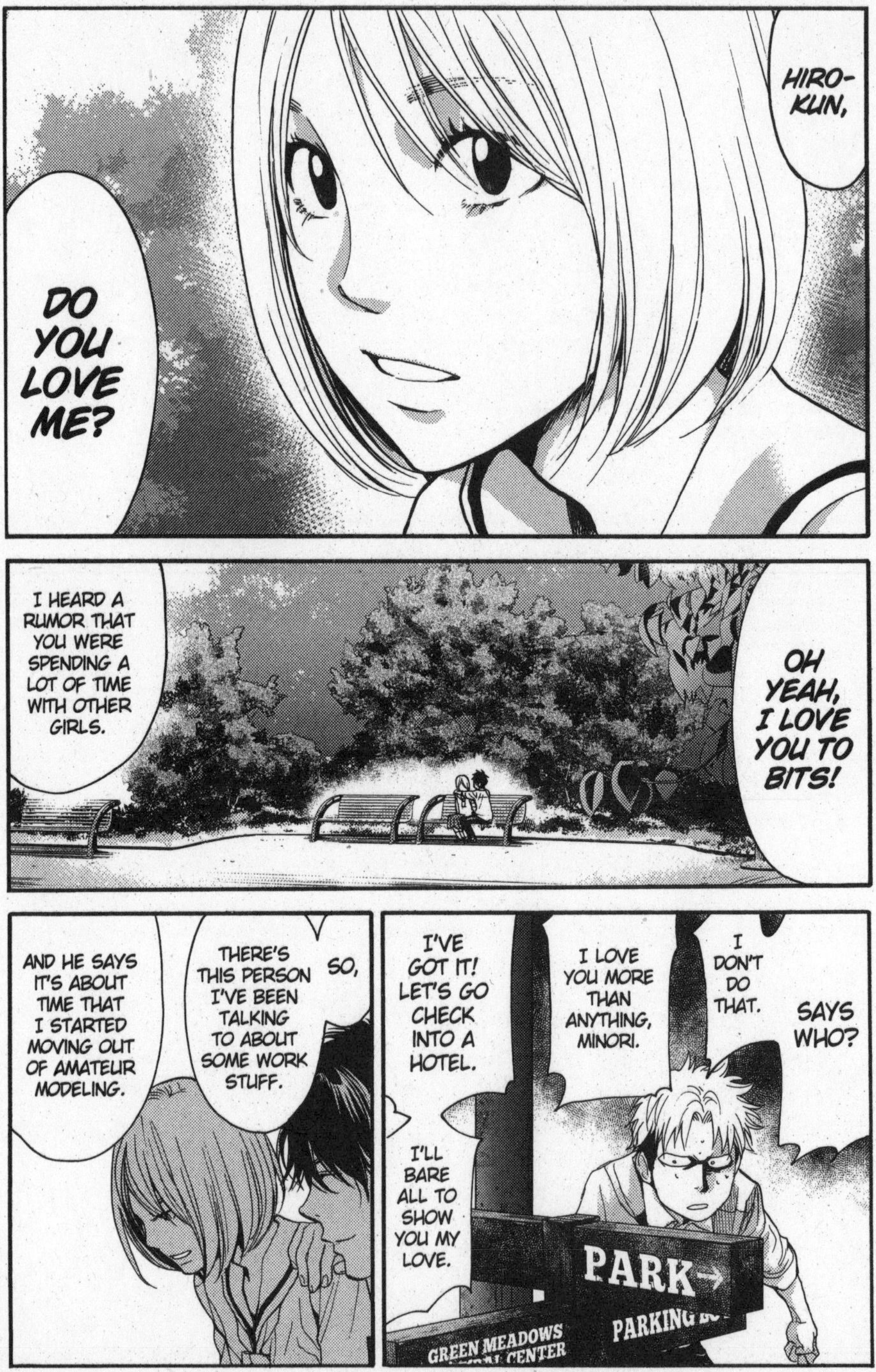
HIRO-KUN,
DO YOU LOVE ME?
OH YEAH, I LOVE YOU TO BITS!
I HEARD A RUMOR THAT YOU WERE SPENDING A LOT OF TIME WITH OTHER GIRLS.
I DON'T DO THAT.
SAYS WHO?
I LOVE YOU MORE THAN ANYTHING, MINORI.
I'VE GOT IT! LET'S GO CHECK INTO A HOTEL.
I'LL BARE ALL TO SHOW YOU MY LOVE.
PARK→
PARKING
GREEN MEADOWS
SO,
THERE'S THIS PERSON I'VE BEEN TALKING TO ABOUT SOME WORK STUFF.
AND HE SAYS IT'S ABOUT TIME THAT I STARTED MOVING OUT OF AMATEUR MODELING.

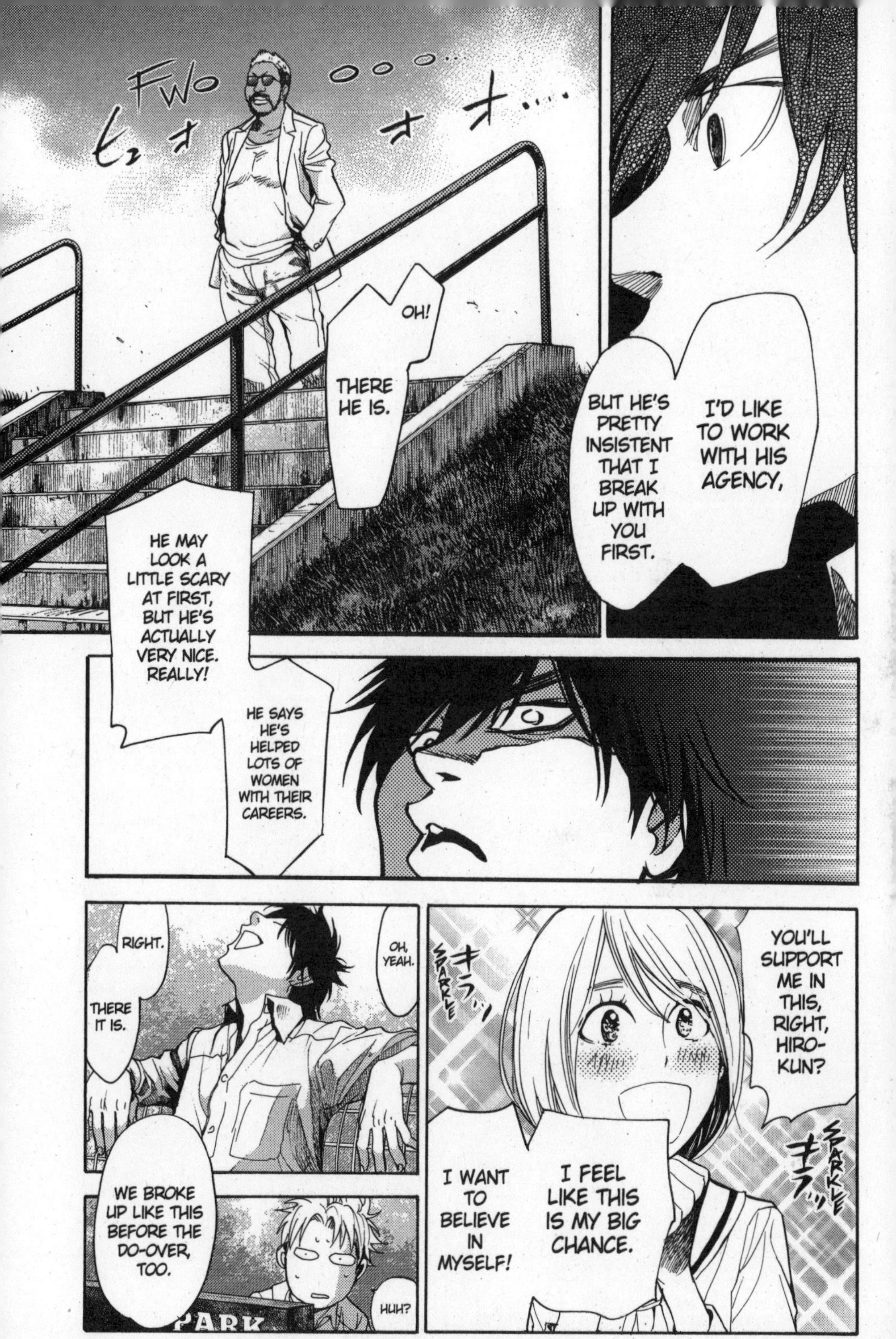
I'D LIKE TO WORK WITH HIS AGENCY,
BUT HE'S PRETTY INSISTENT THAT I BREAK UP WITH YOU FIRST.
FWO OOO...
ヒュオオオ….
OH!
THERE HE IS.
HE MAY LOOK A LITTLE SCARY AT FIRST, BUT HE'S ACTUALLY VERY NICE. REALLY!
HE SAYS HE'S HELPED LOTS OF WOMEN WITH THEIR CAREERS.
YOU'LL SUPPORT ME IN THIS, RIGHT, HIRO-KUN?
SPARKLE
キラッ
SPARKLE
キラッ
I FEEL LIKE THIS IS MY BIG CHANCE.
I WANT TO BELIEVE IN MYSELF!
OH, YEAH.
RIGHT.
THERE IT IS.
HUH?
WE BROKE UP LIKE THIS BEFORE THE DO-OVER, TOO.
PARK

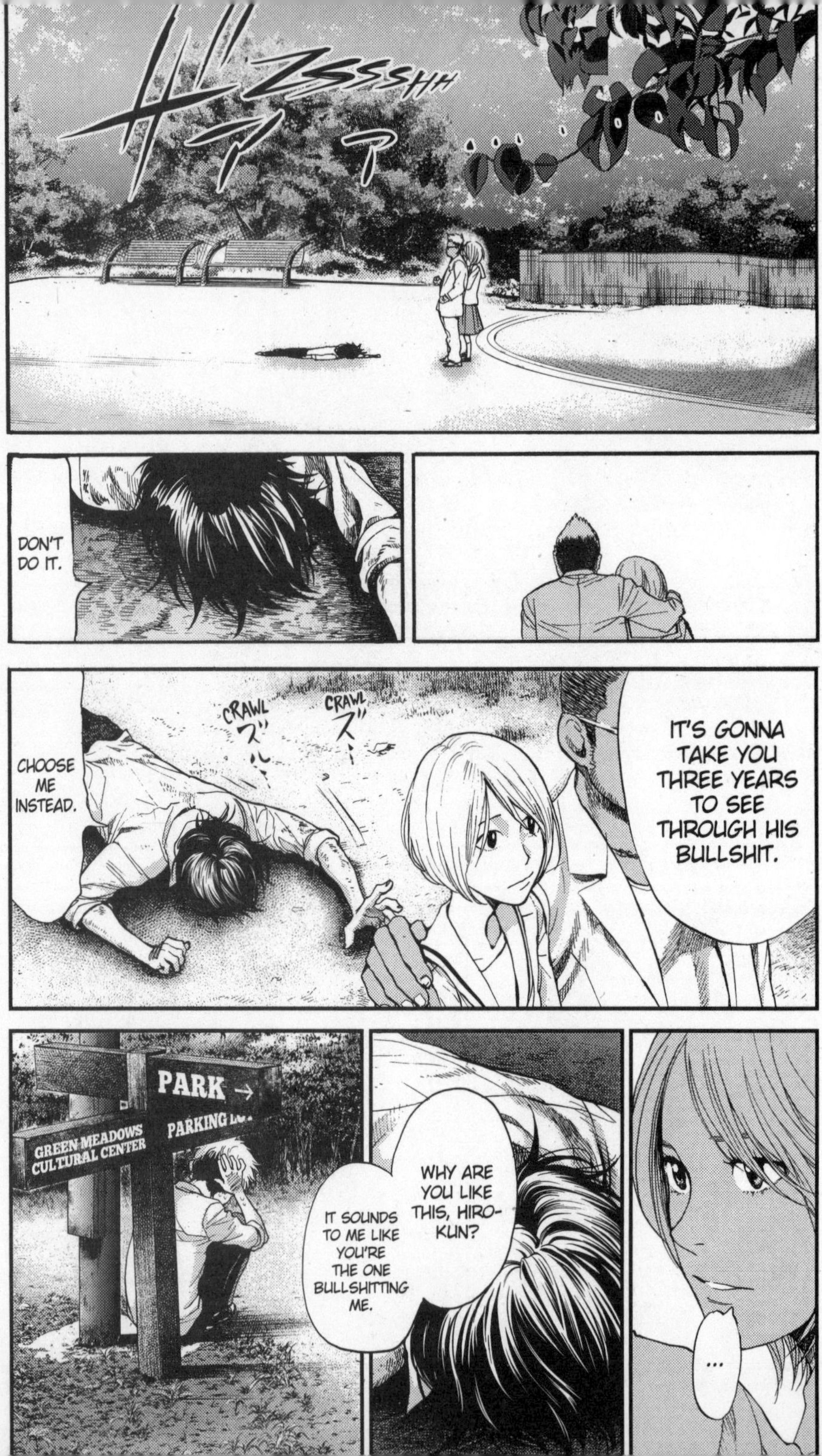
ZSSSSHH
DON'T DO IT.
IT'S GONNA TAKE YOU THREE YEARS TO SEE THROUGH HIS BULLSHIT.
CRAWL
CRAWL
CHOOSE ME INSTEAD.
...
WHY ARE YOU LIKE THIS, HIRO-KUN?
IT SOUNDS TO ME LIKE YOU'RE THE ONE BULLSHITTING ME.
PARK →
GREEN MEADOWS CULTURAL CENTER

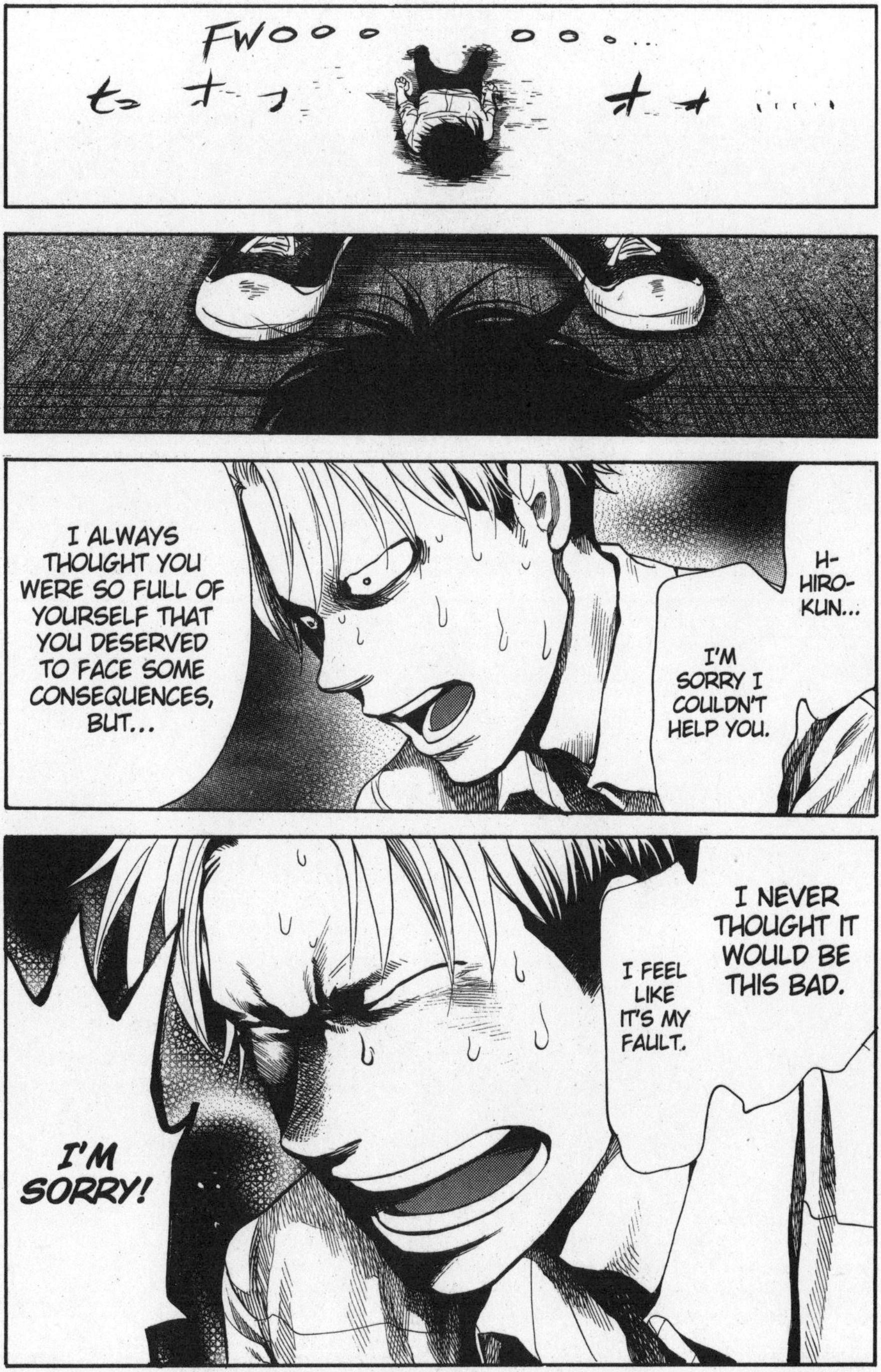
FWOOO OOO...
H- HIRO-KUN...
I'M SORRY I COULDN'T HELP YOU.
I ALWAYS THOUGHT YOU WERE SO FULL OF YOURSELF THAT YOU DESERVED TO FACE SOME CONSEQUENCES, BUT...
I NEVER THOUGHT IT WOULD BE THIS BAD.
I FEEL LIKE IT'S MY FAULT.
I'M SORRY!

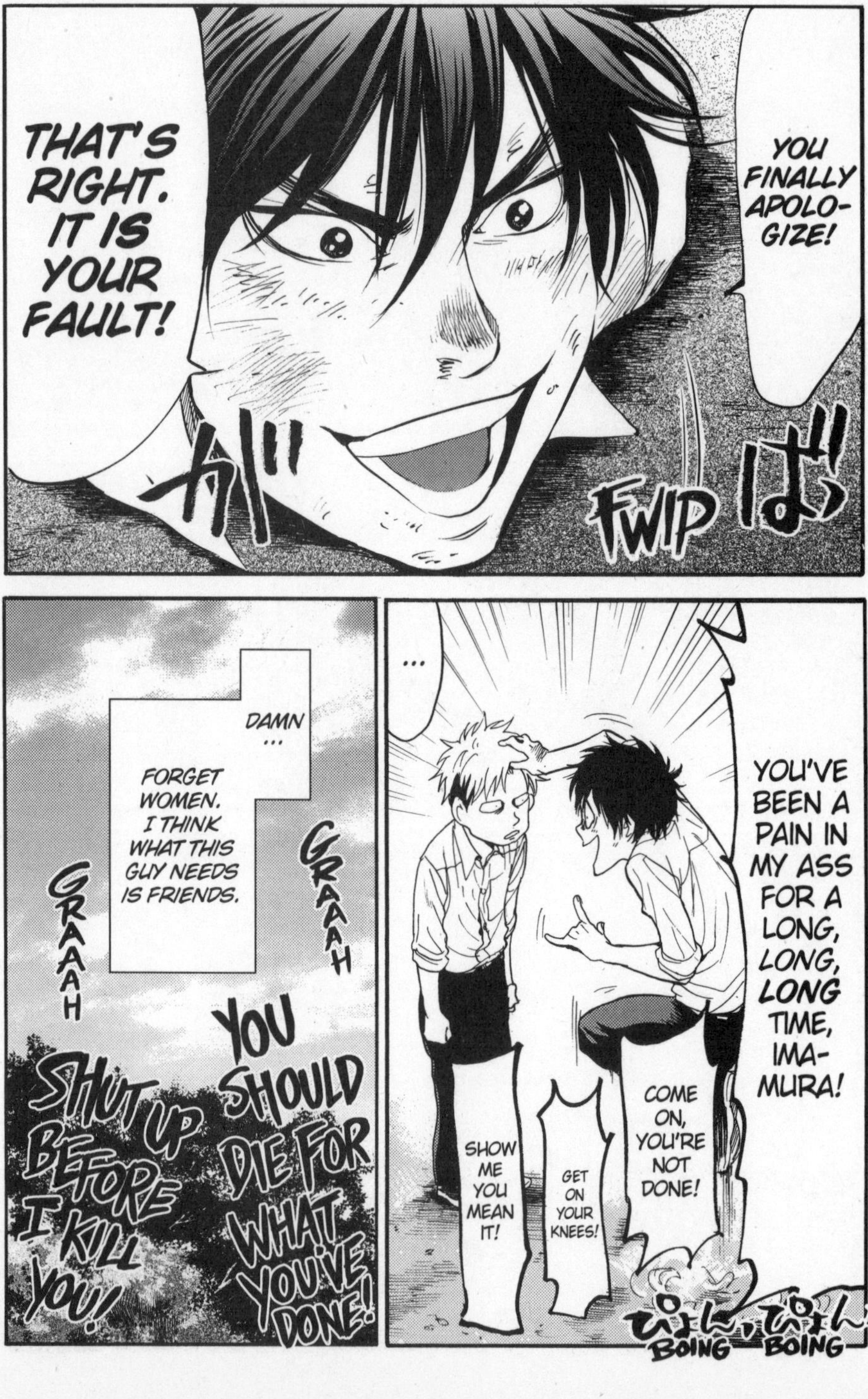
YOU FINALLY APOLOGIZE!
THAT'S RIGHT. IT IS YOUR FAULT!
ば! FWIP
ガ
...
YOU'VE BEEN A PAIN IN MY ASS FOR A LONG, LONG, LONG TIME, IMAMURA!
COME ON, YOU'RE NOT DONE!
GET ON YOUR KNEES!
SHOW ME YOU MEAN IT!
ぴょん、ぴょん BOING BOING
DAMN...
FORGET WOMEN. I THINK WHAT THIS GUY NEEDS IS FRIENDS.
GRAAAH
YOU SHOULD DIE FOR WHAT YOU'VE DONE!
GRAAAH
SHUT UP BEFORE I KILL YOU!

109. NEVER MIND, GRANDMA

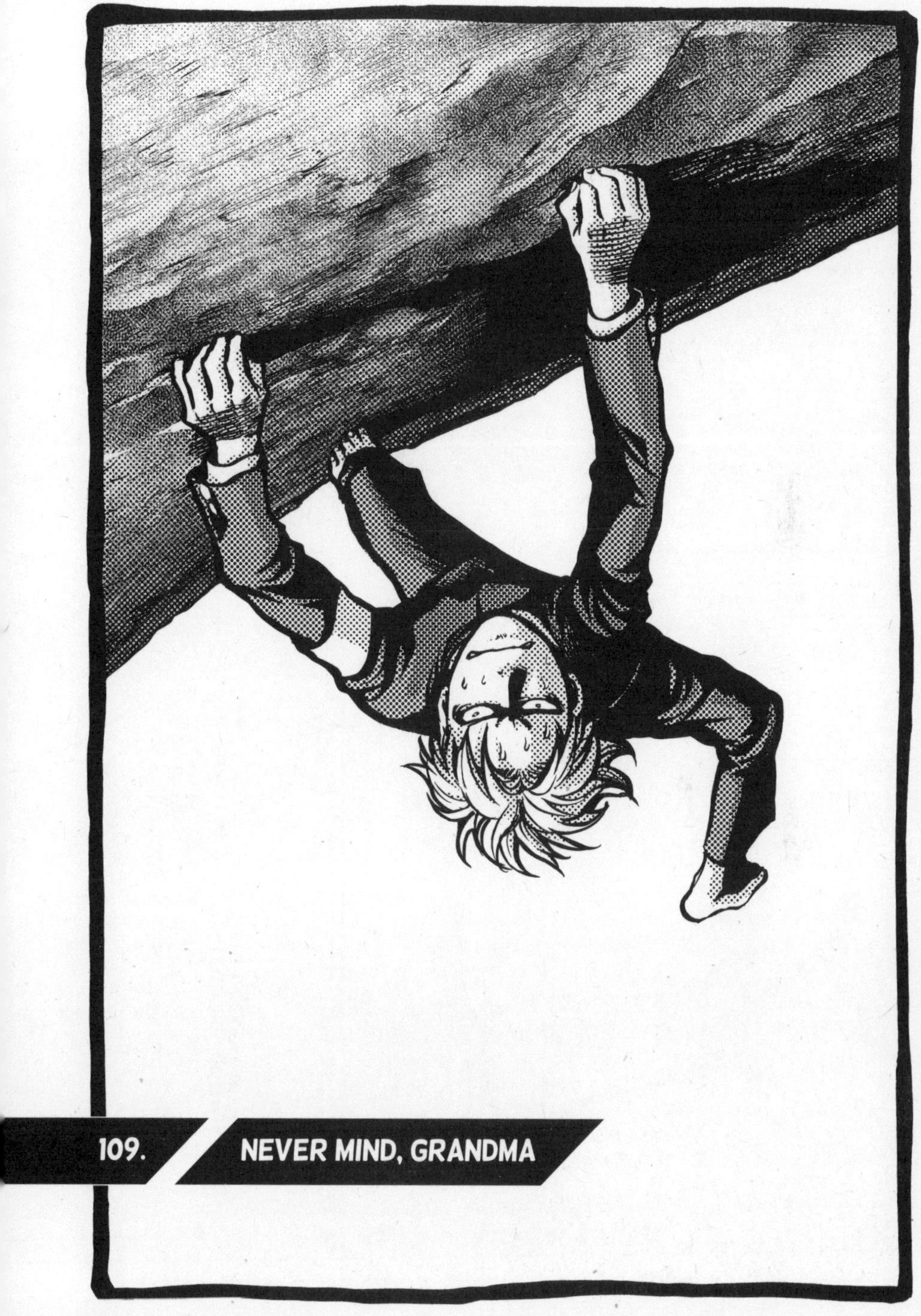

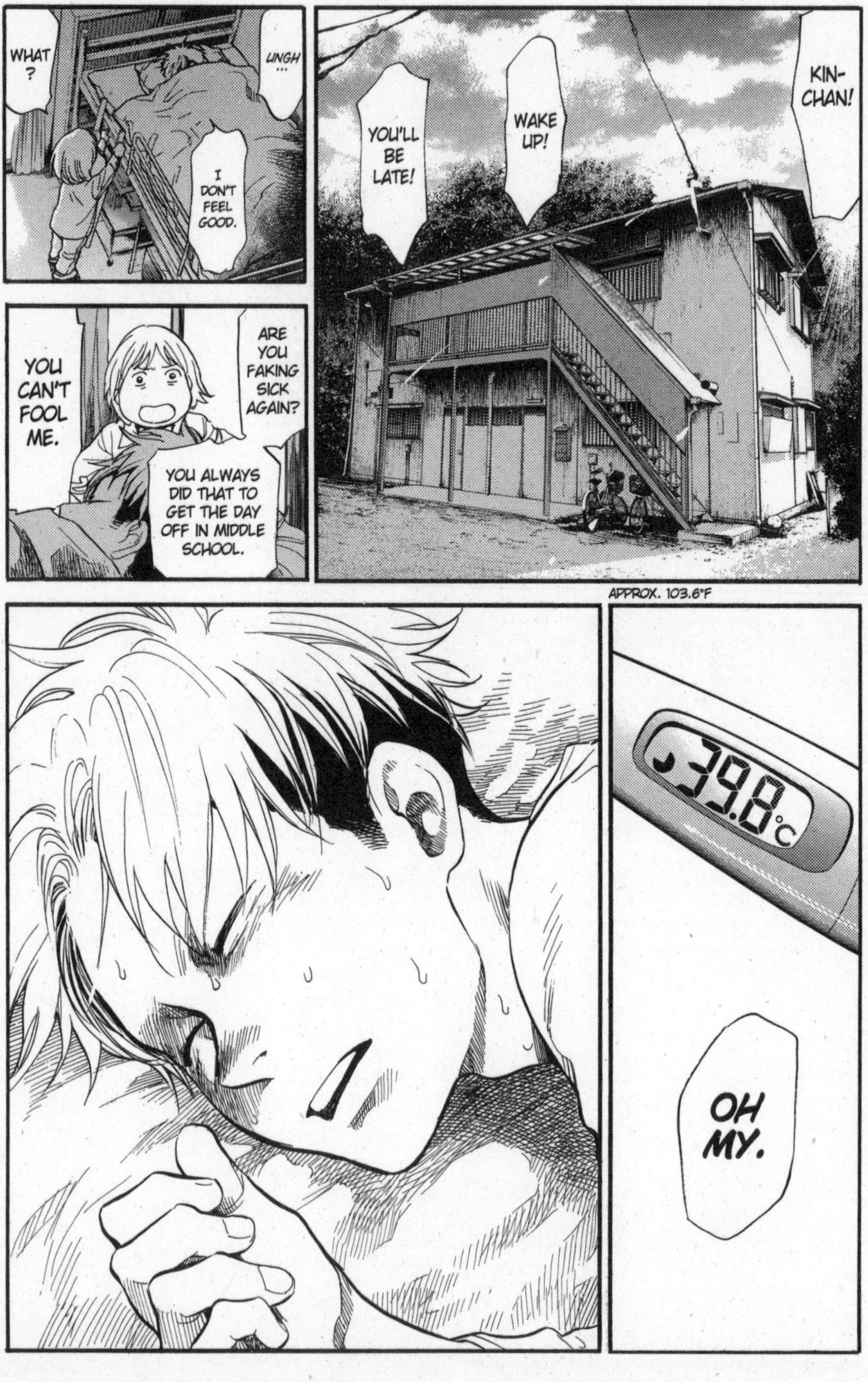
KIN-CHAN!
WAKE UP!
YOU'LL BE LATE!
UNGH ...
I DON'T FEEL GOOD.
WHAT?
ARE YOU FAKING SICK AGAIN?
YOU ALWAYS DID THAT TO GET THE DAY OFF IN MIDDLE SCHOOL.
YOU CAN'T FOOL ME.
APPROX. 103.6°F
39.8°C
OH MY.

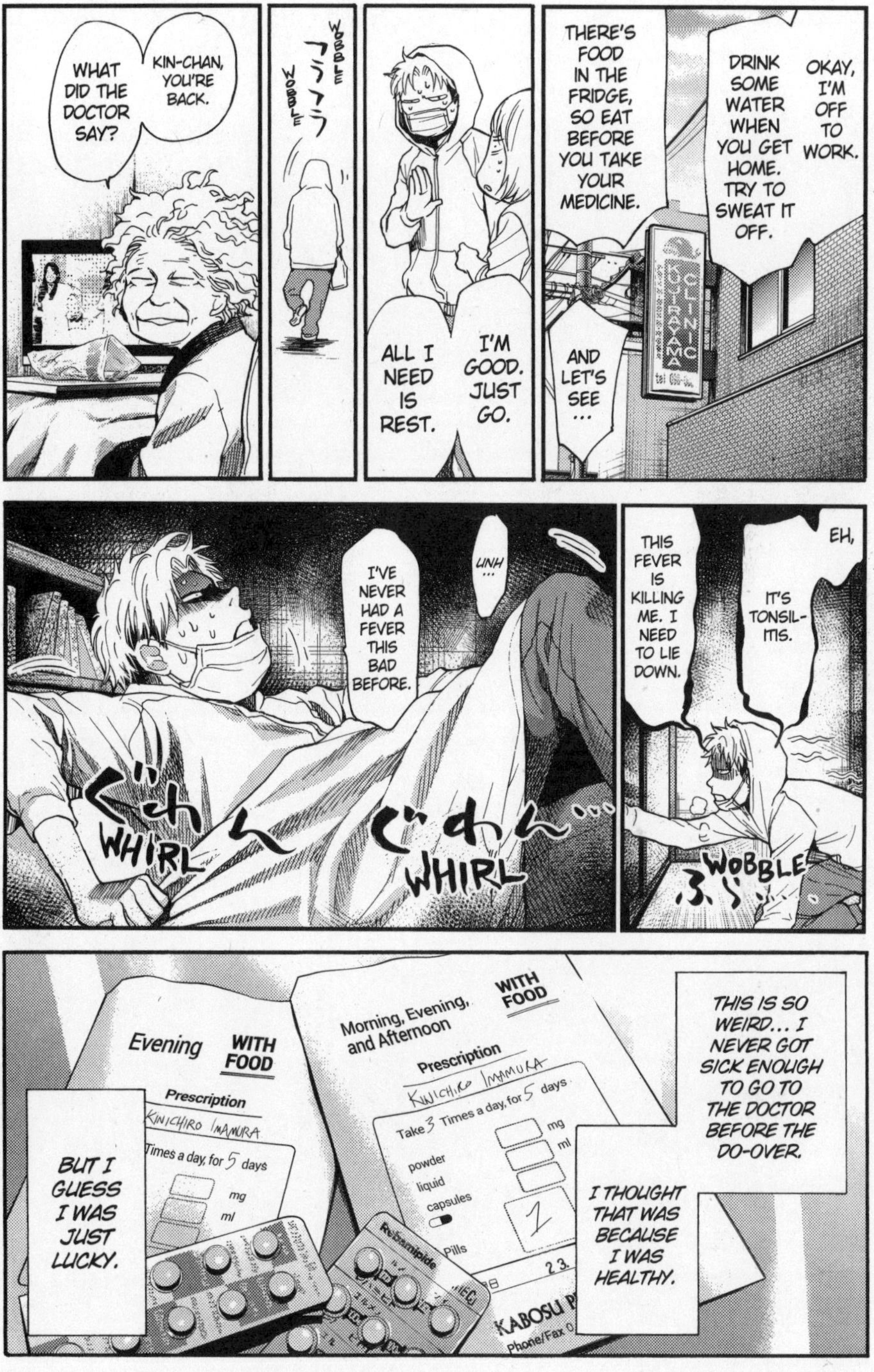
OKAY, I'M OFF TO WORK.
DRINK SOME WATER WHEN YOU GET HOME. TRY TO SWEAT IT OFF.
THERE'S FOOD IN THE FRIDGE, SO EAT BEFORE YOU TAKE YOUR MEDICINE.
AND LET'S SEE …
I'M GOOD. JUST GO.
ALL I NEED IS REST.
WOBBLE
フラフラ
WOBBLE
KIN-CHAN, YOU'RE BACK.
WHAT DID THE DOCTOR SAY?
EH,
IT'S TONSIL-ITIS.
THIS FEVER IS KILLING ME. I NEED TO LIE DOWN.
ふら…
WOBBLE
UNH …
I'VE NEVER HAD A FEVER THIS BAD BEFORE.
ぐわん
WHIRL
ぐわん…
WHIRL
THIS IS SO WEIRD… I NEVER GOT SICK ENOUGH TO GO TO THE DOCTOR BEFORE THE DO-OVER.
I THOUGHT THAT WAS BECAUSE I WAS HEALTHY.
Morning, Evening, and Afternoon
WITH FOOD
Prescription
KINICHIRO IMAMURA
Take 3 Times a day, for 5 days
mg
ml
powder
liquid
capsules
Pills
1
KABOSU P
Phone/Fax
Rebamipide
Evening
WITH FOOD
Prescription
KINICHIRO IMAMURA
Times a day, for 5 days
mg
ml
BUT I GUESS I WAS JUST LUCKY.

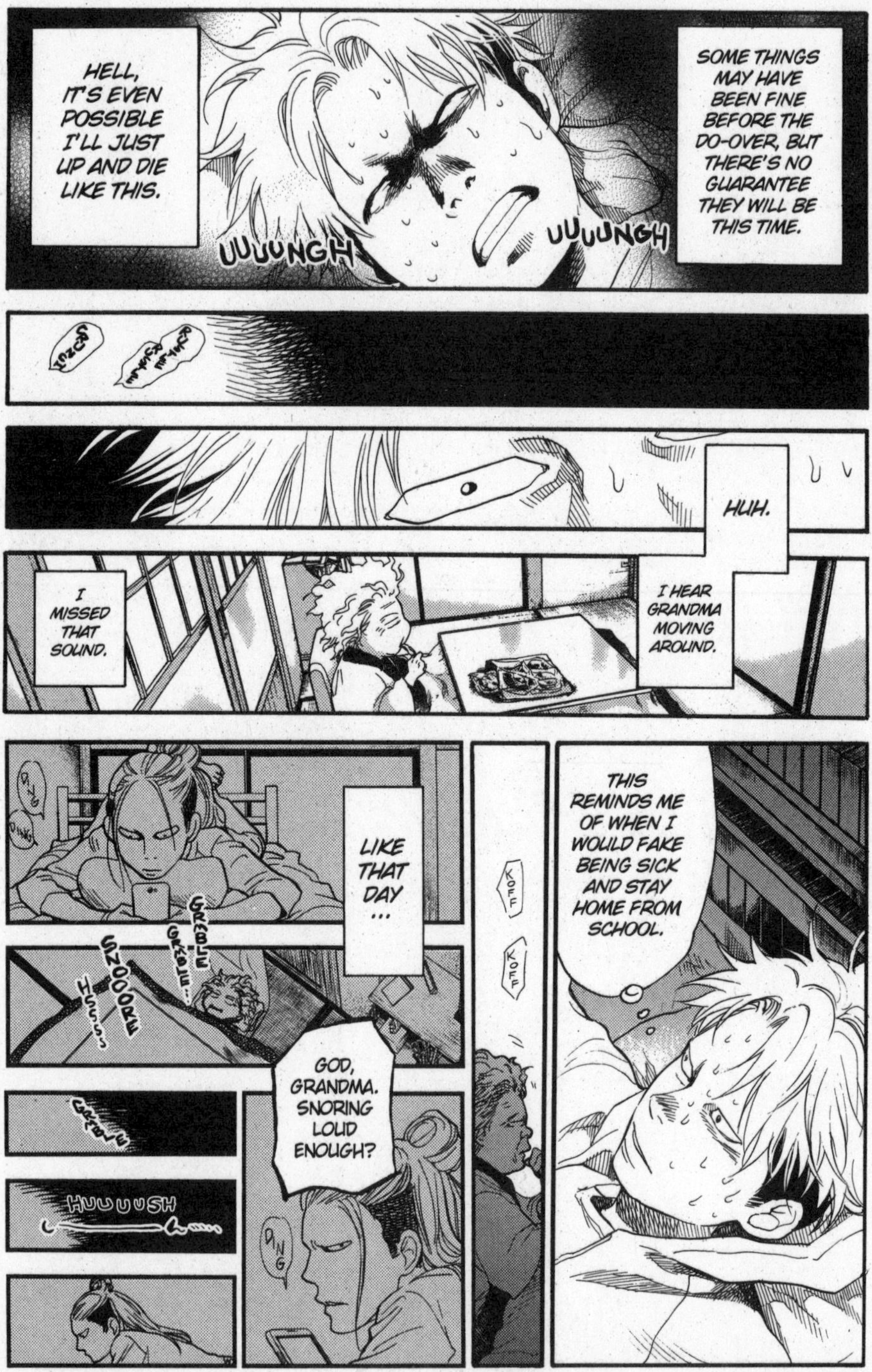
SOME THINGS MAY HAVE BEEN FINE BEFORE THE DO-OVER, BUT THERE'S NO GUARANTEE THEY WILL BE THIS TIME.
UUUUNGH
HELL, IT'S EVEN POSSIBLE I'LL JUST UP AND DIE LIKE THIS.
UUUUNGH
HUH.
I HEAR GRANDMA MOVING AROUND.
I MISSED THAT SOUND.
THIS REMINDS ME OF WHEN I WOULD FAKE BEING SICK AND STAY HOME FROM SCHOOL.
KOFF
KOFF
LIKE THAT DAY ...
DING
DING
GRMBLE
GRMBLE...
SNOOORE
HSSSS
GOD, GRANDMA. SNORING LOUD ENOUGH?
DING
GRMBLE
HUUUUSH

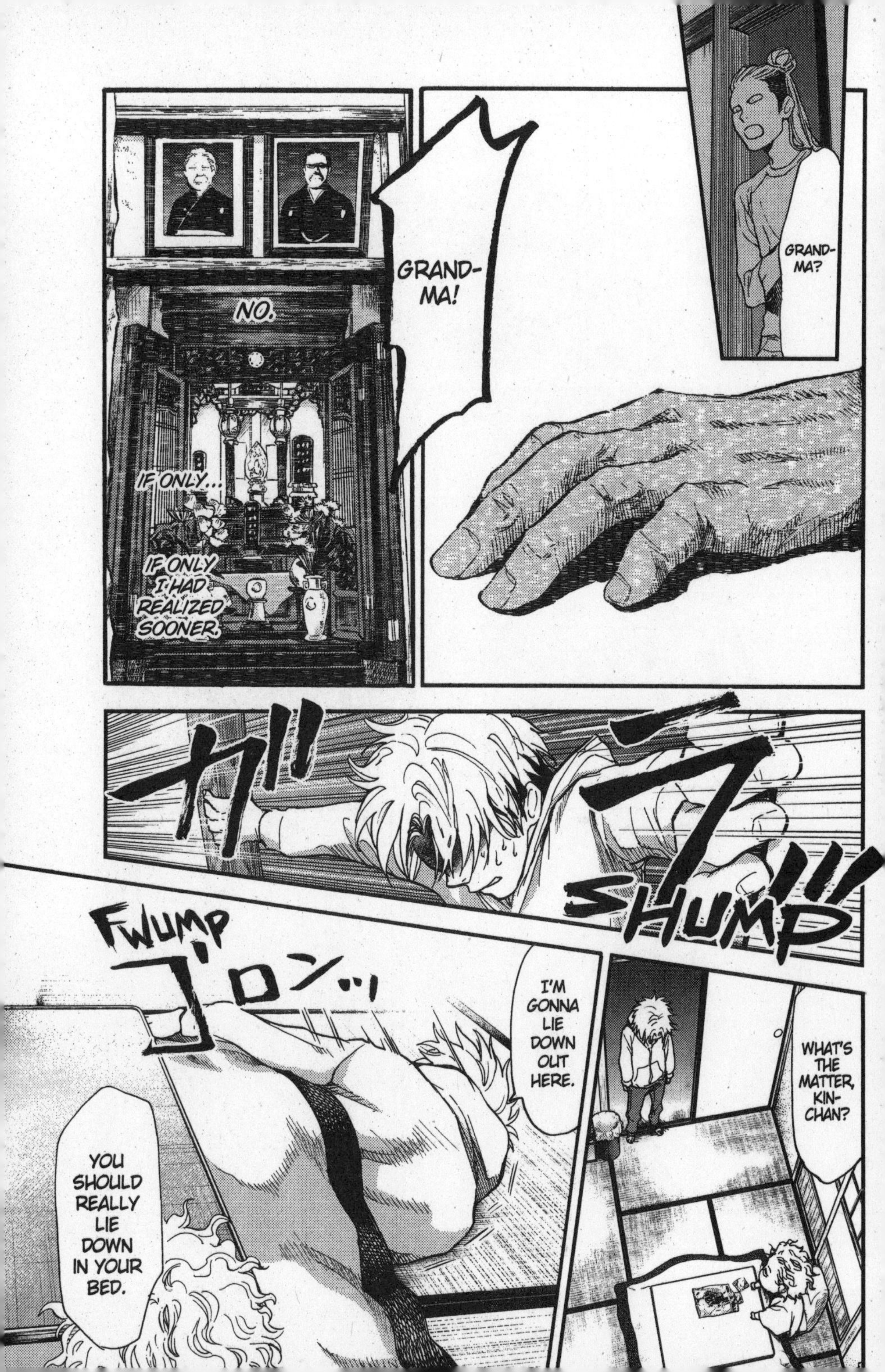
GRAND-MA?
GRAND-MA!
NO.
IF ONLY...
IF ONLY I HAD REALIZED SOONER.
SHUMP
WHAT'S THE MATTER, KIN-CHAN?
I'M GONNA LIE DOWN OUT HERE.
FWUMP
ゴロンッ
YOU SHOULD REALLY LIE DOWN IN YOUR BED.

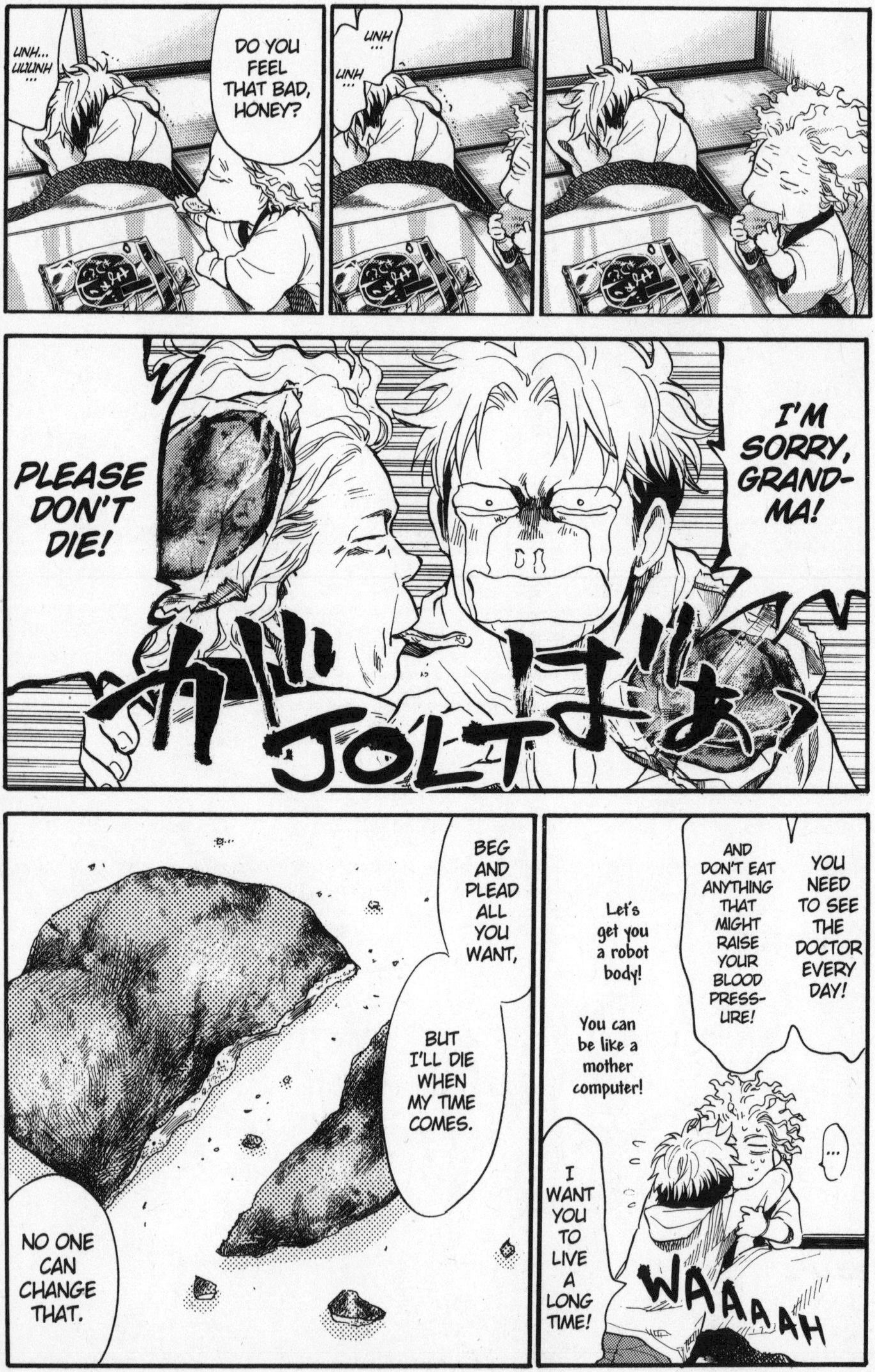
UNH ...
UNH ...
DO YOU FEEL THAT BAD, HONEY?
UNH... UUUNH ...
I'M SORRY, GRANDMA!
PLEASE DON'T DIE!
JOLT
YOU NEED TO SEE THE DOCTOR EVERY DAY!
AND DON'T EAT ANYTHING THAT MIGHT RAISE YOUR BLOOD PRESSURE!
Let's get you a robot body!
You can be like a mother computer!
...
I WANT YOU TO LIVE A LONG TIME!
WAAAAAH
BEG AND PLEAD ALL YOU WANT,
BUT I'LL DIE WHEN MY TIME COMES.
NO ONE CAN CHANGE THAT.

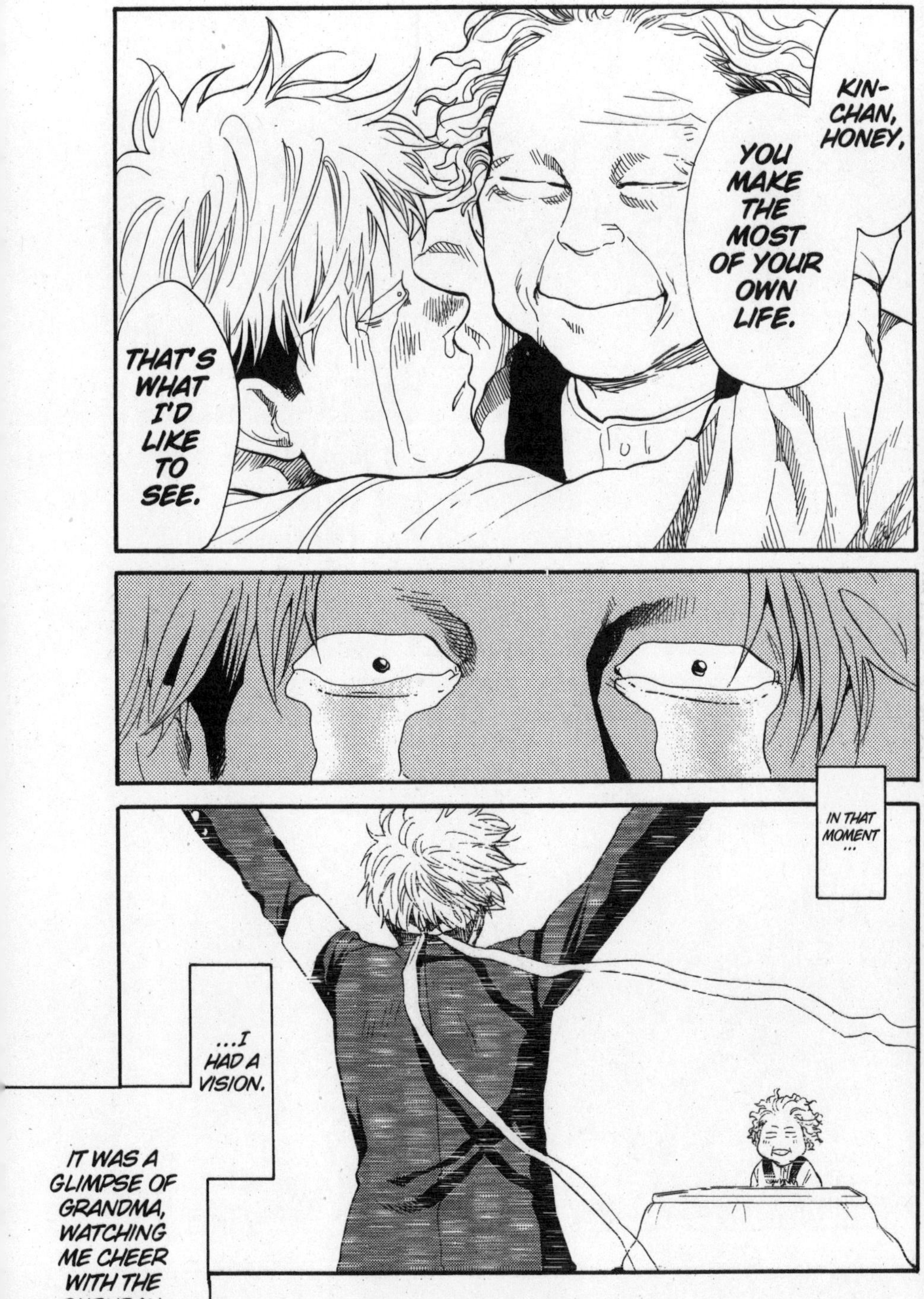
KIN-CHAN, HONEY,
YOU MAKE THE MOST OF YOUR OWN LIFE.
THAT'S WHAT I'D LIKE TO SEE.
IN THAT MOMENT...
...I HAD A VISION.
IT WAS A GLIMPSE OF GRANDMA, WATCHING ME CHEER WITH THE OUENDAN.

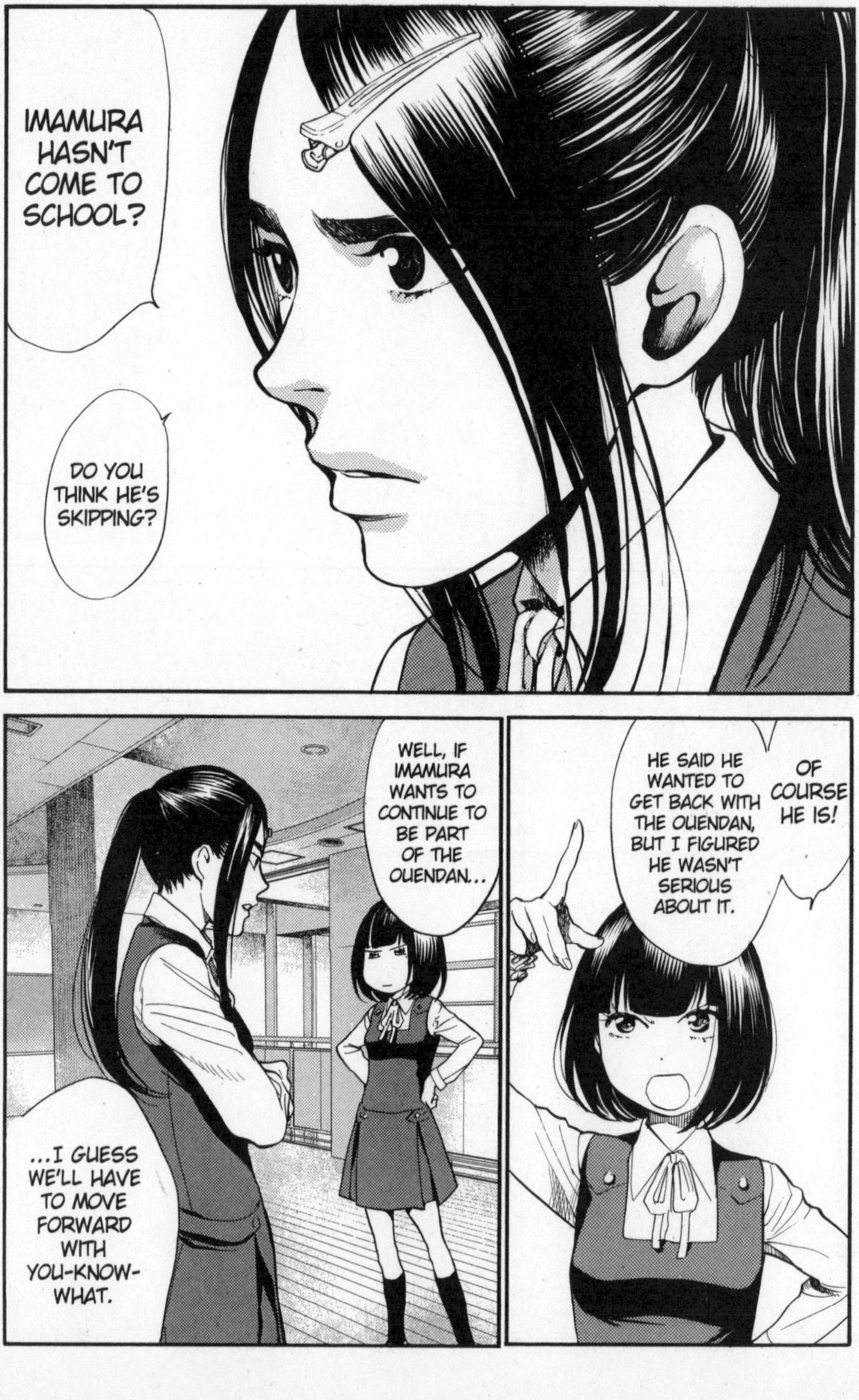
IMAMURA HASN'T COME TO SCHOOL?
DO YOU THINK HE'S SKIPPING?
OF COURSE HE IS!
HE SAID HE WANTED TO GET BACK WITH THE OUENDAN, BUT I FIGURED HE WASN'T SERIOUS ABOUT IT.
WELL, IF IMAMURA WANTS TO CONTINUE TO BE PART OF THE OUENDAN...
...I GUESS WE'LL HAVE TO MOVE FORWARD WITH YOU-KNOW-WHAT.

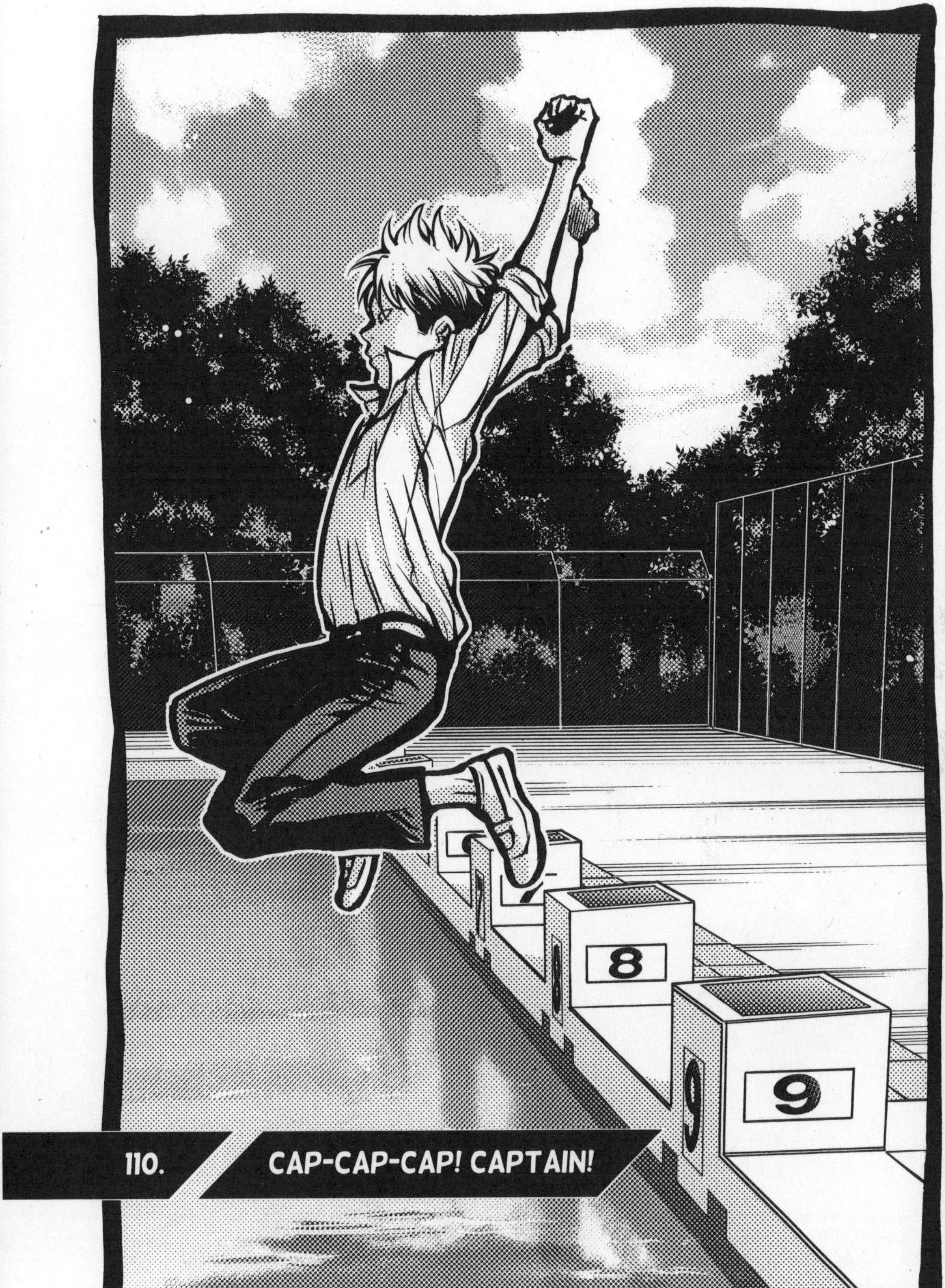
110.
CAP-CAP-CAP! CAPTAIN!

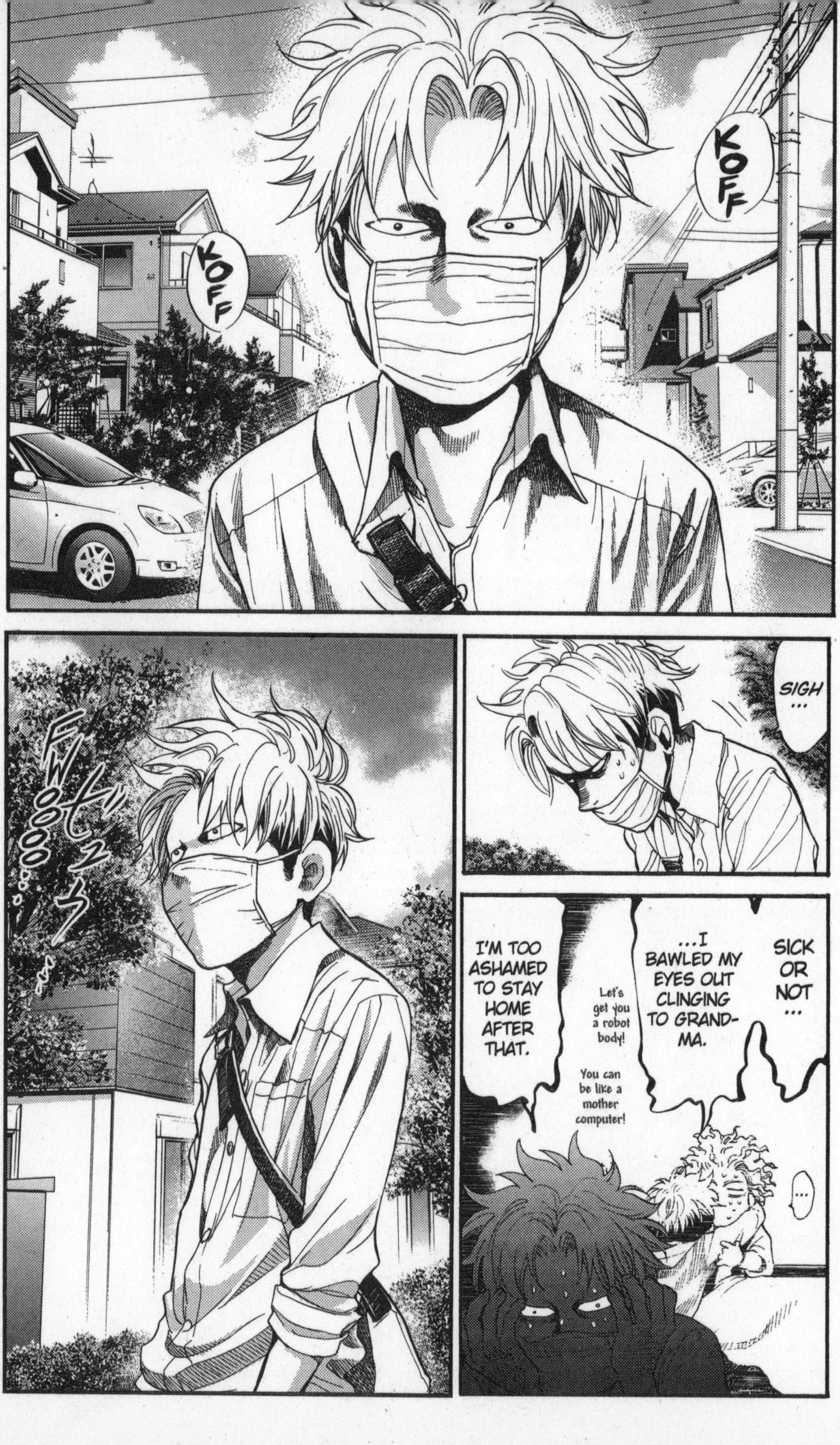
KOFF
KOFF
SIGH...
SICK OR NOT...
...I BAWLED MY EYES OUT CLINGING TO GRAND-MA.
I'M TOO ASHAMED TO STAY HOME AFTER THAT.
Let's get you a robot body!
You can be like a mother computer!
...
FWOOOO...

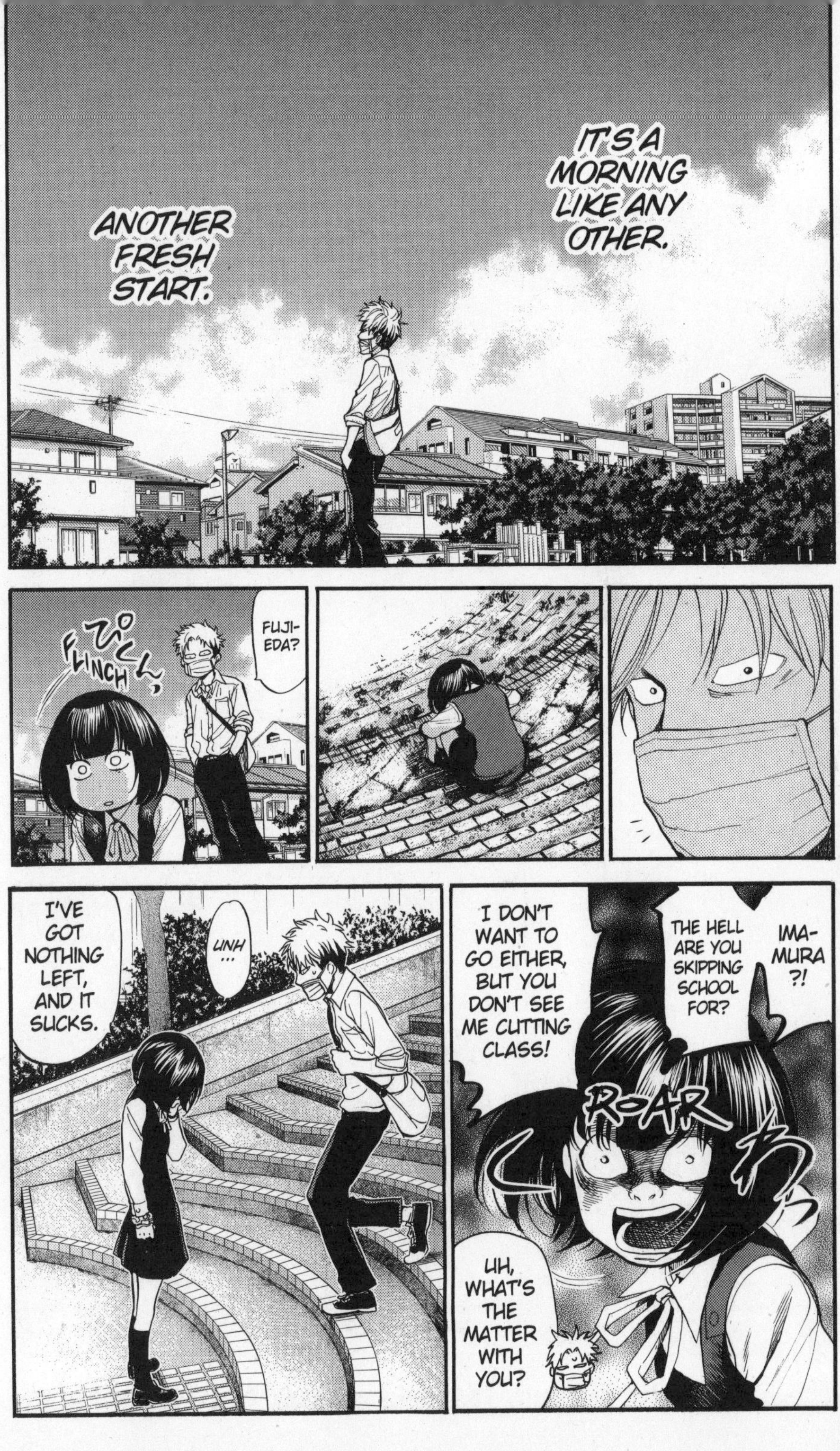
IT'S A MORNING LIKE ANY OTHER.
ANOTHER FRESH START.
FUJI-EDA?
ぴくん
FLINCH
IMA-MURA?!
THE HELL ARE YOU SKIPPING SCHOOL FOR?
I DON'T WANT TO GO EITHER, BUT YOU DON'T SEE ME CUTTING CLASS!
ROAR
UH, WHAT'S THE MATTER WITH YOU?
UNH...
I'VE GOT NOTHING LEFT, AND IT SUCKS.

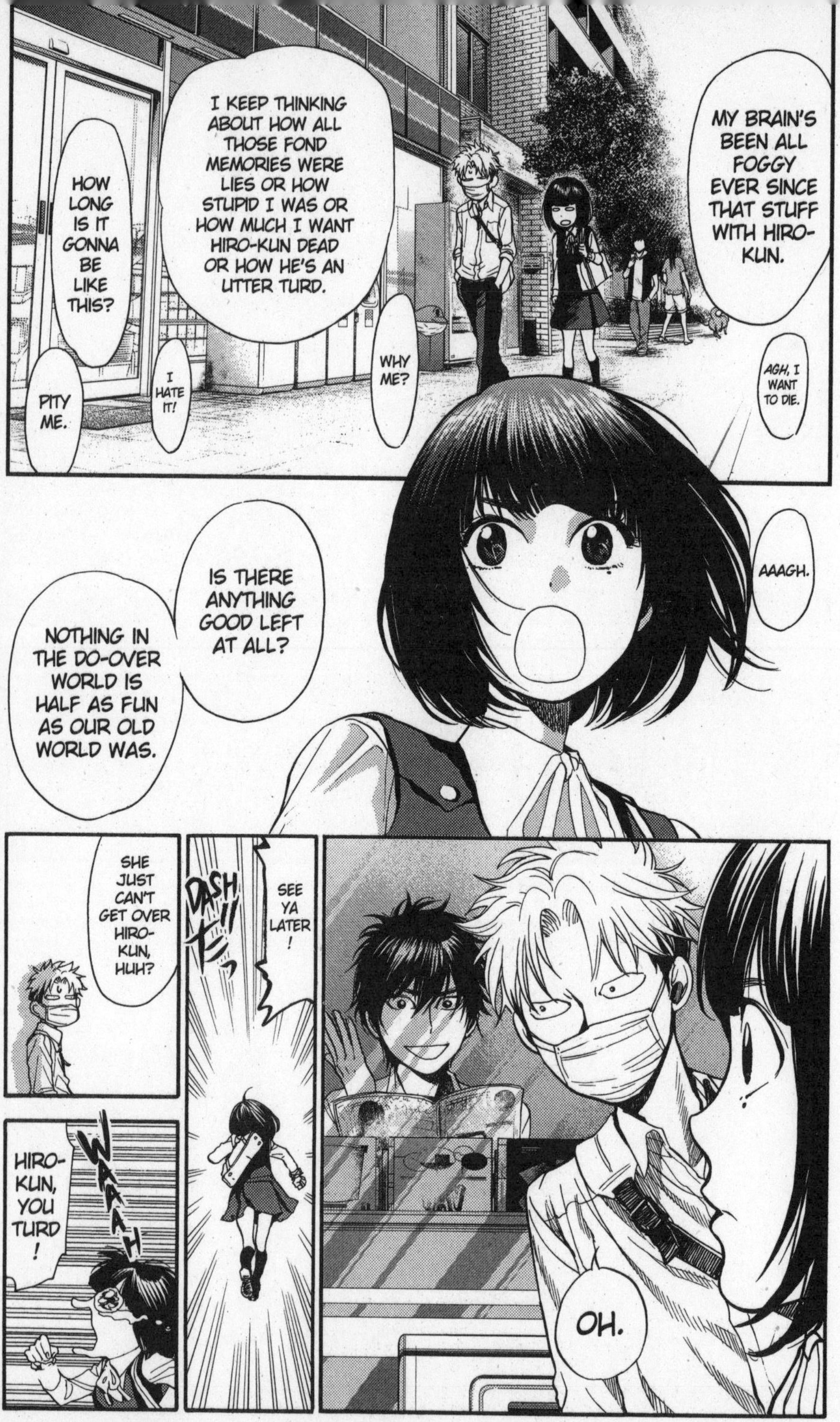
MY BRAIN'S BEEN ALL FOGGY EVER SINCE THAT STUFF WITH HIRO-KUN.
AGH, I WANT TO DIE.
I KEEP THINKING ABOUT HOW ALL THOSE FOND MEMORIES WERE LIES OR HOW STUPID I WAS OR HOW MUCH I WANT HIRO-KUN DEAD OR HOW HE'S AN UTTER TURD.
WHY ME?
HOW LONG IS IT GONNA BE LIKE THIS?
I HATE IT!
PITY ME.
AAAGH.
IS THERE ANYTHING GOOD LEFT AT ALL?
NOTHING IN THE DO-OVER WORLD IS HALF AS FUN AS OUR OLD WORLD WAS.
OH.
SEE YA LATER!
DASH!!
SHE JUST CAN'T GET OVER HIRO-KUN, HUH?
WAAAH
HIRO-KUN, YOU TURD!

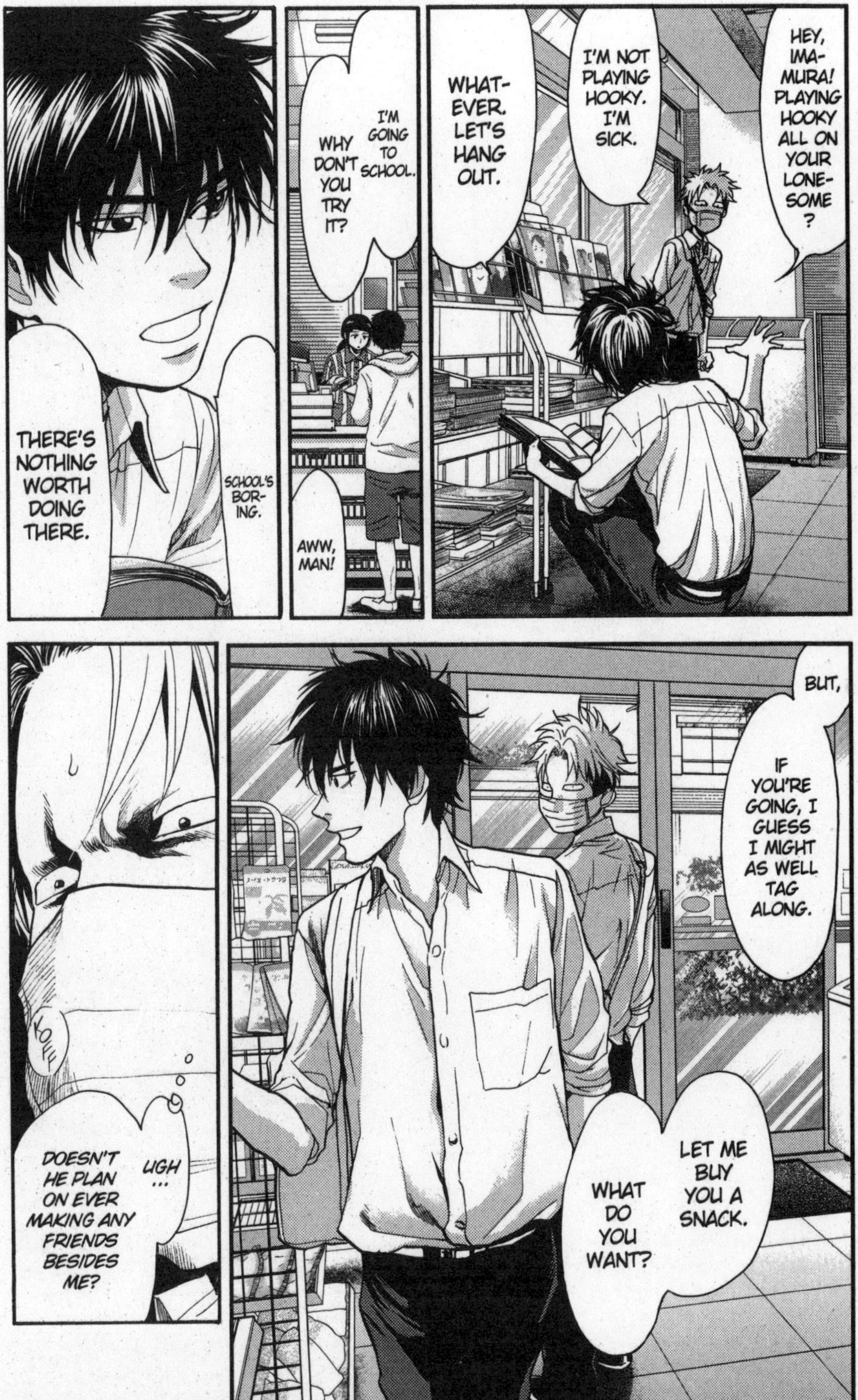
HEY, IMAMURA! PLAYING HOOKY ALL ON YOUR LONESOME?
I'M NOT PLAYING HOOKY. I'M SICK.
WHATEVER. LET'S HANG OUT.
I'M GOING TO SCHOOL.
WHY DON'T YOU TRY IT?
AWW, MAN!
SCHOOL'S BORING.
THERE'S NOTHING WORTH DOING THERE.
BUT,
IF YOU'RE GOING, I GUESS I MIGHT AS WELL TAG ALONG.
LET ME BUY YOU A SNACK.
WHAT DO YOU WANT?
UGH...
KOFF
DOESN'T HE PLAN ON EVER MAKING ANY FRIENDS BESIDES ME?

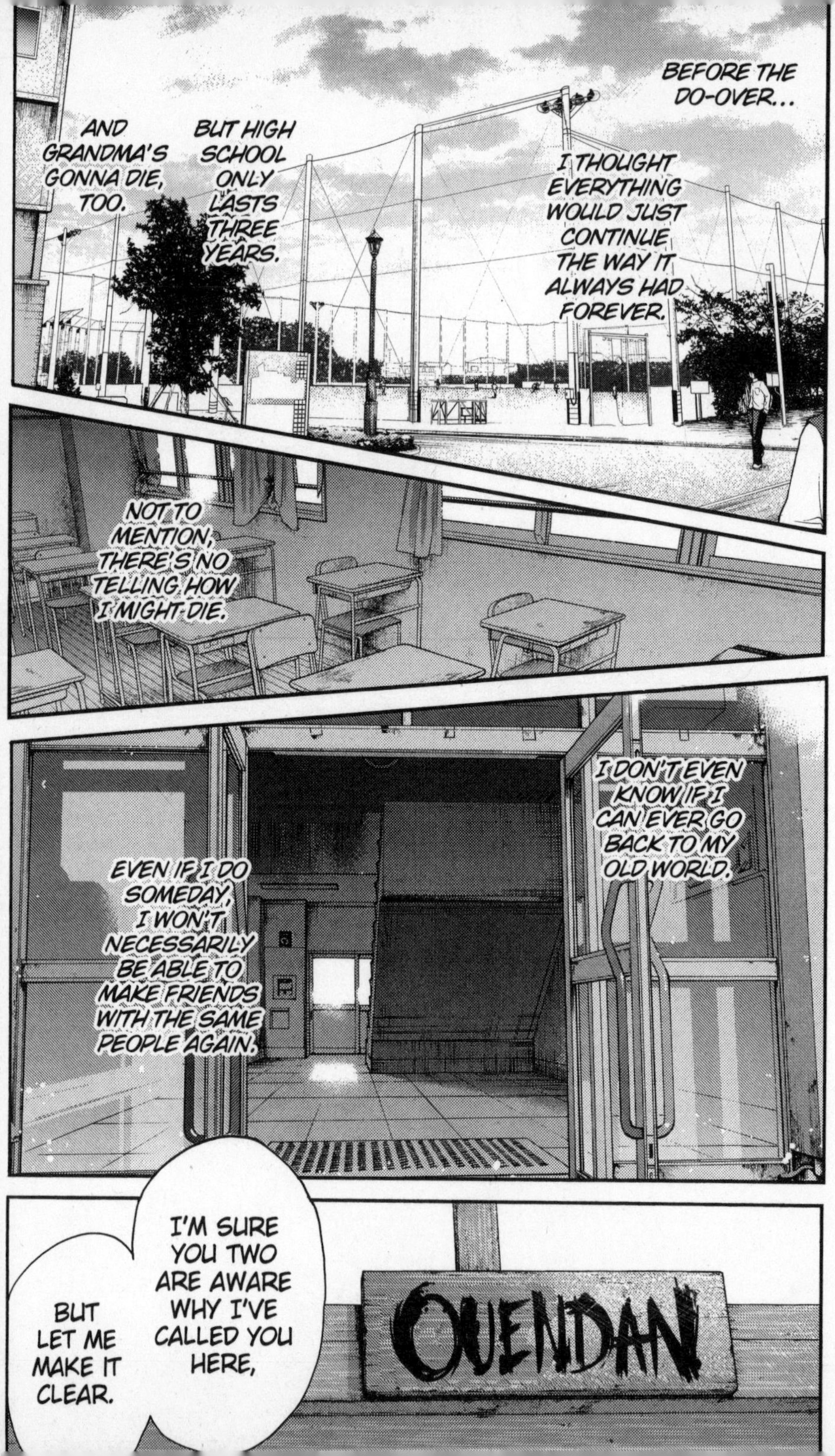
BEFORE THE DO-OVER...
I THOUGHT EVERYTHING WOULD JUST CONTINUE THE WAY IT ALWAYS HAD FOREVER.
BUT HIGH SCHOOL ONLY LASTS THREE YEARS.
AND GRANDMA'S GONNA DIE, TOO.
NOT TO MENTION, THERE'S NO TELLING HOW I MIGHT DIE.
I DON'T EVEN KNOW IF I CAN EVER GO BACK TO MY OLD WORLD.
EVEN IF I DO SOMEDAY, I WON'T NECESSARILY BE ABLE TO MAKE FRIENDS WITH THE SAME PEOPLE AGAIN.
OUENDAN
I'M SURE YOU TWO ARE AWARE WHY I'VE CALLED YOU HERE,
BUT LET ME MAKE IT CLEAR.

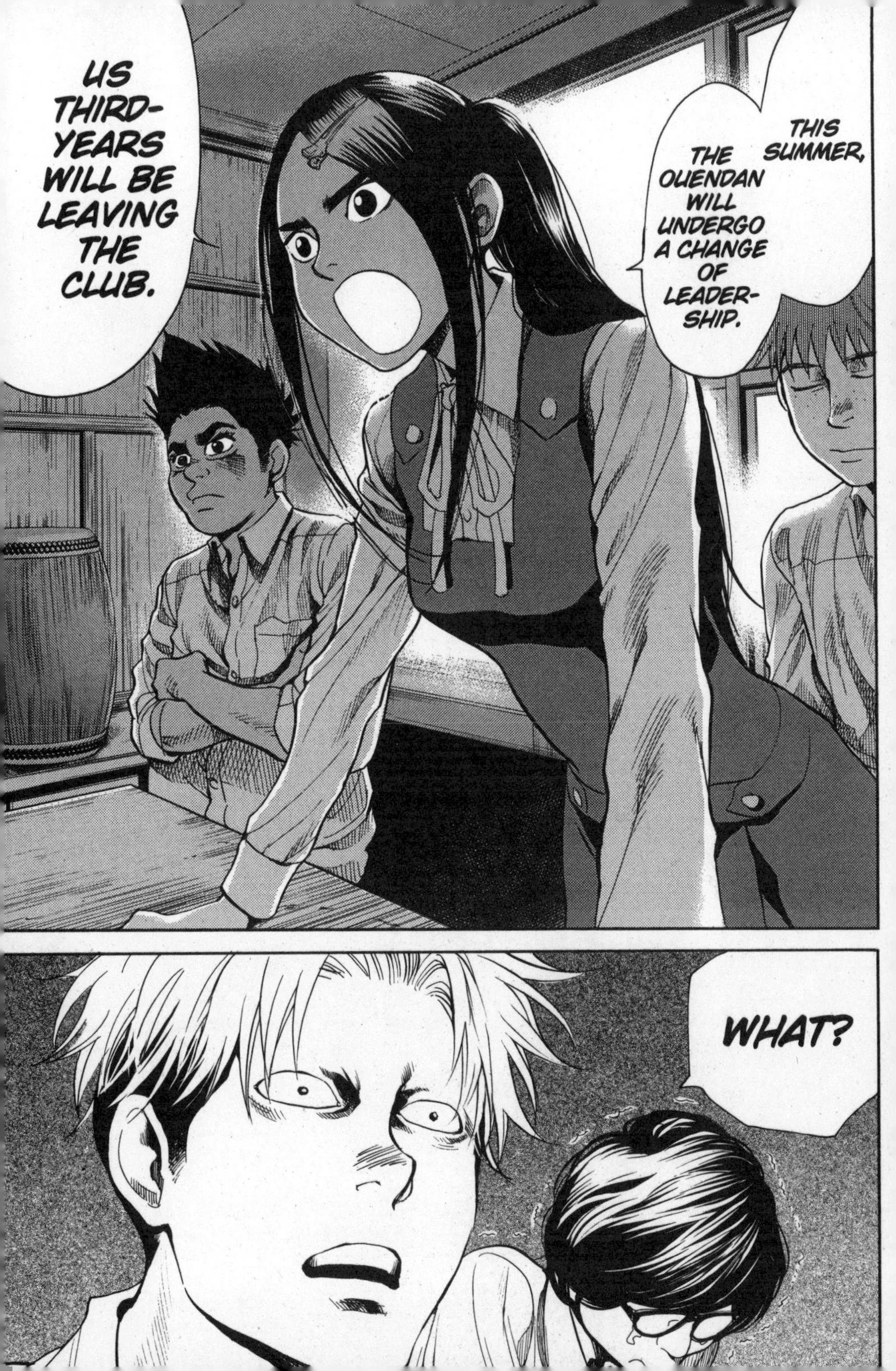
THIS SUMMER, THE OUENDAN WILL UNDERGO A CHANGE OF LEADER-SHIP.
US THIRD-YEARS WILL BE LEAVING THE CLUB.
WHAT?

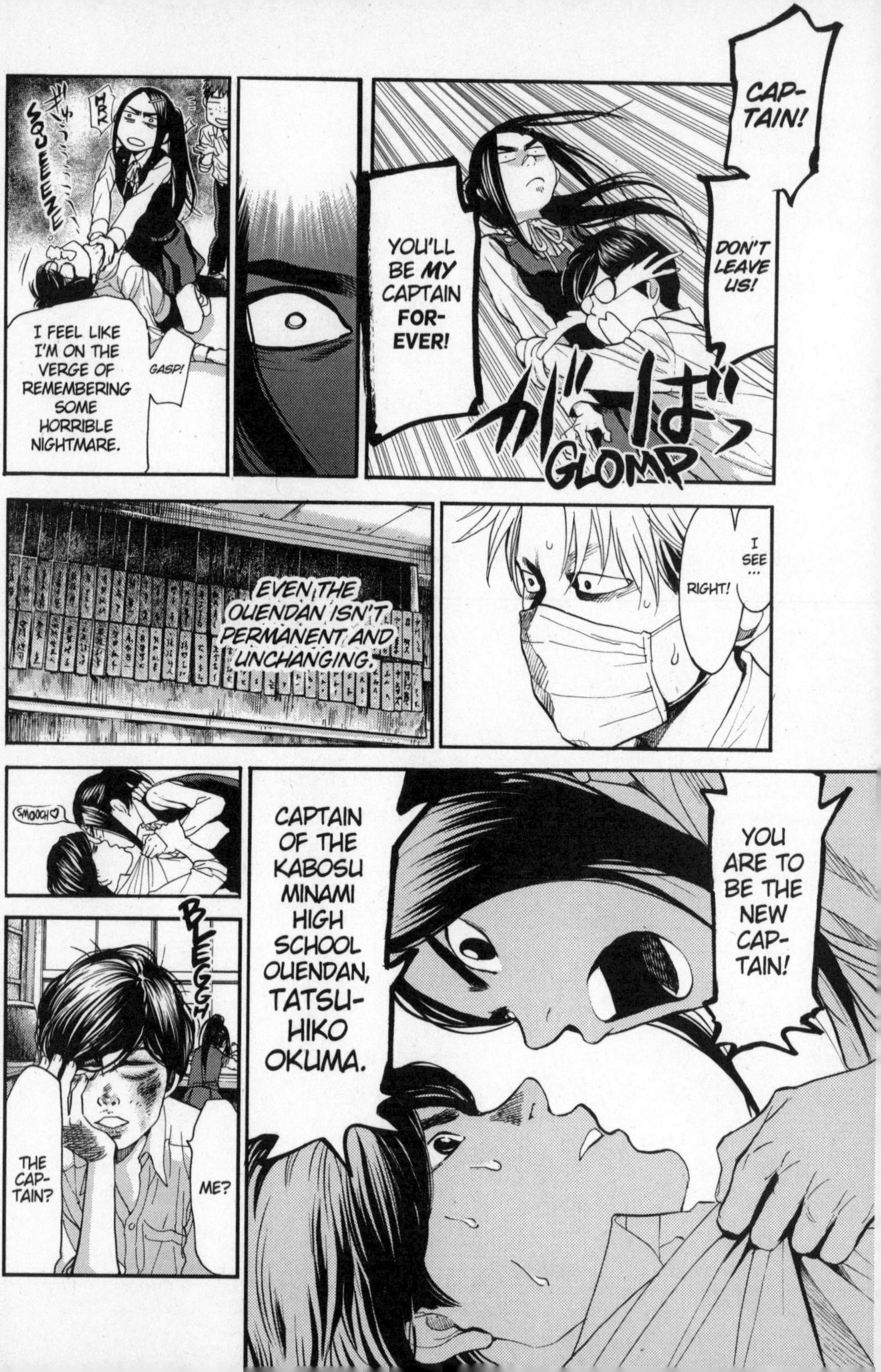
CAP-TAIN!
DON'T LEAVE US!
YOU'LL BE MY CAPTAIN FOR-EVER!
がばっ
GLOMP
HRK
ぎゅううう
SQUEEEZE
I FEEL LIKE I'M ON THE VERGE OF REMEMBERING SOME HORRIBLE NIGHTMARE.
GASP!
I SEE...
RIGHT!
EVEN THE OUENDAN ISN'T PERMANENT AND UNCHANGING.
YOU ARE TO BE THE NEW CAP-TAIN!
CAPTAIN OF THE KABOSU MINAMI HIGH SCHOOL OUENDAN, TATSU-HIKO OKUMA.
SMOOCH♡
BLEGGH
THE CAP-TAIN?
ME?

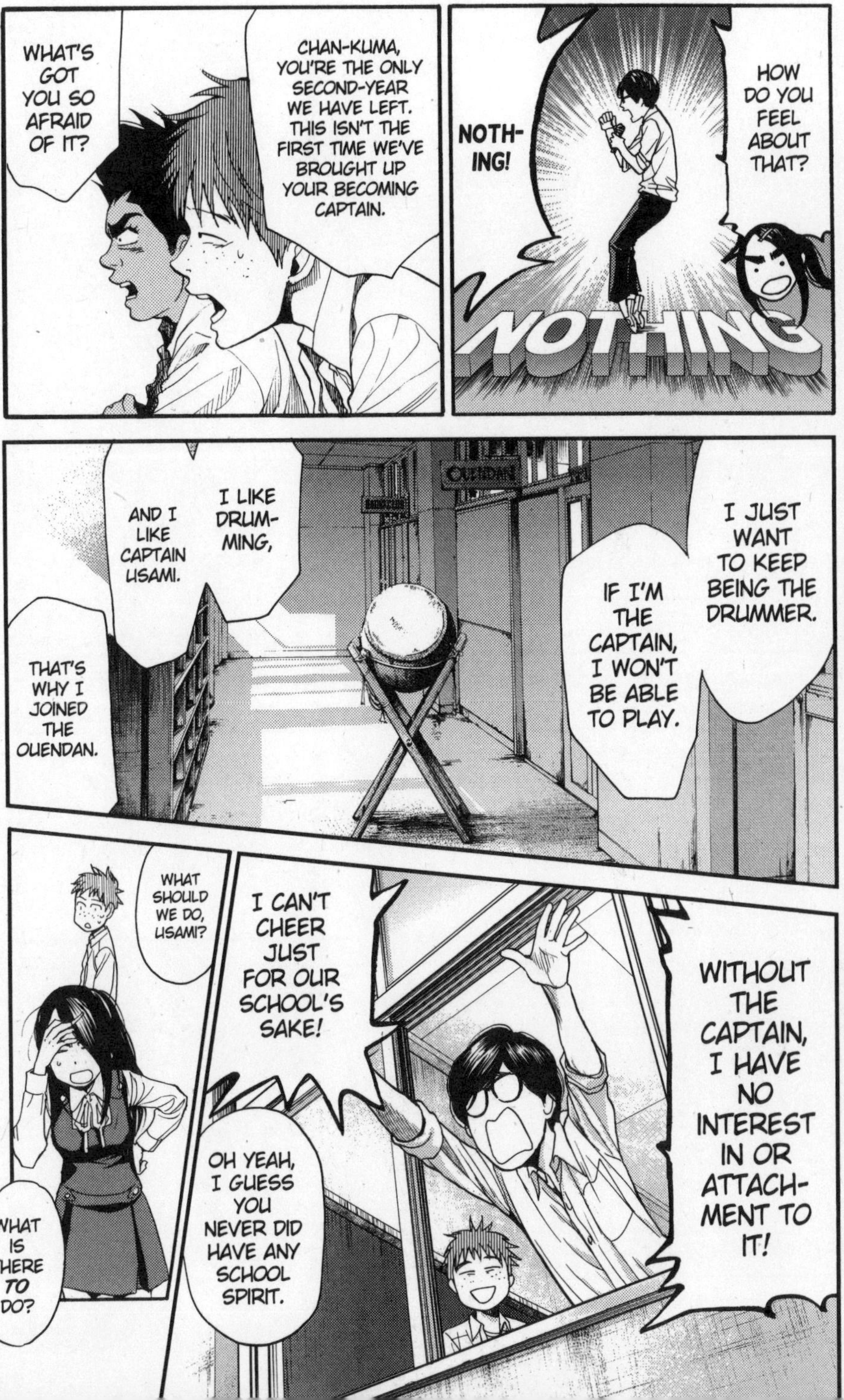
HOW DO YOU FEEL ABOUT THAT?
NOTH-ING!
NOTHING
CHAN-KUMA, YOU'RE THE ONLY SECOND-YEAR WE HAVE LEFT. THIS ISN'T THE FIRST TIME WE'VE BROUGHT UP YOUR BECOMING CAPTAIN.
WHAT'S GOT YOU SO AFRAID OF IT?
OUENDAN
I JUST WANT TO KEEP BEING THE DRUMMER.
IF I'M THE CAPTAIN, I WON'T BE ABLE TO PLAY.
I LIKE DRUMMING,
AND I LIKE CAPTAIN USAMI.
THAT'S WHY I JOINED THE OUENDAN.
WITHOUT THE CAPTAIN, I HAVE NO INTEREST IN OR ATTACHMENT TO IT!
I CAN'T CHEER JUST FOR OUR SCHOOL'S SAKE!
OH YEAH, I GUESS YOU NEVER DID HAVE ANY SCHOOL SPIRIT.
WHAT SHOULD WE DO, USAMI?
WHAT IS THERE *TO* DO?

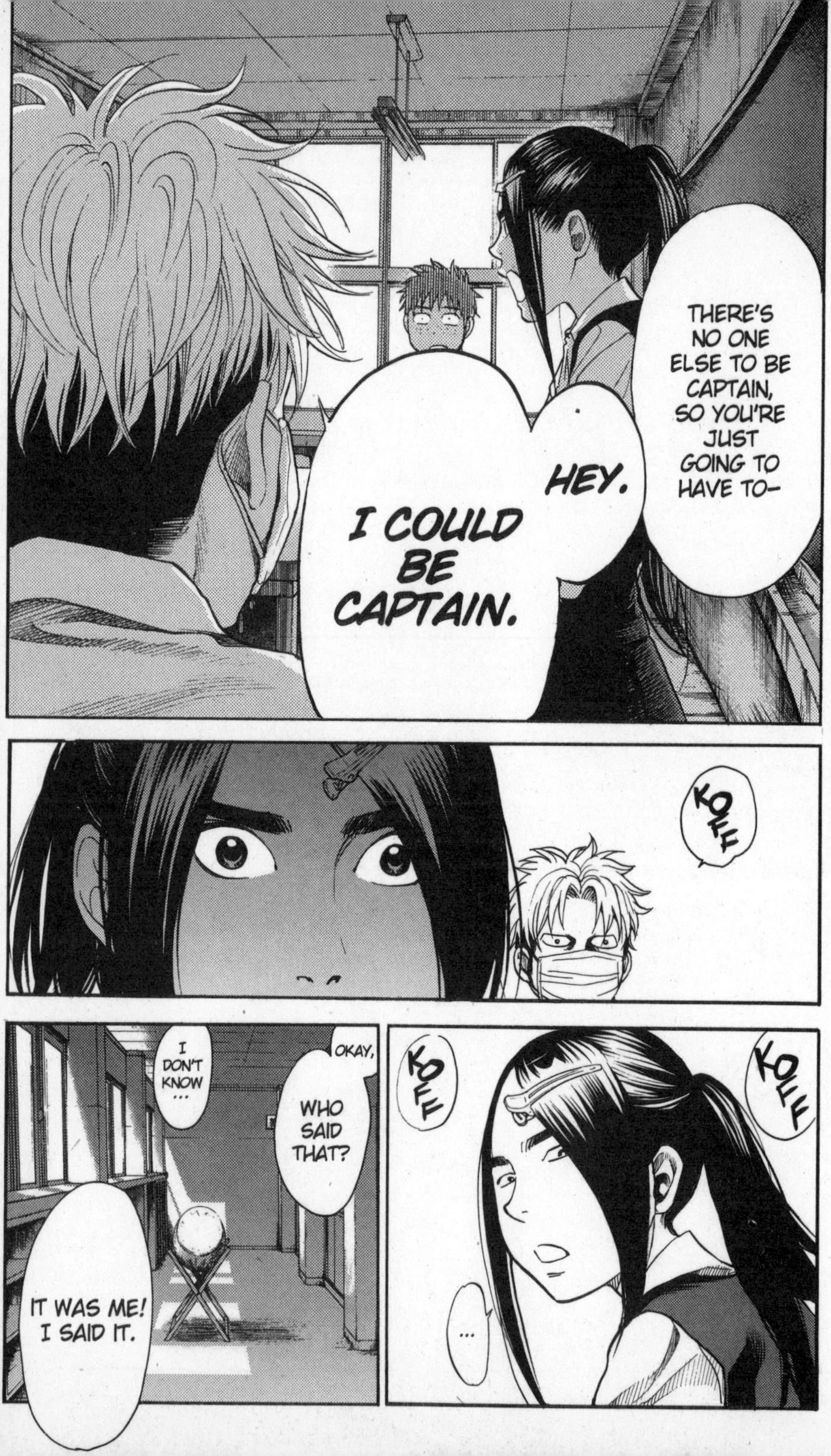
THERE'S NO ONE ELSE TO BE CAPTAIN, SO YOU'RE JUST GOING TO HAVE TO-
HEY.
I COULD BE CAPTAIN.
KOFF
KOFF
KOFF
...
OKAY,
WHO SAID THAT?
I DON'T KNOW...
IT WAS ME! I SAID IT.

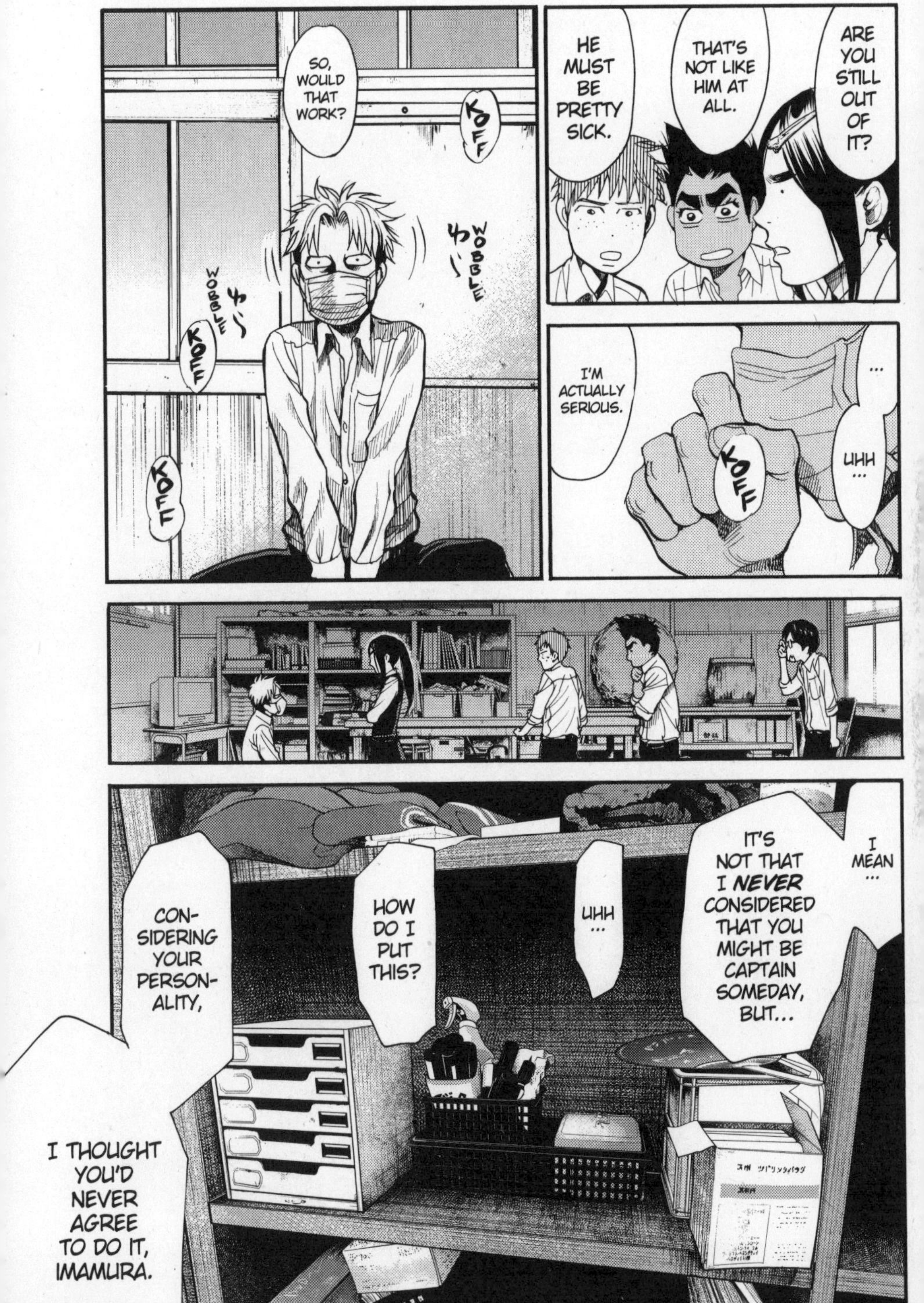
ARE YOU STILL OUT OF IT?
THAT'S NOT LIKE HIM AT ALL.
HE MUST BE PRETTY SICK.
...
UHH ...
KOFF
I'M ACTUALLY SERIOUS.
SO, WOULD THAT WORK?
KOFF
WOBBLE
WOBBLE
KOFF
KOFF
I MEAN ...
IT'S NOT THAT I **NEVER** CONSIDERED THAT YOU MIGHT BE CAPTAIN SOMEDAY, BUT...
UHH ...
HOW DO I PUT THIS?
CON-SIDERING YOUR PERSON-ALITY,
I THOUGHT YOU'D NEVER AGREE TO DO IT, IMAMURA.

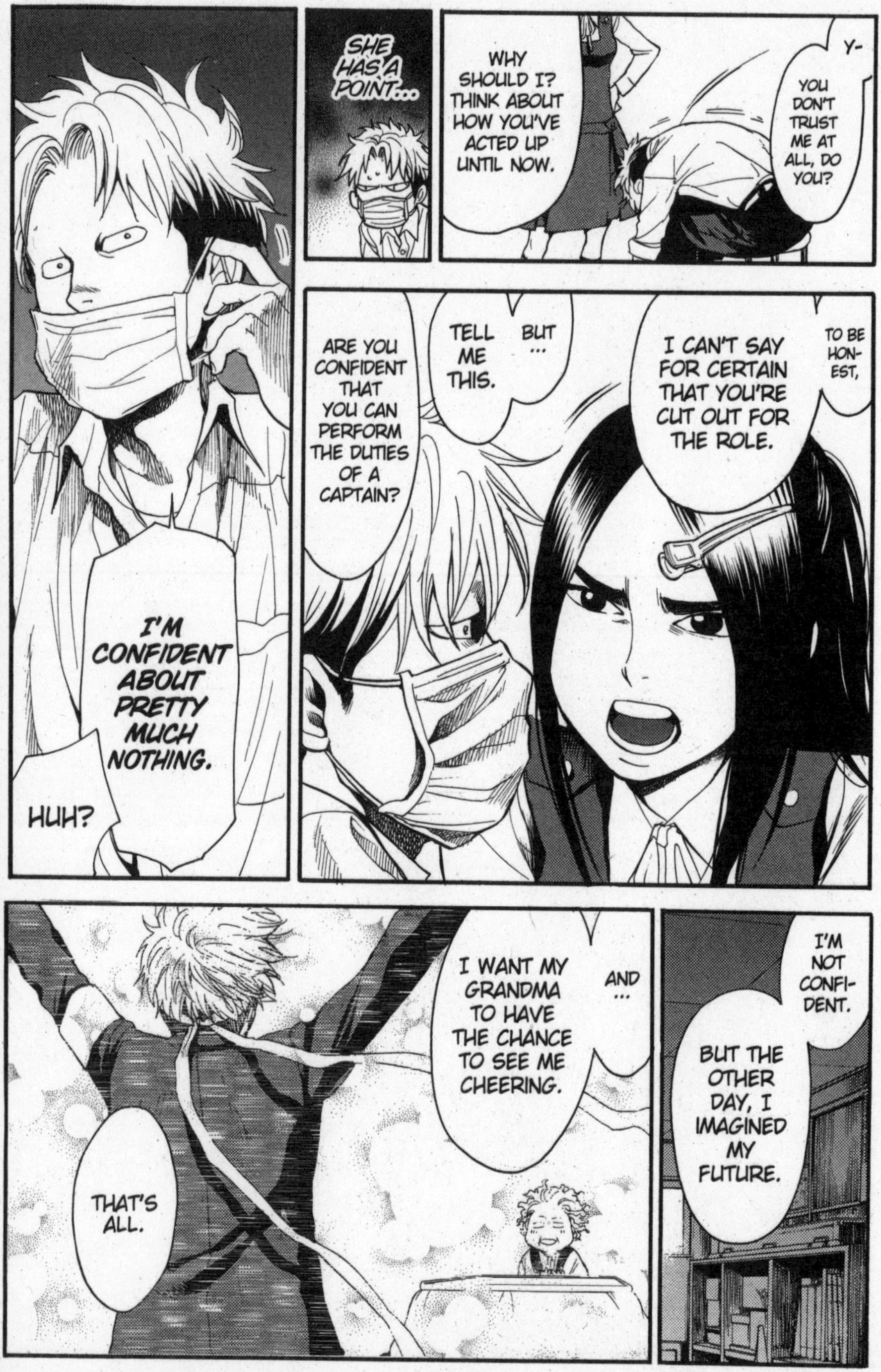
Y-
YOU DON'T TRUST ME AT ALL, DO YOU?
WHY SHOULD I? THINK ABOUT HOW YOU'VE ACTED UP UNTIL NOW.
SHE HAS A POINT...
TO BE HONEST,
I CAN'T SAY FOR CERTAIN THAT YOU'RE CUT OUT FOR THE ROLE.
BUT...
TELL ME THIS.
ARE YOU CONFIDENT THAT YOU CAN PERFORM THE DUTIES OF A CAPTAIN?
I'M CONFIDENT ABOUT PRETTY MUCH NOTHING.
HUH?
I'M NOT CONFIDENT.
BUT THE OTHER DAY, I IMAGINED MY FUTURE.
AND...
I WANT MY GRANDMA TO HAVE THE CHANCE TO SEE ME CHEERING.
THAT'S ALL.

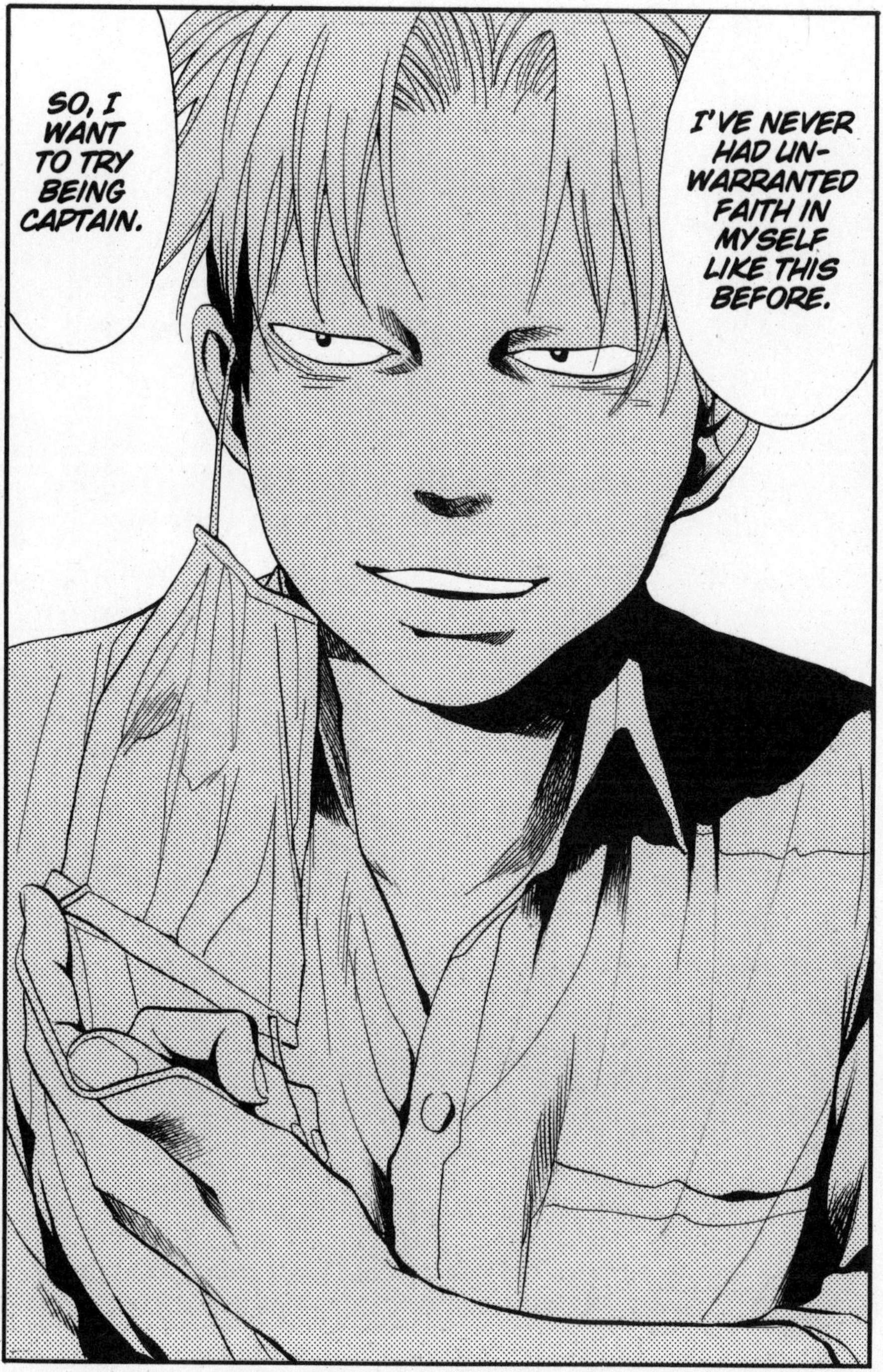
I'VE NEVER HAD UN-WARRANTED FAITH IN MYSELF LIKE THIS BEFORE.
SO, I WANT TO TRY BEING CAPTAIN.

This is the AFTERWORD!

It's the tenth volume! We finally made it!

This is the first time I've written an original serialized work longer than 3-3-7 Byoshi!! (10 volumes).

My heart starts racing when I consider the fact that we're about to catch up with the future portrayed in this manga, considering that it's about going back in time from 2014.

I hope you'll keep cheering on Imamura!

Mitsurou Kubo, October 2013

2013. 10.   久保ミツロウ ☆

☆ My Agent: Hiromi Sakitani
☆ My Assistants: Shunsuke Ono
                 Youko Mikuni
                 Hiromu Kitano
                 Koushi Tezuka
                 Kouhei Mihara
                 Rana Satou
☆ Kuboken Manga Café Staff: Ema Yamanouchi

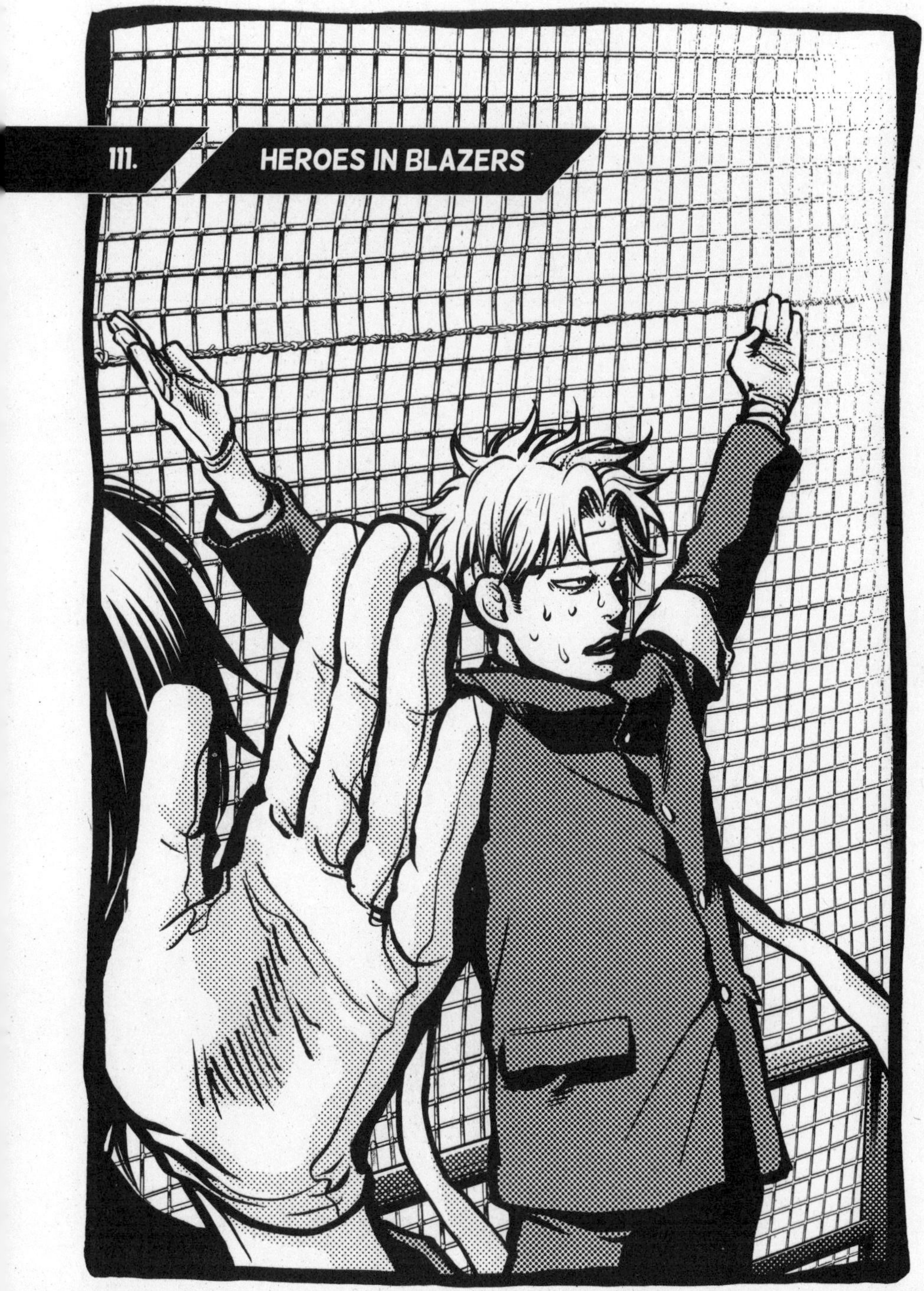
111.
HEROES IN BLAZERS

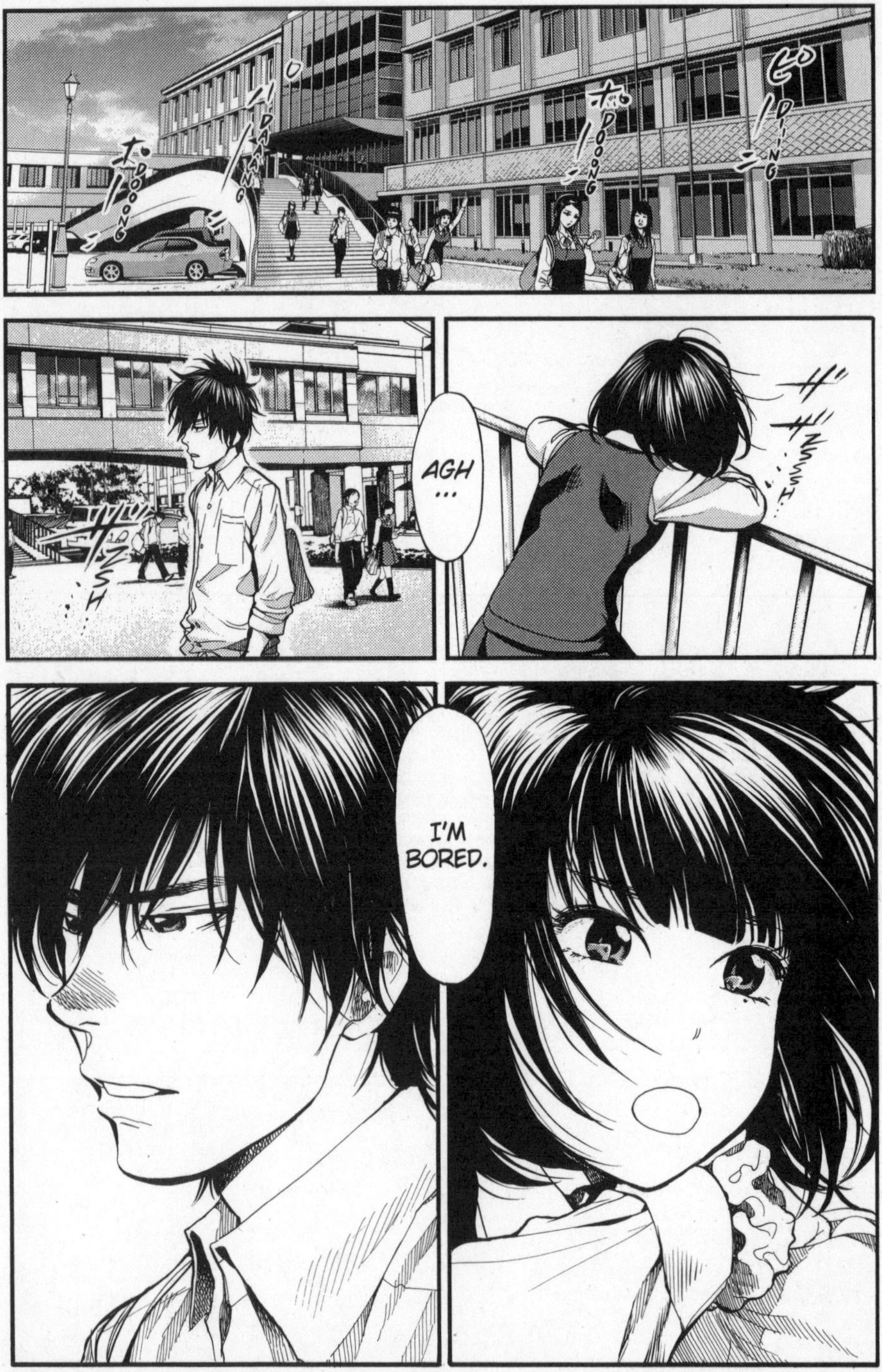
DIING
DOOONG
DAAANG
DOOONG
AGH ...
NSSH...
ZASH...
I'M BORED.

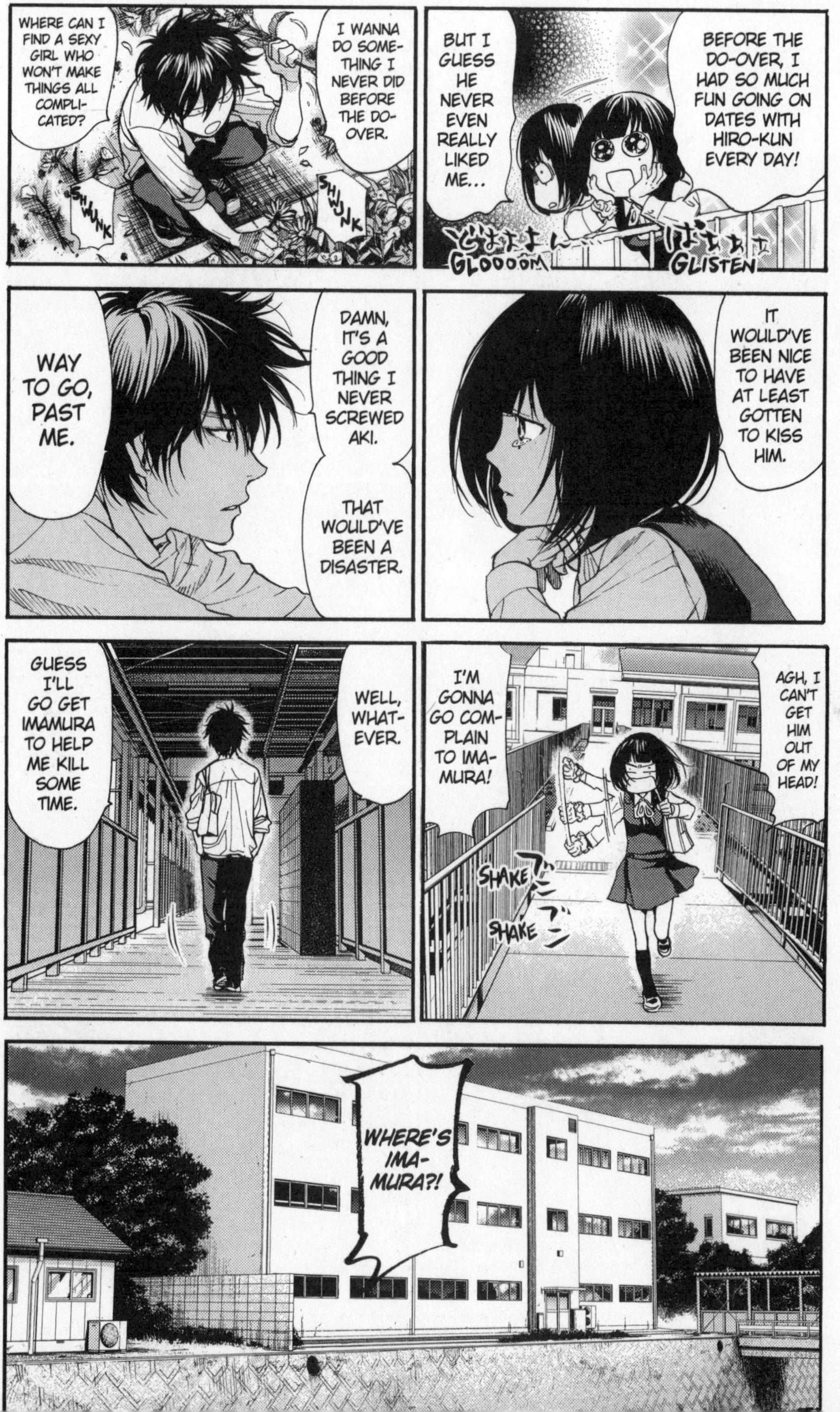
BEFORE THE DO-OVER, I HAD SO MUCH FUN GOING ON DATES WITH HIRO-KUN EVERY DAY!
BUT I GUESS HE NEVER EVEN REALLY LIKED ME...
GLISTEN
GLOOOOM
I WANNA DO SOMETHING I NEVER DID BEFORE THE DO-OVER.
WHERE CAN I FIND A SEXY GIRL WHO WON'T MAKE THINGS ALL COMPLICATED?
SHWUNK
SHWUNK
IT WOULD'VE BEEN NICE TO HAVE AT LEAST GOTTEN TO KISS HIM.
DAMN, IT'S A GOOD THING I NEVER SCREWED AKI.
THAT WOULD'VE BEEN A DISASTER.
WAY TO GO, PAST ME.
AGH, I CAN'T GET HIM OUT OF MY HEAD!
I'M GONNA GO COMPLAIN TO IMAMURA!
SHAKE
SHAKE
WELL, WHATEVER.
GUESS I'LL GO GET IMAMURA TO HELP ME KILL SOME TIME.
WHERE'S IMAMURA?!

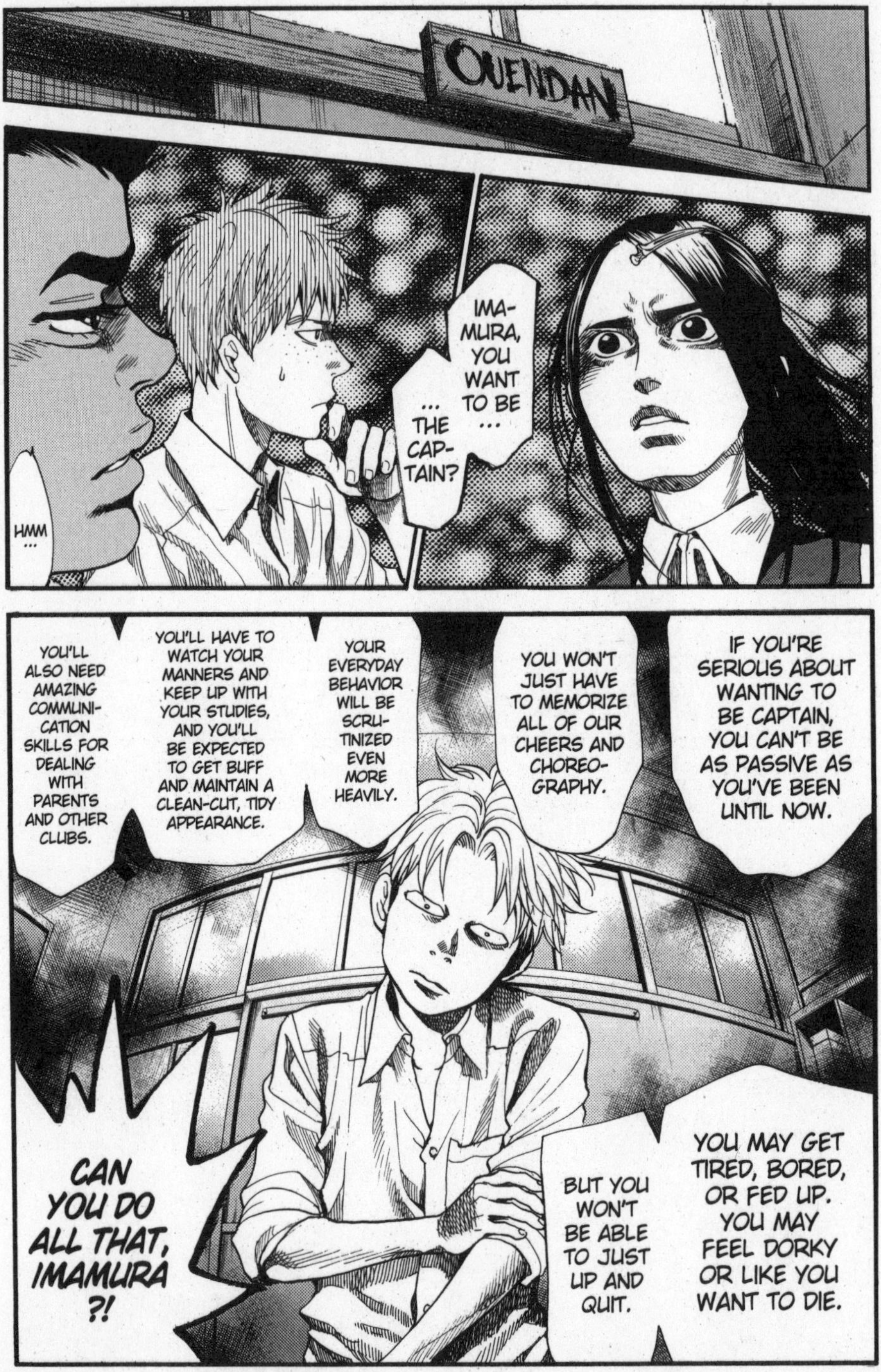
OUENDAN
IMAMURA, YOU WANT TO BE ...
... THE CAPTAIN?
HMM ...
IF YOU'RE SERIOUS ABOUT WANTING TO BE CAPTAIN, YOU CAN'T BE AS PASSIVE AS YOU'VE BEEN UNTIL NOW.
YOU WON'T JUST HAVE TO MEMORIZE ALL OF OUR CHEERS AND CHOREOGRAPHY.
YOUR EVERYDAY BEHAVIOR WILL BE SCRUTINIZED EVEN MORE HEAVILY.
YOU'LL HAVE TO WATCH YOUR MANNERS AND KEEP UP WITH YOUR STUDIES, AND YOU'LL BE EXPECTED TO GET BUFF AND MAINTAIN A CLEAN-CUT, TIDY APPEARANCE.
YOU'LL ALSO NEED AMAZING COMMUNICATION SKILLS FOR DEALING WITH PARENTS AND OTHER CLUBS.
YOU MAY GET TIRED, BORED, OR FED UP. YOU MAY FEEL DORKY OR LIKE YOU WANT TO DIE.
BUT YOU WON'T BE ABLE TO JUST UP AND QUIT.
CAN YOU DO ALL THAT, IMAMURA?!

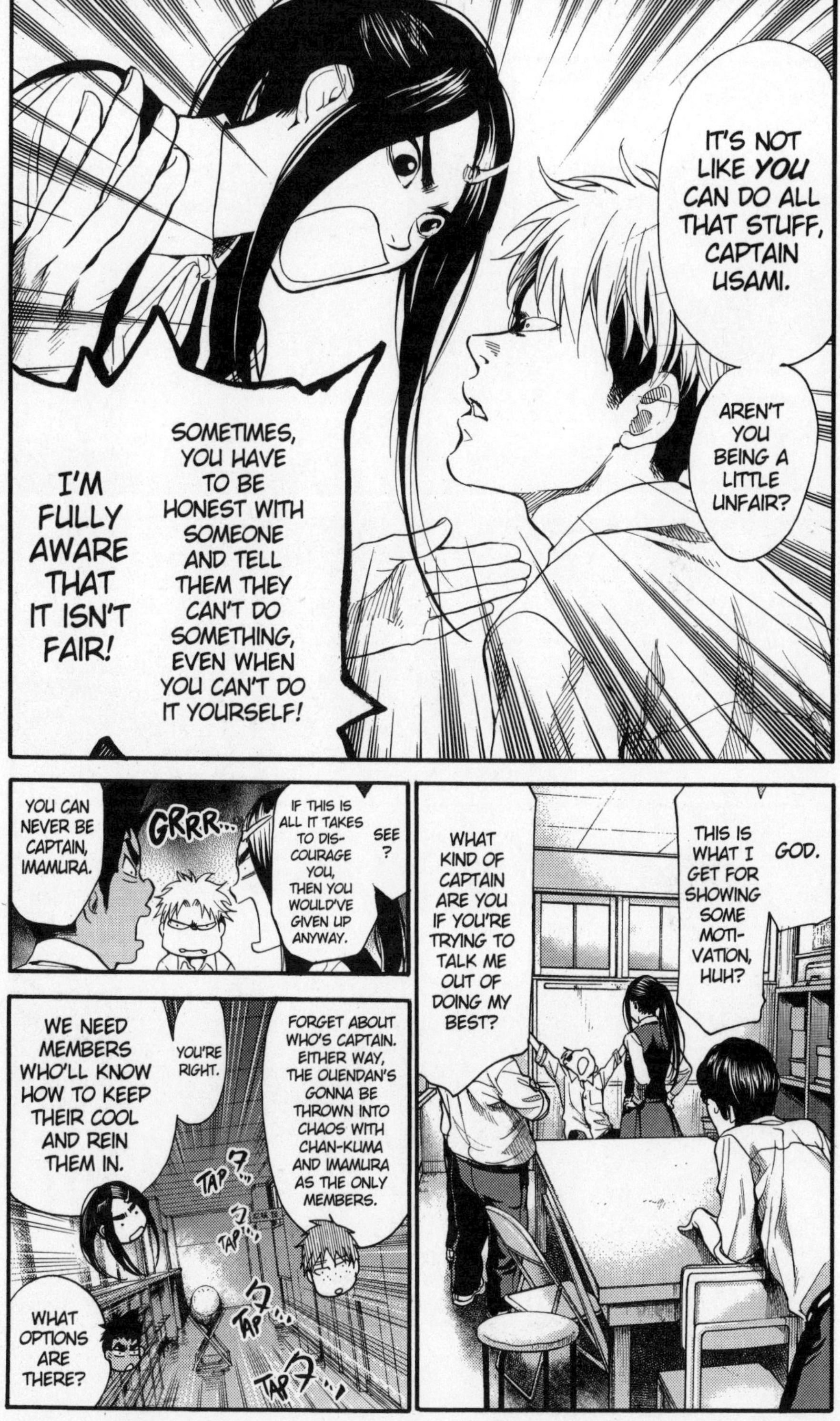
IT'S NOT LIKE YOU CAN DO ALL THAT STUFF, CAPTAIN USAMI.
AREN'T YOU BEING A LITTLE UNFAIR?
SOMETIMES, YOU HAVE TO BE HONEST WITH SOMEONE AND TELL THEM THEY CAN'T DO SOMETHING, EVEN WHEN YOU CAN'T DO IT YOURSELF!
I'M FULLY AWARE THAT IT ISN'T FAIR!
GOD.
THIS IS WHAT I GET FOR SHOWING SOME MOTI-VATION, HUH?
WHAT KIND OF CAPTAIN ARE YOU IF YOU'RE TRYING TO TALK ME OUT OF DOING MY BEST?
SEE?
IF THIS IS ALL IT TAKES TO DIS-COURAGE YOU, THEN YOU WOULD'VE GIVEN UP ANYWAY.
GRRR...
YOU CAN NEVER BE CAPTAIN, IMAMURA.
FORGET ABOUT WHO'S CAPTAIN. EITHER WAY, THE OUENDAN'S GONNA BE THROWN INTO CHAOS WITH CHAN-KUMA AND IMAMURA AS THE ONLY MEMBERS.
YOU'RE RIGHT.
WE NEED MEMBERS WHO'LL KNOW HOW TO KEEP THEIR COOL AND REIN THEM IN.
TAP
TAP
TAP
TAP
WHAT OPTIONS ARE THERE?

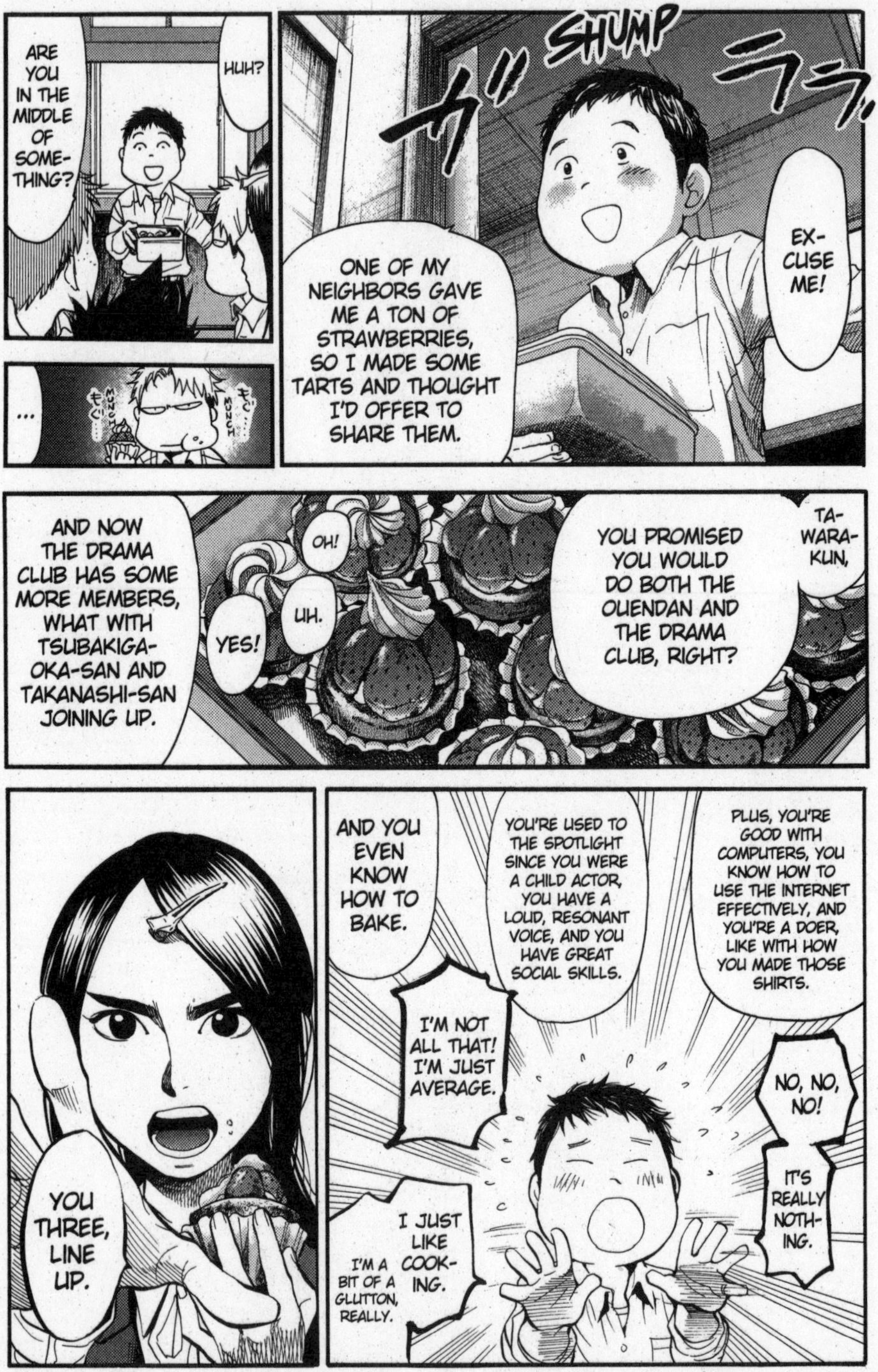
SHUMP
ガララ…
EX-CUSE ME!
ONE OF MY NEIGHBORS GAVE ME A TON OF STRAWBERRIES, SO I MADE SOME TARTS AND THOUGHT I'D OFFER TO SHARE THEM.
HUH?
ARE YOU IN THE MIDDLE OF SOME-THING?
もぐ… MUNCH
もぐ… MUNCH
...
TA-WARA-KUN,
YOU PROMISED YOU WOULD DO BOTH THE OUENDAN AND THE DRAMA CLUB, RIGHT?
OH!
UH.
YES!
AND NOW THE DRAMA CLUB HAS SOME MORE MEMBERS, WHAT WITH TSUBAKIGA-OKA-SAN AND TAKANASHI-SAN JOINING UP.
PLUS, YOU'RE GOOD WITH COMPUTERS, YOU KNOW HOW TO USE THE INTERNET EFFECTIVELY, AND YOU'RE A DOER, LIKE WITH HOW YOU MADE THOSE SHIRTS.
YOU'RE USED TO THE SPOTLIGHT SINCE YOU WERE A CHILD ACTOR, YOU HAVE A LOUD, RESONANT VOICE, AND YOU HAVE GREAT SOCIAL SKILLS.
AND YOU EVEN KNOW HOW TO BAKE.
NO, NO, NO!
IT'S REALLY NOTH-ING.
I'M NOT ALL THAT! I'M JUST AVERAGE.
I JUST LIKE COOK-ING.
I'M A BIT OF A GLUTTON, REALLY.
YOU THREE, LINE UP.

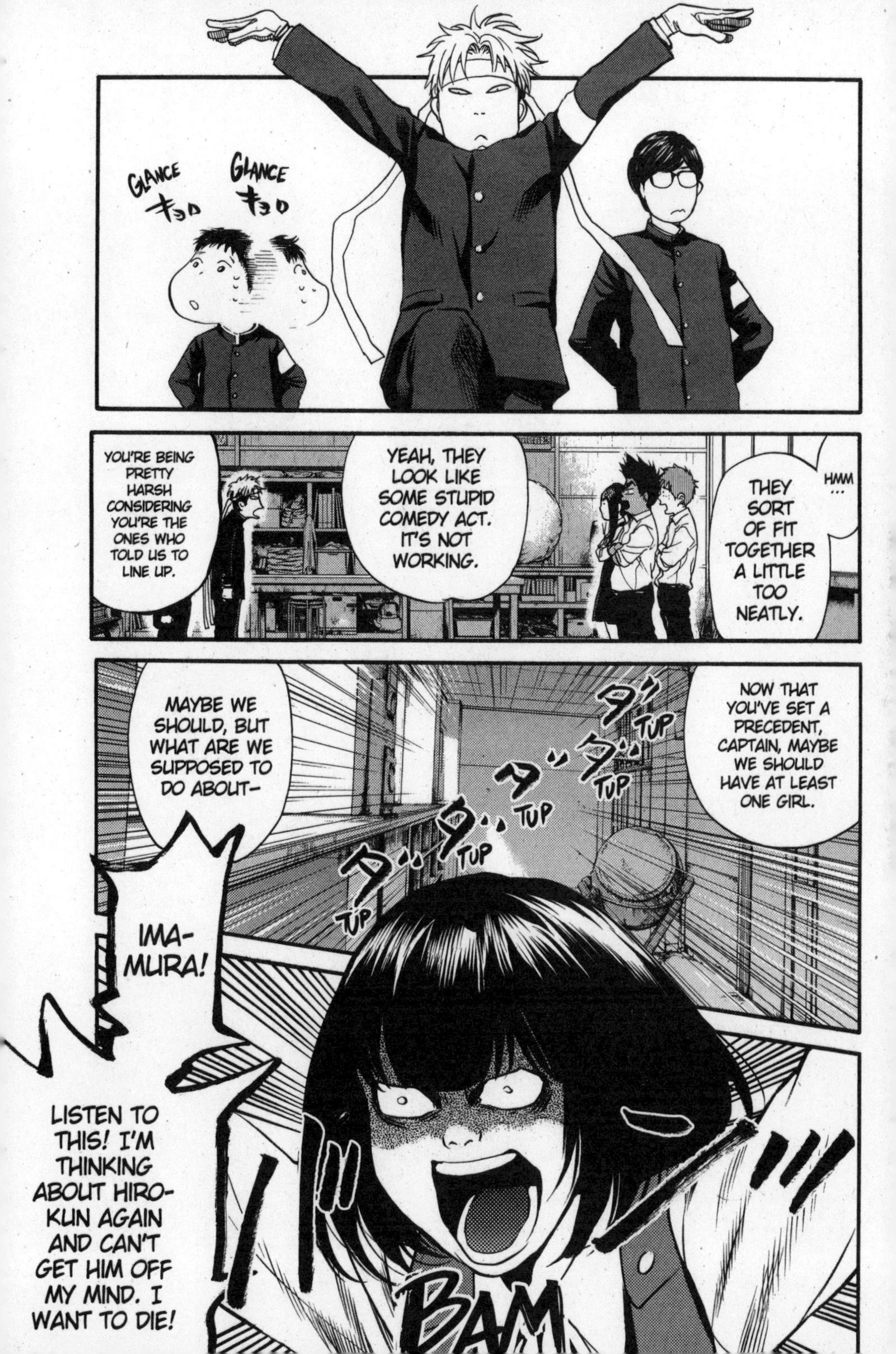
GLANCE キョロ
GLANCE キョロ
HMM ...
THEY SORT OF FIT TOGETHER A LITTLE TOO NEATLY.
YEAH, THEY LOOK LIKE SOME STUPID COMEDY ACT. IT'S NOT WORKING.
YOU'RE BEING PRETTY HARSH CONSIDERING YOU'RE THE ONES WHO TOLD US TO LINE UP.
NOW THAT YOU'VE SET A PRECEDENT, CAPTAIN, MAYBE WE SHOULD HAVE AT LEAST ONE GIRL.
タッ TUP
タッ TUP
タッ TUP
タッ TUP
タッ TUP
MAYBE WE SHOULD, BUT WHAT ARE WE SUPPOSED TO DO ABOUT-
IMA-MURA!
LISTEN TO THIS! I'M THINKING ABOUT HIRO-KUN AGAIN AND CAN'T GET HIM OFF MY MIND. I WANT TO DIE!
BAM

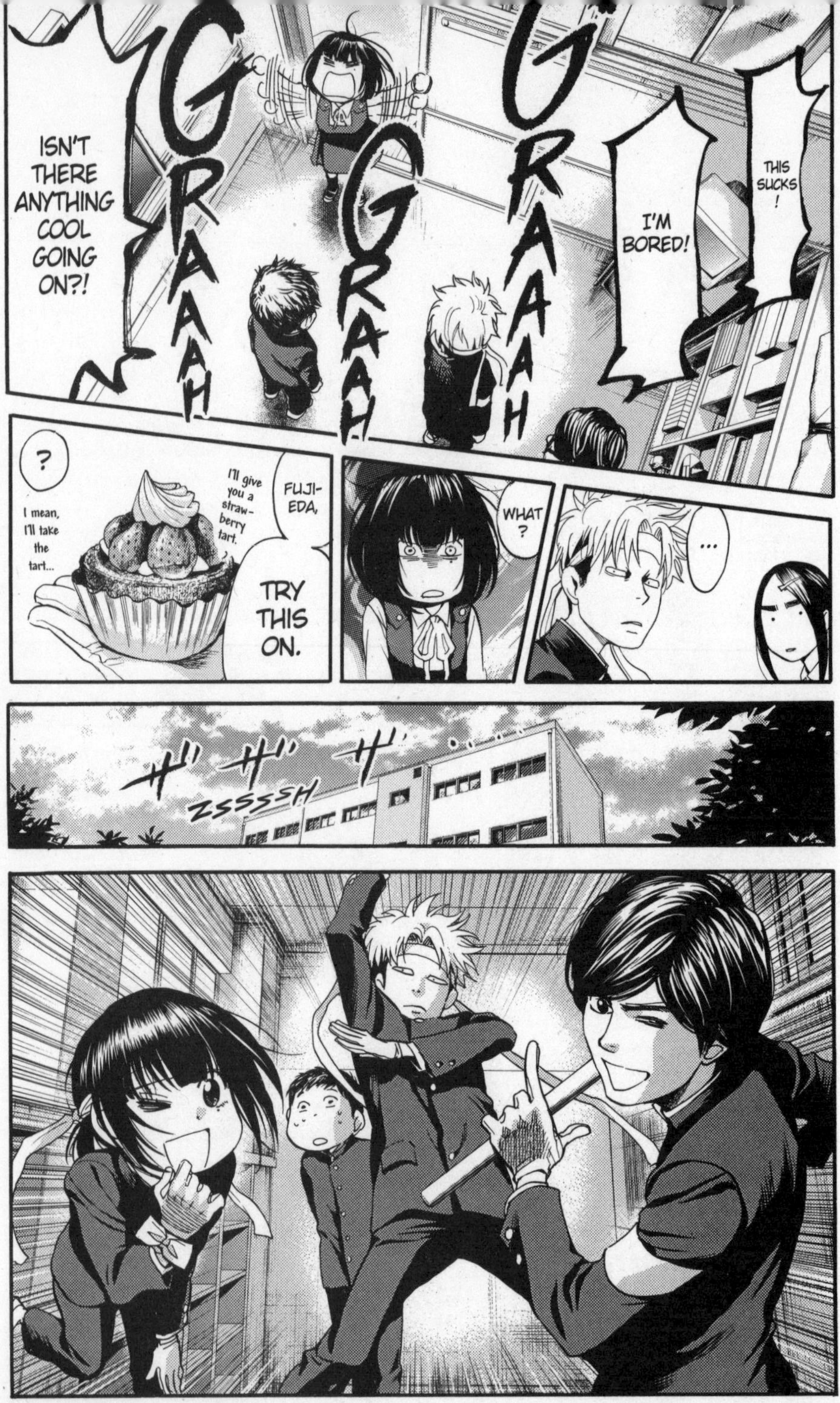
THIS SUCKS!
I'M BORED!
GRAAAH
GRAAH
ISN'T THERE ANYTHING COOL GOING ON?!
GRAAH
...
WHAT?
FUJI-EDA,
TRY THIS ON.
I'll give you a strawberry tart.
?
I mean, I'll take the tart...
ZSSSSH

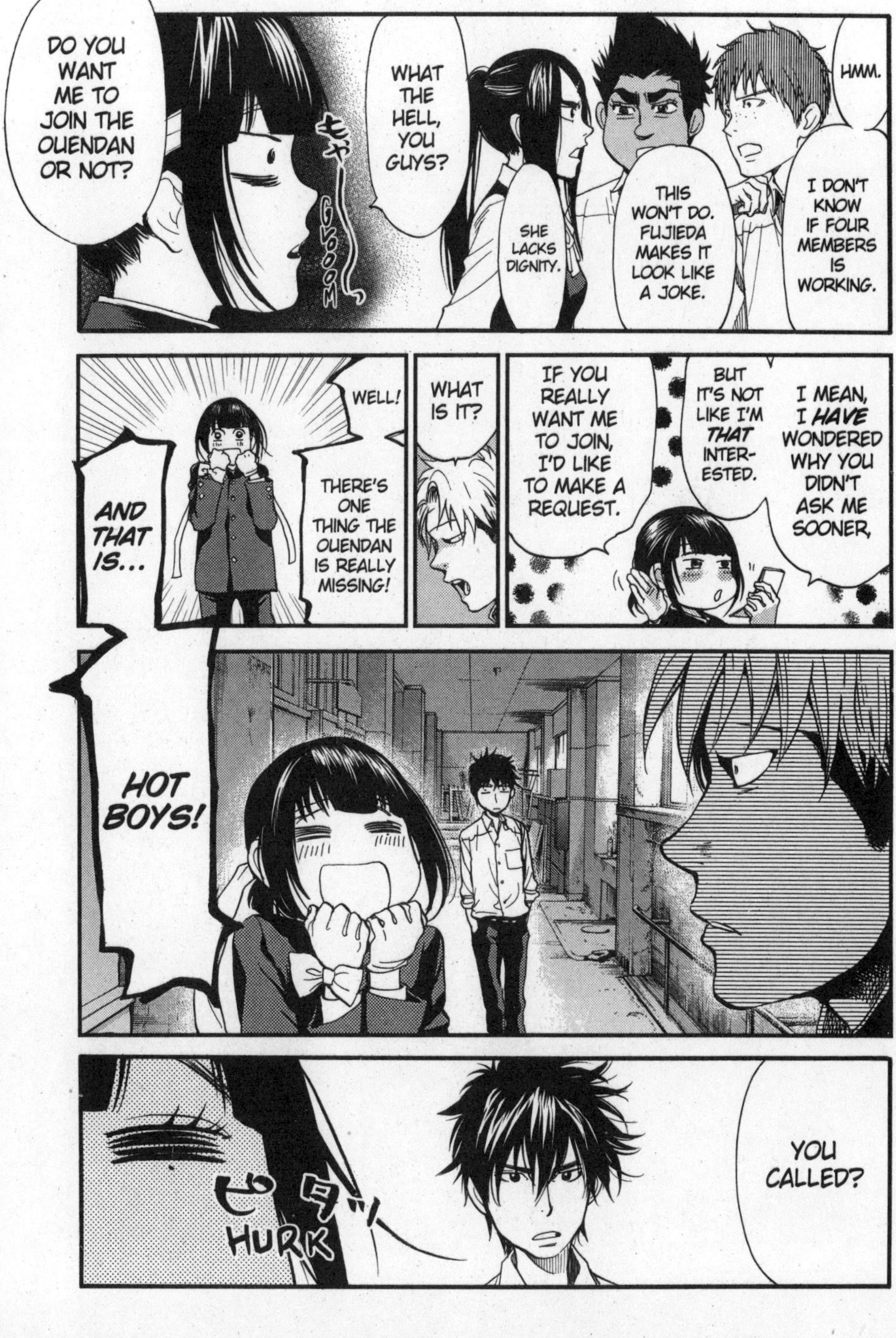
HMM.
I DON'T KNOW IF FOUR MEMBERS IS WORKING.
THIS WON'T DO. FUJIEDA MAKES IT LOOK LIKE A JOKE.
SHE LACKS DIGNITY.
WHAT THE HELL, YOU GUYS?
DO YOU WANT ME TO JOIN THE OUENDAN OR NOT?
GLOOOM
I MEAN, I *HAVE* WONDERED WHY YOU DIDN'T ASK ME SOONER,
BUT IT'S NOT LIKE I'M *THAT* INTERESTED.
IF YOU REALLY WANT ME TO JOIN, I'D LIKE TO MAKE A REQUEST.
WHAT IS IT?
WELL!
THERE'S ONE THING THE OUENDAN IS REALLY MISSING!
AND THAT IS...
HOT BOYS!
YOU CALLED?
HURK

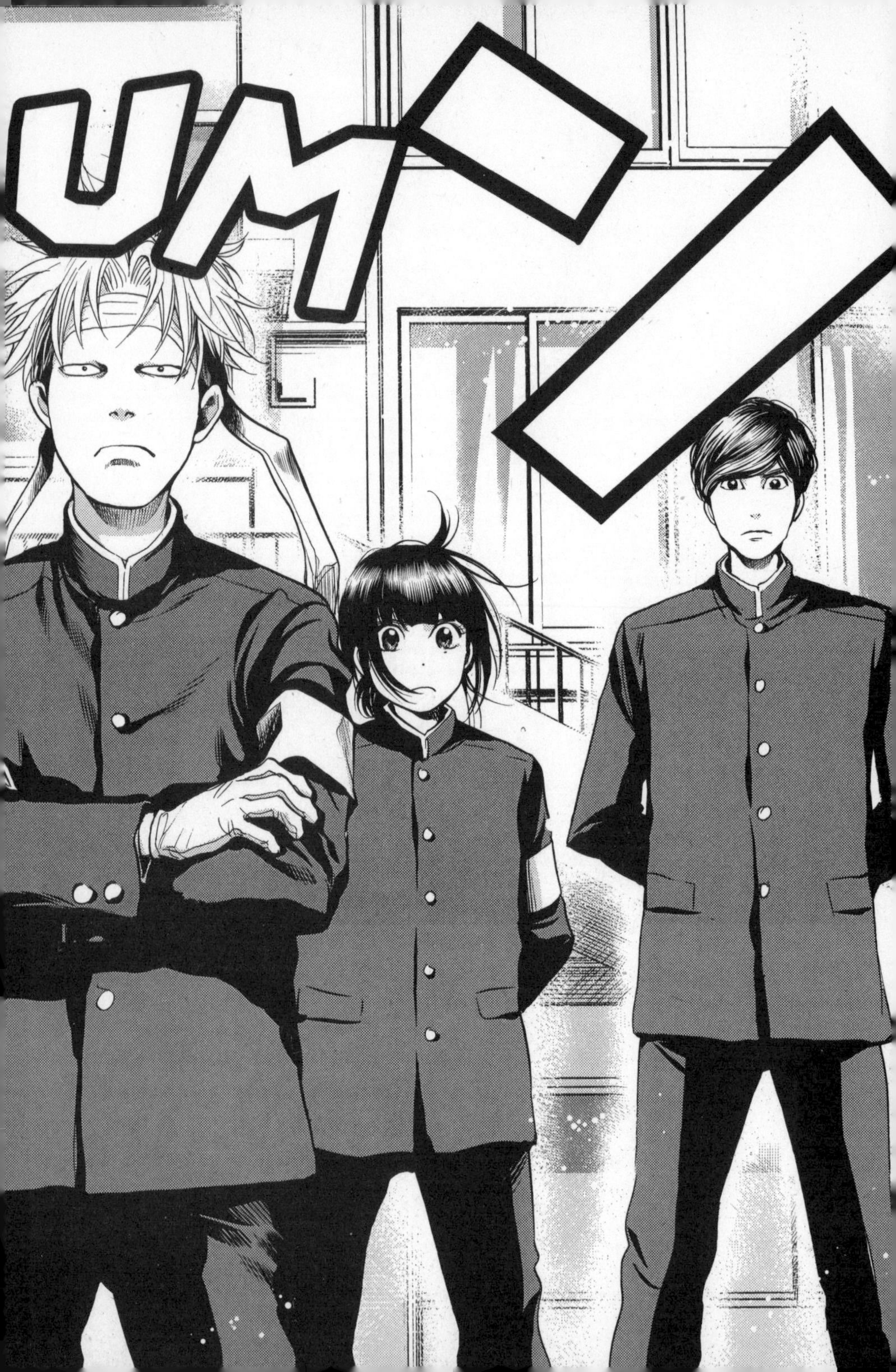
UM—!

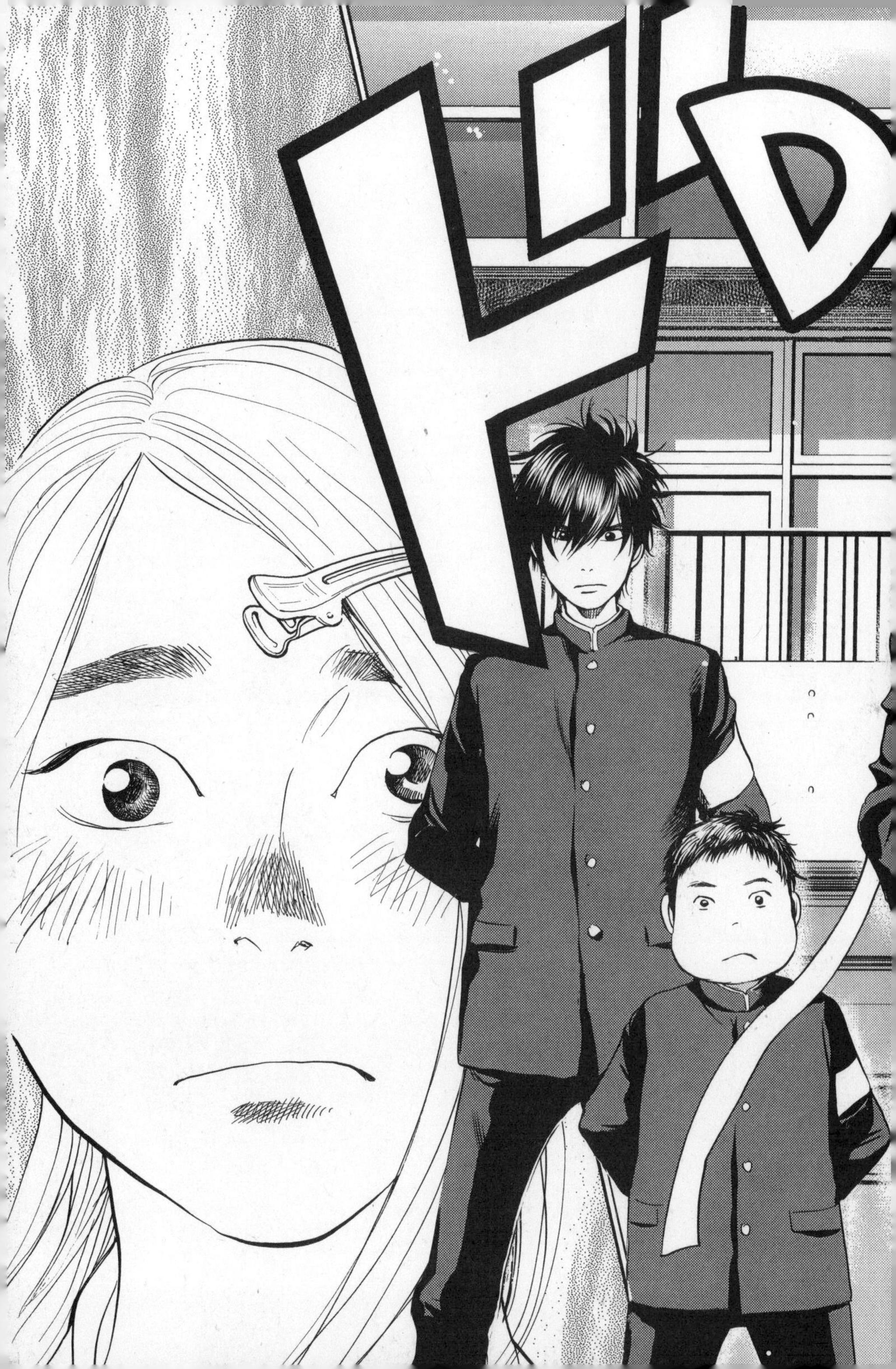

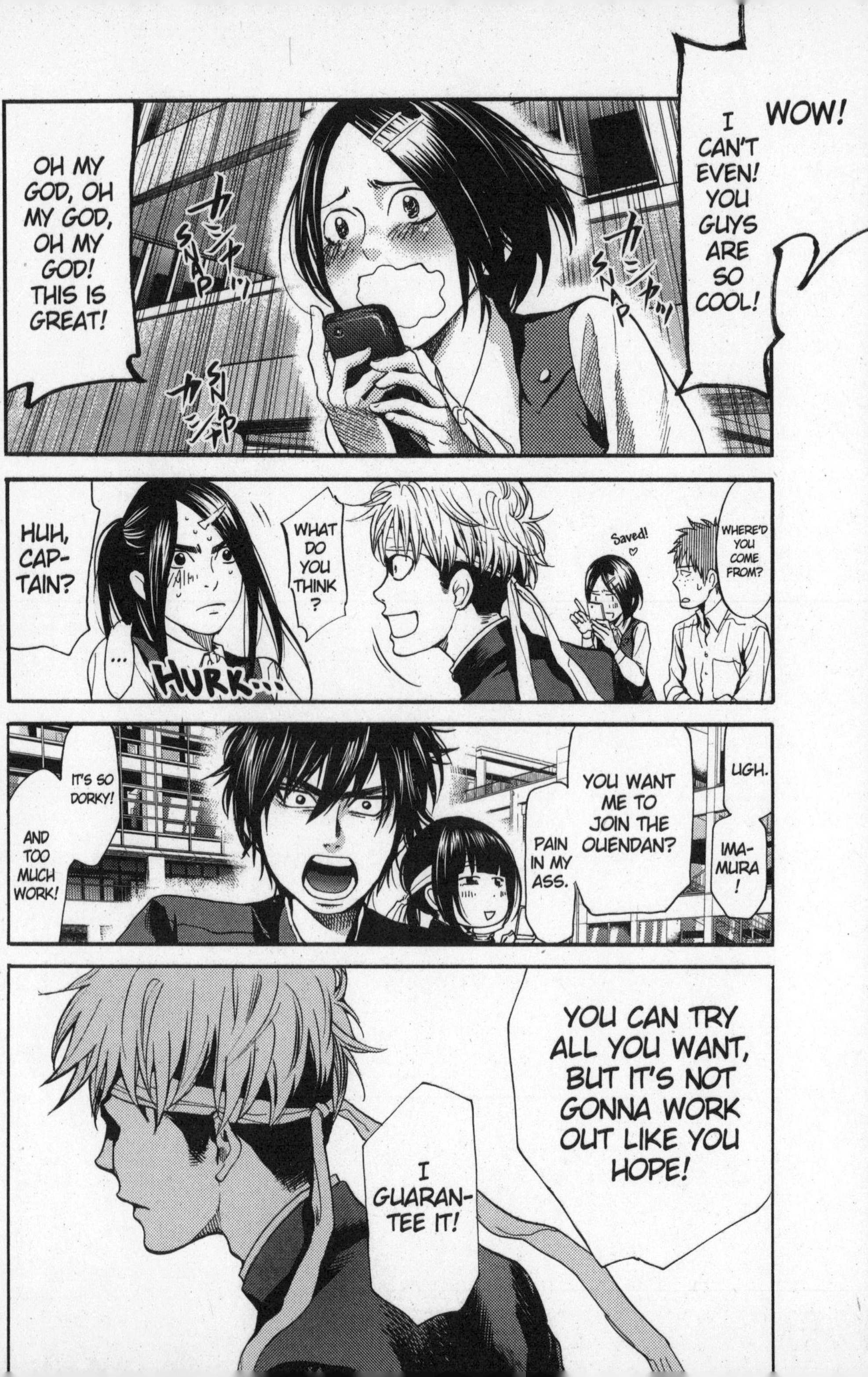
WOW!
I CAN'T EVEN! YOU GUYS ARE SO COOL!
カシャッ SNAP
カシャッ SNAP
OH MY GOD, OH MY GOD, OH MY GOD! THIS IS GREAT!
カシャ SNAP
WHERE'D YOU COME FROM?
Saved! ♡
WHAT DO YOU THINK?
HUH, CAP-TAIN?
...
HURK...
UGH.
IMA-MURA!
YOU WANT ME TO JOIN THE OUENDAN?
PAIN IN MY ASS.
IT'S SO DORKY!
AND TOO MUCH WORK!
YOU CAN TRY ALL YOU WANT, BUT IT'S NOT GONNA WORK OUT LIKE YOU HOPE!
I GUARAN-TEE IT!

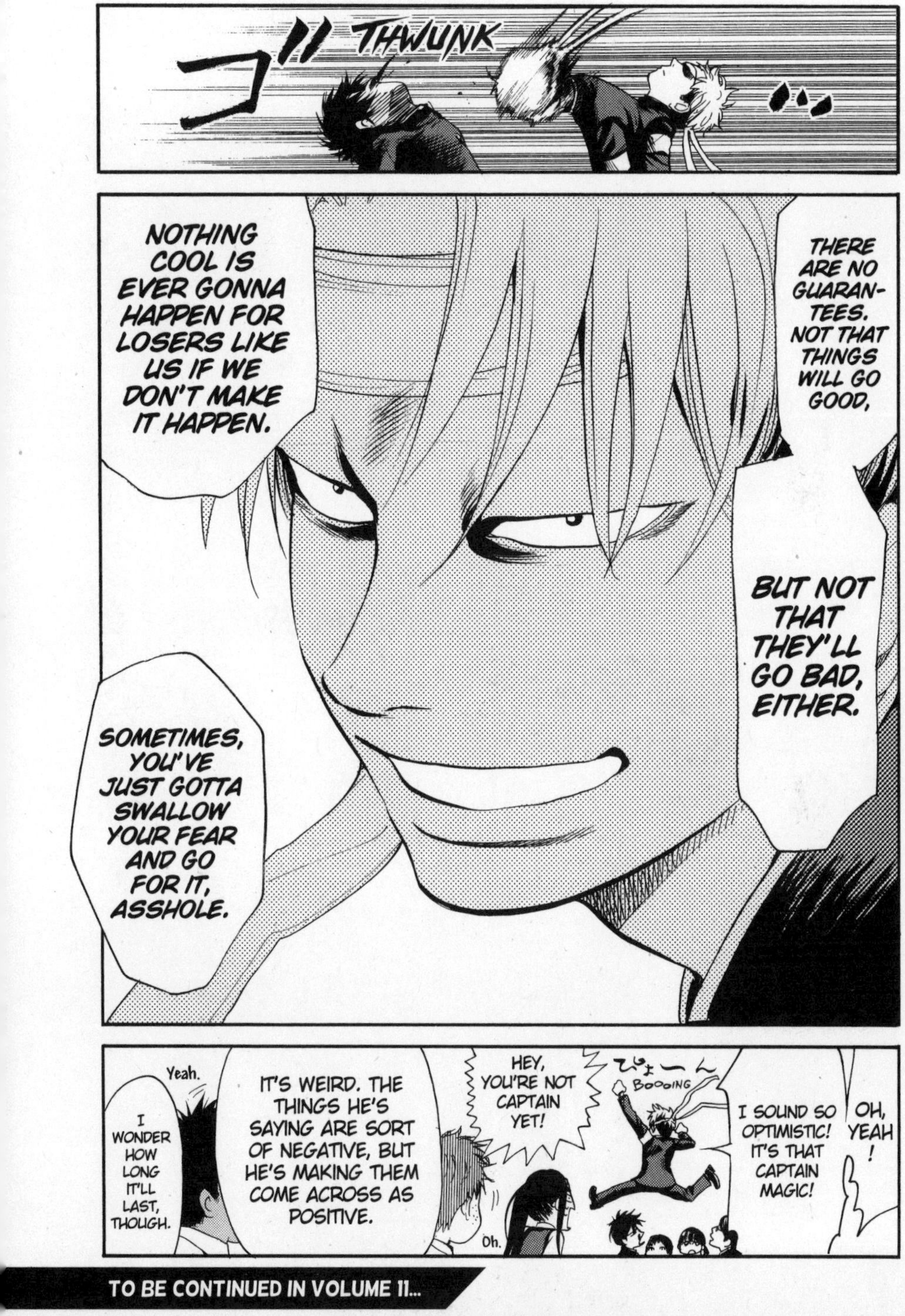
ゴ
THWUNK
THERE ARE NO GUARAN-TEES. NOT THAT THINGS WILL GO GOOD,
BUT NOT THAT THEY'LL GO BAD, EITHER.
NOTHING COOL IS EVER GONNA HAPPEN FOR LOSERS LIKE US IF WE DON'T MAKE IT HAPPEN.
SOMETIMES, YOU'VE JUST GOTTA SWALLOW YOUR FEAR AND GO FOR IT, ASSHOLE.
OH, YEAH!
I SOUND SO OPTIMISTIC! IT'S THAT CAPTAIN MAGIC!
ぴょーん
BOOOING
HEY, YOU'RE NOT CAPTAIN YET!
Oh.
IT'S WEIRD. THE THINGS HE'S SAYING ARE SORT OF NEGATIVE, BUT HE'S MAKING THEM COME ACROSS AS POSITIVE.
Yeah.
I WONDER HOW LONG IT'LL LAST, THOUGH.

TO BE CONTINUED IN VOLUME 11...

A Kodansha Comics Trade Paperback Original.

Again!! volume 10 copyright © 2013 Mitsurou Kubo
English translation copyright © 2019 Mitsurou Kubo

Published in the United States by Kodansha Comics, an imprint of Kodansha USA Publishing, LLC, New York.

Publication rights for this English edition arranged through Kodansha Ltd., Tokyo.

First published in Japan in 2013 by Kodansha Ltd., Tokyo, as *Agein!!* volume 10

ISBN 978-1-63236-782-2

Printed in the United States of America.

www.kodanshacomics.com

9 8 7 6 5 4 3 2 1

Translator: Rose Padgett
Lettering: E. K. Weaver
Editing: Tiff Ferentini
Kodansha Comics edition cover design by Phil Balsman